# CAPTIVITY

# JAMES LONEY

# CAPTIVITY

## 118 DAYS IN IRAQ AND THE STRUGGLE FOR A WORLD WITHOUT WAR

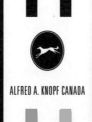

ALFRED A. KNOPF CANADA

PUBLISHED BY ALFRED A. KNOPF CANADA

Copyright © 2011 James Loney

Knopf Canada and colophon are trademarks.

www.randomhouse.ca

Pages 409–410 constitute a continuation of the copyright page.

Library and Archives Canada Cataloguing in Publication

Loney, James
Captivity : 118 days in Iraq and the struggle for a world without war / James Loney.

Issued also in an electronic format.

ISBN 978-0-307-39927-4

1. Loney, James—Captivity, 2005–2006. 2. Hostages—Iraq—Biography.
3. Iraq War, 2003– —Personal narratives, Canadian. 4. Hostages—Canada—Biography.
5. Christian Peace Maker Teams—Biography. 6. Pacifists—Canada—Biography.
I. Title.

DS79.76.L65 2011      956.7044'37092      C2010-904226-3

Text design: Andrew Roberts

First Edition

Printed and bound in the United States of America

2 4 6 8 9 7 5 3 1

For Tom.
For all those who have given their lives for a world without war,
those especially whose names and stories we will never know.
And for my father,
who never got to read these pages.

Sleep Jonah in the belly of a paradox. Now you need have no purpose, nothing to prove, nowhere to go.

You may, as of now, stop talking, stop planning, stop thinking. The God who thinks of you has no need of your thought. The God who loves you has no need of your love. The God who upholds the universe has no need of your strength.

Sleep Jonah, in a motion that is no motion, in a direction that is no direction. Does the unborn child order its mother about, when to sit, when to eat, when to go forth, what words to speak? Be still, then, and know that I am God.

Be still, Jonah, sleep at last. (He sleeps at last.) In the belly of your saviour, in the perilous fathomless sea, where salvation is a miracle and death is most likely—sleep . . .

Until then, I bear you through the pathless sea. Another than you plans for you, another than you breathes for you, another than you loves you, another than you sees before and after, yesterday and tomorrow. While you lie there, ignorant of where you come from, where you might be going, indeed, of who you are.

—from "Whale to Jonah" by Daniel Berrigan,
read to Jim by his partner Dan before he went to
bed, every night that Jim was held in captivity

# GLOSSARY

In general, the terms listed below reflect the author's hearing and understanding of the Arabic used by his captors. This glossary is not correct in every instance, in terms of meaning or transliteration, and should only be used for the purpose of reading this book.

*abiya* – ankle-length black coat worn by women
*abu* – father
*afwen* – you're welcome
*akeel* – food
*aku akhbar* – any news?
*alakum salam* – the response to *salam alakum*, "and peace to you"
*ali baba* – thief
*Allah* – God
*Allah ackbar* – God is great
*Amriki* – American
*ani* – I
*Arabi* – Arabic
*asbooah* – week
*bacher* – tomorrow
*beit* – house
*Britannia* – Great Britain
*cahraba* – electricity
*Canadi* – Canada
*chai* – tea
*chees* – plastic bag
*clatha* – three
*dishdashda* – one-piece, loose-fitting tunic worn by Arab men

duwa – medicine

el messiahiyea – Christianity

el yom – today

faloos – money

firar – escape

Franci – French

frook hind – rub together

Furat – Euphrates River

haji – term of respect for someone who has completed the pilgrimage to Mecca

halal – religiously pure to eat

hamam – bathroom

hum da'Allah – praise be to God

haram – something forbidden, taboo, a moral offence

hazeen – sad

hazeem – escape

helcoom – a type of candy

Hind – India

hooriya – freedom

hubis – bread, money

humburger – hamburger

ianni – means, also a common conversational filler, as in English "like," "so," "well"

imshee – walk, hurry up

inshallah – God willing

Islami – Muslim

isma – listen

Issau – Jesus

jaysh – soldier

jaysoos – informant, collaborator

Jenna – heaven

Jehennem – hell

kabir – big, old

kadim – old

**kaffir** – unbeliever

**killam** – talk

**killeator** – hat

**kineesa** – church

**kool yom** – every day

**la** – no

**leaish** – why

**majnoon** – crazy

**makhtoof** – kidnapped

**mazboot** – truly

**mbhara** – yesterday

**melabas** – clothes

**Messiahiy** – Christian

**mezjoon** – prisoner

**minundra ani gulak** – likely ma'adree ani gulak, which means I don't know,
                         I will tell you later

**mooreed** – sick

**mooseh-dis** – gun

**mooshkilla** – problem, nuisance

**mot** – dead

**mozane** – no good

**mujahedeen** – holy warrior of God

**mumkin** – could I please?

**my** – water

**najis** – spy, piece of soiled toilet paper

**nam** – sleep

**na'am** – yes

**noos** – half

**noos-noos** – so-so

**numibasra** – a sour fruit used for making tea, flavouring food

**Nuzlander** – New Zealander

**ogod** – sit down

**Ordoon** – Jordan

**petrol** – kerosene

**portugal** – orange

**qatil** – murder

**romana** – grenade

**sabha il hare** – good morning

**sabha il noor** – morning light

**sadika** – girlfriend

**salam** – peace

**salam alakum** – peace to you

**sena** – year

**shid ghul** – repeat again, I didn't hear you

**shlonik** – how are you?

**shokren** – thank you

**shoo** – what

**shorta** – police

**shstem** – smell

**shuhada bil Arabi** – how do you say in Arabic

**shwakit** – when?

**shwaya** – little

**sierra** – car

**soba** – heater

**t'al wiyaya** – come with me

**talib** – student

**thnein** – two

**umma** – mother

**wahid** – one

**wardeh** – flower

**whalid** – children

**zane** – good

**zengeel** – chain

**zowage** – marriage

**zowagi** – married woman

**zowja** – wife

# INTRODUCTION

Did it really happen, those four months of handcuffs and chains, terror and uncertainty, excruciating boredom without end? Sometimes, when I'm not sure, I go down into my basement and open a cardboard box to reassure myself. It contains a pair of pants, a sweater, a collared shirt, two undershirts, a pair of socks, two sets of underwear, the green string I used to hold up my pants—and one handcuff. The things the RCMP took from me on the day of our rescue, while I stood shivering in an emergency room hospital gown, in a hospital located in the Green Zone, headquarters for the occupation of Iraq. They said it was for forensic evidence.

I was alarmed. Will I get them back? Even the handcuff? It was the only thing I cared about. Yes, they said. True to their promise, the box came in the mail a year later, each item meticulously folded and wrapped in brown paper. Proof that it really happened.

One hundred and eighteen days. To say "we thought it would never end" would be to dilute an understatement with a cliché. Glaciers moved faster than any single minute of any single one of those days. Each day, each minute was a lash, an open grave, a forced march, an agony and a theft for the four of us held hostage together—Tom Fox, Harmeet Singh Sooden, Norman Kember and myself—and all of our families and loved ones imprisoned with us in that four-month tomb of unknowing.

It is good to be alive. It could easily have turned out differently. The moment of my death might have been recorded on a grainy home video, or I might still be mouldering in the living hell of captivity. Instead I am alive and home free because a unit of crack soldiers risked their lives to secure my freedom. Without regard for my politics or my purpose in going to Baghdad. Simply because it was the duty they accepted. For this I am immensely and perpetually grateful.

I began to record these memories and thoughts in my brother Matthew's apartment in Montreal. He was away for a while and I needed a quiet place to finally start what I had been avoiding for months and months. My heart was heavy. By some strange coincidence, it was Remembrance Day, and Canadians were gathering at cenotaphs, school gymnasiums and churches to honour those who risk their lives in the service of our country. In Calgary, Diane Dallaire laid a wreath at the cenotaph in Memorial Park. She is the mother of 22-year-old Private Kevin Dallaire who, along with two others, was killed on August 3, 2006, in a rocket-propelled grenade attack while fighting Taliban forces west of Kandahar. She said the ceremony was an important reminder of the cost paid for peace. "I hope they remember where their freedom came from," she said.

I felt the calamity of that day deep in my body: a fist clenched tight in my chest. I thought of Diane Dallaire mourning the loss of her son. The grief must be too much to bear. I wondered what I would say to her, were she to ask me, "Do you remember where your freedom came from?"

I do. My living, breathing, everyday-walking-around freedom comes directly from the hand of the soldier who took a bolt cutter in his hands and cut the chain that held me captive for four months. Yet I remain a pacifist, a Christian who believes that Jesus's teaching to love one's enemy is a call to lay down the sword and pick up the cross, to accept rather than inflict suffering.

It is a paradox. I went to Baghdad on a Christian Peacemaker Teams (CPT) delegation in opposition to the institution of war. I was kidnapped by Iraqi insurgents who were fighting against the U.S.-led invasion and occupation of their country. CPT used every weapon in its non-violent arsenal to get us out. There was an international uprising of prayer vigils, solidarity statements, appeals, public witness, moral pressure. Our kidnapping was front-page news for weeks. The constant, unrelenting hope was that our captors would have a change of heart and release us. They didn't. The days piled into months and Tom was killed. It was a secretive Special Forces operation led by Task Force Black—a joint U.S./U.K. unit established in 2003 to hunt down senior al Qaeda operatives in Iraq and rescue foreign hostages—that finally ended the crisis. Soldiers like Kevin Dallaire.

The first Remembrance Day was declared by King George V on November 7, 1919. It recalled the Armistice signed the previous year by Allied commander-in-chief Marshal Ferdinand Foch and Germany's Matthias Erzberger in a secret railway carriage hidden in the Compiègne forest. On November 11, 1918, at 11:00 a.m.—the eleventh hour of the eleventh day of the eleventh month—the First World War was officially over. Twenty million were dead, 21 million wounded. They called it the War to End All Wars.

November 11 is also the feast day of St. Martin of Tours. Martin is the patron saint of soldiers, cavalry and quartermasters. The U.S. Army Quartermasters Corps established the Order of St. Martin in 1997 to recognize the distinguished service of quartermasters. The website reads: "Saint Martin—the patron saint of the Quartermaster Regiment—was the most popular saint in France during antiquity and the early Middle Ages. It is said that French kings carried his cloak into battle as a spur to victory. Usually pictured on horseback dividing his cloak with the beggar, the image of Saint Martin as a Soldier-Provider offers a fitting symbol for Logistics Warriors charged with SUPPORTING VICTORY now and for all time." Their website also tells us that Martin's name comes from the Latin *Marten Tenens* (one who sustains Mars, Mars being the Roman god of war). And that is precisely what quarter-masters do—sustain armies by making sure they have everything they need to do their job: gasoline, rations, bullets, boots.

Martin was born in 316 or 317 in the Roman province of Pannonia (now modern-day Hungary). As the son of a senior officer in the Imperial

Horse Guard, Martin was forced by law to join the army at the age of fifteen. While on duty at the age of eighteen, he encountered a ragged beggar at the gates of Amiens. Moved with compassion, he cut his cloak with his sword and gave half of it to the beggar. That night he had a dream in which Jesus appeared in the half cloak he had given away. "Here is Martin," Jesus said, "the Roman soldier who is not baptized; he has clad me." Shortly thereafter Martin was baptized.

When Martin was twenty, Julian II ordered him into battle against the Gauls. He refused. "I am a soldier of Christ. I cannot fight," he told the emperor. (The early Church prohibited the baptized from bearing arms or serving in the military under pain of excommunication.) When Julian accused him of being a coward, Martin volunteered to go onto the battlefield unarmed at the head of the column. Julian accepted his offer and threw him into prison. The next day the Gauls sued for peace and the battle never happened. Martin was discharged from the army.

Martin travelled to Poitiers to become a disciple of St. Hilary, the local bishop, and then later joined the monastery at Solesmes. In 371, he was acclaimed Bishop of Tours against his will by the citizens of Tours. As bishop, Martin worked tirelessly for prisoners. A general named Avitianus once arrived in Tours with a cohort he intended to torture and execute the next day. Upon hearing this, Martin went immediately to the house where Avitianus was staying. Arriving in the middle of the night, he threw himself on the threshold and began crying out in a loud voice. An angel is said to have awakened Avitianus, telling him Martin was outside. "Don't even say a word," he said upon seeing Martin. "I know what your request is. Every prisoner shall be spared."

In addition, Martin was a staunch opponent of the death penalty. Priscillian of Avila was the leader of a growing heresy that advocated, amongst other things, abstinence in marriage. Condemned by the First Council of Saragossa and excommunicated in 380, Priscillian fled to Trier in southwestern Germany. A group of Spanish bishops led by Ithacius wanted Emperor Magnus Maximus to execute him. Although greatly opposed to Priscillian, Martin petitioned the imperial court in

Trier to have him removed from the secular jurisdiction of the emperor, arguing this was a church matter over which the secular authority had no power to intervene and excommunication was punishment enough. When Maximus agreed and Martin departed the city, Ithacius persuaded the emperor to follow through with the execution. Priscillian and his followers, beheaded in 385, were the first Christians executed for heresy.

Martin hurried back to Trier as soon as he heard the news in the hope of saving the remaining Priscillianists. Once there, he refused to concelebrate with the bishops who had ordered the executions. Fearing a public scandal, the emperor promised to release the remaining prisoners if Martin shared Communion with Ithacius. Martin reluctantly agreed but then was so overcome with guilt for agreeing to this compromise that he resolved never to attend another bishops' assembly.

It is believed Martin died in 397 at the age of eighty-one. He was buried, at his request, in the Cemetery of the Poor in Tours on November 11.

Irony and paradox. A young man who disobeys a direct order to kill becomes the patron saint of soldiers; a pacifist conscientious objector who leaves the army in disgrace is turned into a warrior icon charged with supporting-victory-now-and-for-all-time. The quartermasters have taken the cloak of St. Martin away from the beggar and wrapped it around the institution of war.

The reason, I think, is very simple. Every war needs a cloak. Every war needs something to surround and protect and dignify it, something to conceal that it is really a rotten stinking corpse. Every act of violence needs a pointing finger, a reason, a story to explain why it is necessary. And every soldier needs a blessing. They need to know that the horror of what they are called upon to do has purpose and meaning, that it is legitimate and just, even noble. Without this cloak, this story, this blessing to protect them from the flesh-and-blood consequences of their actions, their work becomes impossible.

Perhaps the quartermasters have chosen more wisely than they know. By enlisting Martin as their patron, they have put him right where he is supposed to be, at the front of the battle column, reminding us that we need not be governed by the imperium of war but that we can, at any moment, lay down our swords and stand up, or sit down, for peace. Perhaps it is those who are most involved in the institution of war—soldiers, quartermasters and cavalrymen—who most need Martin of Tours, the voice who says there is another way.

Christian Peacemaker Teams is an experiment in this other way. "What would happen," CPT asks, "if Christians devoted the same discipline and self-sacrifice to non-violent peacemaking that armies devote to war?"

The question comes from theologian Ron Sider's challenge to the Mennonite Church at the 1984 Mennonite World Conference in Strasbourg, France. Conscientious objection to war is not enough, he said. "Too often we fall into an isolationist pacifism which silently ignores or perhaps profits from injustice and war as long as our boys don't have to fight." Mennonites, he argued, had become "soft and comfortable," even wealthy, staying home from war. "To vote for other people's sons and daughters to march off to death while ours safely register as conscientious objectors is the worst form of confused hypocrisy." In contrast, Sider argued, "Those who have believed in peace through the sword have not hesitated to die. Proudly, courageously, they gave their lives . . . For their loved ones, for justice, and for peace, they have laid down their lives by the millions."

Sider challenged pacifist Christians to get out of their easy chairs. "Why do we pacifists think that our way—Jesus's way—to peace will be less costly? Unless we . . . are ready to start to die by the thousands in dramatic vigorous new exploits for peace and justice, we should sadly confess that we really never meant what we said.

"What would happen if we in the Christian church developed a new nonviolent peacekeeping force of 100,000 persons ready to move into violent conflicts and stand peacefully between warring parties in Central America, Northern Ireland, Poland, Southern Africa, the Middle

East, and Afghanistan? Frequently we would get killed by the thousands. But everyone assumes that for the sake of peace it is moral and just for soldiers to get killed by the hundreds of thousands, even millions. Do we not have as much courage and faith as soldiers?"

The speech created a stir. A 1986 conference in Chicago was convened to discuss how to implement Sider's challenge. A steering committee was organized and Gene Stoltzfus was hired as the first full-time staff member in 1988. The first delegation went to Iraq in November 1989. In 1993, CPT held its first training and sent its first team to Haiti.

Currently, the CPT Peacemaker Corps includes 40 full-time and 170 reservist members, all of whom receive a month of training before joining a team in the field. Full-timers receive a needs-based stipend; reservists cover their travel and living expenses through fundraising. As of this writing, CPT has teams working in Hebron and the shepherd village of At-Tuwani (both located in Palestine), Colombia and Iraqi Kurdistan and with Aboriginal communities in Ontario. We only go where we're invited and generally work in partnership with communities experiencing lethal violence who are struggling to effect social change through the power of non-violence.

We sometimes conceive of our work as *violence-reduction*. Peacemaking is a complex, time-consuming, multi-dimensional dynamic process, and often what we are able to accomplish in a given context is very modest. We look for ways to reduce and limit violence through what we call a "ministry of presence": street patrols; observing in volatile situations with cameras and notebooks; de-escalating body language; physically intervening to protect those facing an immediate threat of violence; accompanying those who have been targeted for violence. We sometimes call this the grandmother effect: you're less likely to stick your hand in the cookie jar while Grandma is watching. While many CPTers *are* grandmothers, an international passport can sometimes have the same effect. In Colombia, for example, paramilitaries and guerrillas tend not to commit acts of violence in the presence of internationals in order to avoid the international scrutiny that would result.

In addition to this ministry of presence, we are becoming more and more involved in the work of documenting human rights abuses. At the time of our kidnapping, CPT was documenting the torture of Sunni men at the hands of Shia-identified departments within the Ministry of Interior. CPT issued a report in November 2003 documenting seventy-two instances where the United States had violated the human rights of Iraqi men they were holding without charges. Seymour Hirsch, who broke the Abu Ghraib story in *The New Yorker* in April 2004, said, "Most of the things that I ended up writing about in Abu Ghraib, most of the general concepts, they [CPT] knew a great deal about earlier, as did Human Rights Watch and Amnesty."

We do not position ourselves in a conflict as third-party neutrals who mediate between, or separate, two opposing but roughly equal sides. We work in contexts where there is an imbalance of power, where a smaller group is experiencing violence at the hands of a larger and more powerful dominant group—violence that is often manifest in systems of social, economic and political oppression. Our thinking is that one cannot remain neutral in the face of injustice, for to do so is to become an accomplice to that injustice. Rather, we see ourselves as allies working to confront, expose and transform the systematic injustices that we so often find at the root of a violent conflict. We are trained in non-violent direct action and are ready to perform non-violent civil disobedience (i.e., break unjust laws) in order to expose injustice and mobilize positive social change.

It's difficult for me to assess just how successful CPT has been in this approach to peacemaking. More often than not, success for us is better measured in terms of what is avoided or prevented from happening. Nevertheless, we have enjoyed a spectacular success now and then. I think of Sara Reschly, her image flashed around the world standing with her arms outstretched in front of an Israeli soldier, preventing him from shooting a group of Palestinians who were non-violently protesting a week-long, 24-hour curfew. I think of Lisa Martens and Cliff Kindy taking around-the-clock media calls during the 2003 bombing of Baghdad, telling the world the truth about war. I think of Lena

Siegers, who videotaped officers from Canada's Department of Fisheries and Oceans officers ramming the boats of Mi'kmaq fishers and then clubbing them while they floated helpless in the water. This videotape was broadcast around the world and embarrassed the Canadian government into a change of policy. I think of Chris Brown and Kim Lamberty, who were attacked by masked settler youth with bats and chains while accompanying Palestinian shepherd children to school. Their cuts, bruises and broken bones captured international headlines and forced the Israeli government to protect the very same children they once said they couldn't.

CPT's budget in 2010 was $1.1 million.

Humanity is in trouble. We have entered the eleventh hour. Half of the world's coral reef species, a third of its amphibians and a quarter of its mammals are at risk of disappearing. The UN issued a report in 2007 that said a major extinction of life caused by human activity is under way. Global warming, peak oil, the loss of arable farmland, growing food and water shortages, alone and in combination, are a clear and present danger to the social and economic systems that undergird human civilization. Meanwhile, unknown thousands are dying every day and unknown millions more are suffering in refugee camps, shantytowns and destitute villages from the violence of poverty. The future is precarious, the present an outrage, and yet the world spent a staggering $1.5 trillion on the institution of war in 2009. It is estimated that the Iraq and Afghanistan wars will cost U.S. taxpayers $3 trillion.

The prevailing wisdom says we have no choice. We must do what it takes, always be ready. War is inevitable, forever looming. War for defence, security, reconstruction, democracy. War to end war. War necessary, right and just.

I too believe that we have no choice. "Men, for years now, have been talking about war and peace," Martin Luther King Jr. said on the eve of his assassination in 1968. "But now . . . it is no longer a choice between violence and nonviolence in this world. It's nonviolence or non-existence."

The choice facing us is as simple as it is stark. A major extinction of life is under way. We can't afford to waste another minute or another penny building and maintaining the war machine. If our children, and their children, are to have any hope of a future, we must make a turn, take a different road, mobilize everything, do all we can—and do it today. But we have been taken captive by an idea. The handcuffs and chains that bind us have been forged in the false confidence that violence will save us. It cannot. Inevitably and irresistibly, it will lead to an abyss of mutually assured doom and catastrophe.

Irony and paradox. Here we are in the eleventh hour. The eleventh day of the eleventh month is when we honour the memory of those who have fought and died in war. It is the day we remember a pacifist saint whose cloak is used to mantle the very thing he walked away from. It is the day that I happened to begin writing this book, the story of a pacifist who was taken hostage in the course of opposing a war and was freed by the very institution he condemned.

This book is the story of this paradox. It is the story of my captivity and what I saw there—of the human spirit and freedom, of violence and the way to find our liberation from it. As with any paradox, there is no answer to it; it can only be lived. I tell this story in the hope that we might yet find another way.

# CHAPTER ONE

## NOVEMBER 26, 2005 DAY 1

We present ourselves to the guards at the main entrance. They're cold, cheerless, brusque. "Passport, passport," they demand. I hesitate. I have never before been asked by an Iraqi security guard to show my passport. I look at Tom. He nods to me and hands them his passport. It must be okay then, I think.

"Camera, camera," they say, pointing to me and Norman and Harmeet. A guard sitting at a desk inspects our cameras with scrupulous care. We empty our pockets and lift our arms. Their hands are rude, gruff, intrusively thorough. I am taken aback. My experience of Iraqi security guards is that they are unfailingly courteous, even gentle, when conducting body searches. "No picture, no picture," they chastise as they hand back our cameras.

"That means you," I say to Harmeet under my breath. He flashes me an innocent smile.

The Umm al-Qura mosque is nothing if not impressive. At the centre of the gleaming complex is a purple and gold dome ringed by four towering minarets made to look like Scud missiles. Surrounding the dome is a reflecting pool enclosed within a rectangular quadrant. The corners of the quadrant are adorned with a second set of four towers, built to look like Kalashnikov rifles. Two big signs stand at either side of the main gate. "This mosque was built according to the orders of President Saddam Hussein. The cornerstone was laid on April 28, 1998, and the mosque was finished on April 28, 2001"—Saddam's birthday. He called it Umm al Marik: the Mother of All Battles. The mosque, with a new name, became the headquarters of the Muslim Scholars Association in 2003, a few weeks after Saddam fell.

Outside the security office, we are met by the human rights officer for the Muslim Scholars Association, a heavy-set man with an abundant brown beard and a parsimonious smile. He leads us through the splendiferous precinct of the mosque compound into a gloomy, bunker-like office. He sits behind a barren desk, sullen and remote, and we sit along a wall in plastic lawn chairs, our notebooks open and pens ready.

Norman introduces us as members of a Christian Peacemaker Teams delegation who have come to Iraq to learn about the realities of life under American occupation. The human rights officer speaks at length about the suffering caused by the thirteen years of economic sanctions that preceded the invasion of Iraq in 2003; the difficulties of life under occupation; the lack of security, electricity and employment; the failure of the United States to initiate a meaningful program of reconstruction; the plight of security detainees. Things were better under Saddam Hussein, he tells us, and he is not hopeful about the prospects for a political solution. He folds his hands on his desk and looks down at the floor. We ask a question. He looks at his watch. Our appointment is over.

We thank him for taking the time to meet with us. He escorts us back to the security office. Harmeet manages somehow to charm a picture out of him. We say goodbye to the grim-faced security guards and trek across the desolate expanse of the Umm al-Qura parking lot to where our driver is waiting. I check my watch. It is 3:10 p.m.

"Did you notice that they didn't bring us tea?" I say to Tom. "In all of the meetings I've had in Iraq, I don't think that's ever happened."

Tom points to the public washroom located outside the mosque entrance. "When I went to the restroom before we went through security, there was somebody in a car watching us. I caught his eyes for just a moment. It was really unusual. I never have these feelings about people, but there was something about him that gave me the creeps. It was like . . . it was like he didn't mean us well."

I wish now that I could remember that walk across the parking lot, the exact number of footsteps it took us to reach the van, how I held my notebook, the things we said to each other as we climbed into the van and took our seats. How I wish I could remember everything about those last, unremarkable motions, this last handful of things we did as free men before being disappeared into the world of the gun for 118 days.

The van door closes. Issam, our driver, takes us through the mosque checkpoint and turns left onto a lonely arterial road bordering the south side of the mosque. I am sitting with my back to Issam, on a bench seat facing Tom and Harmeet, our knees almost touching. Norman is in the seat behind them, at the back of the van by himself. I turn for one last look at the mosque when the driver slams on the brakes. We all lurch forward. "Hey, what's going on?" I say.

A white sedan has stopped in front of us. Three doors pop open and four men with guns pour out, surround us, pull our driver and translator out of the van. There are gestures, urgent voices I can't understand. One of the men gets behind the wheel of our van. Another slides back the panel door and points an AK-47 at us. Two others climb in. Their movements are smooth, quick, precise. They've done this before.

"Get down," one of them says to me. "On the floor." I look at him. He waves his gun and pushes me. "Move," he says. I move. Another gunman sits beside him.

Our translator, Adib, is standing alone, ten feet away from the vehicle. We reach for each other through our eyes. That look on his face—I've never forgotten it. Terror, helplessness, anguish. One human being bearing witness to the last seconds of another.

The last abductor, training his gun at Tom's head, slides in next to him and slams the door. The van pulls away, leaving Issam and Adib standing helplessly by the road. Thank God they didn't hurt them, I think.

I am calm. There is no room, no space for emotion, only observation and response. I look into the eyes of the gunman who has pushed me off the seat. Something tells me he is the boss. He is dark-bearded, twenty-something, impeccably groomed, a steel beam in a navy blue suit jacket. His eyes are hard, cold with murder. He sits ready, AK-47 on his lap, his finger around the trigger. The one next to him is rounder, wipes sweat off his brow, shifts uneasily. The one next to Harmeet slowly chews a piece of gum, his face acne-scarred and villainous.

Tom, Harmeet and Norman are alert, composed, self-possessed. I search out their eyes. Harmeet sees me. We exchange a quick smile that seems to say, "Can this really be happening?"

Harmeet Singh Sooden is a 32-year-old Canadian Sikh, former computer engineer, student of English literature in Auckland, New Zealand. He's casual and sporty in loose-fitting trousers and a golf shirt; his hair is jet black, shoulder-length, his right arm hard and sculpted from years of competitive squash play. Norman Kember is a 75-year-old Briton from a London suburb, husband, father and grand-father, retired professor of nuclear biophysics. He's white-haired, ruddy, robust, bemused and professorial in his tweed jacket, beige vest, brown cotton tie, woollen pants and scruffy oxford shoes. Tom Fox is a 52-year-old American, divorced father of two young adults, retired member of the Marine Corps Band, from Clearbrook, Virginia. He's tall, lean, severe; clean-cut and military in khakis and a moss green button-down shirt.

The van proceeds east five hundred metres and merges onto a divided highway. I watch, try to absorb and remember everything, strain with every neuron to lay down a mental map of where we are being taken. I say to the one in charge, "My name is Jim." His eyes don't even flicker. I keep on trying. "This is Tom"—I point—"and Harmeet, and—"

"No talk," he says.

Tom reaches slowly into his back pocket to get his wallet. The captor with the AK-47 points his gun at him. "It's okay, it's okay, I just want to show you something." Tom takes out his wallet and pulls out a folded-up copy of our "magic sheet." "This says who we are. We are men of peace. *Salam*. See? *Arabi*." The gunman curls his lip and drops the paper on the floor.

The van turns off the divided highway into a neighbourhood of sand-coloured houses hidden behind sand-coloured walls. We turn right, then right, then right again, as if making a circle. The driver honks as he drives through a gaggle of boys playing soccer in the road. We stop in front of a house where two men are holding a gate open. We turn into the driveway and the gate closes behind us. Fifteen, maybe twenty minutes have passed.

Our captivity has begun.


The evening before I left for Iraq, Dan showed me some things he'd found on the Internet: photos of men whose tortured bodies had been found in Fallujah; night-time video footage of U.S. soldiers gunning down an unarmed Iraqi man escaping from a burning truck. I could barely look. "This is why you have to go," he said.

The house filled with friends who came to say goodbye. Joseph and David, a married couple who are friends of ours, took a picture of Dan and me sitting together. I had no way of knowing, but in a few days that picture would be beamed around the world, Dan's smiling face cropped out of it so the kidnappers would not learn about my sexual identity.

As we lay in bed that night, I asked Dan a question. "If we knew this was our last night together, what would we do? Would we fall asleep as usual, or would we do something different?" I was so exhausted I could hardly keep my eyes open.

"I don't know," Dan said. The question floated around us in the darkness. Dan put his arm over me and held me close. I fell asleep.

The next day, Dan went to work and I spent the day in a frenzy of packing and last-minute errands. I borrowed a friend's car and met Dan at his workplace so we could go together to the airport. I pulled out a bar of fair trade chocolate for us to share and slid a disc into the CD player. The Proclaimers began to sing about walking five hundred miles. "It's too bad we're in the car," Dan said. "We could be dancing."

The traffic was a nightmare. In half an hour we moved one kilometre. "You're going to miss your flight," Dan said.

He hates the stress of being late; I love the thrill of arriving just on time. We got to the airport with less than an hour before the flight. We hugged, said goodbye and I dashed off. "Call me if you don't make it," Dan yelled. "Okay," I yelled back.

I arrived in Amman, the capital of Jordan, the next evening at eleven o'clock. I caught a bus to Abdali Square, Amman's chaotic transit hub, fended off the taxi drivers and carried my luggage to the Al Monzer Hotel, CPT's home away from home in the Middle East, where delegations assemble before going into Iraq and CPTers stay before travelling to Israel.

I met Harmeet and Norman for the first time on the morning of Sunday, November 20. After breakfast, we gathered in the room Harmeet and I shared. The agenda for our first meeting was very simple: introductions, overview of the schedule, orientation to our immediate surroundings, review of security measures for travel to and arrival in Baghdad, worship, and a "check-in," the daily CPT practice where team members share whatever they want about what they're experiencing and feeling.

Norman talked about Dietrich Bonhoeffer's notion of cheap grace. Although a lifelong pacifist, Norman found himself in the unusual, and fortunate, position of never having had to pay a cost for his convictions. He'd lived a very good, comfortable life as a professor of biophysics at Barts and the London School of Medicine and Dentistry, and he felt it was time that he took a risk for what he believed, especially now that he was retired and his remaining years of good health might be few. Although she was fully in support of his decision to come, his only worry was about his wife, Pat.

Harmeet was looking for a way to give something back. After an unsatisfying career as a computer engineer in Ottawa, he had moved to New Zealand to be with his sister after losing his job in the 2001 high-tech crash. He went back to school to study English literature and decided to get involved in the peace movement.

Over the next two days—the time it took us to get our visas—we met with representatives of the UN Assistance Mission to Iraq, the Red

Cross and the Mennonite Central Committee. We also met Iraqis who had fled to Jordan for safety. Over a million Iraqis were living as refugees in Jordan, a country of only five million.

We flew out of Amman on a thirty-passenger turbo-prop Embraer operated by Air Serv, a not-for-profit airline that flies NGOs in and out of humanitarian crisis zones. From twenty-nine thousand feet we descended in a tight, gut-wrenching corkscrew over the Baghdad International Airport—a technique used to avoid insurgent fire. A Canadian CPTer named Greg Rollins and Adib, one of the team's translators, met us at the airport. My heart pounded in my chest as I put my luggage in the trunk. The airport highway was the most dangerous road in Baghdad.

Issam, our driver, puffed on a cigarette and chatted nonchalantly as we followed a U.S. military convoy through the slalom course of earthen berms that protected the highway. I sat on the edge of my seat, eyes riveted to the soldier nervously manning a fifty-calibre gun on the rearguard Humvee in front of us. The closer you were, the more danger you were in. The smallest misunderstanding between a driver and a soldier could be lethal.

I began to relax only when we entered the familiar avenues of Karrada Darkhil in central Baghdad. I was overjoyed to see its fruit stands, Internet cafés and barbershops—until gunshots and wild honking rushed towards us from behind. I turned around and looked out the rear window to see a convoy of white pickup trucks barrelling towards us. An urgent voice blared in Arabic from a loudspeaker. The cars around us immediately pulled over. Instead of doing the same, Issam passed the vehicle in front of us and sped through an intersection. "Get over, get over," I shouted. Issam glanced in the rear-view mirror and pulled expertly into the right lane just before the convoy would have hit us. Four white pickup trucks escorting a shiny black sedan roared by. Men in black masks leaned out of windows and stood in the open truck beds, shouting, waving frantically, firing their weapons into the air. Adib sat in the front seat with his elbow resting on his open window while Issam worked his way through another cigarette.

They were deep in conversation, oblivious to the convoy that had just passed us. I touched Adib on the shoulder.

"Yes, Mr. Jim?" he said.

"Sorry to interrupt, Adib, but what was that all about?" I asked, trying to sound casual.

"Oh, this happens all the time. It must be somebody important passing by."

I sat back in my seat and willed myself to disappear as we threaded our way through Baghdad's choking traffic. It was unnerving, the way people looked at us, their faces startled and surprised, as if we were a rare, endangered species.

It was a relief to pull up in front of the CPT apartment. It was located on Abu Nawas Street, a major artery that ran along the Tigris River. Across the street, a sun-baked, rubble-strewn no man's land was all that remained of what used to be a lush paradise of fountains, gardens and footpaths following the river.

Maxine Nash came out to meet us. "Welcome to Baghdad," she said with a big smile.

"Max! It's so great so see you." I reached out to shake her hand, forgetting that public displays of affection between men and women were forbidden.

She shook her head. "Get the delegation into the apartment as quickly as you can."

The team looked weary to me: Tom Fox, Sheila Provencher, Anita David, Greg Rollins and of course Maxine. The Iraq project was a grind. In order to reduce their visibility, they spent long hours holed up in the apartment. There was nowhere to get away, even for a cup of coffee or a cold beer, nowhere to go for a walk to unwind. The lack of electricity, the blazing summer heat and constant winter chill, the suffering of the Iraqi people that they were helpless to alleviate, the daily explosions and gunfire, the relentless, gnawing fear for one's physical safety—all these things combined, accumulated, took their toll.

I had worked with Sheila and Max during my second stint in Iraq. They had been studying Arabic together at the time. Sheila was a

33-year-old Catholic from Boston who radiated warmth, ease, loving acceptance. She seemed to know every child, neighbour and shopkeeper in the team's immediate vicinity. Max was a 43-year-old Quaker from Iowa. She was unflappably calm, decisive, grounded: the kind of person you wanted to have around in a crisis. Anita I had not met before but I instantly liked her. A 59-year-old Presbyterian from Chicago, she greeted me with sparkling eyes and an irreverent grin. Greg I knew as a fellow Canadian CPTer. He was a 33-year-old Mennonite from Vancouver with an incorrigibly dry sense of humour and a relentlessly optimistic disposition. Tom I'd met once before at a CPT retreat in 2004, just as I was starting out as CPT's Canada program coordinator.

After some lunch, Greg took us up four flights of stairs to the new delegation apartment. It was a safer location than the ground-floor apartment where delegations used to stay.* Harmeet and I took one room and Norman took another. We put our bags down and then went to meet Greg and Abu Hani on the roof.

Abu Hani was our landlord, a Christian businessman who owned property throughout Karrada. He was a genial, self-assured man who, unlike most Christians with means, had elected to stand his ground against the bloody chaos that was consuming his beloved city. "There it is," he said, pointing to a newly installed water tank. Ten days before, an errant mortar had struck the roof and destroyed the previous tank. "You can't tell very much now, but it was a mess up here. Metal and shrapnel and roof tiles all over the place." He raised his chin defiantly. "I fixed everything the next day. It was lucky that no one was up here and that it hit the tank. The water absorbed a lot of the blast."

He pointed across the river to a skyline of domes and spires. "Those used to be Saddam's palaces—the Republican Palace and Baath Party headquarters. Of course, now they are the headquarters for the Americans."

---

* The first delegation CPT sent to Iraq was in October 2002. There had been fifteen delegations before us, involving 131 people. The sixth delegation travelled by road to Iraq during the invasion of March 2003.

"What's that big building that's been bombed?" Harmeet asked, pointing to the scorched shell of Baghdad's tallest office building.

"That's why our phone system doesn't work. That's the Tele-communications Building. Destroyed by the Americans," he said. He pointed in the opposite direction, to four smokestacks on a smoggy horizon. "That is the Baghdad electricity plant. As you can see, there is only one smokestack working. Another big headache. After the Second Gulf War,* Saddam had the electricity fixed in a few months. It's been three and a half years since the invasion and the electricity is worse now than it ever was.

"If you come over here," he said, walking to the east side of the roof, "you can see Karrada Darkhil." Before us was a blond and clay-brown expanse of flat roofs punctuated with palm trees, minarets, the occasional tall apartment building. "I have lived here all my life," he said proudly. "There is the Armenian church"—he pointed to a high parabolic arch centred with a cross—"the Shia mosque"—a modestly ornamented minaret—"and the Sunni mosque"—a massive turquoise dome hovering in the smog. "In Karrada, we live together in peace. Or we used to."

"How old is this neighbourhood?" I asked.

"Not very old," Abu Hani said. "Maybe sixty years."

"Really?" I said. "Some of the buildings look a lot older than that."

He laughed. "Everything looks old in Baghdad, especially the people. Baghdad used to be very small. But then there was a mass migration into the city in the thirties and forties and it exploded. Now it's a huge city of six million."

I noted with pleasure that the team's makeshift clothesline had escaped the mortar blast. There is always something that survives war, I thought.

The next day, Waleed, the team's other translator, took us for a tour of Baghdad. Where in my previous two trips we could take pictures and

* Iraqis call the 1980–89 war with Iran the First Gulf War, and the U.S.-led attack in 1991 the Second Gulf War.

walk freely just about anywhere, this time we rarely left the car and had to be very careful where we took pictures. You could feel the tension in the air, the fatigue, the edge of fear everywhere. There were more rolls of concertina wire, more fortressized buildings, more burly men with guns. There were more and bigger piles of rubble dumped along more roadways and boulevards. There was more smog, more burned-out vehicles, more squatters living in windowless buildings. There were more shortages of gasoline and electricity, more helicopters, explosions and gunfire. Otherwise, Baghdad was very much the same. Except for a repaved road here and there, no reconstruction had been done. It remained as I'd last seen it, a crumbling, chaotic, patched-up sprawl of potholes, burning garbage, leaking water mains, bombed and looted buildings, cement barricades and blast walls.

Still, I admired Baghdad. There was something irrepressible about it, a gritty, get-on-with-it, make-do determination that flowed like the Tigris and Euphrates through the chaos, the shortages, the soul-aching grief of war. You saw this spirit everywhere, in clothes hanging on the line, shops that unfailingly opened every day, trucks laden with goods for delivery, homeowners scrubbing down their sidewalks, children riding wildly decorated bicycles, boys hawking newspapers and tissue boxes at grid-locked intersections, the call to prayer punctuating the wheel of each day.

On the morning of Wednesday, November 23, I started a letter to my father.

Dear Dad,

Today is your granddaughter Olivia's birthday, and it's your oldest son's first morning in Baghdad. The Communist Party generator is purring at their big headquarters across the street, the power's out (hence this candlelight writing), and Tom Fox is in the middle of his yoga routine on the living room floor. It is 5:50 a.m. and all is right with the world. In Eastern Standard Time, it's 10:00 p.m. and still a day before. You will have just gone to bed.

I know this is not an easy thing for you or Mom, and I lament this burden of worry you both must carry because of my choices. It is my sense that this burden is increased by your feeling that my being in Iraq is serving no effective purpose. You've said it before, and you said it in the course of our last phone conversation, something like what good is this going to do in the face of the never-ending centuries of the Middle East's ever-escalating internecine violence. (In fact, we are setting our lives against something much larger than that: the apparently eternal violence of Empire itself, in this instance fuelled by an insatiable greed for fossil fuel.) It is my sense that this burden would somehow be easier if it didn't seem so much like a mad tilting at windmills.

When we were in Amman, we met with the top UN and Red Cross officials responsible for the protection of civilians in Iraq: John Pace, the chief of the Human Rights Office for Iraq, and Joerg Gasser, deputy head of the Red Cross delegation to Iraq. As you know, both the UN and the Red Cross were forced from Iraq by suicide bomb attacks and must now conduct their work from the arm's-length safety of Jordan. Both are eager to return but are unable to because of very real security concerns and their ponderous security protocols. Both must rely on intermittent visits. The UN relies on people coming to see them in their Green Zone lockdown, and the Red Cross flies through secure air corridors to permanent detention facilities located on three U.S. military bases. They cannot even get to Abu Ghraib because it is too dangerous to travel there. Their information-gathering systems, the lifeblood of human rights monitoring, are on life support. Both men were envious of CPT's freedom, mobility and access to Iraqis. And I was both surprised and delighted: they not only value but also rely on our reports and documentation. We are able to get to places, meet people, hear stories, witness conditions that the UN and the Red Cross, with all their vast international resources, are helpless to.

These meetings helped me to understand the importance of our work in a new way. We are acting as a kind of intermediary amplifying the cries of those who have no voice, in some small way serving as the eyes and ears of the UN and the Red Cross, a human rights special forces team that can get in close and shine the light where it needs to shine.

I hope I haven't sounded preachy. I'm just trying to find a way to ease this burden you're carrying. Maybe if you can better understand why I think this is worth doing it will be easier for you to bear. Failing that, I guess the best we can do is entrust each other to God's hands.

Well, the day is breaking here. Sleep well, Dad.

With love, James

That morning, we went to Baghdad's electrical power plant, an awe-inspiring complex of steaming pipes, towering chimneys, catwalks inter-connecting everywhere. Despite their best efforts, the plant manager told us, they were only able to get two of the four generators going at one time, often only one. He explained it was because there was a shortage of oil in the country and they couldn't get spare parts. The plant had been built by a German company and Halliburton was in charge of the contract. Why can't Halliburton get the parts from Germany? we asked. I don't know, he said, you must ask Halliburton about this.

Upon leaving the plant, we had to stop at the security gate. "*Ramallah wal day ik*," Adib said to the guard.

"*Hum d'Allah*," the guard answered. Praise be to God.

Adib turned around in his seat as we drove away. "Do you know this saying? *Ramallah wal day ik?*" he asked. I shook my head. "We have many sayings like this. It is part of our custom. When someone does something good for you, you can honour them by saying *Ramallah wal day ik*. It means *May God bless your parents*. I like to say it for the work of the simple man, like that security guard. It tells them they are doing something good. But you can also say it to someone who is doing something bad. It is a way to say a reminder to them—'You are doing the work of the bad man.'"

"*Ramallah wal day ik*," I said. "Thank you, Adib."

"You can use it any time," he said.

I sent my letter on the morning of Friday, November 25, just before Greg, Norman, Harmeet and I left for our meeting with Father Douglas Al Bazi, a Chaldean priest who was the pastor of St. Mari Catholic Church, located in a northern Baghdad suburb. We parked on a quiet residential street and walked towards a leafy property surrounded by concrete barriers and coils of concertina wire. The church itself was enclosed by eight-foot-high walls, and at the main gate there was a little hut that housed two armed guards.

Father Douglas, a hearty, big-bellied man in his mid-thirties, welcomed us with open arms and ushered us into his study. He left the room and returned with a nun, each of them carrying a tray laden with dishes of food. There was chicken, rice, salads, stuffed grape leaves, savoury pastries, grilled fish, lamb, things I'd never seen before. A feast of biblical proportions.

As we ate, Father Douglas talked. Under Saddam, the Christian community had numbered about two million and enjoyed full protection as a religious minority in a secular Iraq. In the turbulent "New Iraq," Christians were in serious peril as forces within the society sought to forge a new national consensus based on the elimination of all differences and enforcing conformity to a narrow spectrum of values and behaviours. Christians selling alcohol had been killed or had their shops destroyed, Christian women experienced growing pressure to wear the hijab, churches had been bombed. St. Mari itself had successfully defended itself against a car bomb attack by the guards who were hired by the church and paid by the government. Father Douglas himself had run outside firing his Kalashnikov. The lack of security and miserable living conditions meant Christians were leaving Iraq in droves. The ones who remained were too poor, too old or too stubborn to leave and kept as low a profile as they possibly could. Of the three hundred families that Father Douglas once served, only a hundred remained.

When our meal was finished, Father Douglas introduced us to one of his parishioners. "This is Lawrence, one of my altar boys. He's going to university now." Lawrence smiled shyly. "Lawrence was kidnapped last year. This is happening every day to Iraqis."

Shocked, we responded with questions. Avoiding our eyes, Lawrence explained how he'd been walking home from school when some armed men forced him into a vehicle. "I have the blindfold, but they not beat me or anything. They make to me to phone my father on the mobile. They make me say to my father you crying you torture you afraid to be kill unless my father to give $50,000." A final ransom of $10,000 was negotiated and Lawrence was released within ten days.*

At dinner that evening, Greg complained that he had laundry to do. The team's laundry facilities consisted of a plastic tub and the rooftop clothesline. "When am I going to get time? I can't do it tonight, I'm with the delegation all day tomorrow, and we leave for Karbala on Sunday. I can't go to Karbala in these," he said, referring to the clothes he was wearing.

"I don't have anything planned for tomorrow," Tom said. "Why don't I take the delegation for the morning meeting and you can get ready for the trip. It's been a while since I've been to Kadhimiya. I like it there."

"Are you sure?" Greg asked.

"Yeah, it's no problem, but I need to be back for the afternoon."

"We can do that, no problem," Greg said. "Our morning meeting is at ten. That'll give you lots of time to get back to the apartment, the delegation can grab a bite to eat, and then I'll take them in the afternoon for the two o'clock meeting at the Muslim Scholars Association."

I had first met Tom in August 2004 at a CPT retreat. He had just completed his training in Chicago and I had just been appointed to the role of Canada coordinator. I happened to overhear him say he had been in the Marine Corps. I was immediately intrigued. How does a former Marine become an activist, pacifist, violence-reduction Christian peacemaker? He explained that he had been a musician, not a soldier. He played the clarinet in the Marine Corps Band. In fact, he had never learned how to use a gun. He retired after twenty years, sold all his musical instruments and took training to become a baker in 1993.

I found this curious. I imagined that if I were a musician capable of making beautiful music, I would never want to part with my instruments. I asked him why.

"Well, I'm an artist. And art is something you give yourself to completely or not at all. You can't do it in half-measures. It's all or nothing."

---

* Father Douglas himself would be kidnapped almost a year later, on November 20, 2006, and held for nine days.

Led by a mutual spiritual curiosity, Tom and his former wife, Jan Stansel, began to explore Quakerism in 1983. A spiritual awakening during his transition out of the Marine Corps Band led him deeper into the practice of Quaker spirituality and he experienced a growing desire to live Quaker non-violence in an active way. When 9/11 happened, he was profoundly disturbed by the hard turn of American policy towards unlimited global warfare. Feeling an urgent call to respond in some way, he began to research different options and found CPT's website. He left his job as a manager in a large organic food chain, went on a delegation and took the CPT training. Now his work was about to begin: he was leaving for Iraq in three weeks.

I asked him if he had any family. Yes, he said, two children: a son named Andrew, who was nineteen, and a daughter named Kassie, who was twenty-four. I asked him how they felt about his decision to work in Iraq. He answered in his matter-of-fact way that they were of course worried but he explained to them this was something he had to do. "Armies expect casualties when they go to war. Those working for peace in war zones have to expect the same," he'd said.

The next day, I got up early to do my laundry. I scrubbed my clothes by candlelight in the bathroom. I was excited about our trip. Karbala was a fabulous city of gold-brick domes and minarets, Byzantine markets, solemn pilgrims, gracious boulevards. And we were going to meet Hussein Al Ibraheemy and Sami Rasouli, the founders of Muslim Peacemaker Teams, a group of Muslim peace activists CPT had trained in January 2005. They had ambitious plans to train twenty teams to do development work and human rights education across the country.

I went up to the roof to hang out my clothes. The sun was rising over Baghdad and the air was remarkably breathable. I lifted my face to the glorious new light. How I loved it up there. The roof was the team's retreat centre, spa and gym, the only escape from visitors, the phone, the confinement of the apartment. There wasn't much to it—a big cement pad furnished with some plastic lawn chairs and piles of junk that had nowhere else to go—but when you were there you could reach up and touch the sky, and for a little while feel that anything was possible. I hung up my laundry and descended the stairs. It was time to leave for our first meeting.

Kadhimiya was my favourite place in Baghdad. At its centre was the Kādhim shrine, a gold-gleaming complex of towering minarets surrounded by a vast, teeming market where you could buy everything from bales of second-hand clothing to major electrical appliances to pomegranates. I had been to Kadhimiya several times before and never felt alarm, but that day I was on hyper–red alert. As we followed Adib into the Gordian market, it felt as if we were walking into a wall of hard stares. I checked constantly to make sure I could see Tom's bald head following behind Norman and Harmeet. If we were separated, it would be impossible to find our way out of the market and back to the van. I didn't want to think about what could happen to a lost foreigner.

We turned right at a tea shop I remembered for its exquisite pyramids of pistachio sweet goods. Imam Ali's house was just around the corner, a modest two-storey brick building marked by a set of concrete stairs on the edge of a labyrinthine world of crumbling arabesque houses.

Two men with bulging arms and machine guns hanging from shoulder straps stopped us in front of the imam's house. The last time I'd visited, we were greeted by an old, bent-over man. Adib explained that we had an appointment with the imam at ten o'clock. They offered us their chairs and brought us tea. At eleven we were invited into the house by the old bent-over man. We took off our shoes and sat on a plush blue carpet in a spartan waiting room decorated with pictures of black-turbaned holy men. At 11:20 we were taken behind an intricately carved wooden screen.

Imam Ali was sitting cross-legged and barefoot on an ornate, hand-carved wooden chair. He wore dark brown vestments and the black turban that signified his authority as a direct descendant of the Prophet. He greeted us warmly, we shook his hand and then sat cross-legged on the floor in a semi-circle in front of him. I guessed that he was about forty, young to be the senior cleric of the third-holiest Shia mosque in Iraq. He was attended by an aide who came and went, whispered things into his ear, handed him a phone.

It had been a traumatic year and a half for the imam and his community. On March 2, 2004, two weeks after I last saw him, fifty-eight pilgrims were killed when his mosque was bombed during the first open celebration of the Ashura since it had been banned by Saddam Hussein. Anticipating the possibility of an attack, Imam Ali had asked CPT to be present as observers at the religious festival. CPTers filmed the immediate aftermath of the bombing from the roof of a hotel located across the street from the shrine. Ashura is one of Shia Islam's holiest days and marks the emergence of Shiism as a distinct tradition within Islam.* On August 31, five months later, rumours of a suicide bomb attack during a Shia religious procession caused a stampede across the Imams Bridge that killed 965 pilgrims. The Imams Bridge connects Kadhimiya with Adhamiyah, a Sunni neighbourhood located directly across the Tigris River with a reputation for armed resistance to the U.S. occupation.

Imam Ali looked to have aged ten years since I had last seen him. Then, I had been impressed by his gentle comportment, his conviction that the two denominations could work together to form a new political accommodation. This time he was full of suspicion and blame. Dialogue and co-operation with Sunnis was no longer possible or desirable. He talked in angry, repetitious circles.

Tom caught my eye and discreetly pointed to his watch. "We've got to wrap this up," he whispered, "or we're never going to make it back to the apartment."

---

* After the Prophet's death in 632 CE, a dispute arose over his succession. A number of the Prophet's companions elected Abu Bakr to be the leader of the Muslim community, while others believed the Prophet had chosen his cousin and son-in-law, Ali ibn Abi Talib. This dispute culminated in the martyrdom of Ali's son Husayn at the Battle of Karbala in 680 CE. The Shia believe in a divinely appointed succession through the lineage of Ali, while the Sunni choose their religious leaders through shura (consultation and election).

It was another half-hour before we could honourably extricate ourselves from the meeting. There was no longer enough time to go back to the apartment to make the switch. Tom called Greg to let him know. We grabbed something to eat in Kadhimiya and proceeded directly to the Umm al-Qura mosque in Ghazaliya.

The Muslim Scholars Association was founded on April 14, 2003, five days after the fall of Baghdad. It was a hard-line organization of Sunni clerics opposed to the U.S. occupation and believed to have links to the insurgency. Aspiring to be the Sunni counterpart to the Shia *marja'iyya* (religious authority) led by Grand Ayatollah Ali al-Sistani, it positioned itself as a behind-the-scenes power broker whose role it was to frame political goals and strategies for the whole Sunni community. CPT had been working for six months to establish a relationship with the Muslim Scholars. Our delegation's visit would be CPT's third meeting with them.

We arrived twenty minutes early for our two o'clock meeting. We pulled over within sight of the Umm al-Qura security gate and waited on a lonely arterial road bordering a middle-class residential area to the south and the open expanses surrounding the mosque complex to the north. There was no pedestrian traffic to speak of, and only the occasional passing car. At 1:50 p.m. we were allowed through the mosque checkpoint and entered the sprawling grounds of the Muslim Scholars national headquarters. The vast parking lot was empty but for a handful of cars clustered near the main entrance.

# CHAPTER TWO

They take us into the house one at a time, Harmeet first and then Tom. It astounds me. This is where they're taking us—a house on a quiet residential street with neighbours all around us? "Come," a voice says when it's my turn. The voice grabs my arm and pulls me out of the van. My mind screams Run! Run! but my body obediently follows. Eight steps to a door, an immediate right, six brisk steps through a dark kitchen and I'm in a spacious living room.

My first impression is of the colour blue, the colour of the room's grubby, threadbare carpet. Then I hear the undulating cry of Quran song, a commotion of Iraqi men around me. Harmeet and Tom are standing against a wood-frame couch. A young, lean man with a moustache walks in front of Harmeet. "Ogod," he snarls, pushing him in the chest.

Harmeet drops like a stone. Young Moustache Man steps sideways. "Ogod," he orders, pushing Tom in the same way. Tom braces himself against the shove. Young Moustache Man glares. Tom sits down slowly and puts his right foot on top of his left knee. The sole of Tom's shoe is dangerously exposed. In Arabic culture one never displays the sole of one's foot unless to show contempt.

Young Moustache Man is not pleased. "No," he says, slapping Tom's foot. Tom holds it in place. "La!" Young Moustache Man says, his voice louder, hitting Tom's foot with more force, then threatening him with his fist. Tom looks at him defiantly. A man wearing a green suit jacket with a gun tucked in his belt touches Young Moustache Man on the arm and says something in Arabic. Young Moustache Man moves away, scowling. Tom puts his foot down.

Above Harmeet and Tom, hanging on the wall, is a picture of a bearded man with puppy-dog eyes. He's wearing a crown of thorns and long flowing robes. His fingers are pointing to a flaming heart in the middle of his chest. It's the Sacred Heart. Who are these people? I wonder. Young Moustache Man grabs my arm and turns me around. "Sit down," he says, shoving me in the chest.

*Don't let him push you around,* my brain screams, but my body stays relaxed and falls into sitting. Norman is brought in next and made to sit on a second bench seat located against the wall on our right.

The process of Observing Everything I Possibly Can begins immediately. Every scrap of information is vital. Who knows which detail will be the vital clue, the key that will open the door to freedom. Doors and windows first. No windows, four doors. There's a glass door opening into an interior window-well in the corner to my left. Another door in the next corner moving clockwise. A door into the kitchen. A door in the corner to Norman's right.

Quran song is coming from a 24-hour Quran channel and Arabic script flows below halcyon images of running water, green forests, blue cloudy skies. The television, with satellite hookup, sits in a white and grey plastic wall unit located along the left wall. There are three worn and scratched wood-frame bench seats: the one Tom, Harmeet and I are sitting on, the one Norman is sitting on, and one against the wall across from me to Norman's right.

In the corner to Norman's left, a waist-high wooden ironing board sheathed with a soiled coverlet. An antiquated iron and a disc made of clay from Karbala sitting on top, a set of Muslim prayer beads hung over the narrowing end. Above Norman, the only other picture in the room, a portrait of Saint Bernadette.

The room is spacious, fifteen feet deep and twenty-five feet wide, with faded lime-green walls and a pink ceiling. A naked light bulb hangs from ornate plaster mouldings in the middle of the ceiling. On the wall across from us, to the right of the kitchen door, there are two plaster arches. Inside each arch a decorative wall hanging has been taped to the wall: On the left, two straggly-looking purple plastic flowers; on the right, a wooden cooking spoon and salad fork crossing each other in an X. To the left of the arches, a broken heart-shaped wall clock, garish, plastic and red. To the right of the kitchen door, a wooden shelf holding a kerosene lamp. To the left of the kitchen door, a Western 2005 calendar turned to September.

Observing Everything I Possibly Can must be done carefully, discreetly, disinterestedly, as much as possible with peripheral vision, the art of seeing without looking.

There is a quick conference of captors in the kitchen doorway. Heads nod and everyone except Young Moustache Man leaves the room. He paces back and forth, rubs his hands together with an excited smile, stops in front of Norman. "My? My?" he asks, forming his hand into a cup and raising it to his lips, eyebrows lifting in question.

Norman shakes his head. "No, thank you kindly," he says.

He turns to us and makes the same gesture. "My? My?" he asks.

Tom and Harmeet both shake their heads. "*La shokren,*" Tom says.

I want to say no. The water must come from the tap, and the last thing I want is to be stricken with diarrhea while kidnapped. Plus, the thought of accepting *anything* from these men, save the immediate return of our freedom, is repugnant to me. "Yes, please," I say. I have to. It's an opening, the first opportunity to communicate, a chance to make them see our humanity. It's a lot harder to kill someone if you see him as a human being.

Young Moustache Man hands me a glass smeared with fingerprints. "*Ramallah wal day ik,*" I say, as Adib taught me.

He looks incredulous, says something in Arabic. The only thing I understand is that he's asking me a question.

"*Ramallah wal day ik,*" I say again, nodding sincerely.

Young Moustache Man laughs and slaps his knee, repeats the phrase again and again. "This *Arabi?*" he asks me.

"No *Arabi.* English. I only speak English. My name is Jim," I say, pointing to myself. Young Moustache Man nods. "Are you married?" I ask. The captor looks puzzled. "Married? Do you have children?" I point to him and use my hand to indicate the height of a small child.

"This? *Whalid?*" he says, pointing to himself, eyes widening. I nod. He shakes his head sadly. "*La whalid.*"

Suit Jacket Man enters the room with four sets of handcuffs dangling from his hand. He is followed by a great big giant of a man. Young Moustache Man laughs excitedly and points at me. He says something to them that ends with *Ramallah wal day ik*. The other men do not smile.

Suit Jacket Man motions for Norman to stand up. "Where is your passport?" he says. Norman gives it to him. "Norman Kember. You are British?"

"Yes."

"You are a doctor?" Suit Jacket Man says.

"Doctor?" Young Moustache Man says, reaching for the passport. Suit Jacket Man shows him where it says *Doctor*. "Ah, doctor," Young Moustache Man says reverentially.

"Well, yes. I'm a retired professor of biophysics, not a medical doctor."

"Your notebook please, Doctor. And everything in your pockets." Norman hands over his notebook, empties out his trousers and jacket pockets. Great Big Man puts Norman's things into a plastic bag. The last thing Norman gives him is a bubble package of medication.

"That's medicine. It's for high blood pressure. For my heart. My heart," Norman says, pointing to his chest. "I need to keep that."

"You have some heart condition?" Suit Jacket Man asks.

"High blood pressure," Norman says.

"You can keep that," Suit Jacket Man says, "but I must to have your glasses."

"Oh dear," Norman says. "Must you take my glasses? I'm an old man. I can't read without them."

"You do not need them for that. But they are right here. Everything is right here." Norman hands over his glasses. "Now I must to search you, Doctor." Norman lifts his arms above his head. Big Man and Suit Jacket Man pat him down thoroughly. "Now put your hands behind your back, Doctor." Young Moustache Man locks his wrists into a set of handcuffs. "Now sit down, Doctor."

It's my turn next. Suit Jacket Man asks me for my passport. "You are Canadian?" I nod. "James Loney," he reads. He puts my passport in his pocket. "I must to take your camera and notebook." I reluctantly hand him the camera. "It's old-fashioned," he says.

"Yes," I say. It's the 35-millimetre camera Dan bought with his own money when he was in grade eight. It goes into the same bag as Norman's things.

"Now your pockets," Suit Jacket Man says.

I pass him a handful of Iraqi dinars, a pen and a cellphone. I watch him pocket the cellphone with a pang of desperation as I realize the only number I know to call for help is Doug's back in Canada.

"Your watch," he says.

"My father gave me this watch," I say.

"You will have it. Everything is right here. We are not thieves. You have everything back. We not take one dinar. Now I must to search you."

I raise my hands for the second time that day. They are thorough, check all my pockets, my jacket, every inch of my body.

"Your hands behind your back," Suit Jacket Man says. Somebody, being very careful, locks my wrists into some handcuffs. As they click down, I wonder how tight they will go, if they will cut into skin, press mercilessly against bone, cut off circulation, as I had experienced at the hands of municipal police when I was arrested for civil disobedience. The clicking stops and there is no discomfort. "Sit down," he says.

Harmeet is next. Suit Jacket Man wants Harmeet's glasses. "I can't see anything without them," Harmeet says, objecting.

"You do not need them. We keep them right here. This not a problem."

When it is Tom's turn, he pulls his last folded-up copy of the CPT magic sheet out of his wallet and hands it to Suit Jacket Man. "This explains who we are and what we're doing in Iraq," he says. "We're members of a peace organization." Tom addresses him like a peer.

"I will read it," Suit Jacket Man says, sliding it into his pocket. Then like the rest of us, Tom is searched and handcuffed. Young Moustache Man picks up a scrap of dusty rag lying on the floor and rips it into four long strips. I note with relief that it looks reasonably clean. They blindfold Norman first, then me. The blindfold is applied gently and sags at the bridge of my nose. I wonder what is going to happen to us as I am taken by the arm and led away. The voice beside me is calm and reassuring. I count twenty steps when a tug on my arm tells me to sit down. I manage to sit cross-legged without losing my balance. I am immediately uncomfortable, sitting without any support for my back. I know I can handle this for a while, Harmeet and Tom probably can too, but this will be very hard for Norman.

There are two more flurries of motion around me and then a long period of silence. I decide to chance it. "Tom? Harmeet? Norman?"

"Quiet. No talk," a voice orders.

I test, probe, analyze every sound, take scrupulous measurements of the direction, force and intention of each footstep, each voice, motion, object being moved or used. Time passes. Discomfort escalates into full-body agony.

*Adib will have called the team, and the team will have called Doug. One of the first things he will do is put together a crisis team. Do our families know? Has Dan been told? Where will he be and what will he be doing? This is going to be rather disruptive for a lot of people.*

The captors come and go, talk in hushed voices, answer cellphone calls. A voice begins to read, in Arabic. It must be the text of our magic sheet. The voice is rich and mellifluous, flows in perfect bass tones. It is calm, deliberate, in charge. The other voices seek instruction from it, respond with deference. Bodies move whenever the voice speaks. It is a voice we will never see the face of. We call this voice Number One.

Time passes. Then a sudden thump, a moan, silence. My heart pounds. Has somebody been struck on the head? I wait another minute and then chance it. "Norman? Are you okay?"

"Sorry. Just making an adjustment," he says. His voice is strained.

"La killam," a voice commands. Silence again. Then the sound of a chain being pulled across a concrete floor. A dog snarling, barking savagely. A voice, crying, begging, pleading in Arabic. Coming from somewhere within the house. Sounds that make my eyes open wide with terror beneath my blindfold. Then, mercifully, the silence returns.

More time passes. Norman asks to use the bathroom. I hold my breath and wait for the answer. I've been wanting to ask myself, as a way of being able to stretch and move a little, learn more about where we are being held, but decided the safer course remained with silence and enduring.

"Yes, Doctor. One minute, please," Number One says.

Then, footsteps entering the room, a voice out of breath. Suit Jacket Man perhaps? "Where are the Italians? Who is Italian here?"

There are no Italians here, we say.

"Who is Indian here? You. Are you Indian?"

"My parents are Kashmiri, but I am Canadian," Harmeet says.

"We are two Canadians, one British and one American. None of us is Italian or Indian," Tom says.

I hear a flurry of Arabic and then, "Doctor, would you like to go to the *hamam*?"

I hear Norman grunting, his body struggling to get up, movement out of the room. A few minutes later I hear steps entering the room, the legs of a plastic chair scraping against the floor, Norman saying, "Thank you."

I am suddenly lifted into standing. They unlock my handcuffs. I look down through the crack at the bottom of my blindfold and am astonished by the bare sandalled feet of one of the captors: they are the biggest, most powerful slab-of-meat feet I've ever seen. The captor locks my hands together at my waist, takes my arm, brings me to a destination thirty steps and two turns away. He stops, opens a door, pushes me into a closet-sized bathroom and closes the door.

I immediately tilt my head back and scan the bathroom through the bottom of my blindfold. There is a small rectangular window above my head. Impossible to climb through with handcuffs on. The toilet is a ceramic squat basin set into the floor. There's a tank affixed to the wall with a pull chain to release water into the basin. A plastic jug on the floor. No toilet paper.

I am surprised at how easy it is to lower my zipper in handcuffs. Try as I might, my urethra won't let go. They bring me back to the room and make me sit in a chair with my knees touching a wall. Norman and Tom are next to me. Harmeet sits behind us on his own. The captors leave the room.

"My blindfold is really loose," I whisper. "It's ready to fall off."

"I know. Mine too," Tom says.

"If my eyes weren't closed, I'd be able to see everything," Harmeet says.

"Should we say something?" I ask. It seems crazy to me. Excuse me, Mr. Kidnapper, but my blindfold is coming off . . . Someone enters. I decide it's better to say something. "Excuse me?"

"Yes?" the voice says, gentle and solicitous. It's Number One.

"Our blindfolds are falling off," I say.

"If you don't want us to see you, then we don't want to see you," Tom says.

"Yes, I see that," Number One says. "I have something for that." He gives an order. A drawer opens and closes. Then, standing directly behind us, he says, "I have a hat for each of you." With exquisite care he removes my blindfold, places a hat on my head and pulls it down over my eyes. "You must not to see me. It very dangerous. For you and for me. Are you hungry? Would you like some food? Some biscuit?" We don't answer. "Doctor, would you like some biscuit?"

"No, thank you," he says.

"Tom? Jim? Harmeet? Something to drink? Seven? Miranda? Pepsi?" I shake my head. The only thing I want is my freedom.

I hear water pouring into a cup, someone drinking. "Thank you," Norman says. More water-pouring sounds, and then a cup being placed in my hands.

"Is this from the tap? If it is, it will make us sick," I say.

"It is good water," Number One says.

"Thank you," I say. I don't believe him and I don't want it, but there doesn't seem to be any choice. I gulp it down. I am thirstier than I thought. He offers me a second glass. "No, thank you," I say.

"I get the phone call from another group," Number One tells us. "You know this group, al-Tawhid wal-Jihad? This very dangerous. They want you, especially you Thomas, and you Doctor. This very dangerous. Iraq very dangerous. There are many groups that take you. I not give you to them. I cannot. *Inshallah*, you will stay with me, and I make sure you release. You safe with me, *inshallah*. We are not terrorists. We are not al Qaeda. We are different. We are Iraqi. We fight for Iraqi freedom." He speaks gently, like a parent reassuring a frightened child.

"Are you Sunni or Shia?" Norman asks.

Number One is suddenly angry. "We are not Sunni, we are not Shia. We are Iraqi! No Shia-Sunni. This something America make. We are Iraqi! Do you understand, Doctor?"

"Yes, you are all Iraqi," Norman says.


The captors chat amongst themselves, yawn, fall into silence. I have to talk to them, open a channel of communication, punch through the muting effect of the blindfold. I rack my brain for some way to engage these men and make them see our humanity. I send mental prompts to the others, hoping they will speak. It is a relief when I can finally think of something to say. "Excuse me," I say when I am sure Number One is in the room.

"Yes?"

"May I ask a question?"

I feel his hand on my shoulder. "Yes, of course."

"Did you read our white paper, the one in Arabic and English?"

"Yes, I read it."

"What did you think?"

Number One takes a breath. "You are the peaceful man. I love the peaceful man. Your group . . . the name of your group . . .?"

"Christian Peacemaker Teams," Tom says.

"I not hear of this. You are the Christian?"

"Yes, but we aren't here to make anybody Christian," Tom says. "We believe in peace, non-violence, *salam*. We are against the war and we are against the occupation. We came to Iraq before the war to try and stop it from happening, and we've been here ever since to try and get the United States to leave. We are independent. We are not part of any government or church."

"Thomas, it very dangerous in Baghdad. Very dangerous."

"Yes, so it seems," Tom says. "But we are a human rights organization that works in war zones. We have a team in Palestine as well. Harmeet, Jim and I have all been to Palestine."

"You go to Palestine?" Number One says to Harmeet.

"Yes. Last year, with the International Solidarity Movement," Harmeet says.

"What you do in Baghdad?" Number One asks Tom.

"We work for justice for security detainees," Tom explains. "Iraqis who are imprisoned by the U.S. We go with families to the American authorities. We document torture and mistreatment. We are here to find out the truth about what's going on in Iraq and we tell people back home so that it will change. The most recent place we visited was Fallujah. We were taken by Sheik Mohammed to the site of the mosque where the video was taken of U.S. soldiers killing Iraqis on the floor."

"What can this do? This can do nothing," Number One says.

"We are in Iraq trying to do the same thing you are doing, which is to get the Americans to leave, except we're trying to do it non-violently."

"Not everyone in America wants this war," I say, jumping in. "Many many people are against it. The media just never talks about us. They make it seem as if nobody is against it."

There is a period of silence. I hear someone walking about the room. Suddenly Number One's voice is at my ear. "See this?" By looking down through the crack at the bottom of my hat I can see he's holding a photograph in front of me. It's a wallet-sized studio portrait of four children. The two oldest stand behind the two youngest in front. Their faces are proud and solemn. "This is a picture of my family. My sister's children. Can you see them?"

"Yes," I say.

"This is a tragic event. They are all killed. All of them dead. Seven members of my family. In one night, at a checkpoint. My sister and all of her family. The Americans shoot them, kill every member of my family. They are innocent! Why! I look at this picture every night. I keep it by my bed." He points to each child, starting with the oldest. "This is Mohanned, and this Mohammed, and Zayneb and Noor."

"Mohanned, Mohammed, Zayneb and Noor," I repeat. "I will remember them."

"Thank you." The oldest is seven, he tells me, the youngest two.

"I am sorry. They are beautiful children."

He hands the picture to Norman. "Doctor, look. Do you see? They are all gone."

"Yes, I am sorry. I have two daughters of my own," Norman says.

"This happen one year ago. I died that night. I am a dead man now. I see their face every night. I can't sleep . . . I *can't* sleep. What can I do? The only thing I can do is stop the American occupation. I am a dead man."

Number One's story transports me back to an emergency room in Balad's hospital. Mahmud Achnud Nejin, a 43-year-old farmer, was lying unconscious on a stretcher, the left side of his hip and abdomen covered in a mass of bandages. He had been shot the day before by U.S. soldiers at an impromtu checkpoint. "He is in shock and has severe bleeding. The bullet exploded in the groin," hospital director Dr. Kassim Hartam told us. "This is not the only case." He estimated that his hospital had treated twenty "innocent civilians" shot by U.S. soldiers at checkpoints in the past six months.

"We know about this," I tell Number One. "I have met several families who had people killed at checkpoints. This is why we come to Iraq. We learn about these stories, document them, bring them back to our countries so people can learn about what's happening in Iraq, and when enough people find out, things will change."

"What good does this do? This does nothing. You say many Americans are against this war. Why do the parents send their children to this war? Why do they send their children to Iraq? Why? One night we make some attack against a Humvee. This north of Baghdad. We make a good attack and kill three soldiers. I see him after, this boy, his face very beautiful. Maybe he is twenty, twenty-one. He is *very* beautiful. I see him, lying on the ground, this boy. He is dead. I see him and I think of his mother. Why this? Why?" His voice is anguished.

Words! I need words. Our lives could depend on what I say. "You know, there is a woman in the United States named Cindy Sheehan whose son—his name was Casey—was killed in Iraq. And she wanted to ask George Bush why her son had to die in Iraq, and he refused to meet her. Many times she asked and he never answered her. So finally, when George Bush was having a vacation at his ranch, she went and set up a tent on the road to his ranch. And the media came, and she got on TV, and then more and more people came, until there were hundreds there with her, all asking for George Bush to come and meet her."

"Yes, I know this. This very famous," Number One says.

"It is usually the poor who end up in the army. They join because they don't have any other choice," I say.

"Yes, I know this," he says, impatient. "There is no way for them to get the education. But what can this do? This does nothing. We must to fight."

"We are in Iraq trying to do the same thing you are doing," Tom says. "I want my country to leave. What my country has done is wrong. It makes me sick to think what we've done. But we're trying to change things non-violently."

"They will never leave. Your way will never work. The only thing we have to do is fight. I have to fight for Iraqi freedom," Number One says.

"If enough people find out about what is happening, they will vote against George Bush. The United States will have to withdraw. In other conflicts non-violence has worked. Take the Badshah Khan in Pakistan. He was like a Muslim Gandhi who forced the British to leave Pakistan non-violently—"

Number One interrupts. "Do you expect us to stand there and let them shoot us? We are not crazy." He turns abruptly and leaves the room.

—

I was vaguely aware in university that there existed a group of people who refused on principle to use violence and that they were called pacifists. The very idea seemed preposterous. Of course war was bad, that went without saying, but if another country invaded yours, or if somebody attacked you, you had the indisputable right to defend yourself—with whatever force was required, so long as it was commensurate with the threat you were facing. This was basic common sense and a self-evident truth. The only alternative was to allow your enemy to walk all over you like a doormat.

I was sharing an apartment with Dan Hunt and William Payne. William suggested we visit a place called Dorothy Day House in Detroit. He said it was a house of hospitality. What's that? I asked. He didn't know exactly, but it was a place where homeless people could go. The auxiliary bishop of Detroit, Thomas Gumbleton, was going to be speaking there about non-violence. He had been arrested for protesting against nuclear weapons. He must be one of those fringe lunatics, I thought. I didn't want to go, but William wouldn't take no for an answer.

Dorothy Day House was an old, dingy, falling-apart place with slanting floors and paint-peeling walls. The furniture looked as if it had been rescued from the curb in front of someone's house. The kitchen was cluttered with jars of strange-looking beans and grains. A man wearing women's clothes who lived at the house sat down beside me. The impulse to switch chairs was overwhelming.

William, who has this annoying gift for inviting people to think about doing something they would never have imagined themselves doing (and inevitably end up doing!), told me they were looking for live-in volunteers. It was my last year of university and I was in agony about what to do next. I shook my head and rolled my eyes. There was no way I was going to live in a place like this.

Dinner was announced and everybody lined up with a plate. They called it a potluck supper. I'd never been to one before. I thought it was rather a good idea. Everybody brought a different dish and you shared whatever there was to share. After supper, people were invited to gather in the living room to hear Bishop Gumbleton speak.

My arms were crossed and my mental defences were ready. He was warm and gentle and spoke with deep humility. He talked about how love of enemy was integral to the Gospel, and the Cross was the way of non-violence. He explained how the first tradition of the Church was pacifist: a Christian could not be a soldier under pain of excommunication and was prohibited from using violence in self-defence. He talked about Martin of Tours and Oscar Romero, Dr. Martin Luther King and Dorothy Day. He talked about the power of non-violence to transform society and heal the wounds of violence. I listened and found it impossible to dismiss what he was saying. I uncrossed my arms. A window had opened in my mind.

That year, 1986-87, Dan, William and I were Basilian associates, which meant we were interested in becoming priests and had accepted formation with the Basilian Fathers. We rented a two-bedroom apartment in Windsor's poorest neighbourhood. We slept in the larger room and crammed our desks into the smaller room. We prayed the office each morning (the ancient prayer required of all those who take vows and enter religious life) and read the day's Scripture reading.

I remember it vividly. The Gospel was vitally alive. It seemed that Jesus was pointing his finger right at me, speaking directly to me. "Go, sell everything you own, give it to the poor, and come follow me."

I began to give what I was feeling a name. I called it the unknown option—the call to leave everything behind, all my possessions, all that was known and comfortable, for a journey along an unknown road where, through a life of radical poverty in solidarity with the poor, I would discover a new way of being, a life of joy overflowing, the Kingdom of God where all live as sisters and brothers in the glorious freedom of the children of God.

At the end of that school year I graduated from the University of Windsor with a BA in history and left the Basilians after deciding their comfortable institutions were not compatible with the unknown option. Dan, William and I went our separate ways for a while: Dan to the University of Toronto to study philosophy, William to Laval in

Quebec City to study geography and I to the University of Toronto to do a master's in social work.

On one of his trips through Toronto on his way to Quebec City, William suggested we visit a Catholic Worker community called Angelus House that, much to my surprise, was located right in Toronto. Over bowls of lentil soup and cups of herbal tea, Lauren Griffen and Charlie Angus (now a Member of Parliament for Timmins–James Bay) explained the philosophy of the Catholic Worker movement to us. "The aim of the Catholic Worker," they said, "is to build a new society in the shell of the old where it is easier for people to be good." The reconstruction of the social order was to be accomplished through the works of mercy performed at a personal sacrifice— feeding the hungry, giving drink to the thirsty, clothing the naked, sheltering the homeless. Every parish would sponsor a house of hospitality and every home would have a Christ Room where Jesus could be welcomed in the face of a needy brother or sister. Voluntary poverty was central: the extra pair of shoes, the extra coat in your closet, belonged to the one who was without. We were to be go-givers, not go-getters. Work was a gift to be freely given for the common good. By firing the bosses we could reclaim our work from wage slavery and build a new economy based on mutual aid and co-operation rather than personal profit. By going back to the land we could heal the earth from the ravages of industrial capitalism and restore our lost sense of communal identity. And we were to love our enemies just as the Gospel said. A disciple of Christ must not enlist as a soldier, work in armaments manufacturing or pay for war through his or her taxes. Christians were not to kill for any reason.

My heart was on fire. I couldn't believe it: here it was, everything I'd been searching for, a practical manifesto for living out the unknown option! I looked over at Bill. Chuck and Lauren must have sensed our excitement. "Why don't you guys start a Catholic Worker house yourselves?" they said.

"How do you do that?" I asked shyly.

"The Catholic Worker is an anarchist movement," they said. "There's no mother house, no rule book, no one in charge. No one needs to ask permission to live the Gospel. You just do it!"

I quit the social work program and went back to Windsor. A high school teacher I knew named Greg Mailloux wanted to start a house for homeless teenaged boys and was looking for somebody to work with. We raised money to buy a house, formed a board, recruited volunteers (William among them for a while) and opened our doors. We called it St. Don Bosco House after a nineteenth-century Italian educator.

The work was good, but I wasn't happy. Greg and I were a mismatched pair. Greg was a charismatic Catholic who loved to sing praise songs and I was a social justice Catholic who wanted to do the Catholic Worker.

In September 1990, we started. Dan, William and I rented a three-bedroom house in Toronto. It was not long before we got a call from a friend who knew somebody who was just getting out of a psychiatric hospital after a suicide attempt. He was recovering from AIDS-related pneumonia and needed a place to stay. Peter was our first guest. We found him a bed and hung sheets in the dining room doorways to afford him a little privacy. The second was a Spanish man named Marco who taught us how to make paella. He slept on the couch until he was deported to Spain.

We found a bigger house downtown: seven bedrooms for half the rent. We scraped, painted, scrubbed, searched for abandoned furniture, scavenged giant glass jars from restaurants and filled them with lentils and beans. We welcomed whoever came across our path: Adrian from the cathedral; Barry and Mike from the Fred Victor; Slash and Margaret Anne from William's school; Jacob who had just arrived from Ethiopia. We hosted a weekly Mass in our living room and had meetings for "clarification of thought"—free-ranging discussions for charting a path from things as they are to things as they should be. We published a newspaper called *The Mustard Seed* that we mailed everywhere and distributed free all over town. People came by for something to eat or just to shoot the breeze. We sat on the front porch in the evenings, drank tea with visitors, trucked laundry to the laundromat, cooked and cleaned and washed mountains of dishes. To pay the bills, Dan worked as a carpenter's helper, William as a high school teacher and I as a youth minister at an inner-city parish. It took us a year, but we finally came up with a name: Zacchaeus House, after the rich tax collector Jesus visited who subsequently gave away all his wealth. "Come down," Jesus had said to Zacchaeus. Come down from your wealth, your status, your power, and live like a brother.

We needed more room. In the summer of 1993 we learned that the Queen Elizabeth Hospital owned a number of vacant houses in Parkdale. They rented us two semi-detached houses with a total of twelve bedrooms for the same rent we were paying downtown. The phone rang and the rooms filled. We took whomever we could sanely live with: people seeking refuge in Canada, people struggling with mental illness, people in recovery, people getting out of jail, people trying to get back on their feet, people who lived better when they were living with others. Sometimes it was for a night and sometimes it was for years.

The rules were simple. Don't come home under the influence. Treat people with respect. Clean up after yourself in the kitchen. Attend a weekly house meeting. No smoking in the house. No television in your room. Home by 11 p.m. for the first few weeks. If things go well, you'll get a key and you can consider yourself a member of the family.

We gathered around two tables in the dining room, sometimes as many as twenty of us. I'd look around at all the faces, people from all over the world and every walk of life, sharing stories and laughter, big bowls of homemade soup and fresh-baked bread. It seemed like a miracle to me, and it was, but sometimes it got to be too much: the noise, the relentless needs, the freeloaders who never helped with cleaning up. I couldn't decide sometimes if I was living in the Kingdom of God or a bus station.

Friends who wanted to be part of what we were doing moved into the empty houses around us and we grew into a little village of households comprising about thirty people. A whirlwind of activity was unleashed. Monthly open-stage cafés for the neighbourhood. An organic pay-what-you-can bakery. Annual apple cider canning bees. Christmas dinner and gifts for fifty, Easter Dawn breakfast for a hundred. A food pantry to get people through to the end of the month. Prison and hospital visits. A worker co-operative sawmill employing twelve people. Vegetable gardens. Protests, prayer vigils, street theatre actions, civil disobedience.

The more I lived with people who had been forced by poverty to seek our help, the more I began to see how violent poverty was. It stained and soured, diminished and degraded, marked with inextinguishable worry and condemned to cheerless drudgery. There were times when I bore the brunt of that violence in the guise of passive-aggressive rages, smashed windows, poisonous accusations and shouts of "Die faggot!" I learned too that violence wasn't only something that happened outside me, it existed within me as well. I had to face the ugly fact that I was fully capable of hatred; those with shrill laughter or lack of hygiene especially evoked my contempt.

"Community is a terrible place," Jean Vanier once wrote. "It is the place where our limitations and our egoism are revealed to us . . . our frustrations and jealousies, our hatred and our wish to destroy. While we were alone, we could believe we loved everyone. Now that we are with others, we realize how incapable we are of loving."

Dorothy Day, founder of the Catholic Worker movement, often quoted Dostoevsky, who said, "Love in action is a harsh and dreadful thing compared to love in dreams." Truer words about community have never been spoken. If ever I thought of myself as a "good" person, community life brutally corrected that illusion. Community was a blast furnace that burned away my every pretence of unconditional love, emotional maturity and equilibrium, of having all my shit together. Community was the place where my little sailboat of hopes and dreams crashed and broke apart on the jagged shore of unmet expectations, emotional frailty, personal limitations, the fear of being vulnerable. The closest I ever came to throwing a punch was at a fellow Catholic Worker who refused to take his dirty shoes off when he came into the house.

In spite of all this, a sense of needing to do something more nagged at me. Soldiers trained and equipped themselves, stood ready to risk their lives in war. What about me? I believed the Gospel was calling us to non-violence. Was I prepared to take the same risks for peace?

It was through William that I first heard about CPT. It was in the years after Dudley George had been shot and killed by the Ontario Provincial Police—the only Aboriginal man to be killed by police during a land claims dispute in twentieth-century Canada. William had joined with a group of Mennonites based in Kitchener-Waterloo who were forming a CPT regional group that could respond in the event of a similar crisis and hopefully prevent such a violent outcome from happening again.

Hobo had heard about it too. He had the same twinkle in his eye as he did the day I first met him. I was sixteen years old at the time, and he was the director of the summer camp I was going to work at. I was afraid. It was my first time away from home. "You're going to have a great summer," he reassured me. He said his name was Bob Holmes but everybody called him Hobo. He was a Basilian priest and a high school principal.

It was the spring of 1998. "How would you like to go to Hebron?" he asked me. He had just been there on a delegation. "I raised double what I needed. I can pay for you to go." At $1,800, it seemed like an impossible amount of money to find. I didn't know what to say at first. "Think about it," he said. "The money's there."

It took me a year to make up my mind. After the ten-day delegation, I joined the team for a month as an intern. I loved the work—monitoring the activities of soldiers and settlers, intervening on behalf of Palestinians at Israeli checkpoints, networking with Palestinian and Israeli peace activists, documenting human rights abuses. When I got home, Doug Pritchard, at the time CPT's Canada coordinator, asked me to consider applying for a regional CPT training in southern Ontario. I couldn't think of a good reason not to and sent my application in. I was trained in the summer of 2000.

I did my first CPT project work that fall in Esgenoôpetitj, a Mi'kmaq First Nations community that had come under attack for asserting its historic treaty right to fish for lobster in Miramichi Bay, first from fishers from neighbouring Baie St. Anne, and then from the federal Department of Fisheries and Oceans (DFO). Esgenoôpetitj community leaders asked for CPT's help after three thousand lobster traps had been destroyed by Baie St. Anne fishers. It had been a tense summer. Masked warriors gathered in Esgenoôpetitj from all over the country. The DFO pointed guns at unarmed Esgenoôpetitj fishers, rammed their boats and pepper-sprayed them after they had been thrown into the water. The RCMP beat and choked an Esgenoôpetitj man into unconsciousness while he was in their custody.

When I got there in early October, the fishing season was all but over and most Esgenoôpetitj fishers were battening down the hatches for winter. I spent the time watching for DFO boats on a grey horizon, visiting with community members and doing crossword puzzles in the team trailer. I told myself this was good; peace and quiet was what we wanted. I battled hard against disappointment. They never told us in the training that CPT work could be so dull.

It would be more than two years before I next served on a CPT project. My excuse was that I was too busy. A group of us had moved to a farm near Durham, Ontario, a Catholic Worker experiment in rural living that lasted only two years. Dan commuted to Toronto to pay the bills and the rest of us worked from dawn till dusk. We tended the garden, renovated buildings, fixed fences, cut firewood, milked a cow, welcomed visitors and washed mountains of dishes. Yes, life was very busy, but if I had wanted I could've made space for CPT. The truth was, I was afraid.

Men's voices drift to us from the kitchen. Silence. The clicking of a nail clipper. Silence. Then, all together at once, a dog barking, vicious and rabid, a chain scraping across the floor above us, the begging pleading crying again, this time cresting in sheer terror. *We are in a house of horror*, I think. *Make it stop. Please, just make it stop.* It stops.

Time passes. My knees are aching. I need to stretch my legs. I can hear Tom deep-breathing through his nose. I turn my wrists and pull at my handcuffs, hoping they'll dissolve like a bad dream. I figure by now our families must know, but I wonder if the news has been broken to the media. There is a sudden commotion of voices and movement, the sound of furniture being pulled across the floor. My heart starts beating faster.

"Hamam? Amriki, Britannia—hamam?" There's a snarl in the voice.

"Yes," Norman says.

"Canadi—hamam?"

Harmeet says yes, I say no. I picture myself as an island of rock rising out of the ocean. I am hard, solitary, invulnerable. I don't need anything from them.

I am taken by the arm, moved through space and abruptly stopped. I risk a quick peek out of the bottom of my hat. Three mats have been laid out on the floor between two beds—sad, depleted rectangles of foam, their cotton coverlets faded and ripped, grimy with human body oils, swarming with brown stains.

They make us lie down in a row, on our left sides, so close we're touching each other. The mat has as much cushion as a piece of cardboard. Three blankets are thrown over us. I wonder whose house we are in, whose sleeping mats we are using, whose blankets are covering us. I am glad for the protection of my clothes. The light goes out. A bed creaks and blankets rustle. "No moving. I am right here," Number One warns. His voice is very close. I lift the hat above my eyes. It's too dark to see anything. I pull the hat down again and tuck my hands under my chin. Somebody coughs.

I consider our situation as though it were an interesting vase or a painting in a museum. We are hostages. I am now one of those I once saw on the news or read about in the newspaper, a rare exotic species I had the luxury of deciding whether or not to pay attention to, learn the names of, care about. Now others will read about us and decide whether or not to be interested.

Sleep is an impossibility. I'm lost and floating in an ocean, time without measure stretching everywhere without end. My left side aches fiercely and my bladder is desperate for relief. The only sound is an unbroken chain of breathing. Sometime, who knows when, somewhere in the middle of that vastness, Norman's voice pokes through the darkness. "Excuse me. Terribly sorry, but I must use the bathroom."

I wait anxiously for the response. Norman is taking a huge risk. I hear a soft groan. Norman speaks again, his voice urgent. "I really must use the bathroom."

"No, Doctor," Number One says wearily. "Sleep."

I hear Norman grunting. He's standing up! "I have to go to the bathroom," he says.

"No, Doctor," Number One says.

"I am going to go in my pants," Norman says, his voice rising in defiance. "I am an old man!"

I hear an exasperated exhalation. A lighter flicks. Number One rises from his bed. "*Hamam hamam hamam*," he sighs.

There's hope. Our captors are not heartless.

# CHAPTER THREE

## NOVEMBER 27 DAY 2

The call to prayer echoes across Baghdad like a promise. Slowly, imperceptibly, by degrees immeasurable, darkness gives way to light. I pull my hat down over my eyes. Birds chatter. A cat meows. We wait. Finally, the captors get up. We hear sounds of scrubbing and washing at a sink, someone getting dressed near us, the TV being turned on, Arabic conversation. I begin sending mental telegrams: *please get us up please get us up please get us up.* Rigor mortis, I am certain, is setting in.

Footsteps enter the room. "Good morning," a voice says.

It's a risk, but I decide to take it. *"Hamam?"* I ask, immediately sitting up.

"Yes *hamam,*" a bored voice says. My bladder is ready to explode. I am ushered through a door, turned left, taken six steps and stopped in front of another door.

I hesitate, wonder if I should close the door or not. I decide to chance it. The captor does not object. A good sign, I think. They respect us enough to let us use the bathroom in privacy. I see that I've been taken to a different *hamam,* though it is the same size as the one I stood in last week, two and a half feet wide and three feet deep. The yellow ceramic floor bowl is caked with shit. I break into a sweat as I wait for my urethra to let go. It won't. I give up, fill the water jug, pour water into the basin—my contribution to good housekeeping—and fill it again so it will be ready for the next customer. I pull my hat down over my eyes and open the door.

The captor takes my arm and sits me down in a plastic lawn chair facing the wall. The others are brought to sit beside me, one by one. I notice right away a round, quarter-sized crater in the wall at the height of my knee. A bullet hole. What else can it be?

—

During my first visit to Iraq, in January 2003, I went to visit Baghdad's Amiriya Shelter. It was my first encounter with the devastation of war. The back of my neck tingled as I stepped into the hellish black cavern. An oval gash of light poured through a curtain of twisted steel into a crater of exploded cement and broken girders. As my eyes adjusted to the darkness, I began to see mangled wires and ventilation ducts hanging from the ceiling, massive concrete pillars stripped to the rebars, black blotches on the floor where the bodies of sleeping women and children had been incinerated. It was one of thirty-four bomb shelters constructed during the Iran–Iraq War. On February 17, 1991, two American "smart bombs" hit the shelter at four in the morning. Four hundred and eight people—women, children and old men—were reduced to ash. An Associated Press reporter wrote, "Most of the recovered bodies were charred and mutilated beyond recognition."

I remember that day very well. Four days before, Dan and I (along with three others) dumped big buckets of ash in front of the Conservative Party headquarters in Toronto. Canada was one of thirty-four countries led by the United States that declared war against Iraq after Saddam Hussein occupied Kuwait. Twenty-six Canadian CF-18s were flying bombing sorties over Iraq. It was Ash Wednesday, the first day of Lent, and we had a message for Prime Minister Brian Mulroney: the only thing that comes from war is ash. We were arrested and charged with mischief.

Talk about mischief. The U.S. dropped sixty thousand tons of bombs on Iraq during the First Gulf War. It deliberately targeted Iraq's electrical grid, dams and power stations and destroyed seventy-five percent of its power-generating capacity. The country's entire civilian infrastructure—hospitals, irrigation systems, sewage and water treatment facilities—was crippled.

Saddam withdrew from Kuwait and the fighting stopped on February 28. The economic sanctions imposed by the UN Security Council in August 1990, however, continued. Medical supplies, chlorine for water purification, firefighting and milk-production equipment—even pencils—were banned. No one could buy from or sell anything to Iraq. The consequences were devastating. The economy collapsed, the middle class was wiped out, child mortality rates skyrocketed, and 90 percent of the country fell dependent on a monthly food ration.

The stated purpose of the UN sanctions was to prevent Saddam Hussein from acquiring weapons of mass destruction. In fact, they were a systematic program of economic warfare. The *Washington Post* quoted a Pentagon war planner on June 23, 1991: "People say, 'You didn't recognize that it [bombing civilian infrastructure] was going to have an effect on water and sewage.' Well, what were we trying to do with sanctions—help out the Iraqi people? No. What we were doing with the attacks on infrastructure was to accelerate the effect of sanctions." Once the sanctions had been imposed, they couldn't be removed until all five permanent members of the Security Council agreed. The United States with its veto kept the sanctions in place until May 23, 2003.

On September 11, 2001, terrorists attacked the Twin Towers and George W. Bush declared a global war against terrorism. He went after Afghanistan first for harbouring Osama bin Laden. Then he turned his sights on Iraq. Saddam Hussein had weapons of mass destruction, Bush said. Weapons inspectors scoured the country while 36 million people took part in three thousand protests around the world in an unprecedented cry for peace.

As war clouds gathered over Iraq, Peggy Gish and Cliff Kindy joined the Iraq Peace Team (a joint initiative of Voices in the Wilderness and CPT) in October 2002. A CPT delegation was leaving on December 26. I took a deep breath and gave Doug Pritchard a call. "I want to join the delegation," I told him.

The fifteen-member team assembled in Amman, Jordan, and travelled overland to Baghdad in a hired bus. We stayed in a hotel in central Baghdad. The city was bracing itself for war. Cliff and Peggy, the delegation leaders, reviewed the different scenarios that were possible during the ten-day delegation. Things could continue as they had been, without war but with escalating pressure from the U.S. The U.S. could start bombing. The Iraqi government could decide to remove us from the country. There could be a coup. "This is probably the most danger-ous scenario for us," Cliff said. "We could be arrested, held hostage, the whole society thrown into the chaos of civil war." I gulped. That was one scenario I hadn't thought of.

The delegation was carefully managed by an Iraqi minder who approved our itinerary and attended our meetings. We were warned by Peggy and Cliff not to ask questions about the political situation—it could get us kicked out of the country or, worse, endanger anyone who talked with us. Nevertheless, we got a clear picture of a country that had been devastated by thirteen years of economic sanctions. Their effects were massive, and they were everywhere. Teachers were making five dollars a month. Ninety percent of the population was dependent on a UN food supplement. An army of children worked in the streets shining shoes and selling tissue paper instead of going to school. The best public infrastructure oil money could buy was a shambles. Half the country's schools were unfit to receive students. Water treatment plants couldn't be repaired. The average Iraqi child suffered fourteen episodes of diarrhea a year from drinking bad water, killing tens of thousands from dehydration. Hospitals couldn't get medicines or parts for medical equipment. The UN estimated that 1.5 million people had died as a direct result of the sanctions.

Azhar was one of the 1.5 million. "She is a six-month-old baby," the doctor told us at a hospital we visited, "brought in last night suffering from diarrhea. She died this morning from dehydration." She was lying on her side, tiny fingers curled gently into a fist. Her eyes were open, her face colourless, cranial, emaciated, a white film about her lips.

On March 20, 2003, the boot of war stomped down on Iraq. They called it Shock and Awe. "There will not be a safe place in Baghdad," a Pentagon official said. "The sheer size of this has never been seen before, never been contemplated before." The bombs and missiles fell day and night, fifty thousand strikes in thirty days.[*] On April 9, U.S. forces rolled into Baghdad and Saddam Hussein fled.

Chaos followed shock and awe. After securing the Ministry of Oil and the Ministry of Interior, the U.S. stood by and watched as libraries, hospitals, schools and every government building was looted and burned. I couldn't help but wonder if the looting of Baghdad wasn't some kind of sophisticated psy-ops operation. Let the criminals and arsonists finish off what the sanctions and the bombing started, while confirming the Western impression that Iraqis (and by extension all Muslims and Arabs) are a barbaric, lawless, uncivilized people.

On May 1, George W. Bush announced the end of major combat operations on the deck of the USS *Abraham Lincoln* behind a giant banner that read *Mission Accomplished*. The toll to that point: 9,200 Iraqi combatants, 7,299 civilians, 139 U.S. and 33 U.K. military personnel.[†] Just a small taste of the death to come. By the end of July 2010, 4,413 U.S. soldiers had been killed. As for civilians, nobody knows. Iraq Body Count, an estimate based on press reports, put the number between 97,143 and 105,994 in July 2010. The prestigious medical journal *Lancet* estimated 601,027 in June 2006. An Opinion Research Business Survey estimated over a million in August 2007.

Occupation followed chaos, and chaos followed occupation. Midnight house raids, the arbitrary arrest and detention of thousands of Iraqi men, the theft and destruction of personal property, checkpoint shootings. The borders were left wide open. The Coalition Provisional Authority disbanded the Iraqi army and police. Unknown quantities of ordnance disappeared from unsecured armaments dumps. It was almost as if the United States wanted an insurgency.

The car and suicide bombs started in August 2003. The United States retreated behind blast walls and concertina wire. Crime swept through the streets like a tsunami. Kidnapping became commonplace, an

---

[*]  "Operation Iraqi Freedom: By the Numbers," USCENTAF Report, April 30, 2003.

[†]  "Iraq Coalition Casualty Count," March 19, 2003, through May 1, 2003, iCasualties.org.

average of thirty every day. Anybody with money became a target. Those with means turned their homes into fortresses protected by armed guards, or left the country altogether. The insurgency grew and the morgues filled—a hundred bodies a day in Baghdad alone. No weapons of mass destruction were ever found.

I returned to Iraq on January 3, 2004. As before, I flew to Amman and travelled overland by bus. I saw two American soldiers on duty at the border: one hardly visible, sitting in a booth, the other slouching in the doorway smoking a cigarette. An Iraqi border guard stepped onto the bus, exchanged some words with the driver, looked at a handful of passports and waved us on. Just about anyone or anything could have entered the country on that bus.

I couldn't believe how much had changed in a year. The roads were choked with traffic. It took hours to get anywhere. The once-ubiquitous images of Saddam Hussein had been blasted, shot full of holes, erased. Giant coils of razor wire surrounded every public building. The streets were littered with garbage. Ragged hordes of teenaged boys laboured under bulging burlap sacks collecting aluminum cans, bottles, scrap metal, anything worth a few cents. Boys sold black market gasoline at the sides of the road and gas station lineups were over a kilometre long. Free speech was in the air like a spring breeze. Men hawked newspapers, and satellite dishes sprouted on buildings like mushrooms. The electricity went on and off at random. Generators belched black diesel fumes everywhere. The city was replete with bombed and looted buildings. There was no reconstruction going on that I could see. Whether or not life was better under Saddam Hussein was an open question.

It surprised me, when I first arrived, to hear Iraqis talk approvingly of George W. Bush. "Bush good, Saddam bad," they'd say with their thumbs up, market vendors, taxi drivers, people in the streets. "Thank Bush, thank America." The long, tyrannical rule of Saddam Hussein was over and everyone, it seemed, had a story about an uncle or a brother or a cousin who'd been threatened, imprisoned or tortured. When Saddam's regime fell, dozens of unions and human rights groups sprang up overnight. People gathered to demonstrate and march, speak their minds, open email accounts, surf the Internet. Few were those who mourned his defeat.

But even during my ten weeks in the country I could see this good-will evaporating. It was like watching a storm roll in. More and more we heard people complain there was no security, no electricity, no gasoline, that things were better under Saddam. "If this is George Bush democracy, give us back Saddam."

The CPT team decided in the summer of 2003 to focus on security detainees when scores of people came to the team with stories of family members who had been detained without charge by the U.S. Army. We accompanied families in search of their loved ones to military bases. A handful we were able to track down, but otherwise our inquiries were met with polite stonewalling or bureaucratic finger-pointing. Nobody seemed to know where the detainees were or when they would be released.

CPT published a report on December 23, 2003, summarizing information gathered from the families of seventy-one men and one woman who had been detained by the United States. A third had been detained after a house raid conducted in the middle of the night. In every case where someone had been arrested during a house raid, the families reported that coalition forces had confiscated their property; 40 percent reported that the person being detained was injured during the raid; 28 percent reported that a member of the family had been injured; two people were reported to have died as a direct result of their injuries. Of the twenty-four men who had been released after being detained for an average of fifty-seven days, none had ever been convicted of a criminal offence and not one of the seventy-two had seen a lawyer. Only a third faced formal charges.

Our impression at first was of an under-resourced system that was nevertheless doing its best to process the thousands of men who were being swept up in the military's clumsy, heavy-handed effort to quell the insurgency. We managed to work our way up the chain of command to get a meeting with Ambassador Richard Jones, second-in-command to Paul Bremer, who was head of the Coalition Provisional Authority. Ambassador Jones admitted they had "no policy," no process for determining guilt or innocence, that the system was "overwhelmed" and they just didn't have the "resources" to deal with "the problem." We reminded him of his responsibilities under the Geneva Conventions and called on him to implement due process for security detainees or else release them. The detainee crisis and the practice of house raids, we told him, were breeding insurgent rage. He asked his aides to schedule a follow-up meeting.

We began to work on an "Adopt a Detainee" letter-writing campaign. We prepared detailed profiles of some of our detainee cases and asked church and community groups to write letters on their behalf. One of them was Kahdhan Munther Ahmed Salih al-Obaydi, a 22-year-old municipal street cleaner who had been detained in October 2003. I met his father, Ismael, a blind man who sang the call to prayer at Baghdad's Abu Hanifah mosque. He told me that Kahdhan and a friend were swimming in the Tigris River when they heard a big explosion. They weren't concerned at first because explosions were commonplace in Baghdad. They became afraid when they heard gunfire, and the two men swam towards shore. U.S. soldiers opened fire on them. Kahdhan was shot in the foot and taken to Abu Ghraib. Ismael explained that Saddam Hussein had exempted his son from military duty in 1997 because of a head injury. This was significant because it meant his son knew nothing about guns or explosives. "I want them to release my son," he told me. "I have no one to support me." His son earned three dollars a day.

Another detainee was Idrees Younis Nuri, a 20-year-old accounting student who also was detained in October 2003. His 30-year-old brother Wakas told me Idrees and five friends were on their way to the market during Ramadan when a sequence of explosions occurred, one of them near a passing U.S. convoy. U.S. soldiers swept up thirty-five people who happened to be in the vicinity of the attack, Idrees and his five friends among them. Wakas told me, "Our neighbour was one of the ones who was detained. He told me they were severely tortured by the soldiers. He heard screams through the night until morning. One of the thirty-five was sent to the hospital. Our neighbour was released after two days." Like Kahdhan, Wakas explained that his brother had been exempted from military service. "He is sick. He has a disease in his colon. And he is still a student, so he has no experience in how to use weapons." Unlike most detainees, Idrees faced an actual charge: "Attack on Coalition."

I remember discussing with Sheila Provencher something she'd written for the Adopt a Detainee program. I had a concern about a phrase she was using, which went something like, ". . . soldiers returning home, having to face in the night the unspeakable things they had done . . ." I thought this should be changed to "unspeakable things they had seen." Yes, things were bad, I argued, but American forces had not yet crossed the line into atrocity. They had not been there long enough to experience the profound dehumanization process that occurred during the Vietnam War. They seemed to have very little interaction with the civilian population, being confined to military bases when not on patrol. It appeared, based on our intermittent interactions with soldiers, that military discipline was intact.

I couldn't have been more wrong. The evidence, in fact, was right in front of me. I just didn't see it—or didn't want to.

There was, for example, the case of Mahadi Al Jamal, a frail 70-year-old man recovering from a hip replacement who was killed while in American custody on December 21, 2003. His son Abdulkahar told me how their home had been raided at nine-thirty in the evening. Soldiers broke down doors, smashed furniture, scattered their belongings everywhere. They handcuffed and hooded Abdulkahar, his father and his uncle. Mahadi complained of not being able to breathe. The men were brought one by one into the back of an armoured personnel carrier, Abdulkahar first and then his father. "My father was in very bad condition at that time. He couldn't talk because of the hood. I could hear him gasping. I pleaded with the soldiers to help my father, but they only said bad words to me. They beat me on the chest with the end of their weapons to make me silent. After that my father stopped moving. One of the soldiers called on the radio, 'The fucking old man, I think he's dead, I think he's dead!'"

Abdulkahar and his uncle were released that night. An officer came to their house and informed them that Mahadi had died of a heart attack. Two days later the commanding officer, Lieutenant Colonel Nate Sassaman, told them the decision to raid their house had been based on false information, and that the U.S. forces would find and punish the informant.

Abdulkahar showed me a formal apology written on CIA letterhead. "We will not rest until this investigation is complete," the letter promised. It was signed, "Mr. Ken, Project Forces Manager." "Mr. Ken" was never heard from again.

Abdulkahar concluded the interview by saying, "In Samarra, everyone expects to be arrested in the night, so now they wear suitable clothes and their ID to bed." At the time, he was working on his Ph.D. in chemical engineering at the University of Baghdad. He was thirty years old.

Then there was Abu Hishma, a town of seven thousand people surrounded by five miles of concertina wire on the orders of Colonel Sassaman. It was an act of collective punishment for the death of Sergeant Dale Panchot, who was killed on November 17, 2003, when a rocket-propelled grenade fired from the town hit his Bradley armoured personnel carrier. Eight sheiks, the mayor, the police chief and most of the town council were arrested. All the men aged eighteen to sixty-five were assigned English-language identity cards. A sign posted at the checkpoint entrance read, "This fence is here for your protection. Do not approach or try to cross or you will be shot." Sassaman said the wire enclosure would remain in place until the villagers turned over the men who were responsible for killing Panchot.

A month before Sergeant Panchot was killed, villagers told us Sassaman's men shot Aziz Taha, a 25-year-old English student at the University of Baghdad. When his brother's wife, Majida, ran to help

Aziz, she was shot and died instantly. Two hours later Aziz bled to death when the soldiers wouldn't let anyone help him. A week later U.S. forces were attacked in the area. Aziz's brother Yasseen was detained on the notion that he would have the motive of avenging the deaths of his wife and brother. Yasseen and Majida had three children, the youngest of whom was fifteen days old on the day Majida was killed.

Then there was Abu Siffa, a farming village about a twenty-minute drive from Abu Hishma. According to villagers we interviewed, on December 16, 2003, at 2:00 a.m., Sassman's men surrounded Abu Siffa and detained eighty men and three teenaged boys (aged fourteen, fifteen and sixteen) in the course of a fourteen-hour operation. Mohammed Jasim Hassan Altaai, one of only two men in the village who were not detained, told us, "The Coalition Forces were searching for one person, but they searched all our houses. It was a rainy night and they surrounded our whole village—about twenty-five houses— with tanks and Humvees. They surrounded the farmers' fields with tanks and destroyed the fences. They destroyed the doors of our houses and kicked down our bedroom doors, or used their weapons to open them, while we were sleeping. They gathered the men together and beat them severely. A 70-year-old man suffocated and died when they put a black plastic hood on him."*

The object of the raid was Kais Hattam, a prominent Baath Party official. According to Sassaman, Saddam was captured with documents linking him directly to Hattam. After detaining Hattam, U.S. forces fire-bombed his home and left his large extended family homeless. On December 31, U.S. forces destroyed the home of Abas Muhamed Abd Wahid, a 41-year-old primary school teacher with a family of sixteen. A third home was destroyed on January 2. "They have detained all the men," Mohammed said. "Jamal and I are the only two men still living in the area. They took about fifteen teachers from the secondary school, so now there aren't enough teachers to give lessons."

---

* CPT was unable to make any further determination about this incident, but it bears an uncanny similarity to the suffocation death of Mahadi Al Jamal.

—

I listened to and documented dozens of such stories. We were so busy, there was hardly time to think. Each story deserved further investigation and determined follow-through, but there were so many, and they just kept on coming. We didn't have the resources to do any of them justice. I'd write them up, file them, send them on to the Chicago office, move on to the next thing. They became bits of language that I assembled and processed.

The stories were astonishing, overwhelming, sometimes impossible to believe. Some I dismissed altogether as rumour and occupation tall tales—stories about Iraqis being pushed out of helicopters, for example, or thousands of detainees being held in ghost prison camps in Kuwait and the United Arab Emirates. An Iraqi cleric, his voice quivering with rage, told us in the Abu Ghraib parking lot that Iraqi women in Abu Ghraib were being paraded around nude, forced into lesbian sex, raped, impregnated. He said a female prisoner smuggled out a note begging for the prison to be bombed. "It is better for us to die," she was said to have written. I heard the same story from a different man in Baghdad's Tahrir Square, where we held public vigils for detainees.

I sifted and evaluated the things I was hearing. I listened cautiously, suspended judgment, reminded myself I was hearing only one side of the story, that I needed to get all the facts, avoid mental commitment. I detached, became a technician of careful listening who collected and analyzed human rights abuses. I wanted to believe in the good intentions of the beleaguered officials and soldiers we talked to, most of whom said they never wanted to be in Iraq in the first place. They were well-intentioned people who seemed to be doing the best they could to follow the rules, run a decent occupation and improve the lives of the Iraqi people. I wanted to believe that the world I belonged to and understood, the world of Western Judeo-Christian civilization and values, was beyond this kind of moral atrocity. It was, I can see now, a process of denial.

Judith Herman, in her book *Trauma and Recovery*, writes: "Those who bear witness are caught in the conflict between victim and perpetrator.

It is morally impossible to remain neutral in this conflict. The bystander is forced to take sides. It is very tempting to take the side of the perpetrator. All the perpetrator asks is that the bystander do nothing . . . The victim, on the contrary, asks the bystander to share the burden of pain. The victim demands action, engagement, and remembering." When Mahadi Al Jamal's son told me about the murder of his father at the hands of U.S. soldiers, I told myself I didn't have time to follow up and left his grief on a piece of paper when I returned to the safety of Canada. The truth is, I was protecting myself from the brutality of what I was hearing, distancing myself from the staggering human implications of a son sitting next to his father as he suffocated under a hood.

Things in Iraq were bad—far worse than I ever imagined. We have only to consider the systematic torture and degradation of detainees at Abu Ghraib. The use of white phosphorus, banned by a 1980 UN treaty, during the siege of Fallujah in November 2004. The murders of twenty-four Iraqi civilians (eleven of them women and children) by U.S. Marines on November 19, 2005, in the town of Haditha. The gang rape and murder of a 14-year-old Iraqi girl named Aber Qasim Hamza in Al-Mahmudiyah on March 12, 2006. The subsequent murders of her mother, father and seven-year-old sister by U.S. soldiers to cover up the crime. The executions of five children, four women and two men on March 15, 2006, shot in the head by U.S. soldiers while handcuffed in a house owned by Faiz Harat Khalaf near Abu Sifa. The July 2007 report by Chris Hedges and Laila Al-Arian published in *The Nation* based on interviews with fifty Iraq combat veterans. Their conclusion: "Dozens of those interviewed witnessed Iraqi civilians, including children, dying from American firepower. Some participated in such killings; others treated or investigated civilian casualties after the fact. Many also heard such stories, in detail, from members of their unit . . . they . . . described such acts as common and said they often go unreported—and almost always go unpunished." The testimony of soldiers such as Cliff Hicks, quoted in the June 12, 2006, edition of *Newsweek*: "People were taking steroids, Valium, hooked on painkillers, drinking. They'd go on raids and patrols totally stoned. We're killing the wrong people all the time, and mostly by accident. One guy in my squadron ran over a family with his tank. Guys would crap into MRE bags and throw them to old men begging for food."

I wonder now who was more naive—me or Lieutenant Colonel Nathaniel Sassaman, the Warrior King who told New York Times correspondent Dexter Filkins, "With a heavy dose of fear and violence, and a lot of money for projects, I think we can convince these people that we are here to help them."*

I met Colonel Sassaman on January 12, 2004, at Forward Operations Base Paliwoda, a commandeered school located on the outskirts of Balad, about sixty kilometres north of Baghdad.† The base had been named after Captain Eric Paliwoda, a 28-year-old officer who had been killed nine days earlier when the base was attacked by mortar fire. Colonel Sassaman himself had lifted the dying man into the medevac helicopter.

We didn't know it at the time, but Colonel Sassaman was one of the most celebrated of the U.S. Army's stable of warriors. He was the commander of eight hundred men (Fourth Infantry Division, Eighth Battalion), the son of a Methodist minister, a West Point graduate, the quarterback who piloted the army football team to victory in the 1984 Cherry Bowl (an army first). He ran a total of 1,002 yards that year while nursing three cracked ribs.

He greeted us just as the day's mail was being unloaded from an armoured personnel carrier. "You're the first Americans I've met since I've come here—besides CBC and CNN reporters," he said, grinning at his suggestion that journalists weren't full-fledged Americans. He shook

---

* Dexter Filkins, The Forever War: Dispatches from the War on Terror (London: The Bodley Head, 2008), 160.

† This meeting was reconstructed with the assistance of delegation member David Hilfiker's report, "Winning Hearts and Minds," posted on Tom Dispatch on January 29, 2004.

hands with each member of the delegation. "Call me Nate," he said. "Come in, come in, we'll get you something to drink." Sassaman was forty years old, his face tanned and open, with a lean, decisive jaw and quick, penetrating eyes, a man who exuded confidence, command, authority. He was vigorously fit and moved with a quarterback's ease.

We were led down a hallway and into a classroom. I stopped at a bulletin board. There was a poster of the Twin Towers with the words "God Bless America and Our Troops," a sign that read "In the absence of orders, attack," and a trophy photo of an Iraqi man lying face down in the dirt, a soldier kneeling on his head, others bending down and smiling into the camera with their thumbs up, his white pickup truck in the background. When I mentioned the picture, the soldier escorting us said, his chest inflating with pride, "Yeah, it took a while, but we got 'em. One of the bad guys."

We sat around a collection of plastic garden tables (the kind with a hole in the middle for an umbrella) on the plastic lawn chairs that are ubiquitous in Iraq: the eight members of the delegation I was leading; Sami, Mohanned and a third Iraqi lawyer from the Balad chapter of the Organization of Human Rights, which had suggested the meeting; and Colonel Sassaman, Captain Blake, Captain Williams and their official translator, Thanya. (Our own translator elected not to come, fearing he might be detained.) Breezes flowed into the room through broken windows. Cold soft drinks were brought on trays.

After formal introductions, Colonel Sassaman began to talk. "I don't think anybody knew what we were getting into when we came in here. When I think of the Iraqi people, I feel incredible sadness and incredible rage at the same time. We can only do so much, and there's far more for us to do here than we're able to do. We've had no support from the State Department. I thought that would be their job, rebuilding the country. We're not equipped or trained for this. We've had to go back to our high school textbooks—it's Civics 101 here. You wouldn't believe the mind-numbing civics lessons we've had to give."

While prepared to use force when necessary, his primary interest was in dialogue with the local people and helping Iraqis get back on their feet. While the soldiers sometimes conducted patrols at night, during the day they were rebuilding local infrastructure. He described with pride how they organized one of the first local elections in Balad. He claimed they had a turnout of between fifty and sixty thousand in a city of ninety thousand. Captain Blake had written a computer program to count the ballots. Balad was a model for the rest of Iraq.

The biggest challenge, he said, was tribal allegiances. "You will constantly fight family ties, tribal ties, in anything you try to do in this country. The only way we're going to get this thing really fixed is for Iraqis to work with Iraqis." They had set up a radio station and newspapers, reinforced the local police and established an Iraqi Civilian Defense Corps of about two hundred people to provide rural security. "I'm sort of like a county sheriff," he said.

Colonel Sassaman held up a newspaper with his picture on the front page. He was bending down next to an Iraqi woman with a lump of raw dough in his hands. "They took this picture when I stopped to bake bread with an Iraqi family," he said. Thanya, an Iraqi-American woman from Detroit who had fled to the United States to escape the brutality of the Saddam regime, told us Colonel Sassaman was so well liked by Iraqis that the base wasn't shelled when he was there.

We asked him about house raids and the treatment of detainees. "I'm not in the detainee business," he said. "We're really into rebuilding Iraq. I feel really uncomfortable entering someone's home. We don't search many homes anymore." They hadn't conducted any house raids in several weeks, he said. "During the first few months we were here, we broke down doors and smashed things, and that was really a mistake. There's been a learning curve, and we know now we can ask for the key. Coming here, we've been trained to do only one thing [to kill], so I have to be constantly retraining my soldiers."

Colonel Sassaman was directly involved in the raids to ensure they were carried out according to the rules. U.S. forces typically took two weeks to "develop their next operation," and every lead about a potential target was corroborated by two independent sources; they did pay informants, he said. When they had to go into a house, they did it in "forty-five seconds of absolute fury." He explained, "You want to make the environment submissive." They only detained "high-value targets," those possessing unauthorized weapons or information about the insurgency. He said they didn't usually handcuff detainees. "That way, if they run, we can use any level of force necessary to control them. Once we cuff 'em, we can't touch 'em."

Most of the Iraqis Sassaman detained were released. Those they decided to hold on to were "processed" and held for twenty-four hours, at most two or three days, before being sent on to Abu Ghraib. Only three people were allowed to talk to the detainees while they were in Colonel Sassaman's custody: Sassaman himself, Captain Blake and Captain Williams.

I liked Nate Sassaman. He was a straight talker who had no time for soft-pedalling platitudes and vague generalities. His desire to improve the lives of the Iraqi people and his frustration with the lack of resources to help him accomplish that task seemed genuine. He appeared to be a man of principle who was doing his very best to carry out an impossible mission with the wrong tools.

We suggested that Colonel Sassaman open a regular channel of communication with the local association of human rights lawyers. The lawyers had a number of concerns about house raids, access to detainees and the misconduct of American soldiers. We asked if the three lawyers, who had been following Thanya's whispered translation, could have a turn to speak.

As soon as Mohanned began to speak, Sassaman's smiling, genial demeanour disappeared. He sat erect, hands gripping the arms of his chair, face hard and jaw a line of steel. He looked through the Iraqis, never at them, as if he were sitting in an interrogator's chair.

Mohanned and Sami talked calmly while Thanya translated. Their concerns were general, about the difficulties of life under occupation. Sassaman clenched his jaw, said he couldn't do anything about that, he was only interested in specific issues, things he could reasonably change. The lawyers referred to an incident in October 2003 in which U.S. soldiers opened fire on a vehicle containing six Iraqis. The car burst into flames and one of the passengers ran from the car. The soldiers forced him back inside. All six were killed.

Sassaman's face went crimson. "That's been dealt with. Why are you bringing that up? That wasn't our unit. That was somebody else, but we had to go in and clean up the mess anyway."

Sassaman turned to us. "You need to understand that these people are Muslim, and their values are not the same as Judeo-Christian values. They aren't for doing things for other people like we are. They're only out for themselves." He seemed to be implying that the lawyers were only interested in financial compensation. Sassaman and Blake told us they'd met every lawyer in town and they didn't recognize these men, nor had they ever heard of the Organization of Human Rights. "You're being used," Colonel Sassaman told us.

We explained that the Organization of Human Rights was a national organization based in Baghdad with which CPT had a long-standing relationship, that the Iraqi men present were legitimate representatives of that organization, and we stated again that our purpose in coming was to try to open a channel of communication between the lawyers and Colonel Sassaman. Sassaman answered, "There'll be a meeting, all right, and the lawyers will be there. And it'll be a humdinger of a meeting." Despite Sassaman's threatening tone, the lawyers agreed and a date was set for January 17.

As we were leaving, we saw dozens of Iraqi men being held inside a fenced-in area behind the school. A delegation member said, "Didn't he say they haven't conducted a house raid in the past few weeks?"

The next day, January 13, 2004, Sami came to visit the CPT apartment in Baghdad with some news. Sassaman had raided Mohanned's house at four in the morning and had detained Mohanned and five of his brothers. They were released at nine that night. Sassaman said later he had nothing to do with it—another unit was working in his area without his knowledge and detained them in the course of looking for their target. "As soon as I saw him, I let him go."

I met Sassaman twice more—both times at meetings with the Organization of Human Rights we helped facilitate at the Balad courthouse. He listened intently, spoke frankly, didn't promise anything he couldn't deliver.

Like Colonel Sassaman, Ba'har Kadhin Al Saady once served his country as a soldier. I first met him in the office of the National Association for the Defence of Human Rights (NADHR). It was a cold January day and the building we were in had no windows. He sat on a frayed chair behind a desk propped up by a brick. One hand held a cigarette, the other a pen that twirled in his fingers. You could see in the creases of his face, the set of his jaw, the spartan lines of his body that he'd had a difficult life.

Ba'har had been conscripted into the Republican Army at the age of eighteen. At nineteen he refused a direct military order to join a unit that was attacking Kurdish nationals in northern Iraq. "When they asked me why, I told them those people are Iraqi people, and they are Muslims. If I kill them, God will be angry with me. I do not want to kill anyone. Because of this, I was accused of being a traitor and sent to jail.

"They sent me to the prison of the Fifteenth Division to investigate me. They tortured me too much. They handcuffed me and beat me with sticks." He pointed to a three-inch scar on his right jawbone. "This is where they beat me with the butt of a pistol." He pulled up his shirt to show me dozens of long white scars on his back. "They gave us lashes with a cable until they cut the meat." Ba'har held out his hands. "They poured water on me and then put electricity on my fingers. They hoisted me into the air on a hook for one or two hours with my hands tied behind my back. They call it 'the scorpion.' This treatment lasted for three months. On August 13, 1994, they sent me back to my military unit. This mistreatment was staying in my mind so that I couldn't bear to continue my military service. They asked me to go on patrol again. I had no choice except to be a deserter in order not to make God angry at me."

Ba'har escaped to a village near Kirkuk in northern Iraq. He stayed there ten days before returning to Baghdad. Ba'har was captured on

October 4. After a series of lashings, he was told he was going to have his ear cut off for desertion.

On October 10, he was taken to a hospital wearing handcuffs and a blindfold. "They gave me an injection in my hand and I lost consciousness. When I woke up, I was in pain. I said to myself, this isn't real, it's a nightmare. But when I felt my bandaged ear I knew it wasn't a dream."

Ba'har turned his head to show me his right ear. The top of it had been cut flat on a downward angle, as though sliced off by pruning shears. The same punishment was inflicted on over 3,600 war resisters and deserters. Some had their whole ear removed. Others lost the end of their nose, a piece of their tongue, or had a minus sign tattooed on their forehead. "It was just whatever they decided to do," Ba'har said.

Ba'har spent the next two years in prison, where he was subjected to continuing physical and mental abuse. "There were nineteen soldiers who were exposed to the same treatment. Some of them had little bits of their ear cut, some had big pieces cut." He was finally released in December 1996.

"At that time, I thought it was the end of my tragedy, but in fact it was just the beginning. Some people, when they gazed at me in the streets, saw me as a bad one. When I was with my friends, they would greet me and say 'Hello traitor' as a joke, but in fact that cut me."

When no one would hire him, Ba'har burned his identification papers and forged new ones that did not record his punishment. Still, marked by his ear, it was impossible to find work. "It became something shameful for me. It affected all my social relationships.

"One day, I asked for the hand of a woman I wanted to marry." Ba'har's voice became strained. He fought back tears. "Her family refused. They said yes, you are good, but you are punished by Saddam Hussein. That is not something honourable for us." Estranged from his family and jobless, Ba'har was living in a looted Ministry of Trade building when he saw posters announcing that the NADHR had a group to assist men in his situation.

"I came to this association at first looking for compensation. I found the people in this society to be very responsible. They helped me.

Meeting the other victims made me eager to volunteer in this organization to work for peace and to work for those who refused wars. So now I like working in this organization and I like my work." Ba'har became the president of the Committee for the People Who Refused Wars. He spent his days organizing on behalf of the 3,600 men who had been branded by the Saddam regime. He helped them apply for compensation, fill out forms, get assistance from the Ministry of Work and Social Affairs, and he listened to their stories. The Ministry of Health had recently agreed to offer surgery. Fourteen auricular reconstructions had been done.

"Before the war, I was humiliated, scorned," Ba'har said. "So now in fact it is not a disgrace, it is not shameful for me." He pointed to his ear. "Now I consider this cut a medal of honour for resisting the strongest dictator ever known."

I asked him to tell me more about how—and why—he made his extraordinary decision to refuse war. He paused, struggled to find the words. "It is . . . a . . . primitive feeling in me." He did not have language for what he wanted to say. "I am the peaceful man . . . I don't like to shed the blood of others. I wish to live in peace, and to realize peace all over the world."

I asked him if he wanted to have his own ear reconstructed. He nodded. "Yes, I want to do that. But only after everyone else gets it done." And then he said, "In spite of my poverty, I want to help others who are in need. Until now I am living in a garden."

I thank God for you, Ba'har. You, and those like you, are the shock absorbers of history. You have set your face like flint against the war machine. Your *no* is the only sharp-edged sword, the only polished arrow that can deliver us from the blind, mad spiral of violence. By your shame we have the possibility of wholeness, by your affliction the possibility of healing. The punishment you accept brings us peace. You are one of the suffering servants of the Lord, all that is holding the world together.

—

As the day of my departure neared, I found myself becoming increasingly skittish. It was early March 2004, just a few weeks before the kidnapping of internationals began. We were right in the middle of our Adopt-a-Detainee Campaign and its daily public vigils in Tahrir Square. I was finding it harder and harder to leave the apartment. The normal everyday code-yellow readiness that's so essential for negotiating the perils of life in Iraq—a strange car parked in front of your building, gunshots up the street, a car full of glaring men pulling up next to you—was building into a paralyzing anxiety. When I mentioned this to Cliff, a veteran of fourteen years of working on CPT projects, he reassured me that this was completely normal. "I always get more cautious as the time gets closer for me to go home. Okay, I think to myself, I'm almost there, I'm going to make it back alive this time. Soldiers talk about feeling that too. It's the horse smelling the barn syndrome."

On March 12, 2004, I said goodbye to the team and one of our translators took me to the bus station. I sat down in my seat and let go a sigh of relief. I had made it. Except, somewhere between Ramadi and Fallujah, on the highway leading west to Jordan, the bus suddenly stopped in the middle of the desert. People sat up and looked out of windows. There were five cars in front of us and, two hundred metres ahead of them, five Humvees straddling the divided highway in a semicircle. Three more Humvees were parked on the left shoulder.

A handful of people got off the bus. I decided to get out too. I could see more clearly what was happening. There were soldiers lying on the ground in firing positions behind the wheels of the Humvees, hyper-charged, afraid, their bodies coiled and ready to kill. A lone soldier stood on the road in front of the Humvees, one hand signalling us to stay back, the other ready on the trigger of his machine gun.

The windows of the middle Humvee on the other side of the road were blown out. Some soldiers ran between vehicles, while others clustered in a tight knot and bent low around what appeared to be someone lying on the ground. I wasn't sure, but I thought I could see a second body lying unattended in front of the damaged Humvee.

More people spilled out of their cars. They lounged on the guardrail, puffed on cigarettes, talked in small groups. An F-16 circled overhead. I looked around me at the tight jam of cars, the vast expanse of desert rolling out flat around us, the brown-skinned people milling around, sitting in cars, waiting with glum faces, some in long flowing clothes, all speaking to each other in incomprehensible guttural sounds. I tried to imagine what the soldiers must be seeing as they kept watch behind their guns in Kevlar helmets and flak jackets. It seemed to me there was only one thing they could see—that they were surrounded by a sea of enemies—whereas I, a lone, unarmed Westerner who was just riding a bus, saw travellers, any one of whom I could approach to ask for help if needed.

After about half an hour, one of the Humvees ventured cautiously into the desert behind five foot soldiers. The men ran in short bursts, dropped to their knees, reconnoitred with their guns ready, advanced again in the same way, gradually securing a perimeter of 150 metres. Fifteen minutes later, a helicopter emblazoned with a red cross landed inside the perimeter. Three teams carrying three stretchers hurried towards the helicopter. The first two stretchers were accompanied by medics. Ominously, the last stretcher was not. The helicopters lifted off in a whirlwind of dust.

Fifteen minutes after that, a convoy of five white Suburbans drove up the shoulder and stopped at the front of the long traffic column. Doors opened and men with cameras and big fuzzy microphones got out. They wore sunglasses and navy blue flak jackets that said CBS. They began to walk towards the Humvees. The soldier who was standing in the road stepped towards them. "Stop! Back!" he commanded.

"We're reporters," the men shouted.

"No! Stop now!"

The men stopped. I asked one of them if he knew what was going on. No, he said. They were on their way to Fallujah to do a story when they got stuck in the traffic jam along with everyone else. I told him what I knew. He said thank you and I went back to sitting on the guardrail amongst the Iraqis.

A few minutes later, the man came over to me, formally introduced himself as being with the CBS *Evening News* and asked me if I'd be willing to talk with them about what I'd seen. He returned with a cameraman, someone holding a microphone, and a tall, craggy, good-natured man, the only one not wearing a flak jacket. "Hi," he said, extending his hand, "I'm Dan Rather with the CBS Evening News."

"Hi," I said, shaking his hand. I immediately thought of my father, who watches the CBS Evening News religiously. I wasn't sure what to say. "I'd heard that you were here covering the story in Iraq," I said.

"Yes, we're here for a week. There's nothing like being on the ground," he said.

"No, there isn't."

"What's your name?"

"James Loney."

"Where're you from, James? You don't look like you're from Iraq."

"Canada."

"What's a guy from Canada doing out here?" he asked.

"I'm travelling on that bus over there. I'm on my way home after working in Baghdad for ten weeks with a peace organization. We're documenting American human rights abuses." His eyes seemed to glaze over when he heard the words "peace" and "human rights."

"So, what did you see?" he asked, pointing up the road.

The cameraman focused in on me as I explained what I'd seen.

"Thanks very much," he said, shaking my hand warmly when the interview was over. "You travel safely now."

"Thanks. You too," I said.

"You'll be on the news this afternoon," the man who set up the interview said, as if announcing that I'd just won the lottery. "Well, actually, it'll be first thing in the morning back home."

"Thanks. Maybe my father will see it," I said, enjoying the thought of his surprise upon watching the news. And then it struck me, looking at all the Iraqi men and women and children standing around in the road, all of them waiting just like me, all of them having seen the same set of events: any one of them could have told the story of what had happened, and yet it was I alone whose witness held credibility and interest. The Iraqis were just an indistinguishable mass. I alone counted because I had the skin colour, spoke the language and carried a passport that mattered. And then, even at that, they had no interest in why I had come to Iraq or what I had seen.

I got on the bus, the Humvees parted and we were on our way again. I thought for a long time about the people on those stretchers. I wondered who they were and what had happened to them. I wondered about their families, what their lives had been like in the past, and what their lives would be like in the future, if they survived. I finally had to accept that I was never going to know. I was leaving Iraq and there were so many things I didn't know. Everything seemed to be a mystery, a half-truth or a lie. The only thing I knew for sure was that war was an outrage, and that nothing good could ever come of it.

When I got home, I found out that Colonel Sassaman had been in the news. On January 3, the day his best friend, Captain Paliwoda, was killed, soldiers under Sassaman's command ordered two Iraqi cousins to jump into the Tigris River. Marwan and Zaydoon Fadhil, twenty-four and nineteen years old, were returning from Baghdad with a truckful of toilet fixtures and plumbing supplies. They were either a few minutes before or a few minutes after the 11:00 p.m. curfew when they were stopped by Sassaman's men just a few hundred metres from their home. The soldiers handcuffed the cousins and transported them by armoured personnel carrier to the Tharthar Dam, where they forced them at gunpoint to jump into the river fifty feet upstream from the dam. Then they crushed the men's truck. Marwan made it out, but Zaydoon was dragged by the current through a water-control gate in the dam. His body was found thirteen days later, a mile downstream.[*]

Sassaman learned about the incident four days later. Rumours were circulating that one of the men had drowned. The platoon officer,

* The full story of Sassaman's role in covering up the circumstances related to Zaydoon Fadhil's death can be found in the *New York Times* article "The Fall of the Warrior King," written by Dexter Filkins and published on October 23, 2005.

Lieutenant Jack Saville, assured Sassaman that he had seen two men walking away soaking wet. Two days later Sassaman met with his commanding officer, Colonel Frederick Rudeshiem. Rudeshiem told Sassaman his men would be court-martialled if he found out they had forced the Iraqis into the water. Sassaman thought this was going too far. When the investigators came, he ordered his men to lie. "I told my guys to tell them about everything," he explained to *New York Times* reporter Dexter Filkins. "Everything except the water."[*] What they had done was wrong, but it was no more serious than a high school prank.[†] He intended to discipline the men himself by making them teach classes on integrity to their comrades.[‡] "I wasn't going to let the lives of my men be destroyed. Not because they pushed a couple of insurgents into a pond."[§]

Three soldiers and one officer faced criminal charges. At the trial, the defence argued Zaydoon was an insurgent who had staged his own death. In his memoir entitled *Warrior King*, published in 2008, Sassaman writes, "It was, in fact, common practice for top blacklisted Iraqi insurgents to fake their deaths in an attempt to divert interest from a particular terrorist cell . . . I believe it's likely this is what happened in the case of Zaydoon Fadhil."[¶] The defence introduced a classified U.S. intelligence report that said confidential Iraqi sources had seen Zaydoon alive and well in Samarra. Army prosecutors argued that the report, drawn up by a member of Sassaman's battalion, was false.

In the end, Sergeant Tracy Perkins and Lieutenant Jack Saville were both convicted of assault. Perkins was sentenced to six months, Saville to forty-five days. Sassaman and two junior officers (Captain Matthew

---

[*] *The Forever War*, 164.

[†] Col. (Ret.) Nathan Sassaman with Joe Layden, *Warrior King: The Triumph and Betrayal of an American Commander in Iraq* (New York: St. Martin's Press, 2008), 246.

[‡] Brian Gomez, "Fallen Warrior Rises to Lead Local Teens," *Gazette* (Colorado Springs), January 14, 2007.

[§] *The Forever War*, 164.

[¶] *Warrior King*, 252.

Cunningham and Major Robert Gwinner) were officially reprimanded for impeding the army's investigation. Sassaman's conduct was called "wrongful" and "criminal." He himself had no regrets. "I did what I thought was right in protecting those men."*

His career in shreds, Nate Sassaman retired from the army on June 30, 2005. He went on to become the athletic director at a private school in Colorado Springs. When asked to reflect on his new role, Nate told a reporter, "My passion has always been helping to teach people how to be responsible for their actions and how to be able to lead courageously in times of chaos and adversity and how to enact justice. You have to have a degree of empathy to help those who are less skilled or less talented than you. I did that in the Army. Now I just don't have to do that in combat."†

In *Warrior King*, Colonel Sassaman tells us about the day he went to the family of Mahadi Al Jamal with a compensation offer of six thousand dollars. He didn't want to do it. It had been only two days since Captain Paliwoda had been killed and Sassaman was angry. "I was frustrated beyond words that I had to pay off a family because their grandfather had died of a heart attack while my soldiers were merely doing their job; however, general army policy dictated these types of reparation payments—that's just how it worked over there."

These payments "typically came [with] much hand-wringing and crying, and occasionally a harsh exchange of words," Sassaman writes. He lost his composure when one of the younger members of the family got in Sassaman's face and started screaming. "There was a fleeting moment in which I thought about putting a bullet in his head. Instead, I got in his face and, with an interpreter by my side, explained . . . 'I know you're upset about your grandfather. I'm upset about my friend, but I'm paying you $6,000; what are you doing for me?'

"Now, I understand how that sounds. It is callous and contemptible; but it reflects precisely what I felt in my soul at that moment. I was

---

*   Gomez, "Fallen Warrior."

†   Ibid.

still the good Christian man who had come to Iraq seven months earlier, but my spirit was broken. This encounter, and my handling of it, represented a significant departure from the way I was raised and taught to be. In a very real sense, I had crossed over to the dark side. In retrospect, of course, I understand the anger and pain this family experienced . . . The truth is, that's not going a long way toward bringing democracy to anybody."*

With regard to the use of military force, however, Sassaman is unrepentant. "We acted with force because force was the only thing that seemed to work . . . the only thing the Iraqis seemed to understand."† If he regrets anything, it's that they weren't given the tools necessary to do their job. "We had a chance to win the war in the first year, and we didn't." Now he says it's time to bring the soldiers home. "We're sending over tired troops on old, worn-down equipment, with an American public that is not as fired up about this as it was in 2003, and I just don't see Iraqis shouldering the load as much as they should. Let them fall into civil war and fight through this on their own."‡

The first foreigner to be kidnapped was a British laundry contractor named Gary Teeley. It happened on April 5, 2004, two weeks after I returned home. By the end of the month, forty-three internationals had been kidnapped. NGOs left the country en masse. Tom Fox arrived in Baghdad on September 24, when the kidnapping of internationals was at its height. He and Matt Chandler from Oregon hunkered down in the CPT apartment while they consulted with the team's Iraqi partners about whether or not CPT should stay. They didn't leave the apartment for a month. Neighbours brought them food.

Margaret Hassan, the Irish-Iraqi director of CARE in Iraq, was kidnapped on October 19. Nine days later it was Borcz Khalifa, a community

---

* *Warrior King*, 235–36.

† Ibid.

‡ Ibid, 303.

development worker from Poland. Both women had worked with the team and had visited the CPT apartment. The kidnappers were practically knocking on the door.

I told Doug Pritchard, CPT's director of program and the project support coordinator for Iraq, that I thought the team should come home. I called Matt in Iraq and told him the same thing. "I know, I know," he said. "I keep wondering if we're like a couple of frogs sitting in a soup pot. We can't tell the water is getting hotter and hotter and we don't know enough to jump out until it's too late."

Our Iraqi partners felt it was still possible for us to continue working, and no one else was doing the work we were doing. The decision was made to stay, and two more CPTers joined the team in November.

Nine months later, in August 2005, Greg Rollins visited me in Toronto on his way home to Surrey, B.C. I asked him what the situation was like now. "It's bad and it's not, if you know what I mean. There's always the risk of being in the wrong place at the wrong time, but Baghdad's a huge city, and the chances on any given day that you're going to be in the vicinity of a bomb are really small. As for the kidnapping situation, for Iraqis it's as bad as ever, if not worse. We ourselves are taking a lot of precautions. We have our own driver now, and we never go out alone outside of our immediate neighbourhood where people know us, and never after dark. The women all wear an *abiya* so they don't stick out as much. We vary our travel routes all the time, and there are some places we just don't go. It's more restrictive, but there's still a lot of work that we're able to do. So far we've been okay. I guess it's kind of an intuitive thing. It just seems like the risk, balanced against the precautions we're taking and the work we're doing, evens out. And the kidnapping of internationals has died down. There haven't been any new cases lately."

I asked Claire Evans, the delegation coordinator, if she was looking for someone to lead the November delegation and she said she was. I took a deep breath and said I'd be willing to go. "Oh, good," she said.

# CHAPTER FOUR

Nothing happens. We sit and we sit. Someone enters the room. Tom asks for water. We are each handed a cup of water in turn. My saliva has grown thick for want of water, but I take only a few sips. There's already enough pressure on my bladder. More time passes. Someone enters the room. Something rustles. "Biscuit?" the voice asks.

"Yes please," Norman says. Something is put into my hand. I look down through the bottom of my hat. Two sandwich cookies with pink icing. They feel like a pat on the head. *Here you are, have a cookie, everything's going to be all right.* Keep your fucking cookies, I want to shout. The only thing I want from you is my freedom. I hear the others munching. My resolve crumbles. They're suddenly irresistible. I eat them quickly. The cookies are stale, chemical-tasting, dry my mouth out even more. I sit in disgust at myself.

We talk to each other in furtive snatches when the captors are out of the room. Every word is a risk. I find out that Harmeet and Norman have been allowed to keep their watches—cheap dollar-store digitals that keep track of the date. Norman is concerned about his supply of blood pressure medication. He has only five days' worth. How can he get more? We'll have to ask the captors. Norman says he doesn't have the prescription. Tom says all we have to do is give the captors the name of the drug and they can get it over the counter at a pharmacy; prescriptions aren't required in Iraq. Who should be the one to ask? Norman, we decide. His age gives him the most leverage.

Harmeet asks if we heard the Iraqi man pleading and crying. Yes. Tom wonders if he's a collaborator.

Norman changes the subject. He asks how he can change his plane ticket and get his luggage from the CPT apartment when we're released.

Tom and I caution him against the expectation of being released any time soon. It could be weeks or months, we say, if we even get out alive.

Norman changes the subject and apologizes for his *hamam* emergency. I ask if anyone else is having trouble going to the bathroom. No. I ask if anyone else has seen the huge, thick feet? Yes.

Somebody wonders whether we have been kidnapped by criminals or insurgents. Tom says Harmeet and I will be safe as Canadians. He says he and Norman could be sold to a group like al-Tawhid wal-Jihad. Norman says he doesn't want to hear about it and changes the subject.

Tom says it'll be a while before the news breaks in the media. He says the team will call everyone they know to try and make contact with the kidnappers, that there's a chance the captors might release us if the right person vouches for us before our disappearance becomes public knowledge.

We agree Number One is the leader. We disagree about how many different voices we've heard.

Sometime in the afternoon we hear voices in the living room. Chatty and buoyant, they move into the room together. A voice from the doorway says, "Good afternoon. How are you?" We do not answer. "Please, you must to take your hats off. We are going to take some picture."

I take my hat off slowly. My eyes blink rapidly against the sudden flood of light.

The voice tells us to turn our chairs around. As I do, I see Suit Jacket Man, Young Moustache Man and Great Big Man standing in front of us. Great Big Man is barefoot and wearing flip-flops; his are the feet I saw last night. There's also a grim-faced man holding a video camera; a little boy, no more than four years old, hanging on the man's pant leg and staring rigidly at the floor; a buxom woman in a long sand-coloured dress watching in the corner, her head covered by a scarf.

I get my first look at the room. It's quite big, about twenty feet by fifteen. They have us sitting in a corner. There's a door in front of us that opens into a hallway. I can see a set of stairs going up and what appears to be a door to the right at the bottom of the stairs. There's a jumble of shoes lying on the floor to the left of the stairwell.

The wall to our left is covered by a gauzy, floor-to-ceiling curtain that turns the light filtering through it a stop-sign red. The window behind the curtain appears to look on to an internal courtyard. The wall to our right is banked by a finely crafted armoire. The tile floor is covered with a green outdoor garden rug. The walls are pink.

There are two single beds in the room. The one closer to us is laden with folded-up sleeping mats, blankets and filthy-looking pillows. The other bed is covered with a rumpled blanket, where Number One must have slept. Next to the bed is a cluttered night table. On the wall across from us, at the height of a man's chest, two exposed wires dangle from an electric heater. I shudder at the thought of what they've been used for. Next to the door is a coat rack burdened with jackets, track pants, shirts, trousers, belts, towels.

I turn to look at Norman, Harmeet and Tom. It is reassuring to see their faces. They look solemn, their eyes are blank, but I sense they're watching everything.

The man with the video camera tells the little boy to sit on the bed. Tom asks if they want us to say anything for the video. Suit Jacket Man says no. This surprises me. If I were a kidnapper displaying my wares, I would instruct my merchandise to at least say their names to confirm their good working order. Suit Jacket Man gives Video Man the signal to start filming. They exchange some words, place candies wrapped in blue iridescent Cellophane into our hands and then turn to leave the room.

"Excuse me," Norman blurts out. The men turn around. "I'm terribly sorry, but may I ask a question?"

"Yes, Doctor?" Suit Jacket Man says.

Norman points to his heart. He speaks loudly, enunciating each word, like someone speaking to an uncomprehending child. He explains that he has high blood pressure and needs medicine.

Suit Jacket Man looks concerned, asks if he's sick. "Tell me, Doctor. What do you need? I will get it."

"Any beta blocker will do."

Suit Jacket Man looks confused. "I do not know this. You must to write this down."

"Yes, of course, but I don't seem to have a pen."

Suit Jacket Man pulls a pen out of his jacket. Great Big Man grabs one of the books lying on the floor next to Number One's bed, tears a page out and hands it to Suit Jacket Man. It shocks me to see a book being treated that way. "Here, you write this," Suit Jacket Man says to Norman.

"This will make Mrs. Kember very happy," Norman says.

Suit Jacket and Video Man leave with their entourage. The remaining captors tell us to put our hats back on and turn our chairs against the wall. I position my chair just a few inches farther from the wall so I can move my legs.

They come back an hour later. They want to do another video. "This time you make some speech," Suit Jacket Man says. I suppress a flash of rage. *I'm not a zoo animal*, I want to say. They take off our handcuffs, put a table in front of us, and I lay out our ID on it.

"This is your money card? American Express?" Suit Jacket Man says to Harmeet. Harmeet nods. "How much money is on it?"

"None," Harmeet says. "I only use it for emergencies. I'm a student. I don't have any money."

Suit Jacket Man picks up another card. "How much money is on this?" he says to Tom.

"It's a bank card," Tom says.

"How much money on this?" Suit Jacket Man demands.

"It doesn't work in Iraq. There are no bank machines here."

Suit Jacket Man turns to me. "Where is your passport?" His voice is hard.

"I don't know. You took it from me yesterday." I wonder what kind of operation this is. They don't know how to document proof of life and they can't keep track of our passports. I begin to shiver. That little blue book is my only link to Canada. What is going to happen to us?

"What is the matter? You are shaking," Suit Jacket Man says to me.

"I'm fine," I say.

"Are you cold? Do you need some jacket?" He takes off his turquoise suit coat and hands it to me. It smells of cologne. I feel filthy putting it on, but I don't dare say no. I suppress the urge to wretch.

Video Man and Suit Jacket Man consult over the video camera. Suit Jacket Man's eyes are intelligent, penetrating, ruthless, his skin smooth and clean-shaven, chin disappearing. He is maybe five foot seven and sports a heavy round paunch. His hair is jet black, cut short, meticulously coiffed. I find it hard to judge his age; he's at most thirty. His clothing and demeanour suggest wealth.

Video Man looks to be about ten years older. His eyes are hard and his face severe. He's losing his hair and the skin around his eyes has begun to crease. He wears a drab, shapeless suit jacket that's just a little short in the arms. He seems anxious and driven, capable of doing just about anything. Something about him gives me a chill.

They turn towards the woman. She laughs and touches Suit Jacket Man's arm. The little boy sits on the bed across from us, sucking his finger. He stares at the floor but sees everything.

Video Man says something to us. We don't understand. Suit Jacket Man steps forward. "We are going to take some picture of you. This is to show to your side you are alive." He steps back and Video Man aims his camera at us, pans slowly from left to right, closes in on our ID. He gives more instructions, points to his left shoulder as if indicating a general's epaulettes. The only thing I understood is, "Thank you Martin. Thank you Martin."

"I'm sorry, I don't understand," I say, shaking my head. Video Man repeats the phrase over and over. I have no idea what he means. The only thing I can think of is an inquisitive-looking animal with a long bushy tail. Then it clicks. He means Paul Martin, thank Paul Martin, the prime minister. Presumably because Canada stayed out of invading Iraq. We nod and smile to signify that we understand.

"Canada good. Canada good," Video Man says. *"Britannia, Amriki mozane. Mozane!"* He points to his feet with contempt. "Bush shoes." For better or worse, I think, we are seen through the lens of our governments' actions.

"You must to make some speech. In a high voice," Suit Jacket Man says. "You say your name, your passport, you have the good treatment, your health is okay, you have some food, and you ask your government to release you. We use this to make some propaganda statement, some publicity for our organization. And then you release. The Canadians I think release first. This is not something hard."

"I don't know what to say. I'm not good at this kind of thing," Harmeet whispers to me. He sounds panicked. I don't know what to say either. My heart is pounding. I can't believe this is really happening.

"Okay. You begin," Suit Jacket Man says to me.

I take a breath. "My name is James Loney. I am forty-one years old. I am from Canada and I am a member of Christian Peacemaker Teams in Iraq. We are against the war and the occupation of Iraq. I am well, um, we are all well. We have everything we need. I urge the Canadian people to work for peace . . . to mobilize its resources for peace in the world instead of war."

Then it is Harmeet's turn. There is a tremble in his voice. "My name is Harmeet Singh Sooden. I am thirty-two and I am working . . . I am a volunteer for the CPT in Iraq. We are all being treated well, we are sleeping okay and, um, we would like to say thank you to our captors for that and hopefully we will be home soon." I cringe at "thank you to our captors." I am not thankful to our captors—for anything.

"Now the British and the American," Suit Jacket Man says. "You must to make some speech, in a high voice. You must to say your name, your passport, you have the good treatment, and to beg your government for your release. You," he says to Tom. "Tell to Bush he must to get out of Iraq. And you, Doctor," he says, pointing to Norman. "Tell to Blair he must to leave Iraq suddenly. Do you understand?" Norman and Tom nod. "The American first."

Tom's voice is flat and calm and direct. "My name is Tom Fox and I am fifty-four years old. I am from the United States and I am a member of the Christian Peacemaker Teams in Iraq. Our treatment has been adequate and we are in good health. As a representative of Christian Peacemaker Teams we feel that continued British and American occupation is not in the best interest of the Iraqi people."

Then Norman, the embodiment of British dignity. "My name is Norman Kember. I am a British subject. I have come to Iraq on a peace mission with Christian Peacemaker Teams. We are being treated well by our captors. I ask Mr. Blair to take British troops out of Iraq and leave the Iraqi people to come to their own decisions on their government."

Video Man nods at Suit Jacket Man and the two men leave, followed by the woman and the boy. Great Big Man and Young Moustache Man handcuff us and turn us back to facing the wall. I notice that each of us has positioned his chair a little farther from the wall, giving our legs a few more inches of space to move in. I smile at this. We're all doing the same thing, pushing for the next tiny increment of freedom. This, I think, is the ceaseless cause of every captive.

Evening. "Okay? This okay?" Young Moustache Man says.

"Okay," I say.

Young Moustache Man hands Norman a black plastic bag. "This *duwa*. *Duwa*. This Big *Haji*."

"Thank you," Norman says.

"*Shokren*," Tom says.

"Do you speak *Arabi*?"

"*Shwaya, shwaya*," Tom says.

"*Shwaya, shwaya*," Young Moustache Man mocks. "This *Amriki*. This CIA."

"*Hamam*?" Norman asks.

"*Hamam*? Yes, *hamam*." No one moves. We wait for him to take us, one at a time, as has been the routine. "*Hamam!*" he snaps angrily and waves towards the door. Now we're to go on our own, it seems without out his escort.

When it's my turn, I can hardly stand. The effort of holding my bladder is physically painful. I navigate my way to the bathroom by scanning the floor through the crack at the bottom of my hat. I close the door and say a prayer. If I don't go this time, I swear I'll explode. I break into a sweat, lean my head against the wall, try to think relaxing thoughts. My urethra begins to let go in tiny increments. There's no captor waiting at the door, so I feel I have time. Then, sheer full-body relief, my bladder finally lets go. I almost skip back to my chair.

When Young Moustache Man leaves, Norman tells us they've brought him a 120-day supply of pills. "That's a bad sign," I groan.

The TV is on. There's enough background noise to cover our voices. I decide to ask Tom a question, something that's preoccupied me from the first moment of our kidnapping. "Are you worried at all about what might happen if they find out you used to be in the Marines?"

"Huh?" Tom says. He's hard of hearing—the occupational hazard of professional musicians. I lean closer to repeat the question. He says he hasn't thought about it. It's out of his control. Whatever happens, happens. He's just trying to stay in the present moment.

I roll my eyes under my hat. How can Tom not be afraid? Is this his way of coping? Is he trying to protect us? I don't want to be protected, and I don't want to be stuck with somebody who's trying to be a stoic hero. If we're going to survive, I think, we're going to have to be as real as we can with ourselves, and with each other.

"The reason I'm asking is because . . . I'm worried they might find out I'm gay."

He seems surprised. "How would they find out?"

"If they googled me. They said they were going to do background checks on us. If they do, they'll easily find stuff I've written about being gay. Or it could come out in the media. If Dan identifies himself as my partner . . . But I'm sure he'd figure that out, or Doug, or *somebody*. But even then, somebody could say something without thinking, and then it'd be all over the media."

Under Saddam Hussein, homosexuality was discreetly tolerated. When the regime fell, Islamic militants began to kidnap and murder gay men. In October 2005, Grand Ayatollah Ali al-Sistani issued a fatwa against homosexuality. "Those involved should be killed in the worst, most severe way possible." Gay men lived in terror as death squads with links to the Ministry of Interior and police ran a campaign of social cleansing.

"I don't think these guys are going to go to all that trouble. You're Canadian. That's all that matters. Your country isn't one of the bad guys.

And besides, I don't think anybody around here has enough English to figure it out. I don't think you have to worry."

"I hope you're right," I say.

The begging and pleading again. A man in sheer terror. Coming from upstairs. Other voices, hard and ruthless, lash, cut, perforate the helpless screaming. The screaming suddenly stops. The other voices continue. They speak to each other, suggest, consult. Men vying against a problem. For a moment of silence. Then movement coming down the stairs. The sounds of struggling, bodies labouring and out of breath. A single voice strains hysterically, impotently, pathetically against a gag.

Each muffled scream jolts me with a thousand volts of shame. Just a few feet away from me a man is fighting for his life. I must do something! Get up from my chair, pull off my hat, walk into the hall, say something. NO! *Haram! Take me instead!* I could grab their arms and try to pull them away, block the kitchen door, create a distraction by trying to escape. I could simply stand at the door with my hat over my eyes. All four of us could. This man's life is just as important. But no. I sit like a statue. Silent, inert, paralyzed by fear. I want to live too much.

This, I see in a flash, is the plight of the Canada Men. "Canada" was the section of Birkenau where the possessions of the gassed and the imprisoned were warehoused. Canada Men met the trains as they arrived, packed to suffocating with Jews from all over Europe. They welcomed the wretched cargo, took their luggage, reassured them they were going to have a shower while helping them onto the trucks that would take them to the gas chambers. The Canada Men knew exactly what they were doing. Bread, marmalade, sausage—survival in exchange for co-operation. The food brought by this daily influx of doomed human beings was keeping them alive.

At the crematoria, another group of inmates called the *Sonderkommando* were busy in a more gruesome transaction. Their job: clear out the gas chambers and move all the corpses to the ovens for burning. The return: food, clothing, cigarettes, a straw bed, medicine, survival for a few weeks until the Gestapo replaced them. The horror of this is beyond imagining or describing.

Never, I used to tell myself; I would rather die than make such a depraved bargain. In fact I am not different. I am striking the same deal they did. I sit and do nothing while a man is being taken to his death. Silence in exchange for survival.

Later I will read the words of Auschwitz survivor Primo Levi:

> We have learnt that our personality is fragile, that it is in much more danger than our life; and the old wise ones, instead of warning us "remember that you must die," would have done much better to remind us of this greater danger that threatens us. If from inside the *Lager*, a message could have seeped out to free men, it would have been this: take care not to suffer in your own homes what is inflicted on us here.

Our personality is fragile indeed. None of us can know what we will do in the bestial hour when we are forced to make the life-and-death choice between complicity and doing the right thing. But let us take care to remember that we are being faced by a danger that is greater than the loss of our life. It is the danger of losing our Self, what happens when we trade away our humanity, who we are and what we believe, for the sake of physical survival. For then we lose everything. It is the ultimate degradation of being the victim. The body lives, but the soul perishes, and we become like the *Sonderkommando*, living corpses who toil without hope among the dead.

Deep in the night. Finally, five deep-sleep breathing patterns. Everyone is asleep. My heart pounds like a parade drum. My legs are free. I can get up, right now, go through the kitchen, slip through the door, climb over the wall, steal my way back to freedom. Is this it, the opportunity to escape that I've been waiting for, my one chance to get away before being shot in the head or worse?

My mind reels with questions. Are the captors really asleep? What if I need a key to open the door? What if the hinges squeak? What if the dog is sitting in the kitchen or outside in the courtyard? What will happen to the others if I do escape?

Nothing. I do nothing. This is me, I think, this is all that I am—a feckless question mark, a convulsion of fear incapable of action, a nothing for others to wipe their feet on.

## NOVEMBER 28 DAY 3

Light in the room. Hat covering my eyes. Sound of bare feet padding on the floor. I steal a quick glance. A man with a green towel over his head is passing through the room. He's wearing a white undershirt tucked into grey track pants. His arms and shoulders are muscle-sculpted. It's Number One.

Half an hour passes. I hear hard shoes clicking on the floor. I steal another glance. It's Number One, in navy blue slacks and a dress jacket, the same green towel over his head, turning into the kitchen. A door slams and a car drives away.

More time passes. It is impossible to find a comfortable position. Everything aches and burns: hips, shoulders, ankles, everywhere my body is in contact with the floor. I am in a rage at the senseless wasting of our lives. *GET US UP NOW! GET US UP NOW!* my mind screams. The captors sleep on.

It is painful to watch Norman struggle and heave to get himself up. It is so unfair to put an old man through this. I groan as my stiff body moves into standing. It is a message of protest against our confinement. Young Moustache Man is not impressed. "Oooooh, oooooh," he mocks, putting a hand on the small of his back. I make a mental note not to do this again.

"*Hamam?*" Harmeet asks.

"Go *hamam*," Young Moustache Man barks. Harmeet leaves the room.

Young Moustache Man is suddenly vigorous, bouncing on his toes, ducking kicking punching in martial-arts-prowess display. "This kung fu. Kung fu," he says, pointing to himself proudly. Then, pointing to us, he asks, "This kung fu?"

"Norman knows kung fu," I say.

His eyes light up. "This kung fu?" Young Moustache Man points to Norman.

"No kung fu," Norman says with a laugh. "This *hamam*."

Young Moustache Man picks up one of our blankets and begins folding it. We stand and watch, unsure if we should help. Suddenly aware that we are watching him, he throws the blanket down and barks at us. You do it, he seems to be saying. We spread the blankets out on the floor and bring the corners together one at a time, the only way to do it when you're in handcuffs. Young Moustache Man points at Number One's bedroom like a drill sergeant. We collect the bedding and follow him. He points to the empty bed. We put the bedding down. He points to our chairs. We sit.

Before long we hear pots and pans being worked in the kitchen, the sizzle-fry of cooking, singing. Young Moustache Man enters the room and presents us with our first meal: a burnt two-inch piece of *humburger* held between two crumbling pieces of *hubis Amriki*, what appears to be a very poor imitation of American sandwich bread. "*Zane*? Good?" he asks anxiously. It has the texture and taste of saw-dust. Yes, we say, "*Zane*. Good."

The whole gang is back. They all seem to be talking at once. Video Man pointing and issuing instructions, Young Moustache Man squatting next to the little boy, the little boy listening, nodding, shaking his head yes or no, the woman giggling and fawning over Suit Jacket Man, Suit Jacket Man with something bright orange in his hand, Great Big Man with a coil of chain.

They remove our handcuffs. Tom and Norman are told to keep their hats over their eyes and stand up. They put two chairs next to

Number One's bed and make them sit facing the opposite wall. Number One's night table is put in front of Harmeet and me. On the table they put two glasses, a bottle of Pepsi, a plate of cookies and some grapes. Video Man urgently motions us to eat. We look at him blankly. He thrusts a glass into each of our hands. I take a sip and put the glass down.

"Eat! Eat!" he commands, forcing a grape into my mouth. I resist the urge to spit it back into his face. "Canada good, Canada good," he says. He takes three grapes from the little cluster and goes to where Tom and Norman are sitting. He barrages them with words and stuffs a grape into their mouths. He bends down in front of the boy and offers him a grape. The boy opens his mouth. Video Man caresses his cheek and pops the grape into his mouth.

"We take some video," Suit Jacket Man says. "Just like before. You make some speech, you say your name, your passport, you have the good treatment. You must to plead to your government for you release."

We nod. He gives each of us a cookie from the plate.

"Here we go again. Take three," I say to Harmeet. "Maybe they never used the one from yesterday."

"I hope not. I can't believe I said 'Thank you to our captors,'" he mutters.

I smile to myself as I imagine standing under a spotlight in a sequined dress holding a big bouquet of roses. *I would like to thank my parents, my goldfish and most of all my captors* . . .

When we finish our speeches, Suit Jacket Man points to where Norman and Tom are sitting. "You sit there. You must to look to the wall. No looking here."

The table and the chairs are taken away. Tom and Norman are made to stand against the wall.

"You must to put these on," Suit Jacket Man says. I peek over my shoulder. Suit Jacket Man is handing Norman an orange jumpsuit. My body starts shaking.

"I'm not wearing this," I hear Norman say, his voice rising angrily. "We're Christian peacemakers, not prisoners of war! *Issau salam!*"

Someone speaks in Arabic. "It might not be a bad idea," I hear Tom say.

I watch cautiously as Norman struggles into the jumpsuit. Young Moustache Man offers to help. Norman ignores him. He's determined to do it himself. The captors wrap a long chain around each of their wrists. The little boy snatches a cookie from the night table.

"Now you will make some speech," Suit Jacket Man says to Norman and Tom. "Like before. Your name, your passport. You must to beg your government for your release. That is all."

Tom and Norman are in great danger.


I take my shoes off with great reluctance. I feel defenceless without them. They represent the possibility of running, the hope we might yet walk out the door. They search each of us, beginning with Tom. I stand up with my arms extended, always with that damned hat over my eyes, while Suit Jacket Man, Young Moustache Man and Great Big Man work together with expert precision, hands probing the entire surface of my body, every inch of my collar, the cuffs of my shirt, each button, the waist and hem of my pants. They take my belt away and make me drop my pants. "I am sorry," one of them says as they move their fingers along the waistband of my underwear. My mind placidly observes; my body shivers.

Suit Jacket Man holds up one of our shoes. "Do any of you have some device in your shoes?" I don't understand. "Some GPS. Some device so the satellite can find you?" His voice is menacing. I shake my head. "You must not lie to me. I will rip your shoes apart to search them." His eyes are savage, threatening.

They throw our shoes onto the pile at the bottom of the hall stairway. "You not need them now," Suit Jacket Man says. "They are right here. When you release—not long, just some time and you release— you shoes are here."

The captors leave. I glance mournfully after our shoes from under my hat. They are at most fifteen feet away, but they might as well be on another continent.

—

We're back in the living room, laying out our sleeping mattresses. I have to keep reminding myself: these men, this situation, the handcuffs around my wrists, it's all very real. In a moment I will be lying on the floor, covered by a blanket, utterly defenceless. The television is on. I monitor it constantly, hoping to catch some mention of us, though I never look directly at it. I don't want them to know I am interested in it. The news is on. There's a soft colour of green I recognize immediately—the Canadian Parliament. My eyes dart to the screen. I watch galvanized, a chaotic scene in the House of Commons, suits milling about, MPs everywhere, some jubilant, others grim-faced. The words are all in Arabic. I want to reach through the television and pull myself home. The channel changes. The government has fallen, I think. There's going to be an election.

# CHAPTER FIVE

## NOVEMBER 29 DAY 4

Young Moustache Man enters the living room in his undershirt. He's cleaning his ears with the same green towel I've seen Number One using. "Good morn-ning," he calls buoyantly. It's time to get up. For a moment I'm not sure that I can. I've lost confidence in my body, no longer know what it can and can't do. My brain sends the signal and, much to my surprise, everything still works. I roll onto my right knee, use my left elbow as a fulcrum against my left knee and ease myself into standing. I immediately reach above my head with my handcuffed hands. A delicious release of tension floods my body.

I look over at Norman. He's struggling to get a foot planted on the floor so he can push himself up. "Would you like a hand, Norman?" I ask.

"No, I think I've got it, thank you," he says. With a Herculean grunt he hauls himself to his feet.

Great Big Man is just sitting up. His eyes are puffy with lack of sleep. He's wearing the same clothes he's worn since Day One—a long-sleeved navy blue denim jacket with three pockets (one at the left breast and two at the waist; keys in the right waist pocket) and matching denim track pants with an elastic waist. The word "GAMMA" is written along the left leg of his pants and his right sleeve. There's no way he could have slept—the couch is two feet shorter than he is. He stands up, arches his back, exits the room.

We fold up our bedding. Young Moustache Man nods approvingly. When our *hamam* rotation is over, we are instructed to go back into the other room and sit down.

—

"What do you mean?" Harmeet says. "It's only been two and a half days."

"No," I say, "it's been four."

"How do you figure? We were captured on Saturday and now it's Tuesday morning. That's two and a half days, not four."

"Saturday was day one," I say, "Sunday day two, Monday day three and today is day four." Harmeet insists that's not correct. "I don't care," I say, almost boiling over. "If it's even one second past midnight, it counts as a day."

"I don't see that it matters," Tom says. "We're going to get out when we get out. The important thing is to stay in the present moment. We don't know how long we're going to be stuck here."

I grit my teeth. The last thing I want to hear is a lecture on "the present moment."

"Okay?" Young Moustache Man says, entering the room. "Come on. *Akeel.*" We follow him into the living room. "Sit down," he says. He turns on the television with the remote and selects an Arabic pop music channel. His eyes light up when he hears the song that's being played. He closes his eyes and sings, hips swaying with the music. Then he goes into the kitchen.

"This is different," Tom says.

"What do you think? Bacon and eggs?" I say.

"I would settle for some crumpets and tea," Norman says.

Great Big Man appears with an oval tray and sets it on the floor in front of us. It holds four glass tumblers, each with an inch of sugar at the bottom, four pieces of the *Amriki* sawdust bread and four foil-wrapped triangles of cheese. "*Chai?*" Great Big Man asks, smiling broadly.

"Yes!" we say.

He pours hot tea from a dented kettle and serves each of us, beginning with Norman, as if we are honoured guests. The tea—warm, sweet, instantly comforting—fills me with ravenous hope. Does this generosity mean we're going to be released? Is today the day? I can't handle another minute of this.

Great Big Man jumps up—he's just remembered something important. He goes into the kitchen and returns with a jar of marmalade.

"Good, good," he says. Our breakfast sits in front of us. We wait to see if they're going to remove our handcuffs. *"Akeel, akeel!"* Great Big Man says, gesturing towards the tray. He takes the bread, breaks it, gives us each a piece. *"Hubis Amriki.* Good." He points to the silver triangles. *"Franci. Zane."* We're eating in our handcuffs.

"This in Canada?" Young Moustache Man asks.

"No, I don't think so." I open one of the triangles. It's some kind of processed cheese spread.

"This in *Britannia*?" he asks.

"Oh yes," Norman said. "It's made in France. It's called Babybel."

It's a difficult procedure, extracting the soft cheese from the foil and getting it onto the bread. The others just use their fingers and lick them clean. I am revolted. In accordance with my mother's strict training in table manners and hand hygiene, I use the foil to spread the cheese on my bread, being careful not to get any on my hands.

We pour the marmalade directly onto our bread from the jar and use our wrappers to spread it. I am aghast when the others lick marmalade off their foil. Proper manners apply even in captivity.

"Good?" Young Moustache Man asks. He's been watching intently, hunching forward with his elbows resting on his thighs.

"Yes, very good," Harmeet says. The rest of us nod vigorously. It's the best breakfast I've ever had.

Back to sitting against the wall. Harmeet asks what the term *haji* means. We've been using it when speaking to the captors. Tom says it's a term of respect for somebody who's completed the *haj*, the pilgrimage to Mecca. It's also an honorific for an older person. Harmeet wonders if we should be using it. He thinks it could be misunderstood. I ask him what he means. He says every war has its terms. In the Second World War it was *kraut*. In the Vietnam War it was *gook*. In Afghanistan now it's *raghead*, and in Iraq it's *haji*. "I don't even like to say those words," he says.

I'm irritated. I feel Harmeet is being overly scrupulous. I say we're using it to communicate respect. Harmeet says we can't be sure how it might sound to them. I say I don't think there's much chance that it'll be misunderstood. Iraqis refer to each other that way, especially when a younger person is speaking to an older man. It's a culturally acceptable way of addressing people—the equivalent of calling someone sir.

"Language changes," Harmeet says. "It can come to mean different things, depending especially on who's speaking."

I feel myself bristling. I can't tell if he's agreeing or disagreeing. I decide to change the subject. "I wish I knew what to call them. Maybe we should give them names, even just to use for ourselves."

Norman says it has to be something respectful. Tom agrees. "Names are important. The names we choose will affect how we relate to them."

We start with Young Moustache Man. "He definitely seems like a junior player," Harmeet says.

"Yeah, he's kind of like a grown-up kid," I say. I throw out Kidnap Kid, The Kid, Boy Scout. They don't like any of these.

"Perhaps we should call him Junior, as Harmeet suggests," Norman says. "He does seem to be the junior partner in this nefarious enterprise."

It is agreed. The Great Big Man is next. "I have the perfect name," I say. "Big Foot."

"It doesn't seem very respectful," Tom says.

"It's like a fun nickname. There can't be too many people in the world with feet that thick," I say.

"I don't like it," Harmeet says. "It makes him sound like a Sasquatch."

"A Sasquatch?" Norman says. "I don't believe I'm familiar with the term."

"It's a legend about a giant apelike creature people have apparently sighted in North America. It's also called Bigfoot."

"Oh dear. I shouldn't think that would be a very good name," Norman says.

None of us can think of a name.

"What about the one who wears the funny-coloured suit jackets, the one who brought the medicine?" Norman says.

"How about Medicine Man?" Harmeet says. We immediately agree. It's perfect.

—

Someone enters the room. It's Junior, I can tell from the breathing. "Come on," he says. "This in TV." We follow him into the living room and stand waiting for his next instruction. "This in TV! *Ogod!*" he says angrily, pointing at the couches. We sit. "This Khazim! This Khazim!" he cries, pointing to a crooning pop star on the television. Junior sits down and watches entranced, softly mouthing the words.

We sit like this for hours. My eyes wander aimlessly, follow the plaster moulding and cracks in the ceiling, return always to the ring of keys on the shelf next to the television.

Sometime in the middle of the afternoon, Great Big Man enters the room holding a large metal can and a skeleton key. He asks Junior a question. Junior, absorbed in the television, doesn't answer. Great Big Man kicks him in the leg. "*La petrol*" is all I understand. Great Big Man opens the door into the four-by-five-foot window well with the key. He leaves it in the lock, steps into the window well and kneels down in front of a rusty barrel sitting on a metal stand. He opens a spigot at the bottom of the barrel and starts filling the metal can. The smell of kerosene fills the room. Junior gets up from the couch, stretches lazily and saunters over to the door. He stands with his back to us, right foot crossed over his left, his right arm above his head, leaning against the doorway.

I put my feet flat on the floor and make ready to spring. Twenty feet, five or six steps, two seconds. One hard shove is all it would take. Junior collides with Great Big Man, the two men lose their balance and fall helpless into the window well. While they struggle to get back on their feet, I close the door and turn the key. And just like that, we are free.

Harmeet flashes me a look. He knows what I'm thinking. He shakes his head. I break from his gaze. There isn't much time. My body is exploding with adrenalin. I have only one chance. What about guns? They appear not to have them. Even if they do, it won't matter, we can easily move out of their line of fire. The crucial thing is the door itself.

It will have to close in a single slam. If it doesn't shut easily, or if the key doesn't turn, the captors will be able to push against the door and stop me from locking them out. Is this the careless moment I've been waiting for?

Great Big Man stands up with the kerosene can and Junior steps back from the doorway. My heart sinks. I've waited too long. I sit back and stare at the television. Great Big Man steps into the living room. I hold my breath and watch carefully as Junior swings the door closed. He has to grab the handle with both hands and lever the door into place with his shoulder before it will close. Thank God. I made the right decision.

The music videos continue. Junior slouches next to Tom, eyes glassy, remote sitting on his stomach. A video suddenly catches his attention. Tight, up-close shots of a scantily clad female vocalist. Junior sits up and bites his fingers. He points to the TV, laughs, turns to Tom with a conspiratorial grin. "Good?" he says. "This in *Amriki*?" Tom nods blankly. Junior turns to Harmeet. "Harmeet! Good? *Sadika*?"

Harmeet shrugs and laughs. "I don't know. She's not really my type."

"Jim!" Junior says, his eyes bright with desire. "This good? This in Canada?"

I nod and smile. Yes, very good, I say. I turn my eyes back to the television and hope that my face hasn't turned red.

I pass the test. Junior turns to Norman. "Doctor! This in television good?"

Norman waves his hand and laughs. "I'm too old," he jokes.

The Sacred Heart comforts and settles me. My eyes return again and again to the picture hanging on the wall, presumably left by the previous occupants of the house. I used to despise this pious, otherworldly Jesus, the vacuous heavenward stare, robes and hair flowing in saccharine cascades. Storybook camp for the spiritually infantile, I used to think, until one summer Sunday in a little country church located on the banks of the Saugeen River, during the second summer of our Catholic Worker farm community experiment, the Sacred Heart changed my heart.

I was early for a change. I genuflected, slipped into a back pew, waited for my eyes to adjust to the stained-glass light. I'd seen them many times before, the statues bookending the altar, Jesus reaching outwards with his nail-pierced hands, Mary pointing towards her chest, both of their red burning hearts exposed. This time, though, instead of being repelled, I was startled by their uncompromising vulnerability, their unflinching openness towards the world. Everything and everyone was welcome. It didn't matter who you were or what you'd done, whether you were an inquisitive child or an aching grandmother, a wild Janjaweed raider or an Abu Ghraib interrogator, the Sacred Heart was ready in greeting, without fear, arms and heart wide open. Thus, I began to see the Sacred Heart as a profound meditation on human freedom and the power of the disarmed life. When you know who you are, a no-matter-what loved child of God, you become like the Sacred Heart, your arms and heart wide open, free and ready to embrace anyone, do anything, go anywhere.

I next met the Sacred Heart during a visit to Auschwitz. It was on the wall of Cell Block 11, the Gestapo hellhole where the most exquisite tortures were inflicted on dissidents and resisters—a young, bearded Jesus etched into plaster, eyes luminous, halo, robes, heart exposed in the centre of his chest, the arm of someone kneeling in front of him and reaching across his waist, the shoulder of the arm stripped to bone. Stephan Jansienski, a member of the Polish underground captured in 1944, had carved it with his fingernail. Tears filled my eyes. Even here the Sacred Heart. Even here.

And here you are again, hanging on the wall of this insurgent safe house. You have found me even though I have been disappeared off the face of the earth. There is no dungeon you will not enter, no suffering you will not accompany. And if you are with me, even if the worst happens, somehow or other it'll be okay.

—

Junior points excitedly at the television. "This action film! Action film!" He puffs out his chest and flexes his biceps. "Action film *Amriki*!" The movie is called *Con Air*.

"Oh dear," Norman says. "I'm afraid *Wallace and Gromit* is more my speed."

We settle in to watch. It's unbelievably bad, an over-the-top bacchanalia of adolescent violence, but still it's a welcome relief from the all-day barrage of incomprehensible Arabic television. Nicolas Cage is Cameron Poe, a highly decorated U.S. Army Ranger on his way home after serving a wrongful seven-year sentence for manslaughter. He's shackled hand and foot on a prison air transport of America's most dangerous criminals.

"Hey, that's just like us," Harmeet says, holding up his hands and pointing to the prisoners in their handcuffs. Junior looks over at him and scowls. We watch as two of the prisoners extract pieces of wire they have embedded in the palms of their hands.

"Don't tell me they're going to pick the lock and escape," I groan. This is exactly what happens.

"Yeah, right," Tom scoffs. It's so ridiculous it has to be lampooned. As if reading my mind, Tom calls out to Junior and mimics picking open his handcuffs. I laugh. Junior turns towards me. I hunch my shoulders, look furtively left and right, grimace with pain as I pretend to pull a piece of wire out of my hand. Junior glares angrily. He doesn't think jokes about escaping are funny.

I try to explain. I point to the television. "This action film *Amriki*, Hollywood. Hollywood action film *mozane* . . . no good . . . stupid." I circle my index finger at my temple in the universal sign language for "crazy."

Junior scowls. I'm only digging myself in deeper. I look chastened and turn my attention back to the movie.

—

It is maybe eight o'clock. They've turned the channel to Al Jazeera. We watch grim footage of burning vehicles, body parts, bloody survivors. Number One stands behind us in the doorway, watching through the green towel. They're angry, gesture at the television, shake their heads.

"Who do you think we are?" Number One says. No one responds. "Who do you think we are? Jim?"

"I don't know. You are fighting for Iraq."

"Doctor? Who are we?"

"I don't know," Norman says.

"Tom?"

"You are *mujahedeen*," Tom answers.

"We are Iraqi. We are not al-Zarqawi. We are not terrorists. We are different. We are fighting for Iraqi freedom."

"In the West you would be called freedom fighters," Tom says.

"What this, Tom, freedom fighters?" Number One says menacingly.

"Freedom fighter. It's a word for someone who is fighting for their freedom," Tom says.

"No," Number One says. "We are *mujahedeen*. We are fighting for Iraq, not for George Bush freedom." He pauses. "We have some video of our organization. Would you like to see it? This very secret." We don't answer. He asks again. Harmeet says yes. My body starts shivering. "Good. I show you. But remember, you must not to look at me. This very dangerous."

Junior points to where he wants us to sit, on the floor in front of the TV. He is excited.

"I hope you guys don't mind. I'm just really curious. Maybe we'll learn something," Harmeet says to us. I don't say anything. I'm profoundly uneasy. I wish he hadn't said yes. What are they about to show us? Where is this going to lead?

Great Big Man inserts a DVD into the player. Junior turns off the light and sits on the floor, hugging his knees. The video begins. Flames boil wildly and fade to black. "This *mujahedeen*," he says, pride fluttering in his voice like a flag. I feel sick. Arabic script rolls across

the screen. Music. Men's voices, haunting, menacing, undulating, march-
ing in a revolutionary anthem. An endless sequence of exploding
tanks and Humvees, burning military vehicles, masked men launching mortars.

Junior jumps up and points excitedly at the television. He rewinds
the DVD. We watch it again: a bomb rips through a Humvee, there's a
spray of black smoke, debris arcs through the air. Junior points to two
black objects twisting in the trajectory of the blast. It's the charred
rag-doll bodies of two soldiers hurtling through the air. "*Amriki! Amriki!*"
he cries, delightedly. I close my eyes in horror. *These were human beings!*
I want to cry out. I swallow hard to hold the words back.

Laughing, Junior rewinds the DVD and plays it again. I shake my
head in protest. No one can see me in the dark. The DVD plays through.
I watch like a block of stone. Yet again, silence in exchange for survival.



The time has finally come for us to go to bed. I thought the day would
never end. We collect our bedding from the other room and set ourselves up in the middle of the living room. One of the mats is thinner
than all the others—the one I slept on last night. I secretly hope someone else gets stuck with it.

"I'll sleep here tonight," Harmeet says, pointing to the thin mat.
"I had one of the thicker ones last night."

"Thomas. This," Junior says, pointing to the outside edge of the
communal bed. Tom moves to his assigned position. Junior points
to the place next to Tom. "Doctor. This *nam*," he says. I end up next to
Norman—on the thin mat. *Of course*, I think. *That's what happens when you
want something too much.* We settle into our places and Junior uses three
narrow blankets to cover us. Harmeet and Tom, on the outside, are
barely covered.

"I have something I'd like to say," Norman whispers. Harmeet and
Tom move closer in order to hear. He wants us to pass a message on
to his wife, in case we are separated and the Canadians are released
first. He chokes up, fights to get the words out. Four things, he says.

He's sorry for what's happened, he asks for her forgiveness, he loves her, and he thanks her for forty good years.

"What this!" we hear. We look up from our huddle. Junior is standing over us with his hands on his hips.

"I was just talking about my wife," Norman says.

"Norman's madam," Tom says.

Junior's eyes narrow. "No talk! *Nam! Nam!*" He turns out the light. I lie on my back and watch the television's blue light flicker on the ceiling.

I must have fallen asleep. The next thing I know, the lights are on and Junior is shouting *"La firar! La firar!"* as he tears the blankets away.

"What's going on?" I say, completely bewildered.

"Shut up!" Junior says. He slaps me in the face and grabs my handcuffs. He locks my right hand to Harmeet and my left to Norman. The ratchet bites into my wrist so hard I can't close my hand. *"Amriki mozane. La firar,"* I hear him say, his voice full of loathing.

Great Big Man locks a chain around the wooden arm of the couch and then around Tom's wrist. This outrages me. *We're not dogs!* Junior gives us another angry blast and throws the blankets over our heads. The lights go out and the television falls silent. The captors converse in low voices as they settle into their places.

I replay the events over and over in my mind. *La firar*, he said. "No escape." Did he think one of us was trying to escape? Harmeet and Norman certainly hadn't tried anything. Had Tom? That was very unlikely. Junior must've been spooked, either by our mimicking of the handcuff escape scene, Norman's whispered message, or both. It makes me realize that the simplest misunderstanding could be a death sentence.

I can't sleep for all the pounding in my ears. Is it fear or rage? Rage. A screaming hurricane of it. I want out. I want this to end. This and the mad, stupefying, demonic waste of war that's put all of this in motion. I want it all to end right now.

When I'm sure the captors are asleep, I tilt my head back and use my chin to fold the blanket down. It takes me several tries but I eventually manage to push it off my face. Calmed by this tiny act of defiance, the storm of rage passes and I gird myself for the long night ahead.

# CHAPTER SIX

## NOVEMBER 30 DAY 5

Staring at the ceiling. Eyes fixing uselessly on scabs of peeling paint, smudges, cracks, a long spatter of something that looks like tomato juice. My back a single sheet of burning. *I can't stand this I can't stand this I can't stand this.* I have to do something. I lift my right knee into my chest, extend my leg out straight, bend it in again, rest it back on the floor. I do this over and over, right leg then left leg. It's somewhere to put the rage.

I thought it would never happen. The captors pull themselves into the day, put their bedding away, move in and out of the room, do things in the kitchen. Finally they unlock us. Getting up is a co-operative effort now that we are handcuffed to each other. Junior and Great Big Man chortle as we struggle to stand. Junior wags his finger at Tom. "*La hazeem, la hazeem.*" He says something in Arabic and slices his finger across his throat.

"*Haji, mumkin hamam?*" Harmeet says.

"No *hamam,*" he snaps. Then, eyes darting to the doorway, he barks, "*Killeators* down!"

Every movement has become complicated. I bend my head towards my hand so I can pull my hat down without pulling on Harmeet's wrist. "I hear about what happen, I hear about this. I am sorry," Number One says from the doorway, his voice grave.

"This must be some kind of misunderstanding," I start to say.

Number One interrupts me. "I am sorry. You must not to escape."

Junior leads us into the bedroom, a blind chain gang of four, our bodies tensing against a sudden collision. "*Ogod,*" Junior says. He maneuvers us in front of a bench in the middle of the room. We sit and Great Big Man chains Tom's wrist to the metal frame of a bed. "Shut up. *La killam,*" Junior orders.

When we speak to each other, it's in whispered fragments, always after checking to make sure no captor is watching. Tom was punched in the chest. Everyone else was slapped in the face. We're all bewildered. No one had been trying to escape. Tom thinks Junior did it to impress Number One. It's ironic, I say, how they're accusing Tom when I've been thinking about escape since the minute of our capture. I tell them how I came within a hair's breadth of pushing Junior into the window well. "I'm glad you didn't," Harmeet says.

I ask if anyone else has been thinking about escape. Harmeet says it's too much of a risk, we should wait to see what happens, they say they're going to let us go. I say I wouldn't put too much stock in that. Norman says maybe he would've tried it in his younger days but it doesn't seem to be much of an option for him now. It's like a puzzle, I say; we just have to figure out a way so we all get out. They only have to make one mistake.

Tom doesn't say anything. I ask him directly. His answer shocks me. "When we've been here a hundred days, maybe I'll think about it."

"A hundred days," I groan. The very idea sends me into paroxysms of despair.

Harmeet says he's worried about how we were separated for the video. "They're treating us differently. That's not good."

I tell Tom I'm sorry, it looks as if they're singling him out. "That's the price of having an American passport," he replies. "There's nothing we can do about it. I'm just trying to live in the present moment. The past is gone and the future doesn't exist. All we have is the present moment. I'm just meditating as much as I can, praying for us, the team, my kids—letting go of everything and just being in the now."

He's right, but I can't help but be irritated. "That's easier said than done," I say.

Norman says he's going directly to the Green Zone when we get out. He doesn't care about his things at the CPT apartment—he's getting the first flight back to London. "I could be back in time to go to church on Sunday. It's the children's annual Christmas liturgy. I haven't missed it in almost forty years." Norman chuckles, "I'm supposed to play God this year."

Tom cautions Norman to be prepared for a long wait. "We just don't know what's going to happen," he says.

"Yesterday was such a good day," I say. "Tea and jam and TV. This must be some kind of plan. They're messing with our heads, trying to throw us off balance. They want us to know they're in control."

"Maybe," Harmeet says.

Sounds. A throat clearing. Bodies shifting. Handcuffs clinking. A helicopter roaring low over the house. Windows shuddering. A burst of gunfire somewhere nearby. The constant chatter of television.

I'm ablaze with pain. I lift, roll, pull my shoulders back, sit straight, slouch, stretch my neck—nothing helps. It astonishes me. What an agony it is to sit like this, without any support for my back.

There's a bird calling out to us from the courtyard. It reminds me that there were swallows darting in and out of their living room, fluttering in the mud nests they'd built high along the ceiling. I tell the story of the day we visited Ahmed and his son Ali at their farm on the outskirts of Baghdad. We took off our shoes at the door and sat on the meticulously swept hand-woven rug that covered the brown dirt floor. Ahmed's wife brought us tea. The door, a sun-faded bolt of cloth, puffed back and forth in a February breeze.

Ahmed was fifty-two years old, the father of eight children, the youngest eleven. His hands were hard, his body thick, his face weathered—the physical accumulations of a lifetime spent in hard agricultural toil. Ali was twenty-six, the father of three children, the oldest four. The line of his hands, the edges of his body were softer and rounder than his father's. He was a driver for the Ministry of Education. Ahmed puffed calmly on a cigarette while Ali simmered under a dark cloud. They had a story to tell, and we had come to listen.

Two weeks earlier, the men had been picked up by the American army, Ahmed on his way home from the mosque, Ali at their home. The Americans were "collecting intelligence" about a nearby bombing incident. For seventy-two hours they were subjected to an excruciating regime of what the military calls *stress positioning*. Hooded with their hands handcuffed behind them for the whole time, first they were forced to lie on their stomachs, then to sit cross-legged on the ground (soldiers kicking their kneecaps to keep them awake), and then to stand continuously, each of these positions lasting for a period of twenty-four hours. They were held outdoors and given only water to drink, no food. Each day they were asked if they knew anything about the bomb incident. Ali was screamed at, kicked in the groin and beaten in the face. They held them for five days and then let them go. There were marks on Ahmed's wrists where the handcuffs had been, and the bone of each of his ankles was covered with a round scab.

"Imagine what they're going through in Guantanamo," Harmeet says. "What we're going through doesn't even compare to that."


The punishment appears to be over. When the ratchet slides free, I immediately grip and massage my wrists, red-ringed from the hours of metal pressing against bone.

"Go *hamam!*" Junior barks. I stand up and arch my back. The relief is instant. I want to jump, dance, cartwheel around the room.

After we go to the bathroom, they lock us up and bring our supper, another *humburger*, as well as a jug and a glass. It takes some figuring out, how to eat and drink when you're handcuffed to the person beside you. Wrist locked to wrist—this is how it will be for the remainder of our captivity.

"*Killeators* down!" Junior says.

From the doorway, the voice of Number One follows. "Doctor, Jim, Harmeet, Thomas. My man tell to me. You must not to escape. Why this? You are safe with me." We try to explain, but Number One interrupts. "My man tell to me this. I know." He moves closer, stands directly behind Norman, rests his hands on his shoulders. "Doctor, you very good with the English. Very good. You must to teach me the English, Doctor."

"Well, thank you, but I—"

"I have some English book."

"I should think Harmeet would be better qualified—he is studying English literature in university."

"But you are the professor. You must to teach me."

"Well, yes, a professor of biophysics, but of course I have been retired for many years now."

"You do not want to teach me, Doctor? Why this? Have I said something bad to you?"

"No, no. It's just not my training." Norman is flustered. "Harmeet would be better. But if you want me to, I can certainly try."

"Thank you, Doctor. I love the English. I want—I *need* to speak better. I need to speak the English so I can express everything—everything that's happened. But there are no words to tell it, to tell everything about the war, the suffering of the Iraqi people. No words." He speaks slowly, almost as if he is in physical pain.

"*Catastrophe? Outrage?*" I offer. He doesn't answer. The words suddenly feel empty, trivial. "There are no words for the horror of war," I add.

"No, there are no words," Number One says. "I wish . . . I wish that I could speak the English. I wish that I take you. I show you everything. Everything that happen, all around Baghdad. I so wish to show you the destruction of the Americans, so you tell to everyone. But I cannot. I not have the English."

"Your English is very good," Harmeet says.

"No, it is not. I need to express everything, and I can't."

"What books do you have?" Norman asks.

"I have *The Old Man and the Sea*. It is about some fish man. And *Faustus* . . ."

"Oh dear," Norman says.

"Yes, it is very difficult. And . . . this book by Fall-ker, it is call *As I Dying*."

"Wow, those are difficult books," I say. "Are you taking a course?"

"Yes. It is for the university. I have some exam on Monday."

"You do?" Norman says. "Perhaps I might help you to prepare for it."

"Thank you, Doctor."

# DECEMBER 2 DAY 7

Tom turns to prayer like a warrior preparing for battle. The long, slow exhalations of his meditation-breathing punctuate the days like an intensive-care respirator. The chain at his wrist clinks softly as it passes through his fingers, one link at a time, as though he's praying the rosary. His resolve and focus are astonishing. "I'm trying to think of our captivity as a *sesshin*," he says.

"I knew somebody who did that," I say. "It was at an ashram in India. Ten days of complete silence, fasting and meditation. All they did was sit and try to clear their minds of all thoughts. They weren't even supposed to scratch themselves if they got an itch. I could never do it."

"What do you meditate about?" Harmeet asks.

It's a compassion practice called *tonglin*, Tom explains. He pictures someone—a member of his family, a CPTer, one of the captors, whoever he feels needs a prayer. On the inhale he breathes in the suffering of the person he is thinking about, and on the exhale he breathes out compassion and healing to them. With each breath he passes a link of chain through his fingers. He holds that person for a cycle of four breaths, praying *With the warmth of my heart* in the first breath, *with the stillness of my mind* in the second, *with the fluidity of my body* in the third, and *with the light of my soul* for the last. At the end of the cycle he pauses and surrounds the person with light.

His example chastens me, rouses me from my self-preoccupation, reminds me it is the one thing I can do: pray for the needs of others and the healing of the world. Sometimes I use my fingers to count off the decades of the rosary. Sometimes I say the Jesus prayer, *Lord Jesus Christ only son of the living God have mercy on me a sinner*, over and over, until it becomes a living force within me. And sometimes I make up litanies to the Sacred Heart. *O most holy open heart. O most holy healing heart. O most holy loving heart.* The obvious thing is to pray for the return of our freedom. But I can't. I don't know why. Something within me forbids it. It's like adding gasoline to a fire. Praying for what I most want will only cause me to suffer more. My prayer is just to be open. Open to whatever comes, and to give whatever is asked of me.

# DECEMBER 3 DAY 8

Late afternoon. We are sitting, as always, in our plastic-chair places, light filtering through the red curtains—a perpetual infrared twilight that wearies me beyond words. Harmeet has been entertaining Norman and me by summarizing movie plots he watched as a teenager. Tom is far away, breathing his way through his meditations.

The television is suddenly silent and there's a stir of voices in the kitchen. Medicine Man enters the room. "How are you?" he says. He stands just behind us against the armoire at our left. We turn to look at him. He's wearing a turquoise suit with a gun tucked into his belt. Great Big Man, standing beside him, looks startlingly businesslike: dark trousers, navy blue suit jacket, baby blue turtleneck. Junior watches from the doorway.

"We have some order. We take you, each of you, to a different place. One here, one here, one here." He points to different places in the room. "Every one separated. We take you by car. In the boot. I go now to prepare." He turns abruptly and leaves.

"I should think this is not an entirely positive development," Norman says.

"That's an understatement," I say.

"I'll go first," Tom says.

"I can go," Harmeet says.

"No, I'll go. I've been preparing for this for a year now. Imagining, praying, meditating about it—ever since I came to Iraq. The way I feel now, I can do this forever."

I turn to look at Tom, astonished that he could say such a thing. His face is illuminated by a serene determination. *Forever is a long time,* I want to say.

"All right," Medicine Man says. "The American, you are the first one. Stand up." His voice is hard, incontestable. Tom stands up. I'd forgotten how tall he is. They lock his hands behind his back. Tom looks straight ahead, face solemn and defiant.

"We take you first," Medicine Man says to Tom, "and then we come for the British, and then you and you. This not be long. Maybe one half an hour. Just go and come back. It is not far." He looks directly at Tom. "We take you in the boot. You must not to make any sound. No crying, no shouting, no disturbance. Nothing. Must I to tape you?" His voice is sharp like a knife. Tom shakes his head. "If you make any sound, I torture and kill you. Do you understand?"

Tom nods. "What about my shoes?" he asks.

Medicine Man looks down at Tom's feet. "You do not need them. The rest of you, I not long. The British is next."

Tom is in grave danger. We are all in grave danger. I feel nothing. There are only facts. The fact that I am sitting in a red plastic lawn chair handcuffed to two other men. That Tom is about to be taken away by a man with a gun. That men with guns like to be obeyed.

Tom turns to look at us. The moment is strangely awkward. I have to say something, but what? *Good luck, take care, God bless? See you later? Jesus loves you, don't be afraid, he is always with you?* Everything sounds trite, pious, ridiculous. I say nothing. "Be strong," Tom says.

Great Big Man blindfolds Tom and leads him past Junior in the doorway. "*Amriki,*" Junior says, his voice full of spitting.

After about an hour Medicine Man returns. "Doctor, we are ready for you," he announces.

"Oh dear, I've never ridden in the boot of a car before," Norman laughs.

"It is not long, Doctor," Medicine Man says. "Fifteen, twenty minutes and you are there. You must not to say anything. Not anything. If you make any sound, I kill you." Norman nods. "Okay, we go."

"See you soon," Harmeet says.

I reach for Norman's hand. "Take care, Norman. Be strong. God is with you."

Medicine Man pulls a second scrap of cloth out of his pocket and uses it to blindfold Norman. "I come for you next," he says, pointing at me. I shudder.

"I have a feeling they're not coming back," Harmeet says when they're gone.

—

We seize upon every movement and sound. Waiting, hoping, dreading Medicine Man's return. Darkness falls. The power goes out. Junior sets a lantern on the floor, enveloping us in a sulphurous gloom. He returns fifteen minutes later with our *humburger* supper. They're not coming back. Harmeet goes back to recounting movie plots. I pretend to be interested.

"Come on, sleep," Junior says. He unlocks our handcuffs and holds the lantern up for us to see. We grab our bedding and follow him into the living room. Our shoes have disappeared from the bottom of the stairway. Junior chains Harmeet to the couch and then handcuffs me to Harmeet. He stands back. His face looks sad. "I am sorry," he says.

I do not answer. There's nothing to say. I turn onto my side and tuck my blanket under my chin with my free hand. Junior goes into the kitchen. "Harmeet, our shoes are gone," I whisper.

"Really? That's not good." We're quiet for a long time. "Good night, Jim," Harmeet says. It sounds like a blessing.

"Good night, Harmeet."

# CHAPTER SEVEN

We breathe, blink our eyes, shift in our chairs. Everything closes around me: emotion, time, space. When things happen in relation to each other I cannot say. There is only waiting. We tread water on waves that rise and fall in the middle of a vast ocean. There is no horizon. Only grey.

On an indeterminate evening, Harmeet and I are sitting, as usual, against the wall. I hear a loud sigh, movement towards Number One's bed, sounds of undressing. Junior asks questions and Number One answers, his voice tired and flat. Their conversation peters out. Number One coughs.

"*Salam alakum*," Harmeet says.

"*Alakum salam*," Number One says. He stands behind Harmeet. His voice is warm.

"How did your exam go?" Harmeet asks.

Number One sighs. "No good, no good. I must to ask my teacher for forgiveness. I cannot sleep. I cannot to think anything. My mind is like—I don't know how to say in English—it is like some thick cloud. I must to change my life." He falls silent for a moment. "At night, when I close my eye, I see everything. It is in my mind like a movie. I cannot to make it stop. I am very tired. Every time I am moving to the different house, every night, every week a different house. It very dangerous here, very dangerous. For me, and for you. I must to change my life. How can I? How can I change my life?" His voice rises in anguish.

I'm astonished—an insurgent commander is asking me how to change his life. His question is a doorway, a portal, an opportunity.

I want to say something about how much God loves us, that we were made for living with an open heart, for joy, that we can only discover our freedom when we give our lives in the healing service of others. I measure, test, knit words together. I must choose carefully. They're all I have. I take a breath, but I'm a millisecond too late.

"Have you seen a doctor to help you with your sleep?" Harmeet asks. I want to curse him.

"I don't know," Number One sighs. "I don't know." Then he is gone.

Harmeet and I are sitting on our sleeping mats in front of the TV, waiting for the order to bed down. We have become used to the sound of gunfire, the explosions that punctuate the days. But this, out of nowhere, something I have never heard before, a sudden cannonade of ear-shattering rapid-fire gun sound, heavy and light calibre, war breaking out everywhere around us. I lie flat on the floor. What is happening? Countrywide insurrection? A neighbourhood feud? A U.S. military action? I want to take cover, but there's nowhere to go.

"What the hell is going on?" I say to Harmeet.

"It sounds like we're in a war zone!" he replies.

Junior and Number One enter from the kitchen, Number One in his green towel. I look up cautiously. Junior points the remote at the television and flicks through the channels. He stops at a soccer team running, jumping wildly, faces ecstatic with victory. Junior breaks into a big smile, speaks excitedly to Number One.

"What's this?" I ask, forming a machine gun with my hands.

Junior smiles. "Iraqi football. In Syria. Iraq yes! Iraq good!" Junior flexes his biceps and puffs out his cheeks.

"Iraq crazy," I say, circling my index finger at my temple. Junior laughs.

An indeterminate afternoon. Sitting. Staring. At hands, wrists, finger-nails, knees. The pink smoothness of the wall in front of us. The bullet hole at my knee. The pebble speckles on the floor. It becomes an obsession: finding, sorting, mind-morphing them into patterns and shapes. A Hercules arm, a clown's face, letters of the alphabet, a foot.

The sharp, cracking sound of a gunshot cuts through this useless thought-babble. I instinctively duck. Adrenalin floods my body. I strain to catch every sound. "Did you hear that?" I whisper to Harmeet. "It came from inside. It was a gunshot."

"How could that be?"

I hold up my finger. We listen. As far as we know, Junior is the only captor in the house. Is he okay? We hear muttering, the clicking of something metal, a couch being moved. "Hello? *Haji? Haji* okay?" I call out.

Junior enters with his arms waving, eyes wide, face flushed, a gun in his right hand. He points it towards the ceiling. "*Mooseh-dis! Mooseh-dis!*" he cries, makes a shooting sound, explains in body language how he'd been examining the gun when it discharged. The bullet nearly struck him in the head, hit the ceiling and sent plaster flying everywhere.

"*Haji* okay?" I say.

He nods. "Yes, okay, but this *mozane*," he says, holding up the gun.


Another afternoon. We're sitting in the living room, under the Sacred Heart, hands free. In front of us, an end table with a plate of cookies, two glasses, a bottle of 7UP. We have visitors: Medicine Man, Video Man, the little boy. Junior squats down to talk with the little boy while Medicine Man, Video Man and Number One confer in serious tones.

I look up at the ceiling. It takes a minute to find it, the round pockmark in the chandelier moulding where the bullet hit. I nudge Harmeet in the arm. "There it is," I whisper. I catch Junior's eye, grin and point to the ceiling. He scowls, puts his index finger across his lips and shakes his head. He doesn't want Number One to know.

Video Man and Medicine Man turn towards us. Number One moves to the doorway. Medicine Man points to the Sacred Heart above our head. Junior takes it off the wall and drops it behind the couch to our right.

"Canada good," Video Man says, offering each of us a cookie with a smile that makes me shudder. "*Shokren*," we say, obediently taking them. He pats Harmeet on the head and gives me a thumbs-up.

"This you release video," Medicine Man says. "We give to Al Jazeera just before you release. You must to look happy." We nod blankly. "You must to smile. This for you release. You have some Seven." Medicine Man fills a glass for each of us. "Drink! Drink!" We drink. "Have some biscuit!" I force myself to smile. "Good. Now we begin. No speech. You just to smile, laugh, make your glasses like this." He holds up a glass as if he's making a toast. "Do like the English."

Video Man stands on a chair to film us, why I have no idea. He gestures towards the glasses.

"Smile!" Medicine Man says. "This you release."

"Cheers," we say, tipping our glasses together. It's humiliating. I feel like a dog sitting up for its master. I look away from the camera. Junior is bouncing in and out of the living room with the little boy on his back. The boy laughs delightedly. I smile at him.

"Good smile," Medicine Man says. "That is all." Video Man steps down from the chair, removes the tape from the video recorder and hands it to Number One. Number One leaves through the kitchen.

"Al Jazeera give us some money," Medicine Man says. "When we release you, Al Jazeera will show the video. Not before. This something exclusive for them."

How long before we're released? we ask.

"Not long," he says. "Three day, four day." What about Tom and Norman? "They are fine," he says. "We separate you for the safety. We take the video of them, just like you. For release. You release first, and then the others. All of you release. Just some negotiation and finish."

He motions for us to stand up. Junior puts our handcuffs back on. Medicine Man pushes the couch back into place and tells us to sit down. The captors chat together in the middle of the room. Junior shows them a gun. Medicine Man releases the safety, checks the magazine, looks down the barrel. He points the gun at the floor, squeezes the trigger, shrugs, hands the gun to Video Man. Video Man looks at it, pulls the trigger, shrugs, hands it back to Junior. Junior throws it onto the couch. The men continue talking.

The little boy wanders over to the gun. He hesitates, puts a finger to his mouth, looks over at the men. When he sees they're not watching, he reaches for the gun. He tries to grip it in his right hand, the way he saw the men holding it, but it's too heavy, he has to use both hands. He examines it reverently, and then, looking up, points it at us. I shake my head slowly. A cold smile spreads across his face.

Medicine Man sees the boy and points at him. The men break into laughter. Video Man pats him on the back and pinches his cheek. He seems to be saying something like, *You will grow up to be a mujahedeen, just like your father.* Whatever it is, the boy beams proudly.

Another evening. Junior is sitting cross-legged and barefoot on the bed next to us at our right, elbows resting on his thighs. If I tilt my head up just a little, I can see Junior's face below my hat. Number One is standing behind us. He interprets as Junior talks.

Junior points to Harmeet. "*Sadika, sadika,*" he says with a curving gesture to indicate a woman's hips. His face is earnest, inquisitive like a 12-year-old boy.

"He see you on television," Number One translates. "Your picture. You are with a girl. She have yellow hair. Very pretty. She is your girlfriend?"

Harmeet shakes his head. "No, I don't know anyone with yellow hair. I don't know who he could be talking about. Unless it's a very old picture. Maybe it's someone I knew in university, but I never had a picture taken with her."

Junior asks if he has any children. No, Harmeet says. Junior asks if Harmeet is married. No. Does he have a girlfriend?

"No *sadika,*" Harmeet says, pretending to cry. " This very sad."

"*Leiash?*"

"I don't know. I'm trying, I'm trying. This not love me," Harmeet says, joking. He pretends to pull a ring off his finger, then draws a big X in the air.

"Mother? Father?" Junior asks.

"Yes, mother and father."

"In Hind?"

"No, Zambia." Junior doesn't understand. "It's a country in Africa."

Junior's eyes widen. "Brother? Sister?"

"One sister. In New Zealand."

"*Nuzlander*?" Junior says, surprised.

"Yes, New Zealand."

"This *Hind*?" Junior asks him.

"This *Kashmiri*," Harmeet says.

"This *Kashmiri*?" Junior's face is full of surprise.

"Yes."

Junior points to Harmeet, flexes his bicep, makes the gesture of a machine gun.

"He say the Kashmiri fight for independence, just like Iraq," Number One says. "He say you have parents in Zambia, you and you sister in New Zealand, but you Canadian, and you Kashmiri. How can someone be all of those things? Are you Muslim?"

"No, I am Sikh." Junior looks puzzled. "It is a religion, like Christianity or Islam."

Number One and Junior converse back and forth. Junior finally nods. "But the rest of you are Christian?" Number One asks.

"Yes," I say.

Number One asks me if I have children. No. Am I married? No. He is surprised. "How old are you?" Forty-one.

Number One explains to Junior. His eyes widen. "Why this? No madame? No *whalid*?"

"I don't know," I say. Junior wants me to explain. I swallow hard. "I don't know why. I just never got married," I say, shrugging, trying to look as natural as possible. I'm in mortal danger. I can't lie, and I can't tell the truth.

"He say you are the handsome one with blue eyes and you not marry. Why this?" Number One says.

"It's a long story," I say.

"We have time."

"It's a long, sad story," I say.

Number One translates. "I am sorry," Junior says.

Number One places his hand on my shoulder. "When you get back to Canada, you must to get married. This very important."

"*Inshallah*," I say.

"*Inshallah*," Number One says. My heart rate eases. I passed the test for a second time.

Junior points to my shirt. It's one of my favourites. It showed up on the porch of Zacchaeus House one day in a bag full of second-hand clothes.

"He says you have a very nice shirt," Number One says. "He ask how much it cost."

"I don't know," I say. "It's second-hand." Junior looks puzzled, feels the fabric of my shirt.

"Was it eight dollars?" Number One says.

"I don't know. Somebody gave it to me. Brand new it would be, I don't know, maybe fifty dollars?"

Junior's eyes widen. "He wants to know if you're rich," Number One says.

"No. I mean yes, compared to most Iraqis I am rich, but in Canada I am not rich. I believe we should only take what we need."

"Thank you," Junior says.

"Does *haji* have work or some business now?" I ask through Number One.

"This . . . taxi . . . in Baghdad," Junior says, forming a steering wheel with his hands. "*Shwaya faloos.*" He rubs his fingers together, making the sign for money.

"How much does a taxi driver make in Iraq?"

"It depends," Number One says. "He say at night it's seven thousand dinars. During the day it's nine thousand. He works at night." It's the equivalent of nine dollars.

"Do you have any brothers or sisters?"

"No mother, no father, no sister," Junior says. He shakes his head, his face sad. Then, looking up, eyes fierce, he points to himself. "This

Fallujah! This Fallujah!" It is like a battle cry. Then, as he speaks, his face and eyes become blank, as if he's stepped away from his body.

"He say the Americans bomb his house," Number One says. "His mother, his father, his sister, his fiancée, his best friend—they all kill when the Americans bomb his house."

"I am very sorry," I say. "This *haram*."

Junior looks down at his hands. "Thank you," he says.

No one speaks for a long time. Finally I say to Number One, "Can you ask *haji* what he would be doing in Fallujah if there hadn't been any war?"

Helping his father in the market, Junior answers.


Harmeet and I pass the time in long, wandering conversation trails, one question and story leading into another. Slowly, word by word, the contours of our lives begin to take shape for each other. I learn that Harmeet is a Kashmiri Sikh born in Zambia and a permanent resident of New Zealand with Canadian citizenship. He tells me his great-grandfather is buried in Iraq. He was a *havildar*, the equivalent of a sergeant, serving in the British Indian army when he died during the Mesopotamia campaign in 1916. There's a memorial maintained by the Commonwealth War Graves Commission near Nasiriya, south of Baghdad.

His great-grandfather had a son in 1913 named Bhagwan Singh, the father of Harmeet's mother. Bhagwan's mother died when he was only ten. He and his brother were looked after by their grandmother, and when she died tragically three years later, they were taken in by a Hindu family. Like his father, Bhagwan joined the army when he came of age. He was a *subedar* (lieutenant) stationed in northern Kashmir, in the town of Gilgit, when the British withdrew in 1947 and British India fractured along religious lines to form the Dominion of Pakistan (later the Islamic Republic of Pakistan and the People's Republic of Bangladesh) and the secular Union of India (later the Republic of India). Kashmir, a kingdom located in the northernmost corner of British India but not under direct British rule, became the epicentre of a bitter contest.

Pakistani-backed forces invaded and Kashmir's Hindu king enlisted the help of India, which promised to allow the people of Kashmir to decide their own future in a free plebiscite.

When his Muslim comrades switched their allegiance to Pakistan, Bhagwan suddenly found himself fighting against men who had once been his friends. He escaped with two gunshot wounds to his leg. It was winter, he was up in the mountains and he had no food. He was captured by Pakistan and taken to a transition camp, where he was saved from execution by a Pakistani soldier who had served under him. He was then transferred to Attock Fort as a POW.

The war ended in a stalemate, with Kashmir divided between India and Pakistan. When Bhagwan returned home a year and a half later, he was horrified to learn that his village was now part of Pakistan and ninety members of his extended family had been killed—basically all the people he had ever known, including his first wife and three sons. It would be seven years before he discovered one of his sons had actually survived. Harmeet's grandfather remarried in 1951 and his mother was born a year later. Bhagwan retired in 1958 after twenty-eight years of military service.

Harmeet's parents, Dalip Singh Sooden and Manjeet Kaur Sooden, were joined in an arranged marriage in 1971 during the third Indo-Pakistani war. They fled to Zambia, where Harmeet's father had been working in a nitrogen plant. Harmeet and his sister were born and raised in the expatriate community that ran Zambia's copper mines. Haunted by the spectre of war and poverty, the young couple were determined to provide their children with the best education possible. At great sacrifice, they enrolled them in British public schools—Harmeet at the age of eleven, his sister at the age of ten. Except for holidays, Harmeet spent his adolescence in British boarding schools.

In 1991, Harmeet was accepted into McGill University to study computer engineering. He graduated in 1997, got a job with Nortel in the techno-boom and became a Canadian citizen in 2001. When the bubble burst that same year, Harmeet was laid off and a long-simmering inner conflict boiled over. Becoming a professional and moving to a

Western country, the path chosen for him by his parents as the means to a secure future, had led him to a soulless corporate career marked by long hours and superficial work relationships. Long troubled by the inequality that ravaged the world and now suddenly free, Harmeet began a lengthy process of rethinking his commitments and priorities. He went to Kashmir and stayed with his grandparents to reconnect with his Kashmiri roots. Then, unsure of what to do next, he followed his sister to New Zealand. After a long search for work, he finally landed a three-month contract with Cubic Defence NZ (formerly Oscmar International), a defence contractor specializing in military training and simulation systems. His savings were running low and he had to get back into the job market or risk becoming professionally obsolete in the swift-moving world of computer engineering. He told himself he'd take the job for a few months while he looked for something else.

Three months turned into a year and a half. A growing unease about his work turned into a full-blown crisis of conscience when he was assigned to a sensitive defence project for Israel that seemed to be in breach of New Zealand export law. He travelled to Israel/Palestine as a volunteer with the International Solidarity Movement (ISM)—a group much like CPT that supports Palestinian self-determination—to learn for himself what the situation was. Concerned that his work was supporting Israel's continuing occupation of Palestine, he resigned and went to study English literature at the University of Auckland, at last embarking on a path that was truly his own.

After completing his first two semesters, Harmeet arranged to begin his summer recess by joining the CPT delegation to Iraq, and from there travel to Palestine to rejoin ISM. Disturbed by New Zealand's decision to support the occupation of Iraq, Harmeet felt it was his responsibility to find out what was going on first-hand.

The excruciating hours and days of nothing-ever-happening-at-all accumulate and compound. Harmeet becomes helplessly garrulous. His normal reserve breaks into a stream-of-consciousness flood. I fall silent, nod my head, answer now and then with uh-huh. The endless flow of words begins to tear at me.

Though I'm desperate for quiet, I can't bring myself to ask for it. I don't want to say or do anything that will impose upon or limit what remains of his freedom. It has become as precious to me as my own. I worry that if I say something, he will feel hurt and withdraw altogether, and that, right now, would be far worse than his talking.

Harmeet has gotten onto chocolate again. "Chocolate—that's at the top of my list. The first thing I'm going to have when I get back home. Thick chocolate cake, and chocolate milk. That's what I always have, late at night, when I'm studying. It's brain food!"

"Harmeet," I groan, "please don't talk about food." *Please*, I want to say, *just for a little while, don't talk at all.*

"When I was in Zambia, you used to be able to get it—chocolate milk. There was this store that sold it—it's still there, with the same logo and everything. They would sell it in tetrahedral containers. That was back in the days when you could still get things like that in Zambia, before the country was embargoed by the West. You could get pretty much anything you wanted—as long as you had the money, of course. Not anymore. The economy has totally collapsed now.

"One time I was in the south—that was during the motor vehicle trip I told you about, when I broke down in the middle of nowhere—I was taking the bus back home and I was hungry. So I asked around for where to get something to eat. They told me to go to the Shoprite—it's a South African chain. It's where the poor shop. It was down the street from the bus stop and around to . . ."

I can see the words gathering within me, along a horizon far away. A voice within me says, *No, don't.* As Harmeet talks, the words come closer and closer. They gather and grow like giant, sky-towering columns of cumulonimbus clouds. *Don't say it,* the voice says, putting up a hand. *Please Harmeet,* my mind starts to beg, *just for a moment, a little tiny bit of quiet. Don't make me say it.*

I can't stop it. The words flash and break in a murderous screaming mind-rage: SPARE ME THE INCONSEQUENTIAL DETAILS OF YOUR

INCONSEQUENTIAL LIFE! Loud enough, it has to be, to smash windows and blast apart walls.

I hang my head, fall prostrate in a cesspool of shame. I feel like I have just dumped poison into the room. Could he have heard? No, thank God, he is still talking. I nod, say uh-huh, go through the motions of listening. *Forgive me, Harmeet*, I say, in the voice he never hears.

It takes me several days. I search the whole of my life. I begin with my childhood and work my way through high school and university, young adulthood and recent middle age. I consider every school year and job, every place I have lived, every group I've been part of. I try to remember every person I have ever known, those who were an integral part of my life and those whose path I crossed only briefly. I visualize each one, embrace and kiss them, thank them for whatever I have learned or received from them. Each person is a shining sun, a face of God, an indelible part of the man I've become. I begin to see that my life has been astonishingly rich, an ever-flowing fountain of friendship and love, a universe of goodness. The joy! So much joy! So much blessing! I thank God for each person, surround them with light, and let them go.

When I am done, a door closes. The desire to think about the people I love—my parents, my brothers and sisters, my nieces and nephew, my friends, even Dan!—disappears. It's not a choice. It simply happens. I have to set my face to the task at hand. Getting through the next five minutes. And the next five after that. That's all there is. There's nothing else.

Deep in the night, the TV is still on, bathing the room in electric blue light. Have I been awake all along? Where's Junior? I hear English coming from the television, a news voice. I'm instantly awake. "Tom Fox of Clearbrook, Virginia," the voice says, "age fifty-four, the father of two, formerly a musician." I steal a glance at the television. I see a picture of Tom. He's smiling. The channel changes. I fight against panic. Could this be the announcement of his death?

# DECEMBER 10 DAY 15

In the morning, Junior unlocks us without saying a word. We gather up our bedding, carry it into the next room, sit in our chairs. Junior follows listlessly, face and body drained of all vitality. After he locks us up again, on his way out of the room, he releases a long sigh. "*Mooshkilla*," he says, just under his breath.

Hours pass. Junior drifts in like a ghost and the room fills with a deathly gloom. "Okay?" he asks vacuously, his face puffy with sleep. The words *Could we have something to eat?* form briefly in my mind. Every cell in my body is trembling with hunger. He's forgotten to feed us. "Okay," we say.

I'm worried. Something's wrong. My mind spirals helplessly. There's been a rift amongst the captors. Somebody's been given an order they don't agree with. Tom and Norman have been sold or, worse, killed. What else could explain the news clip about Tom, Junior's ominous despair?

I take a deep breath and try to bring myself back to what I know—I'm alive, I'm sitting next to Harmeet, I'm not in pain—but there is little consolation in it. I might as well be lying in an open grave. Something is terribly wrong.

Day wheels into evening. Number One returns and Junior revives. I hear his voice, now animated, coming from the kitchen, mixing with the sounds of utensils working in metal bowls and Number One's rich laughter, like a young boy in eager conversation with a parent just home from work.

Junior brings each of us a diamond-shaped piece of flatbread called a samoon. He scoops up our water jug and leaves the room again. The spring has returned to his step. I pull the bread apart to see what's inside. It's the usual, a tiny, overcooked piece of hamburger, but the bread is actually fresh, and the meat garnished with a slice of salted tomato. "Wow, look at this," I say. "We have fixings!" It's the best thing I've ever eaten.

"*Killeators* down," Junior says from the doorway, the order strangely gentle. My hand goes automatically to my hat. Operant conditioning. I hear the soft padding sound of feet on the floor, the clinking of a belt buckle, clothes rustling. Junior moves away from us. I hear them say Norman and Tom, then the word *mot*—Arabic for death. My heart flares wildly. I have to try to find out.

"Excuse me, *haji*?" I say.

"Yes," Number One says.

"May I ask a question?"

"Of course. Anything." He stands behind me, his hand lying gently on my shoulder.

"What's happened to Tom and Norman?"

"Nothing. Nothing at all. They are fine."

"I heard you say Tom and Norman's names, and I heard you say *mot*." I can't keep the anguish out of my voice.

"Do you speak Arabic?"

"No, but I know this word."

"Why do you ask me this? Have you heard something?" I don't know how to answer. "Why you ask me this?" he insists. "Please, you must to tell me. What are you feeling?"

My mind reels with fear. I don't know how honest I should be, what the consequences could be if I tell him what I'm really thinking.

"Please, you can tell me," he says again.

I take a breath. "Last night I saw on the TV for just a second—*Haji* was changing the channel—there was a picture of Tom on the news." I point to Junior. "*Haji* is very sad. Now I hear you say Tom and Norman and the word 'dead.'"

"You must to believe me," Number One says. "They are okay. They not harm in anything. I love the Doctor. I love the peaceful man. They are just in some separate place, for the safety. We are not terrorists. We are different." I nod. "We have some news," he continues. "We kill some man. He is American. He is a contractor. He works as some engineer for the occupation. We take him and we kill him. But we not kill Norman and Tom. We kill only the soldiers. And the collaborator. We not kill Norman and Tom. Would you like to see them?"

The thought of being moved terrifies me. "Well, yes. I'd like to know that they're okay."

"Tomorrow I bring you to them. I promise. Tomorrow you see them," Number One says, patting my shoulder.

# DECEMBER 11 DAY 16

Medicine Man enters the room on a wave of cologne. *"Sabha il hare,"* he says in the middle of a stride, his voice bright and happy.

*"Sabha il noor,"* we say.

Medicine Man stands in the corner facing us, his paunchy body bursting out of his suit jacket, hand on his hip. "How are you? Everything okay?" We are about to answer when we hear an electronicized baby cry. "It is my girlfriend," he giggles, pulling out his cellphone. "She cannot leave me alone."

Their conversation is short. When he is done, Junior asks to see Medicine Man's cellphone. Junior examines it reverently, his eyes full of wonder. Medicine Man pushes a button. The cellphone plays a circus ring tone. The men burst into laughter. "Good!" Junior says.

"It is new," Medicine Man says. "We call this phone a hummer." He pushes another button. We hear "Pop Goes the Weasel." Junior laughs delightedly each time he plays a different tune.

"That is enough," Medicine Man says, suddenly pocketing the phone, smile vanishing.

"How are Tom and Norman?" I ask. "Are they okay?"

Medicine Man frowns. "You see this on TV?" We shake our heads. "We kill a man. He is American. I think he is some contractor with the Ministry of Education. We hold him for two days and we kill him. He have some work with the Americans. But you, I release you all together. All four together."

I will learn later that the man was Ronald Schulz. He was kidnapped on November 25 while doing electrical work for a private security organization. On December 6 the Islamic Army of Iraq released a video threatening to kill him unless the United States released all of its prisoners in Iraq and compensation was paid to Iraqis killed by U.S. forces in Anbar province. The group claimed to have killed him two days later. A video of his execution was released on December 19.

"So Tom and Norman are okay?" I ask again.

"Yes, they are fine. Would you like to see them?"

"We'd like to know that they're okay," I say.

"Very well. I take you there." He looks at his watch. "I bring you today."

Medicine Man and Junior sweep into the room. "This is for you," Medicine Man says to Harmeet, handing him a bottle of water and a package of cookies. He steps back. "All right, I take you now. In the boot."

Junior unlocks my handcuffs, pulls me out of my chair and turns me so I'm facing Medicine Man. Junior's wearing a turtleneck, a navy blue suit jacket, pressed slacks and carefully polished black shoes. He locks my hands behind my back.

Medicine Man grips my shoulders. "Now I am taking you. No talking. No crying, no shouting. Nothing!" His voice is hard. I nod. "Must I to tape you?"

"No," I say.

"If you make any sound—any sound!—I torture and kill you. Do you understand?"

"Yes."

Medicine Man turns to Harmeet. "I back for you in one hour. Not more. You not to make any sound. You not to move. I have the guard who watch the gate for you. Do you understand?"

"Yes," Harmeet says. Junior double-checks the locks on Harmeet's chains.

"Okay, we go," Medicine Man says to me.

Junior takes me through the living room and stops me in the kitchen doorway. The house is dark. Junior is tense, his body coiled. He pulls my hat down over my eyes. A car engine starts. There's a shout from Medicine Man. Junior pushes me down into a squatting position.

"No talk," he orders. I nod. There's a sudden push—the signal to move. I squat-run through the kitchen, turn left through a doorway and step out into air, outside sounds. Through the bottom of my hat I can see the gritty surface of pavement. The breezes on my chin feel like fresh-air kisses. The yearning for freedom flares madly. He takes me to the back of the vehicle. They lift me into the trunk like a helpless puppet. The trunk is empty and clean.

"No talking," Medicine Man says one last time. "It not long. Ten, fifteen minutes and we are there." The trunk lid slams shut. I breathe in. There's a vague smell of vinyl. I lift my head as high as I can but I can't touch anything. I stretch my legs. Six inches is all I can move them. I can just touch the back of the trunk with my handcuffed hands. My heart is beating like a jackhammer, my mind reeling into panic. What's going to happen to me? Am I going to be shot? Are they going to abandon the car with me in it? Am I going to slowly asphyxiate, starve, die horribly in this steel coffin? What happens if there's a flat tire, or the vehicle breaks down en route? What if the car is searched at a checkpoint? *You have to stay calm*, a voice says.

Doors slam. Laughter, voices. Medicine Man and a woman. His girl-friend? It's a perfect cover. Who would suspect a "husband and wife" of transporting a hostage in the trunk of their car? I hear the slide-roll-clang of a gate opening. The clutch engages, the car eases forward, turns left, stops. The gate slides closed. A car door clicks open and slams shut. Junior in the back seat, jabbering excitedly. We're moving again. I feel the turning of wheels, the hum-throb of engine and trans-mission. First gear, second gear, third, roll to a stop, a turn to the left. Another eruption of laughter led by Medicine Man. Somebody turns the radio on. The speaker is just above my shoulder. It's an American army radio station. They're playing something hard and metal.

The car slows to a crawl, bounces through a rough patch of road, turns right onto smooth pavement, accelerates to highway speed and joins the honking stream of Baghdad traffic. I rub my head against the rug floor of the trunk and push my hat above my eyes. I lift my head and look around. It's pitch-black except for a pinhole of light near what I think must be the key lock. I attempt to slide my hat back down over my eyes but I can't get it to return to the same position. I eventually give up and hope they won't notice.

The car is in stop-and-go traffic. We must be approaching a checkpoint. I ready myself to pound and scream if I hear an official-sounding voice. I don't get the chance. We're accelerating again. How long has it been? Ten, fifteen, twenty minutes? Half an hour? I've lost all sense of time. On a far horizon within me, I see a gathering storm of desperation. *Stay calm, you have to stay calm,* a voice within me says. I concentrate on the music.

The car stops again. Cars rush past. Have we stopped on the shoulder of the road? A door on the passenger side opens and closes. There are two voices right outside. What's happening? I go to full-body alert. My mind starts racing. I force myself to breathe. Is this the time? Should I kick and yell and scream for dear life? What if it's an accomplice? They'll ignore me and punish me later. What if it's an innocent bystander? I'll put his life, and mine, at risk. What if it's a police officer? I might provoke a firefight. The decision is wrenching. I remain still.

The door slams and we're moving again. The storm is closer now, moving in, a furious, air-shattering maelstrom. *No,* the voice says, *breathe, stay calm.* I focus on the radio. The DJ is a woman. Her voice is throaty, tough, slightly nasal. She's dedicating a song to a group of soldiers who collected teddy bears and toys for a Baghdad orphanage.

The car stops again and a door slams. The air is suddenly close. I can't breathe. Panic washes over me. My heart feels as if it's going to explode out of my chest. I use my head to push my hat above my eyes again. My whole body is trembling. The car turns and stops abruptly. The engine goes off. Doors open and close. I'm a wild animal on the brink of rampage. The trunk clicks open. Suddenly there's light and air. I'm immediately calm.

Two hands reach in, lift, swing me out of the trunk. It's Great Big Man. My legs find ground and stand. He pushes me down and puts his index finger across his lips—the sign to be quiet. He's giggling. I take a quick look around. We're outside a house with white plaster and big windows, in a yard with a palm tree, bushes, grass. Medicine Man shouts to him from a door at the top of the driveway. We're suddenly running, hunched low, Great Big Man's hand on my shoulder. He's laughing. We enter the house and turn right. He signals me to stand. We pass through a kitchen into a grand hallway. There's a room directly in front of me with an open door. Is that where I'm being taken? No. He turns me to the left, directs me up a flight of stairs into a spacious central landing and aims me towards the one open door.

# CHAPTER EIGHT

I step into the room. There's a smell that makes me want to pinch my nose—sad, stale, rancid, despairing. Ahead of me, a window barricaded with chairs, boxes, piles of junk, stained bedsheet curtains. There's someone behind me. I turn around. It's Norman and Tom, sitting on chairs against the wall. They're pasty, haggard, cadaverous, their faces grizzled with unshaved beard, eyes dull and lifeless. They see me, I think.

"Tom! Norman! Am I ever glad to see you guys!" I burst out. They sit like grey statues, unable to move or speak. "Are you guys okay?"

"Jim," Norman manages to say. Opening his mouth seems to be an effort.

"We thought . . . you had been released," Tom says, speaking in slow motion. They both look pained.

"No, no such luck," I say with a laugh. Neither of them smiles. "We didn't know what happened to you guys. We thought maybe . . . Well, it's just really good to see you again. Really really good."

"We thought you had been released," Norman says. There's dismay in his voice.

"Are you guys okay?"

They nod. I wonder if I look like them and just don't know it. I have no idea how captivity is affecting me.

Junior enters the room. "Doctor! Thomas! Okay?" he says, a big smile on his face.

"Hello," Norman mumbles. "We haven't seen you in a while."

"*Salam alakum,*" Tom says. Junior bristles at his greeting.

"One big happy family all together again," I say.

Great Big Man unlocks my wrists. I stretch and arch my back. He pulls a chair out of the jumble in front of the window and places it next to Norman. Tom is locked by the wrist to a chain that's pad-locked around the door's cantilever handles. Norman is handcuffed to him. Neither of them is wearing shoes. I sit down. Great Big Man handcuffs me to Norman.

"Just like old times," I say when the captors leave.

"Quite," Norman says. "Where's Harmeet?"

"Back at the other house," I tell them. "The captors took me in the trunk of a car, said they'll bring him next." They nod. "How have they been treating you?" I want to know everything.

Pretty much the same as at the first house, they say. The first night, they slept in a room downstairs. Otherwise they've been here the whole time, guarded by the big man. So far he's been treating them well. Unlike Junior, he's calm and steady. When he gets bored, he goes rummaging around the house and brings them things to identify. Little bottles of shampoo. A whisk. A coffee press. Oven cleaner. There's another captor too. He's only stuck his head in the door once, just for a second. He seems shy, almost timid, as if he doesn't want to be here. They think maybe he cooks the food. They've been getting three ham-burgers a day. Just like us, I say. Sometimes they put a tomato in it. They got macaroni once, and eggs once. No fair, I say.

I ask if they've seen Medicine Man. Once, Norman says. Twice, Tom says. Each time they were videoed.

"It was only once," Norman insists.

"No, it was twice," Tom says. "Remember, the first time it was in the room downstairs. They made us wear jumpsuits. And the next day they filmed us again, in the bathroom downstairs, blindfolded, with chains around our wrists, in jumpsuits again. Remember?"

"No, I don't," Norman says.

"Oh my God! That must have been terrifying," I say.

"I don't remember that, and I don't care to," Norman says.

The room falls silent. "Any sign of our shoes?" I ask. No. "What about sleeping?" They sleep right in the room, on the futon heaped against the chairs and the thin cotton mat lying on top of it. "And the bathroom?" It's across the foyer, Norman explains. It has a Western-style toilet and bathtub. The toilet has no running water. The big man lets them go as often as they need to. They point to a filmy one-litre plastic water bottle and two stainless steel cups. They can drink as much water as they want.

We can't believe it, they say again and again. We thought for sure you'd been released. Their faces are dull and vacant. It's as if they're in shock or wearing masks.

I turn my attention to the room. The walls are a soft pink, the ceiling baby blue. I wonder if it might have belonged to a little girl. The floor is eleven pebble-speckle tiles wide and sixteen long. Each tile is a square foot. The window is seven feet wide and four feet high. The left half of the window is covered by a swath of heavy-woven olive green fabric, the right by an unwashed floral-print bed-sheet swarming with brown stains. The windows are covered with vertical bars.

Long jagged strips of paint hang from the ceiling. The plaster above the window and along the walls is extensively water damaged. To the right of the window, in the blistered paint and crumbling plaster, I see a figure with a powerful torso jumping up with one arm above his head. A man reaching for freedom. I wonder if Tom and Norman have seen it too.

I count ten wooden chairs in the barricade in front of the window, many of them with broken thwarts or missing seats. In the left corner of the room there's an imperial-looking throne chair with hand-carved arms and legs. Sitting on the chair is a three-foot-long, two-foot-wide aluminum light fixture with a light bulb the size of an ostrich egg. Poking out of cardboard boxes that are piled on top of and jammed underneath the chairs, a strange assortment of odds and ends: a flat-tened soccer ball, a dark room clock, a Polaroid camera, floor tiles, videocassettes, a red velvet–sided treasure box decorated with a lion's head. Things that have nowhere else to belong.

"What's that thing over there?" I point to a brown, boxy piece of furniture at the edge of the barricade.

"It's a hostess trolley," Norman says. "If you open up the top, you'll see where you can put trays of food to keep warm. It's only useful if you do a lot of entertaining. Something the previous occupants must have done a lot of, judging by the size of this house."

"What about that?" I ask, pointing to a cube covered with grey carpet, two-feet high and a foot and a half square.

"We're not sure," Tom says. "When we asked the big man, he kept saying *zowagi, zowagi* and imitated a woman putting on lipstick. We think it's something a woman must sit on at a dressing table."

I wonder whose house it is, and if they have any idea what it's being used for now. Tom says hundreds of thousands have left the country—anybody with financial means. The houses they leave behind are taken over by insurgents. Who's going to know, much less question, whether or not the occupants of a house have a right to be there—especially under the current circumstances, when asking questions can get you killed.

We hear a vehicle pulling up the driveway, voices under the window, a door below us opening and closing, a high-pitched gurgling laugh. "That sounds like Medicine Man," I say.

Junior enters the room first, followed by Harmeet carrying a massive ball of fiery red blanket, followed in turn by Medicine Man. For a split second Harmeet looks stunned. Then he smiles. "Dudes! Fancy meeting you here."

"We've got to stop meeting this way," I say. Tom and Norman smile weakly. It's a restrained reunion.

Harmeet asks Medicine Man what to do with the blanket. Medicine Man points to the floor next to the beanbag. Harmeet drops it on the floor. Yuck. The floor is filthy. I hope that's not the blanket we're using tonight.

Junior pulls a chair out of the barricade. "Move," he says, directing us to shift our chairs to his left. There's just enough room between the wall and the open door to fit a fourth chair. "Sit down," he says to Harmeet. He handcuffs Harmeet's right hand to my left.

"You see? You are all together again. Everyone is fine," Medicine Man says. "We just have some negotiation with our political arm and you release for the election. We do this to make some announcement to show we are not the terrorist. One day, two day, and you release, case closed." He slides one palm over the other in two quick chopping motions. "Okay? You need something?"

Can you get us some toothbrushes? I say. Yes, he will bring a toothbrush. Four toothbrushes, I say, one for each of us, in a pretty-please-with-sugar-on-top voice. The idea of having to share one toothbrush horrifies me. He raises his eyes in surprise. You want four toothbrushes? Yes, I say. He smiles indulgently. Something else? he asks.

"We seem to have lost our shoes," Norman says. Medicine Man turns to Junior. They exchange words. Medicine Man turns back to us. They're at the other house, he tells us. He will bring them. I fight to disguise my irritation. They're not there, I say. They disappeared right after Tom and Norman were brought here. Medicine Man and Junior converse then laugh. Okay, he says, I'll bring you some shoes. "It must be the big man. Maybe he take them to his farm. Something else?"

Tom says he needs medicine for his stomach. Medicine Man asks if there's a problem with the food. The food is good, Tom says, it's my stomach that's bad. He needs an antacid. "What this?" Medicine Man says. Tom offers to write it down for him. Medicine Man searches his pockets—he has no paper. Junior tears a piece of cardboard out of a box in the barricade and hands it to Medicine Man. Medicine Man hands Tom the cardboard and a pen. "Anything else?" We shake our heads. "Okay. I go."

The kitchen door slams. A car pulls away. I become aware for the first time of the rushing sound of traffic, horns blaring, an occasional shout. The outside world is very close. Only a curtain and a window's width away. I look at the three men I am locked to, listen to their breathing, their bodies shifting in their chairs. *We're alive!* "It's good to see you guys," I say.

"I hope you don't take this the wrong way," Tom says. "I wish I could say the same, but I'm not. We really thought you'd been released."

"How was your trip over?" I ask Harmeet. "What was it like riding in the trunk?"

"The worst part was waiting. The house was so quiet it was creepy. I didn't know if they were going to come back for me or if I was going to be left there. I thought about trying to escape, but there wasn't much I could do locked to the bed, and I didn't know if there really was a guard outside. They gave me some biscuits and some water, but I didn't eat them just in case they didn't come back for me. It seemed to take forever, but it was only a couple hours. I didn't like it. When Medicine Man and Junior came back, they handcuffed me and made me lie on the floor in the back. I didn't have to go in the trunk."

"That's no fair. Did they blindfold you?"

"No, just the hat over my eyes. I didn't have my glasses. Medicine Man said if I made any noise or tried to run away, he'd kill me."

"Did you think about trying to escape?"

"No. There wasn't much I could do the way my hands were handcuffed."

Slowly, in tiny, incremental steps, we fashion as best we can a home for ourselves in our paint-peeling room of gloom. One of our first tasks is to make a bed. We fold and tuck the cotton mat against the wall and lay the futon next to it to form an area of mattress wide enough for us to lie side by side. We place two folded-up curtains (giant gun-barrel-grey bolts of dust-reeking fabric) and two "pillows" (filthy brown pancakes I can hardly bring myself to touch) on the floor along the length of the futon to cushion our legs and feet. Later, in January, when we are all-day shivering cold, we will use these pillows to insulate our feet from the floor.

I sweep my hand along the floor and hold it in the light of the kerosene lantern. It's covered with dust, sand, hair, crumbs. I sweep my hand across the surface of the futon. It's full of little gritty bits. I get down on my hands and knees and brush the futon madly with my hand.

"What're you doing?" Tom asks.

"The futon's covered with dirt. I'm cleaning it before we have to sleep on it."

"We've been sleeping on it for a week. It doesn't matter," Norman says, impatient.

*Yes, it does,* I want to say. *I don't want to sleep in filth.* "It'll just take a second." There's too much of it. I sense the captors are getting impatient with my housekeeping efforts. I'll finish the job tomorrow.

Tom hands each of us a bulky, lead-weight pillow. What are you going to use? we ask. He says he'll roll up his sweater and use it as a pillow. We offer to share. No, Tom insists, he'll be fine.

The captors put Tom on the outside of the bed by the door so they can chain him to the door handle. We ask if Harmeet and I can sleep between Tom and Norman so that Norman can have one hand free. "*Kabir, kabir,*" we say, reminding them of Norman's age. They agree. Junior kicks off his flip-flops and steps onto the bed. We hold up our wrists. He locks Harmeet to Tom, Harmeet to me, me to Norman.

"Okay?" he says as he closes each handcuff. "Okay," we say, just before the handcuff becomes uncomfortably tight. He nods and clicks it down one more notch, just to be sure. He grabs a length of chain and bends over Norman's foot so that his face is only inches away. He wraps the chain around Norman's right ankle, then struggles to get the padlock shackle through two links of the chain. He wants it tight. He scowls, Norman clenches his jaw, the lock clicks shut. Junior stands up and moves to Tom's foot. Norman touches the chain, as if testing to see if it's real. Junior, physically repulsed, touches Tom as little as possible as he locks Tom's left ankle with the chain that leads to Norman's right.

I grit my teeth as the captors drag the big red blanket across the floor and heap it at the foot of our bed. We open it up and pull it flat. It's a heavy polyester fleece material decorated with a profusion of green leaves on a screaming red background. It isn't big enough to cover all four of us. I cross my arms and shiver. "The blanket is too small. We need another blanket," I say to the captors.

Junior shrugs. "No blanket."

"You must have something," I say. Junior shakes his head. I fight to contain my anger. "From the other house? Or the market?"

Junior scowls. Great Big Man leaves the room and returns with an armful of fabric: white latticed cotton with delicate floral embroidery lined with a sheen of cream-coloured silk. He drops the fabric on Tom's legs.

"What the hell's that? It looks like a bridal gown," I mutter.

"I can make this work. I don't need a lot of blanket," Tom says. The chain at his right hand clatters on the floor as he teases the fabric apart. "It's a curtain. They must've ripped it off a window." He folds it in thirds and slides himself between the rustling layers. We'll take turns, we tell him. "No, it's okay, I'll be fine," Tom insists.

Great Big Man puts a finger to his lips. "Shhh. No *killam*," he says, pointing to the window. We nod, say good night. They turn the lantern down, set it outside the door, make their way downstairs. Diesel generators hum in the night around us. The street outside is curfew quiet. The murmur of television rises up through the stairwell.

There's too much light. I can count the brown stains on the bedsheet curtain. I hear Harmeet, Norman and Tom shifting in their places, trying to get comfortable.

"Tom, can we close the door a little? It's awfully bright in here," I say.

Tom pulls on the door. A sharp groaning reverberates through the second-floor foyer. I hold my breath, listen intently. The television chatters on. "I'll have to work on that," Norman says.

I look up at the angular shadows on the ceiling cast by the lantern.

"Good night, Tom," Harmeet says.

"Good night, Harmeet," Tom says.

"Good night, Norman," Harmeet says.

"Good night, Harmeet," Norman says.

"Good night, Jim," Harmeet says.

I start giggling. "Good night, John Boy," I say.

"John Boy?" Norman says.

"They're characters from a seventies TV show called *The Waltons*," I say. "It always ends with the characters saying good night to each other. Do you remember it, Tom?"

"Good night, Mary Ellen," he says.

I'm so glad we're together again. I can't imagine going through this alone. I want to say this, but don't. I don't want to sound maudlin.

I lie awake for a long time.

# DECEMBER 12 DAY 17

Sometime in the early hours of the morning, before the first call to prayer, I'm awakened by an engine-roaring procession of vehicles. A military convoy, vital occupation supply line, very close, no more than a hundred metres away. I want to leap up, hurl open windows, scream for help with every ounce of breath and strength. The last truck passes. Silence pours back into the room, flooding me with despair.

Every night at about the same time, another convoy will barrel past, heard but not seen. Help so close, and yet so far.

Great Big Man unlocks us while Junior, leaning against the wall with his arms folded across his chest, watches irritably. Tom goes to the bathroom. Harmeet gathers up the big red blanket and drops it on the floor near the barricade, sending up a cloud of dust. I get down on my hands and knees and vigorously brush the futon with my hand. When I'm done, Harmeet and Norman fold the futon in half and drag it across the floor towards the barricade, cutting a swath through dustballs, candy wrappers, sunflower seeds.

"*Haji*," I say to Great Big Man in My Most Polite Hostage Voice. "Do you have a broom?" He looks at me. "A broom," I say, demonstrating with my hand. He shakes his head. "The floor is very dirty. *Mooshkilla*," I say. I wipe my index finger on the floor and show it to him.

Tom returns and I take my turn in the bathroom. It's directly across from our room. There's a Batman sticker on the door. I assume it as a right and close the door. No one objects. It's an eight-foot-by-eight-foot room. There's a puddle of water around the base of the sink and a long slimy effluence leading to a drain near the tub. I'm suddenly very conscious of my stocking feet. The white tile floor is even dirtier than the floor in our room. We're going to need *hamam* shoes.

Above the tub, up near the ceiling, light pours into the room through a translucent rectangular window a foot high and two feet wide. The window, divided into two parts, opens outwards. Each half of the window is fitted with a cantilever handle. The window ledge is cluttered with old toothbrushes, a Snoopy bath toy, a rotting hairbrush and a crumpled Irish Spring box.

I quickly assess that it would be possible to pull-hoist myself through the window headfirst. But then what? The window must be twenty-five feet off the ground. I could call or signal for help. No. That would lead to a military rescue operation, and the very real possibility of somebody getting killed.

The pleasure of being alone is intoxicating. There's no one to observe me, no one to answer to or worry about obeying. For a few moments I can do whatever I want. I step to the driest part of the room to jump in the air and twirl my arms. There's a mirror over the sink. I gaze into my eyes, frown, smile, wiggle my eyebrows. I'm pasty, thinner, my hair is oily and matted. I smell myself, check the state of my underwear, pull up my shirt, run my hand across my belly. I guess that I've lost fifteen pounds.

All of the bathroom fixtures—vanity, toilet and bathtub—are baby blue. The toilet is the ceramic-bowl type common in the West. It's caked with brown, and a noxious stew of urine and shit festers at the bottom. The water supply to the toilet has been shut off. I lift the lid off the tank, being careful not to make any noise that would arouse suspicion. The flush mechanism is hopelessly corroded. We're going to have to get a water pitcher to flush it manually.

There's a cracked yellow plastic toilet seat on the floor. I put it in place and sit down, being careful to avoid pinching my thigh in the broken plastic. I hop over to the sink with my pants hanging about my knees. I wet my left hand, squat down, wipe, trying not to drip water on the floor. I make a mental note to ask for a *hamam* jug.

There's no soap. I take a quick look around the bathroom. There's a rotting string bag hanging from the shower faucet that holds several cracked bars of soap. I take one and wash my hands. The water is ice cold. I'm perplexed. Norman and Tom have been here a week and haven't even thought to take some soap for themselves so they can wash their hands. It seems as if they've made no effort at all to improve the conditions of their captivity. They've been living without hope, like men condemned.

I see a rubber squeegee with a long broom-handle pole leaning against the wall. I make a plan to clean the floor tomorrow. I'm excited. Something useful to do.

When I return, Harmeet, Norman and Tom are sitting in their chairs against the wall. I sit between Norman and Harmeet. Junior locks our wrists together.

Standing near the hostess trolley, Great Big Man pivots on his toes like a dancer and grabs four *samoons* lying on the dirty surface of the trolley. He pivots again, crosses the room in two steps, hands us our breakfast. "*Shokren,*" we say as he leaves.

"Well, here we are. Day 17," I say.

"Day 16," Harmeet says. I chuckle. "How did everyone sleep?" he asks.

"Fine," I say.

Tom says he isn't sleeping well. Only a couple of hours a night. It's the acid in his stomach. "I don't know what's going to happen if this continues. I can't function without sleep." Norman sleeps okay until his side starts to hurt in the middle of the night. He can hardly bear it sometimes. He says it would help if he could move around. Why don't you stand up and stretch? I ask him. He says he doesn't want to bother me. That wouldn't bother me at all, I say. We'll see, he says.

I suggest that we have a meeting. "That's a good idea," Tom says. "Shall we make an agenda?"

"I shall have to check first to see if I'm available," Norman says. "Let's see . . . No, I don't have anything else scheduled right now." I think he's joking, but I'm not sure.

First item: futon. Can we avoid dragging it across the floor? I ask. No problem. Can we always fold it over the same way so we can keep the side we sleep on clean? Sure. Can we put the blanket *on top* of the futon instead of on the floor? Yes. Can we use the Quality Street tin for garbage? Okay.

We need to get a broom, I say. I can't stand the filth of this place. Wait, someone says, are there other things we need before that? We make two lists: one for the guards and one for Medicine Man. Broom, water jug and *hamam* shoes go on the guards' list; stomach medicine, street shoes and Norman's reading glasses go on the Medicine Man list. I suggest another blanket for Tom. Tom says no, that's not necessary. Norman suggests a bible. I say no, we should only ask for what they can realistically get; how're they going to find a bible in Iraq? Tom wants us to ask for sleeping pills. Norman wonders if they're readily available given the conditions in the country. "Half of Iraq is taking sleeping pills," Tom says.

Last item: we still don't have names for two of the captors—the big one and the shy one. "He was really quite kind when it was just the two of us," Norman says of Great Big Man. "He was almost like an uncle."

"Hey, let's call him Uncle," Harmeet says. It's agreed.

"What about the other one," somebody says. "He seems kind of timid, almost like a captor-in-training."

"Like a nephew," someone else says. We all laugh. Nephew. It's perfect.


Slowly, our persistence wins results. One day there's a pair of grungy plastic *hamam* shoes at the bathroom door, the next a yellow water jug. When Uncle enters the room holding a little hand broom, I almost want to kiss him. "Thank you! Thank you!" I say. He flashes me a big smile.

I get to work cleaning the next morning. The broom, the water jug, the *hamam* shoes—these are crucial recognitions of our human dignity, signs that our captors are not going to kill us. At least not right away. And it feels good not to live in filth.

The struggle to assert our humanity, improve our living conditions, expand our knowledge about the geography of our hostage prison is unceasing. Every interaction is a strategic testing, an opportunity to examine the habits of our captors. Who knows when or where we will stumble across something—the open window or door, the misplaced key, the act of kindness or thoughtless mistake—through which we can escape this nightmare existence? It is in every thought, word and action: the irrepressible, burning urge to be free.

The next victory in this invisible war is our morning exercise routine. It happens gradually, imperceptibly, over the course of several days. It begins our first morning in the second house when the captors arrive to get us up. They step heavily, faces dull like Monday morning factory workers. They stand and watch as we fold our bedding and set up our chairs for the day. We work quickly, almost urgently, why I don't know. Maybe it's because it feels so good to be doing something, or maybe we're sending a message to the captors. *See, you can trust us. We're doing what we're supposed to do—quickly, efficiently, in the best way we can. We won't take advantage of you by taking more time than we need.*

We finish this morning chore before the first person is done in the bathroom. We stand waiting, charged, ready, alert to everything, like deer in the middle of a clearing. The energy in our bodies irrepressibly seeks release. We start bending, twisting, stretching, reaching. It's instinctive, primal, can't be stopped. A prisoner must exercise.

The room becomes crowded with movement, and the captors, suddenly in our way, move into the foyer. We exercise with the singular focus of Olympic champions. The same thing happens the next morning, and the captors leave the room earlier. I do my exercises in the doorway to give the others more room. We don't go back to our chairs until the captors tell us to. The morning after that, the captors don't spend any time in the room at all. I ask Uncle if I can stand just outside the door. There's not enough room, I explain in body language. He says yes.

The morning after that, Harmeet moves into the foyer too. They don't object. With every passing day, we take longer in the bathroom. From fifteen minutes, we push our little envelope of freedom to half an hour.

One morning, Uncle waves us into the foyer, arms flapping in jumping jack motions. The foyer is shaped like an L. Our room, the bathroom and another bedroom open onto the short side of the L, an area about eight feet wide and eight feet long. The second part of the L is much bigger, maybe fifteen feet wide and twenty feet long. A modernist concrete stairwell with open risers is located to the right of the bathroom. Each set of stairs, one leading to the roof, the other descending to the ground floor, pauses at a landing halfway up and halfway down. Heavy red velour curtains cover the lower-landing window while light pours into the foyer through the upper-landing window.

I move hesitantly into the open expanse of the foyer. The walls are high and white. It feels strange to be surrounded by so much space and light. I stand for a moment, unsure of what I should do. I count four more doors, all of them closed. Not counting the bathroom, six rooms open off the foyer. I look longingly at the stairs. They must go to the roof. The curtains, I think—if the door to the roof is not locked, we could tear them into strips, tie them together and make our escape by climbing down the building.

"Come on, Jim! Exercise." Junior puffs out his cheeks and pumps his arms. He's uncomfortably close.

I smile and step back. "Yes! Exercise good!" I say, matching his enthusiasm with some jumping jacks. It's good to feel my heart pumping again.

I lie on my stomach with my palms against the floor. I have to see how many push-ups I can do. Normally it's thirty-five or forty. It takes everything I have to get to fifteen. I sit back on the floor, my body trembling like a leaf. My eyes meet Junior's. He looks away quickly. He doesn't want me to know that he was counting, measuring himself against me.

Those first two weeks at the second house are a swirling mass of inchoate waiting. Nothing has form or shape. We sit, we lie on our backs, we drift and float, anchorless on an ocean of grey. Medicine Man's promise of release echoes in every footstep, phone call, door opening and closing. We wait on pins and needles, ask the guards for news. "*Shwaya, shwaya,*" they say. Every minute is a lash.

One of the few things I can remember about those interminable days happens one afternoon. We ask Junior and Uncle if we can go to the bathroom. They say yes and unlock us one at a time. When it's Tom's turn, Junior becomes agitated. What's he doing in there? he cries. Why is he taking so long?

We hear a clang in the bathroom. Tom has dropped something on the floor. Junior rushes to the bathroom door. "*La firar! Amriki! Amriki!*" he shouts, pounding with his fist on the door.

"Just a second," I hear Tom say.

Junior bangs harder on the door.

I find it curious. There's no lock, nothing to stop Junior from just going in. This is good. Junior feels bound to respect Tom's privacy. He sees him as a human being.

The door opens. There's a flurry of angry Arabic from Junior. Tom returns to his chair, defiantly calm. Junior follows close behind, his face red. "This CIA. This *hazeem*," he says, pointing at Tom. He locks Tom up and goes directly to the bathroom to investigate. Later we see that he has wrapped a piece of wire around the window handles to make sure it can't be opened.

"What happened?" we ask Tom.

"I don't know. I just knocked the water jug over and the next thing I know he's pounding on the door," Tom says.

When Junior brings us our *samoon* supper, I try to explain that Tom was not trying to escape, he just knocked the water jug over. Junior is not interested. "No, this *Amriki najis*. This CIA. This *jaysh*."

At lock-up, Junior tells Tom to move his legs closer together, he's going to chain both his ankles because he tried to escape. Tom tries to explain that if his legs are chained too close he won't be able to move them during the night and they will cramp up. No, Junior says, move them closer. Tom refuses. Junior tries to push Tom's feet together. Tom resists, sending Junior into a rage. "No! This *mozane*," Junior snarls. He tries once more to push them together. Tom braces his legs and tries one more time to explain. "No. Shut up. This *najis*!" He grabs Tom's shirt and threatens to punch him in the face. Tom looks at him without blinking and moves his feet together.

# DECEMBER 15 DAY 20

It's election day, the first under Iraq's new constitution, ratified in a referendum on October 15. The ballot includes a staggering list of 228 parties and 21 coalitions. Junior is in a buoyant mood. He opens our handcuffs with care and joins in our exercise routine with some stretching of his own. I'm relieved to see that he's no longer angry with

Tom. We ask Junior and Uncle if they're going to vote. Uncle shakes his head. "No," he says. "*Ali baba*." He thinks all politicians are thieves.

"Yes," Junior says solemnly. "This *Islami*. This *Sunna*." He says he's voting for Party 649.

Election day is followed by two days of curfew. Any news? we ask. No news, they say. When is Big *Haji* coming? we ask. When the curfew is over, they say. When the curfew is over we ask again. They don't know. Can you phone *Haji* and ask him to come? Yes, they say.

Norman smuggles a soft piece of soap out of the bathroom. His idea is to use it to lubricate the hinges, so we can close the door at night without the captors hearing us. It works beautifully.

# DECEMBER 18 DAY 23

Medicine Man enters the room with a whoosh of authority, Junior and Uncle following behind him. Junior puts a bulging black plastic bag on the floor near the barricade. "I have something for you," Medicine Man says, smiling. He hands each of us a toothbrush. "They are the different colour. So you know to take them separately."

"Thank you, thank you!" I say, holding the toothbrush against my chest.

Medicine Man laughs and hands Norman a box of Sensodyne. "This your toothpaste. For the sensitive teeth." *Shokren*, we say. *Afwen*, he says. He points to the bag on the floor. "I bring you shoes."

*Our shoes! Walking, freedom, going home!*

"And I bring you your medicine. For the stomach," Medicine Man says, handing Tom a bottle. Tom is effusive with thanks. Medicine Man nods, stands back with his hands resting on his hips, the flaps of his suit jacket gathered behind his arms, exposing his bulging gut, a gun tucked into his belt. "Is there something else?" he asks.

Norman asks about his reading glasses. "They are at the other house," Medicine Man says. "For all of you. All of your things—your camera, your notebook. I bring for you. We not take anything."

Norman wants to know if he can send a message to his wife. Medicine Man looks at him blankly. "To let her know I'm alive," he says, his voice breaking.

Medicine Man looks puzzled. "She know you alive. We take some video to show this."

"Yes, but I should think a video of me in a jumpsuit—"

"There is one more thing," I interrupt, worried things are moving in a bad direction. "Tom is having trouble sleeping. Would it be possible to get something to help him sleep?"

Medicine Man looks at Tom. "This is not a problem. What do you need?"

"Valium. Just something that will help me sleep."

"I bring for you." Medicine Man's face turns instantly ruthless. He steps towards Tom and grabs his shirt. "I know you. You must not to escape. If you try this, I kill you. I know who you are." Tom answers with the barest nod. Medicine Man releases Tom's shirt and steps back.

"Tom didn't try to escape," I say. "He knocked a jug over in the bathroom and the sound must've startled haji."

"We are trained," Medicine Man says. "He cannot fool me. I know who he is. He is not like you. I can tell, the way he look to me. He is cold, not smiling. He is a hard man. Like the CIA. I know this. This is something we have the training for."

My heart sinks. "Tom is a peace activist. He's been working in Iraq with CPT for almost two years."

Medicine Man shakes his head. "I know this. I have the training for this."

Medicine Man edges towards the door. He's about to leave and we haven't asked the most important question of all. "Is there any news?" I blurt out.

"There is some change," he says. "We have some negotiation for your case. One week and you release. Not more. You are home for Christmas."

—

Time edges towards Christmas, the hope of release in every breath. We eddy and whirl in a grey fog of waiting. I lose track of the days, what happens when. There is only Christmas, blinking like a navigation light on a faraway radio tower, a red eye flashing in the darkness.

At first I am hopfeul. A Christmas release would be perfect, I say, a public relations coup! Think of the headlines: HOSTAGES REUNITED WITH THEIR FAMILIES, TERRORISTS NOT SO BAD AFTER ALL. INSURGENTS GIVE THE GIFT OF PEACE. They've even given us our shoes back!

Harmeet will call his family and then make his way to Palestine where he'll join the International Solidarity Movement team in Nablus. Norman will attend the Christmas Eve service at his church and sip ginger wine afterwards with Pat. Dan and I will go to Sault Ste. Marie where there'll be tons of snow and we'll go tobogganing with my nieces and nephew.

Tom is the lone holdout. "We really don't know how long we're going to be stuck here. I'm just trying to stay in the present moment."

Then I am irritable.

"What would you do for Christmas if we do get free?" Harmeet asks.

"I don't want to think about that. I'm just trying to stay in the present moment."

*Present moment, present moment! Fuck the present moment. If you say that one more time, I'll ram it down your throat and make you choke on it!*

"What would you *usually* do for Christmas?" Harmeet presses.

"Well, for the last couple of Christmases—this is only the second Christmas since Andrew moved out on his own—Kassie and Andrew and I have a meal together on Christmas Eve and then we go to a Quaker meeting together."

I am prickly, venomous, rabidly impatient. My mind circles around and around, like a vulture in search of carrion, something to leap on, criticize, attack. Harmeet's wriggling toes. How Norman digs in his ears. The slow-motion way Tom blinks his eyes. The hours of aimless chatter, every word a flagellation! A voice in my head screams for silence. I fight with everything I have to hide and contain it. This is my problem, not theirs.

The black plastic bag with our shoes sits there for days. I stare at it hungrily, compulsively. Harmeet says it's too small to hold his boots and all our shoes. I'm desperate to find out. We all are, I think, but none of us dare. We're not sure. Could we have misunderstood? Did Medicine Man really mean for us to have our shoes back? What if they hear the rustle of the bag or catch us getting up out of our chairs?

It is Harmeet who takes the first illicit peek, one morning during exercise. "Hey guys, I have bad news. Those aren't our shoes," he reports as soon as the captors leave.

"Are you sure?" I ask. He has to be wrong.

"I'm sure," he says.

Norman investigates next. "I'm afraid Harmeet is right. They look like Keds sneakers."

My spirits plummet.

A day or two later, Junior points towards the bag and then at our feet. "Shoes. This shoes." We nod and say thank you. He holds the bag out to us: what are you waiting for, he seems to be saying, go ahead, you can wear them. I want to leap at it. Shoes! *Escape! Freedom!* It's okay, we tell him, we're used to not having them. Junior shrugs, puts the bag within Norman's reach and leaves. Still we don't open it. It infuriates me. A strange and compulsory indolence has taken hold of us. We've lost our initiative and will, our ability to act. Our spirits have been taken captive too.

Finally, during a long stretch of afternoon, it is Tom who suggests we have a look at our new shoes. We open the bag and discover they're black, dollar store tennis shoes, decorated with a lightning flash decal. I examine the tread, bend the toe, fit my hand inside. The biggest shoes, size nine, are hopelessly small for Tom's size-eleven feet. Harmeet, with the smallest foot, finds a pair that fit perfectly. Norman and I are just able to squeeze into ours.

"Hey, look at this!" Harmeet says, holding up a one-inch tack. "It was stuck into the sole of the shoe."

"Wow! That could be really useful," I say.

"It almost looks as if somebody stuck it there," Harmeet says.

"Remember when we watched *Con Air*?" I say bubbling with excitement, "how they picked their handcuffs with that piece of wire?" Everyone laughs. "Do you think that's just Hollywood, or do you think it might actually work?"

"It's just Hollywood," Tom says.

"Maybe we should try it?" I say.

The room grows very quiet. My chest tightens uncomfortably. *This might actually be a way for us to escape.* No, they say, it's not worth the risk. I'm not sure whether to be angry or relieved. I deliberately change the subject. "I think we should ask for bigger shoes. It's the least they can do after stealing ours. These certainly didn't cost them anything."

Tom says they'll stretch. Norman says he's not planning to run any marathons. Harmeet says his fit just fine. I remonstrate with Tom. "You have a right to a pair of shoes that fit," I say. I want to shake him, them, all of us. Shake us out of this strange creeping passivity, this fatalistic waiting, this lethal drug of resignation.

"I can make do with these," Tom says, adamant, in that infuriating it's-final-don't-argue-with-me tone.

Tom rarely wears his shoes. They just don't fit. Norman slides in and out of his as if they were a pair of slippers, wearing the heel collars flat. Harmeet wears his loose, laces untied. I wear mine laced up tight. They stretch and fit just right. I fall in love with them. They protect my feet from the cold and the filth of the floor. And they are ready, should a door suddenly open, to help me run.


Nephew emerges slowly from the shadows. There's an air of regret about him, something kind, even apologetic in his eyes. He tells us he's thirty-six, but his face, round and smooth, looks much younger. He's five foot seven, squat, bursting with stomach like a retired football player. He is tentative and shy at first, stands back, watches, smiles. When he comes in during the day to check on us and we ask if we can go to the bathroom, he holds up his finger and goes in search of Junior or Uncle. He begins by carrying the lantern when the power is out, holding the handcuffs and chains for Junior and Uncle, giving us our food. As the days pass, he graduates to issuing instructions—hurry up in the bathroom, sit down, lower your voices—and then, sometime in the new year, he is given charge of the keys. We suspect this must be his first mission.

The nights become unbearably cold. We lobby our captors for permission to close the door at night to conserve the heat our bodies generate. They say no at first but then eventually relent. This seems to have a negative effect on the air quality in the room. A few mornings later Junior gags when he comes into the room, pulls his shirt over his nose and makes a beeline for the window. He pushes the bedsheet back and opens the window a crack. A shaft of clear gold light streams into the room. I'm transfixed. Junior turns to us, scowling and pinching his nose. I am surprised. I'd been paying close attention, monitoring myself and the others for the emergence of noxious odours. I sniff my shirt. There is a hint of staleness, but nothing strong or malfeasant. "Is it because of us?" I say to the others under my breath.

Junior bends down to unlock the chain around Norman's ankle. He breathes heavily through his nose, lip curling in disgust. "Najis," he says, gritting his teeth. "Naaa-jisss."

Uncle comes into the room, coughs, waves his hand in front of his nose. Junior turns to Uncle, his arms full of gestures and complaints. Uncle breaks into knee-slapping laughter. They turn and point at Norman. "Najis," they say, erupting in more laughter.

This is how the najis treatment begins. For a while it is gruelling and relentless. Every time the captors interact with Norman, when they unlock him in the morning and lock him up again at night, when they give him his food, when he passes them on the way to the hamam, he has to endure this word and its contemptuous tone. He steadfastly ignores them, carries on with unalterable dignity. I watch, furious at the captors and ashamed at my silence.

When Junior and Uncle aren't around, I ask Nephew what najis means. He frowns, holds his nose, grimaces, shakes his head. That's what it means. Something that is repulsive.


It is a growing concern for me, how to maintain a basic level of hygiene as the days pass into weeks. "Dudes, look at my socks! These used to be white!" Harmeet says one day. They've turned dishwater grey. We laugh though I can't help but wonder, is this what's happening to us too? Are we turning grey?

Cleanliness is next to godliness when you're a captive. Your life depends on being seen as a human being. If you look and smell loathsome, you will be treated with loathing. Our worst enemy is the contempt of our captors. And, perhaps just as dangerous, getting sick.

Some things we have control over, such as the handling of our cups. It becomes quite a skill, passing a cup back and forth in handcuffs. Some of us, at first, have the unfortunate habit of gripping the lip of the cup, a major sanitary faux pas when you consider that's exactly where you put your mouth to drink. It takes a bit of coaxing and some gentle reminding, but everybody eventually learns: when passing the cup, please and thank you, always hold it at the base.

A lot of things we don't have control over, including being able to wash our hands, the preparation of our food and washing of our dishes, how often and when we have access to the bathroom. This is a constant worry for Norman. Our diet is having an unfortunate effect on his digestive system, causing what he calls "loose bowels."

It first happens in the days before Christmas. Norman is seized by an immediate need to use the bathroom. He rushes to the hostess trolley and we follow him in our handcuff line, a vector sweeping across the room in an eight-foot arc with Tom as the pivot. Norman grabs a glass tray from the hostess trolley, pulls his pants down and sits over it. He does as much as he can with his left hand, his right being handcuffed to my left. I squat down beside him and turn my head away.

I would have been mortified, but Norman is remarkably composed. "I think I can do this with a minimum of mess," he says, as if describing a scientific procedure. "I just have to make sure I have the tray in the right position. We don't want any accidents. I kept some pillow stuffing handy for just such an emergency." When it's over, he laughs. "Sorry about that, chaps, but that's what you get being chained up with an old man."

It is the vulnerability of age that makes Norman a target. The long hours of inactivity are taking a toll. His body is stiff and non-compliant. He moves slowly, carefully, reaching for chairs and walls to steady himself. Uncle and Junior scowl and complain. "*Imshee*. Hurry up. *Najis*," they say, feeding on each other's contempt. I sometimes worry Junior is about to strike Norman.

Norman blocks them out, avoids their eyes, looks through them. He gives up trying to understand what they say to him. This increases the captors' frustration and interferes with his ability to understand what they want and respond appropriately.

I worry even more about Tom. He's lost weight and he's not sleeping. His face is a bleak, impenetrable mask, sullen, impossible to read. When I sometimes imagine how our captors must see him, something within me hardens like a fist. But when he smiles, the effect is very different. Then there's life, buoyancy, warmth in his eyes, and the fist gently opens.

I debate long and hard. In the end I figure there's nothing to lose and everything to gain. They might be hurt or offended, but their lives just might depend on a little bit of coaching. I swallow hard and begin with Tom. I know it might be a strange thing to say, I tell him, but you might consider smiling more for the captors. Your face is often, well, difficult to read, and it's hard to know what you're thinking. If you smile more, it might shift something in the captors so they'll want to react more positively to you.

I'm relieved. Tom is not defensive. "I guess you're right about that. I call it my poker face. It used to upset my kids, especially if we were having an argument about something. They said they could never tell what I was thinking. Maybe that was unfair to them sometimes. I guess it's the way I deal with things. Put on my poker face. It does come in handy sometimes."

I talk with Norman next about how he interacts with the captors. "I don't understand anything they say," he says. "I'm just terrible with the Arabic. You three are much better at it."

When they're disrespectful to you, I say, ignoring them can be the best strategy. But if they're being neutral or positive towards you, ignoring them risks frustrating them. Every interaction with them is an opportunity to make them see our humanity. It's the only thing that protects us. If you look at them in the eyes and smile, that reinforces your humanity and makes it harder for them to treat you disrespectfully.

Norman agrees and tries to interact more with the captors. Eventually, though, he figures out his own solution to the *najis* treatment.

We're lying down, locked up on our communal bed. Junior enters the room with a gun. He points it at Tom, at his head, in firing stance, feet planted firmly at shoulders' width, arms straight and locked at the elbows, finger around the trigger. He stands this way, glaring, for ten long seconds, then is gone.

## DECEMBER 23 DAY 28

I've been thinking about it for days. On the surface things are going well, but in the spaces around and behind our words I sense tension, and it's building, like seismic forces deep in the earth. We need a safety valve, some kind of routine, a structure to help us communicate, make decisions, ease the inevitable frictions of our pressure-cooker existence. I want to propose that we think of ourselves as the CPT Kidnap Team, that we assume the disciplines of team life: daily worship, check-ins, even formal meetings. I don't know why—it's my job, I can see exactly what needs to be done, I am the delegation leader after all—but I just can't bring myself to say the words. I detest and abhor my inability to act. I too am infected with the creeping paralysis of captivity.

I almost laugh when Tom makes the suggestion. It's as if he took the words right out of my mouth. Everyone agrees. Daily check-in and worship will start tomorrow, Christmas Eve. Norman volunteers to lead our first worship.

Tom also wants to do a daily Bible study. "How would you propose to do that without a bible?" Norman asks.

"From memory," Tom says. "It could be a paraphrase of a story, a single verse, a word or a phrase. Just say it aloud and we can discuss it together. When I did Bible study with the Young Quakers, I would pose four questions. What is the meaning of this Bible verse to me? How does it accord with my experience? What do I find difficult or troubling about it? How might it change my life?" Tom offers to lead the first Bible study.

I'm so relieved. The yoke of inertia has been broken. It's now official: we've become a team.

Voices downstairs. There's a formality, a politeness that's different. One of the voices is higher, softer. A woman. Uncle enters the room on tiptoe. He has a gun in his hand. He looks at us sternly, puts his index finger against his lips. "Shhhh," he says, moving with a hunter's stealth.

Being careful not to make any sound, he pulls out a ring of keys and opens the padlock that locks the chain around the door's cantilever handles. He gathers the chain together, sets it on the hostess trolley, then closes and locks the door. He waves his finger in warning, pretends to cough into his fist, shakes his head, pulls an index finger across his throat. *If you make the slightest noise, I will kill you.*

Footsteps and voices coming up the stairs. Uncle stands to the right of the door. The footsteps and voices move into the foyer and gather in front of the bathroom. The bedroom door to the left opens and closes. Uncle is ready with his gun, smiling, eyes twinkling. He's enjoying this! The footsteps and voices move in front of our door. The door handle turns, rattles. A voice with a question in it. Somebody is trying to come in. Who could it be? A landlord perhaps?

My body explodes with adrenalin. A mad screaming fury of *Help! Help! Help!* thrashes in my chest. Uncle looks at me, touches his index finger to his lip. I sit like a stone. There's no other choice. I'll put whoever is on the other side of the door in danger too.

The voices and footsteps move away. Uncle steps back from the door, giggling, blows on the muzzle of his gun, tucks it into his waist. The voices make their way downstairs. He opens the door and peeks out. My head falls in despair.

I am haunted by the old joke about the man caught in a flood who takes refuge on the roof of his house. He's on his hands and knees praying to God when a boat passes by and asks him if he wants help. No thanks, the man says, God will save me. Another boat passes by. They ask him if he wants help. No thanks, he says, God will save me. The flood waters rise higher and higher. A helicopter comes and lowers down a rope. No thanks, he says, God will save me. The water sweeps him away and the man drowns. When he gets to heaven, he says to God, "I prayed and prayed for help. Why didn't you save me?" And God says, "What're you talking about? I sent you two boats and a helicopter. What more could I have done?"

I burn in a crucible of questions. Was this the helicopter waiting to lift us to safety? Was our freedom only a shout away? Did we doom ourselves with our silence? There are no answers. And, therefore, no relief.

# CHAPTER NINE

## DECEMBER 24 DAY 29

I have no idea where I am or what is going to happen to me. There are steel bracelets around my wrists. Each bracelet is connected to another by a single link of chain fastened by a swivel eye. Right hand first, then left, I move my handcuff towards the one next to it. The two links sag together as the swivel eyes touch; then, being careful not to pull against my neighbour's handcuff, I move it away until the chain becomes tight. I do this again and again.

My beard is itchy. I bend my face towards my wrist so I can scratch myself without pulling against Harmeet's handcuff. I've been wearing the same clothes for twenty-nine days. There's a long vertical tear in the front of my shirt. My pants are saturated with the oils from my hands. I'm ravenously hungry.

My mind wanders to Dan, my family, the Catholic Worker community, CPT. I visualize the various dinners people will be having— Dan in Owen Sound with his mother and brothers; my family gathered at my sister's in Sault Ste. Marie; the Zacchaeus House potluck dinner line snaking out of the dining room into the hallway—the yuletide spreads of tourtière, turkey, mashed potatoes, mincemeat, shortbread. It is Christmas Eve and the people we love don't even know if we're alive. I remember with dread the chocolates and hand-painted cards I left for my sister to give to my nieces and nephew before I left for Iraq. I hope she's forgotten about them. I wave these images away. It's all too painful.

Norman clears his throat. "Shall we sing some Christmas carols?"

"Yes!" I say. I love singing. I wish the others wanted to do more of it. When we sing, our handcuffs melt away and I am free. With the help of Norman's prodigious memory, we reconstruct parts of thirty-nine

Christmas carols. My favourite is "Ding dong! merrily on high, In heav'n the bells are ringing; Ding dong! verily the sky, Is riv'n with Angel singing; Gloria, Hosanna in excelsis!" The long, breathless descent of the *Glo-o-o-oria* fills me with celestial joy and transports me to that holy, heaven-singing night when the darkness was broken open by astounding angel words. Words delivered on seraphic wings to a bunch of lousy, mutton-odoured, good-for-nothing shepherds out in the middle of nowhere where nothing ever happens. *Do not be afraid, I bring you good news of great joy that will be for all people. Glory to God in the highest, and peace to God's people on earth.*

Do not be afraid. The good news is peace. Peace, do not be afraid. Peace, the cry of every child's birth. Peace, the birthright of every child. Peace, a baby wrapped in rags lying in an animal trough, God born into history. Peace, not by the hand that holds the gun, but by the hand that holds the newborn child.

When carolling has run its course, Norman leads us in worship. Afterwards, I turn to look at him. His face is drawn, haggard, grizzled. Dark pouches hang under his eyes. His hair is matted and wildly askew, but he's shining and beautiful. I'm immensely grateful. To be here, with Norman, Tom and Harmeet, these three brothers. Somehow, through our helplessness, though I have no way of knowing how, God is bringing something new to birth.

# DECEMBER 25 DAY 30

There's a constant chill seeping through my cotton shirt. I'm envious of Norman with his tweed jacket and Harmeet his jumper. I remember thinking as I got dressed that Saturday morning, the last day of our freedom, I won't need a sweater or a jacket, it's going to be a warm day. If only I'd known then what I know now. If only, if only . . . I feel a bad mood coming on. I almost pitched breakfast, a *samoon* filled with a tablespoon of rice. It was hardly worth eating.

—

Norman points to the wall near the hostess trolley. Down near the floor he's drawn a barely discernible star with a piece of soap and written the first letter of each of our names around it. "As you'll note, it's rather hard to see, so I got busy last night and sketched a star with my thumbnail in my little corner over here. Something to do in the middle of the night when I couldn't sleep. I'm afraid it's not much of a star. The plaster is very hard and it was jolly difficult to make the points. It's a little lopsided, but there you have it, a five-pointed star. You can't see it right now because my chair's in the way. The captors won't see it unless they get down on their knees."

"We should add all of our names!" I say. "Wouldn't it be neat if the owners were to see these strange English names one day. I wonder what they'd say if they knew what their house was being used for." I turn to Harmeet. "Where's that little nail?"

"I lost it."

"You lost it!" I don't believe him.

"It must've fallen out of my pocket when I was sleeping. I searched the blanket and all around the floor, but I couldn't find it. I'm sorry. I'll keep looking."

I look down at my hands and clench my teeth. I mustn't say anything, not a single word.


The day drags like a fallen muffler. I avoid thinking about my parents, Dan, anything at all related to the celebration of Christmas. Instead, I consider the *idea* of Christmas—the day God was born into the world, two thousand years ago, in a cave on a scrubby Palestinian hillside. A sentence drifts through my mind. *In you and through you, everywhere and in everything, God is giving birth.* Was it from a sermon I'd heard, a quote from somewhere, a Christmas card?

I look down at my handcuffs, the grungy hems of my shirt cuffs, the long tattered strips of paint peeling off the walls, the tiresome clutter blocking the window. Everything I see is stained in the hopeless, pallid light filtering through the soiled curtains. It astounds me, how your life can change, just like that, in the snap of a finger, the blink of an eye: you're taken into a place you could never have imagined, and you're stuck there, in it, with no way out.

What can it possibly mean, to give birth to God here, in this grim twilight, where NOTHING ever happens and each day looms like a guillotine? We might as well be on life support. How did it go, that poem by T.S. Eliot? "We are the hollow men." That's us, the hollow men, the handcuffed men, the empty waiting men. We are shape without form and shade without colour, a paralyzed force, gesture without motion. We lean together, headpieces stuffed with straw, our dried voices quiet and meaningless when we whisper together. There is no birth-giving here. We are stillborn in a tomb of waiting.

Damn this place. Damn this suffocated existence. I *hate this!* I want to scream. *I want my life back!*

A memory gathers in my mind. Two days before I left for Baghdad, a friend named Julie, one of the most loving people I know, invited Dan and me for supper. She was telling us about her work as a home care nurse. One of her favourite patients, a gay man, was dying. His parents had just left after a two-week visit. It was hell. They took over the household, ignored his partner, battered him with advice about medical treatments and all the things he should do to get better. They just couldn't accept the fact that he was dying. "What am I going to do?" he said to Julie. "They say they're moving in when they come back. "

Julie sat down on the bed beside him, smoothed his hair, took his hand. "Frank," she said, "this is your life. Right now, right here. Don't waste it on what you don't want to do. Enjoy your partner, the light streaming through the window, your drinks, your music, your visits with your friends. Each day that you have is a gift. If you don't want your parents here, you don't have to have them here."

*This is your life. Right now, right here.* I tap a handcuff against the arm of my plastic chair. I look at Norman, Harmeet, Tom, their dull, waxy faces. How is it possible to live your life when it has been stolen?

—

"What time is it?" I ask.

"It's 5:30," Norman says.

"I have 5:32," Harmeet says.

The time between nightfall and supper is the gloomiest, when hunger throbs loudest and our stamina for sitting is at its lowest. "I wonder what's for supper," I say. Before the words are out, I want to take them back. I've carelessly reminded us of the Christmas dinner we're missing.

Footsteps in the foyer. I'm suddenly alert. We hear the glass lens of the lantern being lifted, the flick of a lighter. Amber light breaks into the room. Uncle enters with a lantern. "*La cahraba, la cahraba,*" he says. He sets the lantern down and plops four *samoons* onto the hostess trolley. He rubs his arms and blows on his hands. He spins suddenly on his heel, quickly disperses our supper, steps back, smiles, rubs his hands together again. "*Haji Big, Haji Big,*" he says. He turns and is out the door.

My heart quickens. Maybe, finally, the news we've been waiting for. A Christmas Day release.

"What flavour of *samoon* are we having tonight?" I say.

"White rice," Tom says, opening his *samoon* and tilting it towards the lantern light.

My spirits dive. I force myself to take a bite. The *samoon* is fresh and the rice is still warm. Beyond delicious. I practically inhale my supper.

"There you go, chaps, I'm full," Norman says, handing me the last bit of his *samoon*. It's become a ritual. After every meal Norman breaks and shares a piece of his bread. If we object, he always has an excuse ready. "I've lots of extra padding," he'll say, or "I'm not really a fan of *samoon*," or "You just don't eat as much when you're an old man."

I pass it to Harmeet. "This is for you," I say.

Harmeet passes it to Tom. "This is for you," he says.

Tom takes a small piece and passes it back to Harmeet. "This is for you," Tom says.

As he always does, Harmeet passes it back to me without taking a piece for himself. Always I object and always he prevails. Except tonight.

"This is for you too," I say, refusing the bread.

"I'm full," he says.

I laugh. "Yeah, full of hot air." I shake my head. "It's Christmas. You have to share in the Christmas feast."

This gets him. He breaks off a piece of bread and eats it. "There. Satisfied?"

"Yes." I smile. "Very."


Medicine Man coughs and pinches his nose as he enters the room. Junior and Uncle follow behind, Junior holding two black plastic bags. "How are you, Doctor?" Medicine Man says, a look of concern on his face. We have been pressing the captors for days to bring a course of antibiotics.

Norman lifts the leg of his trouser, turns his foot outwards and touches his calf. "As you can see, it's quite red and swollen. I believe it is cellulitis," Norman says.

Medicine Man bends down to look. He gives Norman a box containing capsules of an antibiotic, then to Tom, Valium and antacid. He also has four sweaters that he says come from the market, and a bag the contents of which he doesn't reveal. Thank you, we say. Medicine Man nods but does not smile. We ask if there's any news. "Yes," he says. "We have some negotiation for you. Our negotiator is in the UAE. When he call me, you release. Three day, four day, maybe one week, you go. Not more. I wish you release before now, but this take time. Only time now. You, and you, are safe," he says, pointing to Harmeet and me.

"What about Norman and Tom?" I say.

"All of you are safe. Just some negotiation and you release, all of you." He smiles. "You very famous. Especially you and you." He points to Norman and me. "All of you very famous. When you release, this a whole different life for you. You interview on CNN, NBC—Al Jazeera. You can speak for your cause." He points at Norman. "Your wife, she is on the TV. She is pleading for you. You," he says, pointing at Tom, "your daughter is on the TV for you." To me he says, "For you, your mother is on the TV. And for you," pointing to Harmeet, "your sister."

"But we don't want to be famous," Norman says. "We want to be free!"

"Do not worry, Doctor. All of you release when I have the order. This only some time. Three day, four day. Not more." Medicine Man looks at his watch. "I must to go. Tomorrow you have some shower. With the hot water."

"Shall we have a look at our Christmas presents?" Norman says when they've left. He holds the sweaters up one at a time. The first is grey and patterned with black triangles. The collar is wide and floppy. *Yuck. Totally depressing.* The second is a turtleneck covered with orange and black zigzags. *God, I hope I don't get that one.*

The third is slate-blue and grey with a crewneck. *Tolerable, but barely.* The fourth sweater is a creamy, tight-ribbed knit with a quarter-zipper front and suede shoulders. "Oh, I like that one!" I burst out. I'm immediately embarrassed by my display of greed.

"I don't care which one I get," Tom says.

"Neither do I," Harmeet says.

"Shall we see what's in the bag?" Norman says. "There's all kinds of interesting things here. Let's see—four sets of socks, four boxer shorts, four pairs of tracks pants and four vests."

"Vests?" I say.

"We call them undershirts in Canada," Harmeet says.

Norman piles the clothes on the *zowagi* cube. The track pants are purple, baby blue, lime green and navy blue.

"That's an interesting assortment of colours," I say, secretly hoping for navy blue.

"I don't care which colour I get," Tom says. He takes the purple. Norman ends up with the baby blue, Harmeet the navy blue and me the green.

"Norman, would you mind passing me a sweater," I say. "I might as well put one on. I'm cold."

"How're you going to do that?" he asks.

"Oh, yeah, of course," I say. I'd forgotten. You can't put a sweater on when you're in handcuffs.

—

The sweater I like is the first one on the pile. We stack up our chairs, sweep the floor, lay our bedding down. I can't keep my eyes off it. The first one who takes a sweater will get it. I have to restrain myself from grabbing for it. I'm relieved to see it's still there when I return from the bathroom. "I'm going to put one of these sweaters on. I'm cold," I announce, reaching for it. This is not opportunism, I tell myself. Somebody has to take the first one.

There's a tag. *Made in Italy*, it says. *50% LANA-WOOLLE-LAINE-WOOL, 50% SETA-SEIDE-SOIE-SILK.* I put it on. I revel in the movement of my arms through each sleeve. The sweater has a dry, factory smell. It immediately cuts the chill. The zipper pull-tab is a ring of bronzed metal fashioned into the shape of a heart. *That's funny*, I think, *it must be a woman's sweater.* I look at the sweater carefully. No, it's definitely a man's sweater. How interesting. You'd never catch a man wearing a sweater with a heart-shaped pull-tab in Canada.

The captors turn out the light and go downstairs. As always, it is a relief. The long trek of day is over and I can escape into the sweet oblivion of sleep. My eyes fix on the bracket of light cast onto the ceiling by the lantern.

"I'm sorry, Jim. I need my arm for a second. My head is itchy," Harmeet says. His voice is apologetic.

"Of course," I say. My arm follows as he raises his hand to his head. I hear the sound of his hat rubbing against his hair. "Sorry, now I have to adjust the blanket," he says. I bend my arm so he can pull the blanket up to his chin. This is very important. If the blanket doesn't cover your neck and shoulders, you freeze.

Harmeet's movements pull my part of the blanket down. Now I have to make an adjustment. "Sorry, Norman," I say. "I need my hand for a second."

There's a trick to it. You pull the blanket as high as you can, grip it with your chin, then slowly slide your hand under the blanket until it rests beside your hip.

"Good night, gentlemen," Harmeet says.

The soft droning of a mosquito grows loud and then stops. It's landed on my cheek. I rub my cheek against my shoulder. The mosquito buzzes away. The blanket falls off my shoulder. "Sorry, Harmeet, I need my hand again," I say. I tuck the blanket under my chin. The mosquito lands on my cheek again. I sigh and let it feed on me.

*How I hate this,* I think to myself. I start to pray. *O most holy sacred heart, free me. O most holy healing heart, deliver me. O most holy loving heart, open me.*

Then it strikes me. The pull-tab on my sweater. You can see through it. It's open. Just like the Sacred Heart! A giggle ripples through my larynx. Even here the Sacred Heart. Even here.

"What's so funny?" Harmeet says.

"Oh, nothing," I say.

# CHAPTER TEN

## DECEMBER 26 DAY 31

There's a big aluminum tub full of hot water sitting on a ledge at the back of the bathtub. Curling fronds of steam rise and disappear. It's my turn to bathe. Norman and Tom have already gone. Harmeet and I will share this tub of water.

I search out the cleanest, driest part of the floor and set my new wardrobe down. I take off my clothes and drape them carefully over a towel rack affixed to the wall near the door. I stand in front of the mirror for a moment, shivering in the stark ceramic air, amazed at the emergence of ribs and pelvic bones, the muscle my body has retained despite so much inactivity and so little food.

The tub is filthy with grime and hair. I frown irritably. Norman and Tom never bothered to clean it. There's a small pot with a handle lying next to the aluminum vat. I fill it with water from the tap and clean the tub as best I can. It exhilarates me to do this, one small thing to change and improve my environment. I step into the tub and dip my finger into the vat. The water is scalding. I fill the pot halfway and add cold water from the tap. I hold my breath and pour the water over my head.

Oh my God! It's beyond describing, the euphoric pleasure of hot water pouring down my body. I grab the soap and scrub my body with my hands. For a moment I'm alarmed—I'm suddenly covered with long, stringy black worms—until I realize it's just my skin. This must be what happens when you don't bathe for a while, the friction of your hands rolling up dead skin.

When I'm done, I squeegee myself dry with my hands. I move quickly so the remaining water won't be cold for Harmeet. I step over to my clothes then stop. For a moment I am paralyzed. The thought of putting on the captors' clothes repulses me. My clothes are all I have left, the last physical link to my stolen life. They looked like rummage sale derelicts when they emerged from the bathroom in their captor outfits, the violent clash of colour, fabric, design, Tom in the purple track pants and hideous grey sweater, Norman in his tweed jacket and the baby blue sweatpants. What will I become if I put on these slave garments? I wonder. Is this another invisible step in a continuing process of losing who I am?

I rub the sleeve of my shirt. The fabric is brown, saturated with grunge, impregnanted with oils from my body. I consider the clean clothes lying on the floor. Socks, underwear, undershirt, track pants, sweater. Nothing of my own. I pick up the sweater and finger the Sacred Heart zipper tab. It's okay, I tell myself. I'm a child of God. As long as I remember this, it doesn't matter what I wear.

## DECEMBER 27 DAY 32

Using the *zowagi* cube as a desk, Norman meticulously folds and rips the cardboard backing our socks came packaged in. We are fascinated. What are you doing? we ask him.

"Something for our amusement. Perhaps a game," he says.

"What kind of a game?"

"I don't know, we'll have to see," he says.

He tears the cardboard into twenty-five pieces. One side is blue, the other manila. Norman, Harmeet and I work together to create an elaborate version of tic-tac-toe. The first one to lay down four cards of the same colour (blue or manila) within a five-by-five grid wins. Do you want to play? we ask Tom.

"I guess I could try."

It's okay, we say, you don't have to if you don't want to.

"I'm sorry," Tom says. "I'm just not much of a games person. But I can try." He never does.

—

When Nephew sees us playing the game, he's immediately suspicious. "What this?" he says, frowning.

Norman holds up one of the cards. "It's a game. Would you like to play?"

Nephew takes the card and examines it carefully. He wants to know where it came from. Norman shows him a remaining piece of the packaging. Nephew sits wearily on the folding chair. He looks at the floor, arms cradling his round gut. "No happy birthday. No *kineesa*. I am sorry," he says. We don't understand. Nephew repeats the phrases. We still don't understand. Nephew forms a cup with his hands, drinks from it, then offers it to us. "No *kineesa*," he says. "No *kineesa*."

I suddenly get it. "Christmas, he means Christmas."

Nephew nods. "I am sorry. No happy birthday *Issau*." His face suddenly brightens. "*Bacher*, tomorrow," he says, "I bring cake for happy birthday Jesus." Thank you, we say. I won't hold my breath, I think.

Nephew asks each of us if we're married. My chest tightens. No, I tell him. He accepts my answer without comment. We ask him if he is married. Yes, he says, smiling. We ask if he has any children. Five, he says, holding up his hands. He whinnies like a horse and pumps his pelvis. We ask how old they are. He shifts in his chair, suddenly uncomfortable. He answers reluctantly. The oldest is fourteen. A boy. Does he go to school? He's in grade eight. How old are the others? Nephew shakes his head. This is a secret. His wife, his children, his parents don't know that he is a *mujahedeen*.

"I am sorry for the English," he says. He used to be good at it when he was small, "*talib, talib*," a boy in school. But he was conscripted, got married, became a father, and now he can't speak it anymore.

Were you in the Iran–Iraq War? we ask. Yes, he says. *Clatha sena*, he says. Three years.

We ask him where he's from. His face darkens. Fallujah, he says. The Americans bombed his house. Now he and his family are forced to stay with relatives in Baghdad. He holds his head as if he has a headache. The house is too small, there are too many people, too many children, always too much noise. "*Mooshkilla, mooshkilla.*" We are cursed to have oil, he says. We have fruit, we can grow food, we have water—we don't need this. Let them have the oil and let us have peace. All this fighting—*mooshkilla*, he says.

He stands up heavily. "*Bacher*, I bring happy birthday Jesus cake." Then he leaves.

# DECEMBER 28 DAY 33

Evening. As usual, the power is out. The cacophonous jostling of Baghdad traffic disappears as dusk turns into night. The hum-throb of countless diesel generators, broken by sporadic gunfire, rises from the city like an industrial keen. The lantern Uncle brought for us is sitting on the floor, just out of our reach, the lens clouded with soot.

My body is suddenly alert. The captors are coming upstairs. Junior enters first, carrying a lantern. Nephew follows with an oval slab of cake on a metal tray, and Uncle behind him with a bottle of Pepsi. Junior leads the singing of "Happy birthday to you," his head bobbing like an enthusiastic choirboy. They unlock us and put the *zowagi* cube in the middle of the room. Nephew sets the cake down on the cube and stands solemn and erect with his hands clasped behind his back. The cake is decorated with a thick layer of white icing, pink and blue flower-edging, a palm tree with green leaves and a brown trunk, a pink and blue slab of crystallized sugar with Arabic writing. Harmeet asks what the words mean. "Happy birthday," Nephew says, beaming with pride. His wife got the cake in the market.

We sing "We Wish You a Merry Christmas." "*Zane! Zane!*" Junior exclaims, clapping his hands with delight.

Uncle tears a piece of cardboard out of a box in the barricade and gives it to Nephew to cut the cake. He serves us in the order of our age: Norman first, Harmeet last. Uncle pours Pepsi into one of our beakers and shares it around. Cake and Pepsi. Sweetness explodes like a fireworks of pleasure in my mouth. I can feel energy surging through my body. It is almost too much.

After we've eaten, the captors each take a piece for themselves. Junior wants us to sing again. The captors become very still with listening. The melody flows out of us like a prayer. *Silent night, holy night. All is calm, all is bright.* No more bombs, no more guns. Then we shall all live as one. *Sleep in heavenly peace, sleep in heavenly peace.*

Uncle shakes his head sadly. "*Issau salam. Messiahiy. La kineesa, la kineesa.*" He cuts each of us a second piece of cake. Then, grunting like a pig, he plunges the great paw of his hand into the remaining slab and shoves fistfuls of cake into his mouth. Nephew and Junior laugh so hard they have to grip themselves.

Then, just as if a switch has been thrown, the party's over. "*Hamam, hamam. Nam!*" Junior orders. We stack our chairs and move them out of the way. I reach for the broom to do a quick sweep. There are cake crumbs all over the floor. "*La, la,*" Junior says. The cleanup will have to wait until tomorrow.

We go to the bathroom and Junior locks us up. "Sorry, Harmeet. Sorry, Jim," he says, stopping to look at us before he leaves, four men lying on a ragtag bed, faces peeking through hats and a carpet-like blanket. The omission of Tom's and Norman's names hangs ominously in the dark. Good night, we say.

# DECEMBER 29 DAY 34

"*Shlonik?*" I ask Junior as he hands us our *samoon* lunch.

He looks pained and shakes his head. "*Mozane, mozane.*"

"I am sorry," I say.

"This *mozane*," he says, pointing to himself. "This no Fallujah. No mother, no father, no madame. *Kool yum in beit.* George Bush *najis.* Bush *mozane. Jaysh Amriki* in Fallujah, Baghdad, Ramadi. *Kabir, kabir.*"

"I am sorry," Tom says. "What my country has done is very wrong."

Junior nods. The Iraqi government is dominated by the Shia, he says, traitors and collaborators who are controlled by Iran. There's no hope. Armed resistance is the only option. His face is dark and fierce with hate. He explains with his hands how he's going to drive a car packed with explosives next to an American Humvee and blow himself up. He points to the ceiling. *Jenna*, he says. He will go to heaven and join his family, his fiancée, his best friend. He points to the floor and stamps his foot. *Jehennem*. The Americans will go to hell. I look at him dumbly. This can't be happening. He repeats the same sequence of gestures. No, it really is. I am listening to a young man tell me he wants to be a suicide bomber.

There is a sudden high-pitched whirring sound, a loud metal clang. *"Isma!"* Nephew cries. Junior freezes. Nephew bolts to the window to peek through the curtains. He turns from the window, their eyes lock, Nephew runs out of the room. Junior grabs the handcuffs and locks us up as fast as he can. His eyes are cold and round like beads of steel. "What's going on?" Tom says.

"Shut up!" Junior barks. *"La killam, la killam!"* He forms his hand into a gun and points it at his head. *This is what will happen to you if you talk.* He hurries from the room.

"It sounds like a tank," Tom says. "It must be some kind of patrol." Fear courses full-throttle through my body. Is this the nightmare scenario, a military rescue, the open-fire, gun-and-bomb fight to the death we've been dreading?

I strain to catch every sound. The whirring moves closer. Downstairs, furniture scrapes across the floor. Nephew's and Junior's voices are urgent, panicked, arguing, then silent. I look helplessly at my hand-cuffed hands. There's nothing we can do to protect ourselves. There are clipped shouts, voices in the street giving orders. The whirring moves away slowly and fades into the night. Junior and Nephew return shortly afterwards. Junior looks at us intently. His eyes are sinister, almost crazed. *We could've been killed*, they seem to say. *The soldiers, the occupation, the danger we're in, it's all your fault. You're going to have to pay for this.* He's holding something in his hand. I can't tell what it is. It's not a cell-phone. Nephew steps forward to unlock us.

Norman begins the rotation through the bathroom while Harmeet and I start setting up our bed. Tom approaches Junior. "What happened? What happened outside?" he asks, pointing to the window. Junior gives him a menacing look. "This soldier? *Jaysh Amriki? Britannia?*" Tom presses.

Junior steps towards Tom and jabs him in the chest. "No *Amriki*. No *Britannia*. This no *hazeem*—no escape."

Tom shakes his head. "*La hazeem*," he says. He turns away from Junior and busies himself with setting up our bed.

Junior sits down. He stares vacantly at the object in his hands. I can't tell what it is in the dim light. "*Shuhada bil Arabi?*" I hear Harmeet ask.

"*Romana,*" Junior answers.

"In English we call that a grenade."

My head turns and my eyes lock onto the object in Junior's hands. Oh my God, he *is* holding a grenade! Junior looks up and sees me watching him. There's a mad gleam in his eyes. He stands up and makes as if to pull the pin. "Boom," he says, opening his arms in a slow-motion display of a bomb exploding. "*Amriki mot.*"

Nephew holds out his hand for the grenade.

"*La mezjoon, la mezjoon,*" he says, holding up his wrists as if they were handcuffed. He points at us and repeats the action of throwing the grenade. If they try to take him prisoner, he will fight to the death and take us with him.

Nephew gestures towards the grenade. He is calm, friendly, cajoling. Junior shakes his head. He doesn't want to give it to him. They talk back and forth. Nephew waits patiently. Junior reluctantly gives him the grenade. Nephew continues to hold out his hand. Junior, petulant, takes a second grenade out of his pocket. Nephew flashes me a look as he turns towards the door and leaves the room. He too is relieved.

Sleep is impossible. I can't get it out of my head. "This in car and BOOM," he'd said. *This is my body. Exploding for you. Take this. What you have done unto me, I shall do unto you. Limb for limb, life for life, ash unto ash. It is necessary. It is righteous. It is just. For my family's blood I will be a martyr.* At least then it will be done, I think. He won't be able to kill anymore.

But no, it will never be done. Hate is never finished. It sickens me. The shrapnel-blasted lives, the futile cycle of reprisal and vengeance, the blind self-righteousness, the endless grief, the calamity and waste of war. This is not what we were made for. God did not give us our amazing, beautiful bodies for hating and killing. We were given life to give life. Eyes for seeing the wild beauty of the world. Ears for hearing the sweet songs of children and birds. Hearts for loving. Hands for blessing and healing and giving.

How do I tell Junior this? How do I tell him that his life is sacred, his body a wondrous chariot, that he must not do this, foreclose every possibility of good in an irrevocable act of hate? I struggle to find words, for some way of communicating across the divide of language and power. He is captor and I am captive. I am slave and he is master. Words, I decide, are useless. He needs to taste and see, *feel* the goodness of God in his body. Only then will it be impossible for him to turn himself into a bomb.

Human touch. That's how to do it. My heart starts pounding. It's ridiculous, crazy, insane. I immediately sweep the idea out of my mind. One does not massage one's captor.

# DECEMBER 31 DAY 36

Morning exercise. The second-floor foyer is awash with light. How I love the reach and stretch of arms, the bend down and twist of waist, the all-around move of my body handcuff free, the feeling of being myself again.

Junior and Nephew are leaning against the stairway railing, talking. Junior is massaging the back of his neck with his hand. There's a look of pain in his face. Something seizes me. The next thing I know, the blue folding chair is in my hands and I'm standing beside Junior. He looks at me. I point to the chair, touch my shoulder, make a massaging gesture with my hands. Junior looks at me strangely. "Massage, massage," I say, demonstrating on my shoulders.

He looks at Nephew. Nephew shrugs. Junior takes off his sweatshirt and sits down. Now what? I stand behind him, take a deep breath, rest my hands on his shoulders. I can't believe it. I'm actually touching one of the captors.

The edges of his white undershirt are yellow and worn, the fabric saturated with his body oils. I'm surprised by the animal warmth of his skin, the ordinariness of his body. His back is covered with acne scars and blackheads. His shoulders and biceps are thin, soft, lacking definition. Such a strange contrast to the bulging strength of his forearms. For a moment I am seized by the desire to close my hands around his neck. He looks flabby and weak. I could do it, choke the life out of him. No, I think, Nephew is right there.

I put my fingers and thumbs to work. I search, press, knead, strip the muscles of his neck and upper back, gently at first and then with increasing pressure. His back is a mess of knotted cords and tight little fists of muscle. "*Zane, zane,*" he groans, melting into the chair. I breathe deeply and pray for this young man whose name I don't know. I pray for the healing of his spirit, that he might know the amazing goodness of God in every cell of his body. I start to hum, "Go now in peace/go now in peace/let the love of God surround you/everywhere, everywhere you may go," a song Tom taught us.

The massage prolongs our exercise period. Nephew directs Norman, Tom and Harmeet to return to their chairs. Sensing Nephew's impatience, I pat Junior's shoulders to indicate that I've finished. "Come on, Jim. Massage, massage," he protests. I continue for another five minutes and then return to my chair. Nephew handcuffs me and leaves.

"Well, that was pretty crazy," I say. I worry that I've crossed the line. I want to know what they think.

"No, that was good," Harmeet says.

"It gave us more time for exercise," Norman says.

"It was like you soothed the savage beast," Tom says.

I feel uneasy. "I wonder what I've started. I just hope he doesn't expect me to do it all the time."

"He was really out of shape," Harmeet says.

"Yeah, I noticed that too," I say. We are agreed. Of the three, he would be the easiest to subdue.

—

New Year's Eve is a popular wedding day in Iraq. All day and into the evening we hear waves of honking, celebratory gunfire and blaring music as exuberant wedding parties make their way through Baghdad in hired vans and buses, women and men in separate vehicles. "I love it," Tom says. "How even in the middle of all this uncertainty about the future, and all the terrible suffering that's come with the occupation, people just keep living their lives."

That night we have a special New Year's Eve visitor. We can hear him yukking it up downstairs with the guards. "He better come up and see us," I fume. We've been waiting on pins and needles ever since he told us three day, four day, Big *Haji* in UAE. He comes without party favours, but he does have news. "The negotiations are almost finish. Just some small thing and you release. All of you. One day, two day. Not more." He holds up his cellphone. "I get the phone call. Money in Baghdad and you release."

## JANUARY 1, 2006 DAY 37

Laughing in the stairwell. The captors are coming. "*La cahraba,*" Junior says, entering with a lantern, followed by Nephew. "*La cahraba,*" we say. Uncle enters quietly and eases himself carefully into a chair. He appears to have been limping.

Nephew steps towards us with the keys: his first time unlocking us. "Sleep, sleep," he commands, but his fingers are nervous, clumsy. He doesn't know how to position the handcuffs, which way to turn the key in the keyhole, when to shake the ratchet loose. Junior snickers as Nephew struggles a fourth time to open Norman's handcuff. Nephew's face is red when he comes to open my handcuff.

When we are unlocked, Norman goes to the bathroom and we start right away to set up for the night. As I stack the plastic chairs and put them next to Uncle, I happen to look down at his feet. He's barefoot and his right ankle is massively swollen.

"What happened? *Shoo* this?" I say, pointing to his ankle.

"Football, football," he says, lifting his bruised ankle off the floor.

"Have you seen a doctor?" Norman asks.

"No doctor," Uncle says.

Harmeet bends down to look. "You should see a doctor. This *mozane*."

Uncle shakes his head. "Iraqi doctor *mozane*. No Iraqi doctor."

"This massage?" Junior asks me.

"This no massage. Massage *mozane*," I say.

We try to explain with our handful of Arabic words the best way to treat a sprain. Harmeet is something of an expert, having suffered several bad ones from playing squash. The one thing we seem able to successfully convey is that he should rest it as much as possible and keep it elevated. Then, without explanation, Tom is on his hands and knees, hands wrapping gently around Uncle's ankle, eyes closed. Puzzled, Uncle and Junior look down at Tom and then at each other.

"*Shoo?* What this?" Junior asks, frowning.

I fold my hands under my chin and point to heaven. "He is praying to Allah. For *haji*."

Junior nods reverently. The room is quiet and still for a full minute. Then Tom stands up, eyes blinking rapidly as if emerging from a trance. "I was trying to draw the pain out," he says. "Sometimes I can draw the pain out." Junior and Uncle look at each other blankly and shake their heads. They are completely bewildered.

I'm the last one to go to the bathroom. When I return, the three captors are talking quietly. Norman and Tom are chained to each other by the ankle as usual, and Harmeet is handcuffed to Tom. I slide under the blanket between Norman and Harmeet.

"*Shwaya, shwaya,*" Junior says, earnest like a choirboy. Only a little longer to wait.

"*Hubis, hubis,*" Uncle says, miming a jet taking off with his hands.

"*Mooshkilla, mooshkilla,*" Nephew says, shrugging his shoulders.

We say good night and the captors depart. I'm shocked and amazed. They left without locking me up! I'm free as a bird! I feel myself starting to panic. I don't know what to do. I slide my wrists against the blanket. I can't get enough of it. The direct, smooth-gliding contact of wrist against blanket is delicious comfort. "What should we do?" Harmeet asks. He wants to know if we should lock ourselves up or let them discover their mistake in the morning. *This is the wrong question,* I want to shout.

No one speaks for a long time. I can hardly breathe. Is it now? Is this the time, the open window, the key to the door, the helicopter rescue hoist coming down? Adrenalin roars through my body like a cataract. There's nothing to stop me. I can get up, find out if the windows in the other rooms are also barred, see if the door to the roof is locked, creep downstairs when the captors are asleep and try to get out by the kitchen door, or find some other avenue of escape.

But! What if, in opening one of the bedroom doors, it creaks, or there's an alarm on the door to the roof, or I knock something over while feeling my way through the pitch-black kitchen? And if I'm successful, what will happen to the others when the captors discover I'm gone? Do I act to save my life or do I throw my lot in with the others? I'm frantic with indecision. Freedom! I want it desperately. But it means risking everything. Why are they so silent? We should be making a plan—acting! Don't they know, can't they see, what an opportunity this is? Damn them. Damn their passivity and resignation.

They're waiting for my answer. "I'll put them on in the morning," I force myself to say, "before the captors come. So they don't realize their mistake." The thought of handcuffing myself is repugnant.

"Well, I'm certainly going to enjoy having my hands free," Norman says. "Now I'll be able to stand up for a bit in the night."

"We're all going to sleep better," Harmeet says. "Good night, gentlemen."

I'm suddenly exhausted. I turn onto my side, curl my hands under my chin and fall asleep.

—

# JANUARY 2 DAY 38

"It's time," I say to Norman, sometime after the call to prayer, when the streets of Baghdad are still quiet and the day's light is gathering. I close Harmeet's handcuff around my right wrist. He sits up with a grunt and uses his free hand to lock us together.

There, I've done it. Chosen slavery over freedom. I lie back on my pillow in a stupor of self-loathing.

# CHAPTER ELEVEN

T.S. Eliot was wrong. January is the cruellest month, not April. January is an open wound and a sealed tomb, a door that won't open, a gate that leads nowhere. We drift like broken bits of Styrofoam in a ceaseless ocean. Our lives are a breath held in suspended animation. There are no words to describe the pain of this waiting. A minute feels like an hour, an hour like a day, a day like a week.

January is named after Janus, the Roman god of gates and doors, beginnings and endings. He's a two-headed deity with two minds and two faces who sees the past and looks into the future at the same time. He's the point-in-between that keeps watch as things move from one condition, one time and place to another. He's the god of change.

Alas, it is a betrayal. Nothing changes. The gates and doors of January never open to us. There is only waiting.

It begins hopefully, with our hearts set on Medicine Man's most recent promise: "Big Haji in the UAE, negotiations almost finish, money in Baghdad and you release." Tom, however, cautions us. We're in the endgame, he says. He says the image of a marathon came to him during one of his middle-of-the-night meditations. Every marathon runner says the last mile is the hardest to run. You're almost there, but your body has used up everything. They call it hitting the wall, when a person is most likely to injure themselves, drop out or die, and getting across the finish line becomes an excruciating mental game. Now that we're in the endgame it's only going to get more difficult, and we're going to have to work even harder. Except the difference for us is, we have no idea where the finish line will be.

I don't know whether to be encouraged or despair.

January is cold. I wear every article of clothing I have: socks over socks, underwear over underwear, sweatpants over pants. We huddle together under the big red blanket and wrap our shoulders with some upholstery covers Tom found in the barricade, the curtains we use as part of our bedding. "We're cold," we tell the captors. "*Soba?*" we ask. "*La petrol, la petrol,*" they say, "Bush *najis.*"

In January, Tom hits the wall. It happens slowly, almost imperceptibly, the eroding away of the impossible resolve and stoic leadership of those first days. Fear, boredom, gnawing hunger, incessant cold, the lack of sunlight, exercise, time alone—these things accumulate, take their toll. "I can't get warm," he tells us in his check-ins. "My body is just not getting enough protein." "My stomach is full of acid. It just can't handle this diet." "I don't know what's wrong. I just can't sleep." His face becomes grim and skeletal.

Tom's response is to dig in, fight with our captivity, try and wrestle it to the ground. He exercises constantly, rotating his shoulders, stretching his neck, extending and lifting his legs in his chair. "I want to be able to hit the ground running when we get out of here. I've got to do everything I can to keep healthy," he says. When he's not exercising, he's meditating. His long in-and-out breathing punctuates the days like a respirator. He tells us about his experiments with different images, prayers, patterns of breathing. He's determined to spiritually prevail; it's a matter of hard work and applying the right technique. "I'm just trying to stay in the present moment. I'm not going to be controlled by negativity," he insists over and over. It's a life-and-death struggle: his will against the captivity.

He sees God as a kind of non-personal energy, an energy of love, perhaps best described as light, which suffuses and imbues everything. There is no limit to this energy. Its desire is to grow and expand infinitely. A little bit of this energy, or light, exists in every human being. "There is that of God in everyone," the Quakers say. Thus, every human being is connected to God and our task is to perfect this connection. Jesus points the way, shows us how to do it. While not the Son of God, Jesus had a unique and privileged understanding of his connection to

God, something he achieved through a life of hard spiritual work. We too are capable of perfecting our connection by going all the way in the spiritual life just as Jesus did. In so doing, we will be working towards an increase in the total amount of love energy in the Universe, and the time when everything becomes transformed into love.

Tom's dread fear is that he'll be overcome by "negativity" and begin to hate and dehumanize the captors, thus losing everything he's worked so hard to achieve in the spiritual life. He fights tooth and nail against this, redoubling his efforts each day to pray, meditate and breathe. It's as if salvation for him is a process of hard work and sacrifice—a project of the will rather than a gift to receive.

It's not working. He tells us one day that he's going to take a second Valium. His mind becomes foggy. His perceptions grow rigid, his ideas fixed, he's less able to incorporate new information, we have to repeat things. "I don't know what's wrong," he tells us. "I'm trying, but I just can't shake this negativity." He alternates between long periods of silence and helpless rambling. His judgment is becoming erratic. I begin to worry that he's losing the ability to cope altogether.

It pains me to see him in this struggle. It seems futile. There's no way of prevailing against the boredom, the hunger, the uncertainty, the fear. It's all too big and too much. I concluded early on that there was no way to fight it. Whatever my inner creativity, force of will or capacity to endure, the captivity would always win, like a vast and limitless cloud, insensible to both rage and despair, swallowing whole. The strength to get through would have to come from outside me. Coping was not a matter of projecting my will but of opening myself to receive a gift. The gift of grace. The spontaneous, unmerited self-giving of God. What can never be earned or achieved, only awoken to, discovered, received. *God loves you more than you can possibly imagine,* I want to tell Tom. *Your connection with God is already given. It's permanent and irrevocable. There's nothing you need do but fall into God's arms. Surrender and He will carry you through.* I worry his ceaseless striving is causing him to suffer needlessly, that it may lead him to a breakdown and compromise our safety. But how do you say this to a person whom you are handcuffed to, without sounding preachy and judgmental and calling into question every cherished thing they believe?

It comes from the poverty and isolation of his childhood, I think, this unwavering faith in the power of his will to get him through adversity. It was the way he survived, and indeed, triumphed. It almost breaks my heart when he tells us his story. He was born in 1951 in the town of Graysville, Tennessee, the only son of Virginia and Henry, aged forty and fifty-five. His grandparents on both sides had died, and there was no extended family to speak of. When he was five, they moved into a poor Chattanooga, Tennessee, neighbourhood. They were the only white family on the street. His father, a First World War Marine, suffered from emphysema and couldn't work. Tom believed his father's health condition was the result of a battlefield gas attack. His days were spent reading and exchanging letters related to a keen interest in an obscure philosopher. His father never played with him; he couldn't because of his health, Tom said.

The responsibility for keeping the family going fell to his mother, who worked for a beer distribution company. She started to drink as soon as she got home. Tom would spend the first half-hour after school visiting with her—he used to love that time with her, when she was sober—and then he would go to a friend's house, only to return late in the evening. He was forever arranging things so that he didn't have to be at home.

Tom's street dead-ended onto a woods. He took refuge there, spent countless hours wandering, exploring, playing. He loved the trees, the creek, the sun dappling through leaves. It was where he truly felt at home, the only place where he was free.

He found solace in the clarinet. He practised endlessly in his room, and sure enough, had quite a flair for it. When he didn't have enough money for his private music lesson, the instructor waived the fee. His hard work earned him a music scholarship to Peabody College, where he met Jan Echols in his first year of study. They married at the end of his junior year, shortly after the death of his parents. He graduated in 1973 and successfully auditioned for the Marine Corps Band. The young couple moved to Washington, D.C., and Tom began a life of travelling the world and playing at glittering White House functions. Their daughter, Katherine (called Kassie), was born in 1980, Andrew in 1984. He and Jan divorced in 1990. He spoke of it with regret. "I wasn't paying attention. I should've seen it coming," he said. After playing his clarinet for four successive presidents, Tom retired in 1993 and trained to become a baker.

He told his story without emotion. It was just what happened, the facts as they were. I wanted to cry, hold him tight, undo what could not be undone.

## JANUARY 5 DAY 41

Norman finishes his course of antibiotics. The cellulitis in his leg has disappeared. We're all very relieved. Medicine Man appears like a fat genie popping out of a bottle. He says there's been no contact with Big Haji, but this is not a problem, everything is fine, you'll be released any time now. He reassures us with smiles and shrugs. I want to strangle him. We ask him if he can bring us notebooks to help us pass the time. This is not a problem, he says, the next time I come.

## JANUARY 6 DAY 42

It happened on a Monday, three years ago today, the eighth day of the delegation, during my first trip to Iraq. It was an accident that could have happened anywhere. We were on our way back to Baghdad after spending two nights in Basra, a convoy of three white-gleaming, late-model Suburbans travelling at 120 kilometres per hour on a divided highway, no one else on the road. It was a perfect blue-weather morning, already hot and it wasn't even eight o'clock. None of us was wearing a seat belt. It's not the done thing in Iraq. The back tire exploded, our vehicle skidded out of control, flipped end over end, and crash-landed on the roof.

I relive the accident frame by frame. The sound of the back tire exploding. The wild fishtailing and long skid towards the shoulder. My body bouncing helplessly up and down. Sand flying in grey light. The

Voice: *I am with you I am with you.* The sudden silence and stop of motion. Everything crazy and upside down, knees jammed into my chest. The calling out, *"Is everyone okay?"* The slide out through the smashed window. The overturned wreck of the vehicle. Luggage scattered across the desert. The lifting of George Weber's body onto a stretcher.

Razza (our driver) and I escaped without so much as a scratch. Larry Kehler from Winnipeg and Pat Basler from Wisconsin were cut and bruised. Michele Naar Obed from Duluth broke her nose. Charlie Jackson from San Antonio wrenched his back and cracked his ribs. It would be two weeks before he could travel home. But George . . . We found his body lying on the sand, thrown clear of the vehicle, his face an unrecognizable mass of blood and brain and bone. He died instantly. Razza was inconsolable.

At the time, George and I were country neighbours. He lived in the town of Chesley, twenty minutes from the farm where I was living. We had done our CPT training together in 2000. He was a retired high school teacher with a dry sense of humour and an unflappable distaste for platitudes, social bromides, pretence of any kind. You would often find him on the other side of an argument, poking holes with his devil's advocate stick, a boyish grin on his face. "What are you going to do when the bombs start falling?" he'd asked me three weeks before we left for Iraq. He was testing me.

I said something about war not being imminent, but if it did happen the Iraqi government would likely evacuate us in advance of hostilities, as it did in 1991 when the Gulf Peace Team was camped in the desert between Saudi Arabia and Iraq. I tried hard to sound nonchalant, but in truth the prospect terrified me.

A veteran world traveller, George chuckled in reply. "When the war comes, there won't be any government left to do anything. It'll be chaos. What you'll need is two thousand American dollars in your pocket to hire someone to drive you out of the country. But don't worry." He smiled. "I'll look after you."

Perhaps it is the ineluctable habit of reading back into things, the effort to make sense of the capricious and the absurd. At the airport, waiting for our flight, watching the jets ferry back and forth, George had said, "You know, I've lived a long life, and it's been a good life. Of course, I want to come back, but if I don't, I'm okay with that." He laughed. "When I think of some of the taxi trips I've taken in Hebron, the way some of them drive, I always think I'm much more likely to die in a car accident than I am doing actual CPT work."

In Amman he purchased an exquisite silver necklace for his wife Lena, a perfect and beautiful memento of his love. In Baghdad he ordered a tailor-made suit. He said it was "to help the local economy." It ended up being the suit he was buried in. Then, on that fateful morning, contrary to his established habit of sitting up front with the driver, George sat in the very back in the place where Michele always sat. She couldn't help ribbing him. "George," she said, "what're you doing back here? You should be up front, in the seat of honour!"

"What? Are you kidding?" he joked. "That's the death seat."

I always wondered, did George know? Did some part of him, perhaps in the wordless deep of his spirit, intuit what was to happen? I reach out to him with my spirit, the first CPTer to die in the course of duty. *Are you watching over us now, George?*

## JANUARY 8 DAY 44

Uncle stops in to tell us he's heating up water for a bath, the second of our captivity. While we're waiting, Norman asks if we've seen the gecko. No, I say, what's that? A little creature, rather like a lizard, but smaller, he explains. Harmeet has seen it too. "I quite like it," he says. "Sometimes when I'm in the bathroom I just sit and watch it."

"Yes, it's rather nice to have a living creature around. Something that's free, rather unlike ourselves," Norman says.

We hear sounds in the bathroom, then a loud whack. The door to our room, closed during the day now to keep the heat in, opens. A dead gecko rolls into the room. Uncle appears in the doorway, grinning from ear to ear. He flicks the gecko back into the foyer with the bathroom squeegee and disappears without saying a word. I almost burst into tears.

—

Uncle has brought us a kerosene heater. For the first time in weeks we are warm. The dark foreboding of January lifts just a little and I start to feel good. Now, if only we could have a cup of tea.

When Harmeet returns from his bath, his long hair is dripping water onto his shoulders. We move the *soba* in front of him. He leans over his knees and flops his long black mane forward so that it can hang freely in front of the heater. He squeezes the water out of his hair and combs the tangled strands apart with his hands. It takes almost an hour for it to dry. Not long after that, Nephew shuts off the kerosene heater. "*Bush najis. La petrol,*" he says.

We ask every day for the use of the heater. Each time, they say the same thing: "*Bush najis, la petrol.*" Finally relenting, they put the heater on for a couple of hours in the evening before we go to bed. The blue dancing kerosene flames introduce a tiny bit of cheer into our lives and ease the chill out of our bodies for a while.

In a fit of boredom one day, Uncle pulls a prehistoric electric heater out of the barricade. It has no plug. He strips the sheathing off the cord with his teeth and inserts the exposed wires into an electrical outlet. With a sudden electric hum, some snapping and sparking, the coils come glowing to life. The room fills with the dry smell of burning dust. Uncle shakes his head and points at the electrical outlet. It's dangerous, he says.

# JANUARY 10 DAY 46

There are two Eids in the Muslim calendar. Eid al-Fitr marks the end of Ramadan and the month-long discipline of fasting during daylight hours. Eid al-Adha commemorates Ibrahim's willingness to sacrifice his son Ishmael (in the Judeo-Christian tradition, the story of Abraham and Isaac). Today is Eid al-Adha. To celebrate, Junior solemnly announces that he is going to cook.

He delivers lunch on an ornate metal tray—a plate of rice and a bowl of thick lentil stew—and sets it down on the *zowagi* cube with a restrained flourish of pride. My eyes fix greedily on the food. Nephew instructs us to move our chairs around the cube. I grab a spoon off the tray and note with relief that it is clean. I'm ready to start eating. Junior shakes his head, waves his finger, points towards the bathroom. We have to wait for Tom, he says. Today is an occasion, it seems; proper manners are required.

When we're all gathered, Nephew smiles and points towards heaven. We're starting the meal with a prayer. He repeats a phrase over and over: "*Bismillah al rahman al rahim.*" In the Name of God, Most Gracious, Most Merciful. The first words of the Quran, Tom tells us later. When we've each taken a turn stumbling our way through the words, Nephew signals for us to begin. Junior watches closely as we take our first bites. The stew is rich and warm and soul-nourishingly good. We express our gratitude with lip-smacking hmmms, nods, *shokrens*. Junior beams.

Tom and Harmeet shovel food into their mouths with tunnel-vision urgency. I watch with dismay as the lentils and rice start to disappear. I measure and count compulsively: for every spoonful Norman and I take, Tom and Harmeet take two. I feel as if I'm at a feeding frenzy at the zoo. If I want my fair share, I'm going to have to compete, match them spoon for spoon. I slow down, eat less, smile. Inside, I rage.

Some rice falls onto the floor from Norman's spoon. "*Najis! Haram!*" Junior cries, waving his arms angrily. Norman ignores the reprimand and keeps on eating. Junior scowls, picks up the rice and carefully puts it on the tray.

"You never let food fall on the floor where it can be stepped on," Tom says to Norman. "It's considered disrespectful." But then some rice falls off Tom's spoon. He doesn't notice. Junior's eyes dart to the floor. I pick up the rice and put it on the tray.

"*Najis,*" Junior scowls contemptuously. He points to Tom's left hand and scolds him. "*La, la,*" he says. In Arabic culture, the left hand is considered unclean and never used at table or in greeting.

"It's because I'm left-handed," Tom says. Junior glares and Tom switches the spoon to his right hand.

Junior points at me. "*Shoo?* What this?" He apes the way I've been eating by taking small bites from an imaginary spoon and chewing with exaggerated delicacy. "*La Iraqi*," he says disdainfully. He points at the others. Eat quickly, he seems to be telling me, with gusto like them, this is the Iraqi way.

"*Iraqi, Iraqi*," Nephew says, nodding in vigorous support.

I pat my stomach and smile. "*Akeel* good. *Shokren*," I say. Junior shakes his head irritably. I don't mind. If the way we eat matters so much to them, it means they aren't planning to kill us any time soon.

I tell myself it isn't Harmeet and Tom's fault. Hunger is a fierce, indomitable force. It gnaws at you, possesses you like a demon, reduces you to your basest instincts. They were simply hungry. But, try as I might, I can't talk myself down. The rage won't stop. I swallow hard. Saying something means breaking the unspoken rule that has governed us rigidly since the first day of our captivity. We work valiantly at it, in every interaction, with generosity, respect, sensitivity to feelings, asking for permission, offering apology for imposition, restraining emotion. It is a relentless discipline. Avoid conflict at all times and in every instance. Our lives depend on it.

Miraculously and marvellously, it has worked for the most part, but now I am chafing against this silent imperative. I can't do it anymore. Yes, the prospect of an uncontrolled conflict fills me with dread, but unless we can find a constructive way to deal with it, someone is going to explode, and it most likely will to be me. I clear my throat. The time has come.

First, the carefully prepared opening statement. "I'm sorry to have to bring this up. I debated all day about whether or not I should. I tried really hard to let go of it, but I just wasn't able to." Then the benefit of the doubt. "You may not have been aware of it, but . . ." The naming of names. ". . . Tom and Harmeet . . ." And the point of no return. My breath catches. I hesitate. Maybe I shouldn't. Anger forces the words out. "You ate really fast and took more than your fair share. I felt like I had to race to keep up with you. I never want to be put in this position again."

Tom apologizes right away. Harmeet, stricken, mortified, shrinks into his chair. In some way I hadn't anticipated, my words have wounded him. "It's all right," I say, reaching desperately for some way to take back what I've said. "It's easy to happen. We're all so hungry."

Harmeet doesn't answer. He can't. His silence feels like a lash. Tom throws me a lifeline. How can we prevent this from happening in the future? he asks. Norman suggests dividing the serving into four. We don't need to be slavish about being fair, I say, as long as we're attentive and eat at the pace of the slowest person. Tom promises to pay more attention.

"Thanks, Tom," I say. For being so gracious.

Harmeet disappears into a shroud of silence. Tom, Norman and I converse in fits and starts of small talk. We hobble through the day like a dog with a broken leg. For the first time in our captivity we go to sleep without saying good night to each other. I toss and turn all night in self-reproach.

## JANUARY 11 DAY 47

Morning exercise. Harmeet's face is ashen. He avoids my eyes. I wonder if he will bring me a glass of water, as he always does, when he finishes his turn in the bathroom. He doesn't. I approach him in the middle of some sit-ups. "I'm sorry," I tell him. "I shouldn't have said anything."

"No, I'm the one at fault," he whispers. "It's me." I barely hear him. He turns onto his stomach and begins a round of push-ups. He has nothing more to say.

*It's going to be a long day,* I tell myself.

Uncle enters the room with a big smile on his face. "*Melabas, melabas,*" he says, pinching the cuff of his shirt. We don't understand. "*Frook hind.*

Frook hind." He pulls at his shirt, sniffs it, makes a face, makes a whirling gesture with his hands.

Our faces break into joyous smiles. He's going to let us wash our clothes! My imagination leaps wildly. Does this means we're going to be released for Eid?

There was no Eid release, but we did get to do laundry. It is draped all over the barricade now and hanging on the banisters in the foyer. It was a relief to be handcuff free for a while and doing something useful, hands working vigorously in warm-water balm, a relief to get away from Harmeet's funereal mood. He didn't say a word all day.

It is during our check-in that he finally breaks his silence. "About what happened yesterday . . . I . . . what I did . . . that's not . . . my grandfather went through much worse than this. He would never have done what I did. He went hungry to save somebody else, and I took more than my share."

Harmeet is referring to the dark, famished months when his grandfather was a prisoner of war in a Pakistani concentration camp. A veteran sergeant in his mid-thirties, the same age as Harmeet is now, he took two Sikh soldiers under his wing. No more than boys, he counselled them when they were losing their faith, nursed them through sickness and fed them his rations to keep them alive. It is the singular act of solidarity and sacrifice that governs Harmeet's moral universe. When I confronted him for taking more than his share from the common dish, something he hadn't been aware of, he went into a spiral of shame. He had failed the example of his grandfather, and therefore failed everything he had ever hoped to be.

When the captors depart with the lantern, and all is finished for this day, Harmeet's nocturnal benediction returns. "Good night, gentlemen."

"Good night, Harmeet," we say. He cannot see, but in the dark I am smiling. Harmeet has found his way back to us. All is right with the world again.

# JANUARY 14 DAY 50

Nephew is standing in the doorway, all smiles. "Big *Haji* in Jordan," he says excitedly.

"*Faloos, faloos*," Uncle says, bending over our wrists, locking us up for the day. He puts one hand on top of the other, slides his palm forward and lifts his hand into the air. "Schoooo," he hisses, mimicking the sound of a jet taking off. "*Canadi, Britannia, Amriki*." The two men leave.

"I'll believe it when I see it," Norman says.

"I'm just trying to stay in the present moment," Tom says.

"It's probably just another false alarm," I say.

"We can't believe anything they tell us," Harmeet says.

But we do. They bait their hooks with little morsels of hope and we bite down hard. It's a paradox. The days when we know nothing will happen, when we know there is no chance of being released—these days are easier. Much, much easier, in fact. We float and frolic in the stories we tell, the games we invent, the riddles we pose to each other. On those days we swim in pulsing currents, surf on curling waves. At the end of such days we say to each other, "You know, today went by quickly," or "Today wasn't too bad."

But on days like today, when there is even the faintest hope of release, time grinds to a halt. Every minute and every hour becomes a piercing lance. *Today, tomorrow, any day. I get the call and you release. Not long now. Just some small negotiation.* Such days move slower than glaciers and pass through us with the screaming agony of kidney stones. *When! when! when!* our minds and bodies cry. We obsess, speculate, hypothesize, argue about contingencies. Now isn't soon enough. We burn in the fire of our expectations.

*Present moment, present moment.* It sends me to the brink every time he says it. But Tom's right. There are moments when the four of us, all at the same time, slip out of our handcuffs and chains and lose ourselves in the story we're telling, the game we're playing, the riddle we're solving. I call it breaking into the present. It seems to only happen when we let go of all expectation. Then the walls around us disappear and we're simply four friends sitting together enjoying each other's company. We could be drinking beer on a front porch or pitching horseshoes on a summer day. We have entered the Palace of Now, the only place where we are truly free.

# JANUARY 16 DAY 52

"You know, last night I had this dream," Tom tells us during his check-in. "We were sitting here in the room and Junior came in. His face was a mask of evil. He said somebody has been sold. One of you has to go. He had a gun in his hand. We looked at each other. Nobody moved. 'Come on,' he said, 'one of you must decide.' Then I stood up. 'I'll go. I'll be the one.'

"That's when I woke up. My heart was pounding and I couldn't get back to sleep. I began to think, over and over in my mind, could I do that? Could I really do that? And it struck me, you guys are my friends. Yeah, I could do that, I said to myself. I really think I could do that."

No one speaks. For a moment I'm angry. *Why are you telling us this?* I wonder. I steal a look at Tom out of the corner of my eye. His face is open, searching, reaching. He wants some response. I don't know what to say. Tom's nobility astounds and shames me. This, in fact, is a scenario I've secretly tested in my imagination. Would I be willing to offer my life in the same way? I have to force myself to admit it: no, probably not.

Someone coughs. Norman continues on with his check-in. Our lack of acknowledgement feels like a betrayal. We are captives indeed.

# JANUARY 18 DAY 54

"*Haji kabir* in Baghdad," Nephew announces. We are confused. Is he referring to Medicine Man or the negotiator? He puts his hand above his head to indicate someone with greater authority. It's the negotiator. What about, *Haji Shwaya?* we ask—Medicine Man. Can you call him and ask him to come? It's been *thnein asbooah*. Two weeks. Nephew says okay and leaves. He returns a few minutes later, pointing to his watch. "*Haji* one o'clock in house. News good."

We wait on pins and needles, our ears leaping at every sound. Could this be the Phone Call, the Footstep, the Voice that brings The News? One o'clock comes and goes. At two o'clock we hear the kitchen door open and close, the rattle of the gate, the arrival of a car. Medicine Man enters the house on a wave of laughter. Voices collect at the bottom of the stairs. Finally. His shoes click briskly in the stairway. He crosses the foyer in five steps. He's in a hurry. "News good," Medicine Man says. "One week and you release. We have some negotiation and you release. All of you. The Canadians first."

"What is involved with these negotiations?" Norman asks.

"Negotiation with your government. The Canadians are no problem. The British have some little problem. The Americans, they have some problem. They not negotiate. Anything else?"

I ask about the notebooks. "I am sorry. I forget. I bring for you." He slips out the door and is gone.

"Oh God, not another week," I moan.

"At *least* a week," Tom says. He's gently reminding me. "Canadians first." I'm jolted by shame. I was so preoccupied with my own release that I failed to see the devastating implication.


"Hey, look what I found!" Harmeet exclaims. He's holding the nail he found stuck in his shoe before Christmas.

I stare as though it has magical powers. "Where was it?" I ask.

"Buried in my pocket."

"The whole time?" I try not to sound suspicious.

"It must've been. I found it when I switched back to wearing my track pants this morning."

I ask him for it. "Remember that movie," I say, "how they opened their handcuffs with a piece of wire? Let's try it!" No one says anything. "How does it look, Tom? Coast clear?"

"Yup. Nothing's happening that I can hear," Tom says.

"We can use a little amusement," Norman says.

It is an act of defiance that both thrills and terrifies me. I stick the nail into the keyhole of my left handcuff and start digging. "Any joy?" Norman asks.

"I'm afraid not. Why don't you give it a try." Norman inserts the nail into his handcuff and pushes counter-clockwise, increasing the force until his hand shakes. "Be careful of the mechanism," I say. "It'll be difficult to explain if the handcuffs suddenly don't work." Norman continues with less force. "Pull up on the handcuff," I say to Harmeet. He pulls, there's a click and the handcuff releases.

"Joy!" Norman says.

I can hardly contain my excitement. I have to try again. I turn the nail counter-clockwise and pull on the ratchet. It opens like a charm. I can't believe it! I examine the handcuff carefully. The design is startlingly simple. The ratchet passes through a housing and catches against a spring-loaded pawl. The key turns against the pawl and the ratchet swings free.

"It's quite strange," Harmeet says, "how the nail was sticking into my shoe. Do you think someone could have stuck it there deliberately?" The idea of a secret ally is exhilarating.

"If I had to pick somebody, it would be Nephew," Tom says, as if reading my mind.

My body shivers with excitement—or is it fear? We now have the capacity to escape.


Tom is keen. Unlocking our handcuffs will help him to sleep better. Norman is too. He'll be able to turn more easily onto his side and stand up to stretch in the middle of the night without disturbing me. Harmeet thinks it's worth trying. I don't. It's an unnecessary risk, I tell them. We're gambling away the possibility of escape for the luxury of a better night's sleep. My voice is hot. If they discover the nail, they'll take it away. We should only use it for trying to escape.

"Tom and Norman are chained up," Harmeet says. "We can't all escape." We might figure something out in the future, I say. Harmeet disagrees. "We have to deal with our circumstances as they are in the present," he says. "It's not an option for everybody, and I'm not going to try until it is. But since we have the nail, we might as well use it to make things easier."

"Maybe there's some way we can pick the locks," I say lamely. No one answers. I have to make a choice: I can share the risks faced by Norman and Tom by saying yes, or I can protect the possibility of escape for myself by saying no. I'm willing to try it, I say, but we have to minimize the risk of getting caught.

"Do you have the Instrument of Grace?" Norman says to Harmeet.

"The Instrument of Grace?" Harmeet asks.

"Why, your little nail, of course!"

Harmeet chuckles. "Yeah, it's right here in my pocket."

Norman opens his handcuff in a matter of seconds. The rest of us struggle, but we manage. We practise locking up quickly in the event the captors come to check on us. The fastest we get is twenty-three seconds.

I object. That's too slow. Tom says he'll block the door. I say the captors will know there's something going on right away. Tom says he'll pretend he's using the hamam bottle. What about the sound of the handcuffs clicking closed? We practise closing them as quietly as we can. It's still too loud, I say. Tom says he'll pretend to have a coughing fit. I'm not convinced. Tom insists it'll be okay. Norman and Harmeet really want to do it. It's against my better judgment, but in the end I agree. We sleep with our handcuffs unlocked.

I love it—the ability to cradle my head, swat mosquitoes with impunity, rest my hands on my chest or move them wherever I please. But I don't sleep. I'm braced, girded, ready to move at the first sign of danger. I toss and turn in an agony of questions. Are we sealing our doom, Harmeet and I, by not acting to escape? What happens if we do try to escape and we're successful? How will we find someone to help us? What if this is an insurgent neighbourhood? Would we be jumping out of a frying pan into a fire? Where would we hide? A trash bin? Someone's garden? A construction site? What do we do then—flag down a car, wait for a military convoy, run into a store or an apartment building? Will this put innocent people in jeopardy? And if we do find someone to help us, how do we explain our situation? I don't know how to call the police—I don't even know the team's phone number! And what about Norman and Tom? The consequences could be fatal. On the other hand, isn't it better to spare at least one family terrible grief than have all four of us perish? But then, if we try it and fail, there is the prospect of merciless beatings, excruciating punishment, death. It's a zero-sum game. We can wait it out and risk getting killed, or risk getting killed in trying to escape.

The night passes in a merry-go-round of buts spiralling around what-ifs. It's a relief when daylight creeps into the room. "Are you guys sleeping? It's starting to get light," I whisper. "We better put our handcuffs back on."

It is only when my wrists are safely handcuffed again that I fall fast asleep.

# JANUARY 20 DAY 56

The voices—loud, excited, running into each other—move to the bottom of the stairway. It sounds like a party. The voices subside. Footsteps in the foyer. Junior and Uncle appear. "T'al wiyaya," Junior says. "Downstairs."

Uncle unlocks us. I scramble to put my shoes on. I'm irritated with myself. I should be ready, always ready. You know neither the day nor the hour.

"La shoes. Come on," Junior says. My chest tightens like a drum. Where are they taking us? What's going to happen to us?

We follow Junior through the dark foyer and down the stairs. Nephew, waiting at the bottom, directs us to turn left through an open door. The room we enter is grand, at least fifteen by twenty feet. The walls are plum grey and crowned with butterscotch-coloured mouldings. A ceiling fan hangs between two cascading chandeliers. The floor is covered with a hard-worn Turkish rug. The walls opposite the door and to my left are banked with cobalt drapes that reach from floor to ceiling.

There's noise, confusion, people everywhere at once. Video Man is at the door holding a camera. He grips my arm and leads me towards three plastic lawn chairs lined against a blank expanse of wall. He turns me around and pushes me into a chair. He grabs Harmeet's arm and ushers him towards the chair next to me. Tom is next. "No, I can stand," he objects, pointing to the empty chair. "For the Doctor. Old man. *Kabir, kabir.*"

"*Ogod!*" Video Man barks, face reddening. Tom offers to get a chair from upstairs.

"Sit down," Junior orders, jabbing Tom in the chest with his index finger.

"Chair for Norman. Doctor *kabir*," Tom says.

"Sit down," I hear another voice say. I look up. It's Medicine Man. He takes a step towards Tom. His eyes are blazing.

I'm incredulous. *Tom—what're you doing?!* "It's their show," I try to warn him. "Just sit down."

Junior takes hold of Tom's shoulders and forces him to sit. Video Man's face and gestures are urgent, almost frantic. He points to Norman and Tom. Medicine Man shrugs his shoulders and steps back. Video Man is clearly in charge. He pulls me out of the chair and leads me to a bed heaped with clutter located against the wall. He wants me to sit here instead. I move a plate encrusted with food to make space to sit down. He brings Harmeet to sit next to me.

Then I notice the little boy. He is leaning against a second bed located against the curtain-covered wall to my right, fingers in his mouth, staring at the floor.

Norman has been standing in the doorway to my left. Uncle instructs him to sit down in the chair next to Tom. Norman doesn't understand. "*Imshee,*" Uncle says. When Norman doesn't move, Uncle grabs him by the lapels and jerks him towards the chair like a rag doll. Norman's eyes are wide, startled, full of fear. Medicine Man touches Uncle's arm. Uncle lets go with a laugh, fixes Norman's lapels and steps back.

"I am sorry, Doctor," Medicine Man says to Norman. "The big man, he is joking. Always he is joking."

Video Man shoves sticks of gum into Tom's and Norman's mouths and lectures them in Arabic. They nod blankly.

Medicine Man steps towards us. He looks pressured. "It's good to see you," I say.

He rolls his eyes and exhales. "We have nothing but problems. The border is closed now for two days. *Mooshkilla!* Our negotiator cannot get back to Baghdad."

Medicine Man turns back to Norman and Tom. I return my attention to the little boy. Junior is squatting beside him, talking quietly. He turns towards us and points. The boy looks at us cautiously. Our eyes meet. I smile and wink. The boy looks away. *"Zane, zane,"* I hear Junior say. He takes the boy's hand and brings him towards us. The boy hangs back. Junior smiles. I smile.

"Good, good," he says to the boy, shaking my hand to show I'm a friend. He encourages him to do the same. I hold out my hand. His hand moves towards me for a brief moment, but then he pulls it away and runs back to the other bed. Junior shrugs his shoulders.

My attention shifts back to Tom and Norman. Video Man is standing in front of them, gesturing, castigating. "We don't understand," Tom says. *"La Arabi."*

Medicine Man steps in. "You speak to the camera that you are in good health, you have the good treatment, everything is okay. Just like before. In a high voice. You speak to the camera for the immediate withdrawal of the American soldier. You must to speak against the occupation. That is all. Do you understand?" Tom nods.

As Medicine Man is talking, Video Man approaches us. *"La ilaha illa Allah, Muhammadu Rasul Allah,"* he says. There is no god but God, Muhammad is the Messenger of God. His eyes roll piously upwards and he points his right index finger towards heaven. He searches our faces intently. "This Quran. *Allah wahid. Allah wahid.*" Video Man looks heavenward with open palms. An ecstatic look flashes across his face. "*Allah*," he mumbles reverently, as if praying. He makes the sign of the cross on his chest. "*Mozane. El messiahiyea mozane.* No good," he says, his eyes flashing hate.

A cold chill sweeps through my body. Medicine Man calls to him. Video Man turns away abruptly.

"What the hell was that?" I whisper to Harmeet.

"Disturbing," he says.

Video Man is standing on a chair, pointing his camera at Tom. "Okay, you begin," Medicine Man says to Tom. Tom faces the camera and takes a breath. He speaks calmly, authoritatively. Medicine Man signals Norman. As he begins to speak, he is interrupted by the baleful mewing of a cat. Somebody giggles. Medicine Man barks at Uncle.

Uncle parts the curtain and taps gently on the window. "Shhhhh," he says, putting his finger to his mouth. The cat stops mewing. Uncle turns from the window and stands with his hands behind his back, a soldier at ease.

"Again," Medicine Man says to Norman. When Norman is finished, Harmeet and I exchange places with him and Tom. As Video Man stands scowling in front of us, behind him Junior is bending down to the little boy. The boy is restless, wants to move about the room. Junior lifts him onto his knee and whispers in his ear. The little boy nods his head and settles obediently.

Video Man speaks to us in Arabic. "*La Arabi, la Arabi*," we say. He turns to Medicine Man in frustration.

"He want you to say that you have the good treatment," Medicine Man interprets. "You must to beg the Canadian government, the Canadian people, to release you. And you must to beg the Pope for your release, say to him he must to withdraw from Iraq."

Harmeet and I look at each other. "The Pope?" I ask. "What do you mean?"

"You must to beg the Pope for you release. He tell me the Pope have some forces here."

"That doesn't make any sense," I say, shaking my head. "The Pope doesn't have any forces here. It will just look silly if I say that."

The two men confer. Video Man looks at me sharply. Medicine Man turns back to us and waves his hand. "It does not matter. Just your government then." When we've both made our speeches, he signals us to stand.

"At least I didn't say 'thank you to our captors' this time," Harmeet says in a low voice.

"You did great," I say. "An Oscar-winning performance."

Medicine Man and Video Man confer. Video Man issues instructions to Junior and Uncle. Junior moves the three chairs out of the way and Uncle lines the four of us up against the wall. *I hope they offer us a cigarette before they shoot us*, I think.

Video Man stands on the bed where we were sitting. He looks into the camera, points, gives directions to Medicine Man. Medicine Man gives directions to Junior. Junior moves us together until our shoulders touch.

"This video is to show you live," Medicine Man tells us. "Our negotiator have some meeting and he give this video to show you live. Now you just to say your name and the day. That is all. You know the day today?"

"January 20," Tom says.

We each state our name and the date. Video Man pans over us one last time. Confusion immediately follows. Video Man grabs Tom's arm, Junior chases the little boy, Uncle talks to Norman. I step towards Medicine Man to ask if he can tell us more about the negotiations. He's stressed, wipes his brow. "Just some small thing. I think you— and you"—he points to Harmeet and me—"you release in four, maybe five days. We have some exchange of money, file closed and go."

I am just about to ask another question when Video Man grabs my arm and hustles me out of the room. It is all I can do to stop myself from smashing him in the face. He releases me at the bottom of the stairs. I go back to our room and sit in my chair.

# JANUARY 25 DAY 61

Our third bath day. Uncle fires up the kerosene heater for us. Life is not so bad. We're warm for a change and I feel human again. After many days of requests, Uncle has finally brought scissors so we can trim our mous-taches. It's been driving me crazy, the growth of beard over my lip, the way it gets in my mouth every time I eat. And Harmeet has news, both good and bad. The bad news is that the door to the roof is locked. Harmeet snuck up the stairs during laundry, when the captors weren't looking. The door is secured with a heavy padlock, he says. There's no way to open it. As for the good news, Nephew has told him there's a prisoner exchange under way. Four hundred and fifty Iraqi detainees for the four of us.

It seems too fantastic to believe. Still, I can't help myself. "That would make this worth it," I say. "If our kidnapping results in the release of a few hundred Iraqis." The hope of release burns in me all day like an out-of-control wildfire.

## JANUARY 28 DAY 64

Medicine Man comes to see us with news. "This very secret," he tells us. "The Americans will not negotiate for Tom. So we make the pris-oner exchange instead. They release 450 of our men, four of our womens. We are just waiting now for two of our womens to be release, and one of our men in the U.S.—Omar Abdel-Rahman. He is the blind sheik. The Americans never say they make this release because of our negotiation. They say this is normal, we just to make the normal release. But it is not. This is our negotiation." He pauses for breath. "The Canadian money is not a problem, but it not in Baghdad. The negotia-tions are complete, except for some money from Jack Straw. The British are cold. Only some time now. One day, two day, and go. Canadian money in Baghdad and go. File closed."

"What about the notebooks?" I say.

He hits his forehead and laughs. "I am sorry. I am bad for this. I bring for you. They are just in my car." Then he is gone.

"One day, two day, and go," Harmeet says, imitating Medicine Man.

"File closed," I say.

—

We dissect, analyze, parse every word. It appears they're trying to roll a three-pronged negotiation—a prisoner exchange for Tom masked as a routine security-detainee discharge with separate British and Canadian ransom payments—into one release package. It seems like a coherent narrative, but there are two ominously discordant notes. "The British are cold," Medicine Man said. What does that mean? And the release of Rahman-whoever-he-is. That's an unrealistic demand. They'll never agree to that. (Upon our release I learn he was convicted for his involvement in the 1993 al Qaeda bombing of the World Trade Center.)

Tom is convinced this is good news. He latches on like an acrobat gripping a trapeze bar. He's so convinced, he decides to make a confession. "I didn't want to say anything until I was sure things were going to work out. I didn't want you to worry. I've been feeling sick about it, that I've put you all in danger. Maybe you saw it on the table when they filmed us with our ID. But when they kidnapped us, I had my military retirement card on me."

I turn to look at him. First I'm shocked, astounded, flabbergasted, then sick with dread. This is bad. Very very bad. "Why would you have done that?" I ask, straining to keep my voice even.

"I know, I'm sorry, it was stupid. I always thought it would be helpful if we came to an American checkpoint or had to deal with military officials. The team warned me against doing it, but I thought it might really help us sometime."

That's how he could be. Maxine will tell me a story later. Restless and a little stir-crazy after weeks of confinement in the apartment, Tom decided one evening after dark to gather some soil from the boulevard in front of the apartment so he could grow some plants on the roof. She told him not to. Military vehicles routinely passed there. Anyone watching would think he was planting an IED—Improvised Explosive Device. He could be shot on sight. But Tom, having made up his mind, did it anyway. "We all did things like that," Maxine said. "You had to sometimes. It was a way of protesting against all the restrictions the war imposed on you. But that . . . that was going too far."

# JANUARY 29 DAY 65

A month after her kidnapping, she declared on an audiotape that she had changed her name to Tania and joined her captors as a member of the Symbionese Liberation Army (SLA). Two weeks after that, she was photographed with an M1 carbine robbing a bank. A year and a half after that, she was arrested by the FBI in an SLA safe house.

I think about her constantly—Patty Hearst, the 19-year-old American newspaper heiress and socialite who became the 1974 poster child for Stockholm Syndrome, what they call it when a hostage becomes emotionally attached to her abductors and sympathizes with their aims, even to the point of defending them against law enforcement officials.

It disgusts me every time I hold out my wrist for the captors. *Here, go ahead, lock me up, I don't mind.* I feel like a trick poodle jumping through a hoop. I am making it easier for them. Easier to negotiate their goddamned ransom, buy more weapons, kill more people. Sometimes, in a storm of rage, I say to myself, *No, enough of this, I will not play your game anymore. Release me or kill me, you must decide. Until you do, I am taking my clothes off and I am going to sit here, naked, refusing everything—your food, your chains, your instructions. I would rather die than co-operate with murder.*

Perhaps if I were stronger, more courageous, had more faith, this is what I would do. But I don't. Day after day I hold out my wrist, eat their food, follow their instructions. I want to live too much. It becomes a kind of dance. Where to draw the line? How much can I co-operate without becoming an accomplice to my own captivity? It's a constant tension. I sometimes wonder if I, if we, have become like Patty Hearst, victims of Stockholm Syndrome who have internalized subservience for the sake of survival. I must continually remind myself: no, we are not the same. They are the captors and enslavers; we are the captives and slaves. Until the day our freedom is restored, we are *ipso facto* locked in existential combat. There is no escaping it.

Last night during lock-up, Uncle asked Harmeet to go and get one of the chains in the foyer. Without thinking, Harmeet went to get it. This was crossing the line. "Harmeet," I said to him later, as gently as I could, "I know it's a risk to say no when they ask for something, but

I'll never do it. They're the ones holding us captive. It's their chain. If they want to lock us up, okay, I don't have any control over that, but I'll never go and get their chain. And I don't think you should either. There's a line between us and them. We have to always remember that or else we'll lose ourselves in the captivity."

I was right, he admitted. He hadn't thought about it. He won't do it again.

Tonight, Harmeet is put to the test. Uncle is unusually playful at the start. He provokes Junior with pinching and jostling, grabs him in a headlock, forces him onto his knees by twisting his ear. When Norman passes him on his return from the bathroom—slowly, cautiously, holding on to fixed objects, so different from the vigorous man I met in Amman two months ago—Uncle steps towards him and shakes his keys in his face. "*Najis*," he taunts elfishly. "*La hubis.*" Norman eases himself onto his knees, moving as if in slow motion. "Hurry up," Uncle says, waving his hands with comedic urgency. Refusing to be hurried, Norman turns onto his back and stretches out his leg. "*Najis*," Uncle says, gripping Norman's ankle with the chain.

"Ow!" Norman protests. Uncle laughs and yanks Norman's leg. "That's my leg!" Norman cries out, his voice breaking with anger.

Uncle sits down, chortling as if this is the funniest thing. He points to the foyer. "*Zengeel, zengeel,*" he says, ordering Harmeet to go and get the other chain.

Harmeet shakes his head. "This *haram*."

"*Haram?*" Uncle says, getting up from his chair, indignant and threatening. He clamps a giant hand around Harmeet's crossed forearms and squeezes as hard as he can. "*Haram?*" he repeats, hoping to force Harmeet to cry out in pain. Harmeet looks at him, silent as a stone. Uncle lets go and reaches for Norman's chain, but Norman pulls it away before he can grab it. "*Najis*," Uncle cries. Junior slaps his knee with laughter.

"*Haram!*" Norman says, his voice a foot stomping down. "Old man. I'm an old man!"

Uncle tosses his keys at Junior and storms out of the room. After this, the *najis* treatment ends.

—

"Uncle is definitely angry," Tom says, reflecting later on Uncle's antics during lock-up.

"What do you mean?" I say. We do it all the time, analyze and parse our captors' moods, their glances and gestures, what they say and don't say, alert for any sign of danger or release. We test and formulate different hypotheses gleaned from our various perceptions and understandings, always searching for the most accurate interpretation. We have to get it right. The smallest misunderstanding could be lethal.

"He's always saying it," Tom says. "He's angry because there's no *hubis*." *La hubis*. No money. Uncle says it every night. Sometimes it's an explanation, sometimes it's a tease or a promise. Yes, I think, Uncle was angry, but it wasn't about ransom money. It was because Norman and Harmeet defied him. I try to explain this, but Tom refuses to consider any other explanation. He insists it's because there is no money. I'm perplexed, irritated, concerned. His perceptions are becoming more and more fixed, his mind closed, his judgment askew. If he is unable to adjust his thinking in this matter of little importance, what will happen in a matter of life and death?

## JANUARY 30 DAY 66

I'm awakened by a shaft of lantern light pouring into the room. We're unlocked! My body goes instantly to red alert. It takes me a second to realize it's only Tom, kneeling at the edge of our bed, readying himself to pee into the *hamam* bottle. There's a sudden clattering sound. "Sorry," he whispers. He's knocked the bottle over. I hold my breath and listen intently for the captors.

I hear Tom removing the lid of the pop bottle, a soft click as he places it on the floor, the brittle crinkling of plastic, urine streaming into a bottle. "I'm sorry to disturb you like this," he says. "It must be the acid in my stomach." I wince. His voice is too loud.

"It's okay, you don't have to apologize," Harmeet whispers. Tom closes the door and settles back under his covers.

A sudden rush of fear. I'm not sure. I think I can hear something, a noise from downstairs. Every cell in my body listens. I hear rustling. Tom is standing up. I'm about to say something when there's a sudden racket of chain hitting the floor.

"Tom!" I whisper fiercely.

"It's all right," he says. "The chain's all knotted up."

*Please, Tom—be quiet!*

He cracks the door open again. "I need a bit of light. The chain's all knotted up." I hear it again. Now I'm sure. Voices, movement at the bottom of the stairs, very soft. I lift my head from the pillow. Another thud of chain falling. I can feel the vibration of it in the floor.

"Tom!" I hiss.

"It's all right. I'm just unknotting the chain." His voice is much too loud.

"LISTEN!" I whisper-shout. He drops the chain again. "TOM! STOP!" I hiss.

He stops. I listen. Nothing. After a minute I hear a door closing. The danger has passed, thank God. I rest my head back on the pillow, shaking with rage.


"*Najis!*" Junior says, pinching his nose as he enters the room. He rushes to open the window and turns to us with an angry gale of Arabic. The contempt on his face tells me everything I need to know.

Uncle stands at the door dressed in civvies: collared shirt and suit jacket—even shoes. He talks briefly with Junior before leaving. Junior kicks off his sandals, steps onto our bed and bends down to unlock Norman's ankle, his face writhing with disgust. When the lock clicks open, Junior stands above him with his hands on his hips, lecturing. He unlocks the rest of us and leaves in a huff.

"It looks like somebody has some time off," Harmeet says, referring to Uncle's brief appearance. "My arms are bruised where he grabbed me."

"He promised we could do laundry today," Tom says. "I'll check that with Junior. It'll break up the day."

"I don't know, Tom. He seemed pretty grouchy this morning," Harmeet warns.

"It won't hurt to have a try," Tom says.

Harmeet asks Tom how he slept. Not well, he answers, even with the medicine. He doesn't think it's working. I look at him closely. He's glassy-eyed, disconnected, moving like he's under water. He asks if he can use the bathroom first. Go for it, we say.

I gather Harmeet and Norman together. I'm really concerned about Tom, I say. It's like he's in a fog all the time, and it's getting worse. Last night, when I thought I heard noises downstairs, he wouldn't stop rattling that damned chain. We have to keep our wits about us if we're going to have any chance of surviving. We have to talk with him, I say, get him to cut back on the Valium. Norman and Harmeet agree. They nominate me. I reluctantly agree.

My mood immediately changes when I walk into the middle of the foyer for morning exercise. The sunlight pouring down the stairway is pure therapy. I lift my hands into the open-air space of the foyer and begin my stretching routine. *It's great to be alive,* I want to shout.

Tom emerges from the bathroom. Norman goes in carrying our water bottle and metal cups. Tom walks straight towards Junior. "*Sabha il hare,*" he says.

"*Sabha il noor,*" Junior grunts without looking up from the cellphone.

"How did you sleep last night? *Nam zane?*" Tom asks.

Junior shakes his head. "*Mozane. Kool y um mozane.*"

"This no sleep too," Tom says, pointing to himself. "*Kool y um mozane nam.*" Junior doesn't answer. "Are we going to be able to do laundry today? Laundry? *Frook hind?*" Tom asks, demonstrating with his hands.

"No," Junior says, still not looking up.

"*Mbarha,* yesterday, *haji* say, 'Today laundry.' *El yom* laundry."

Junior looks up from his cellphone. "What this, *mbarha* laundry? No *mbarha* laundry. No laundry *el yom.*"

"Yes," Tom insists. "*Haji* told us we could do laundry today. El *yom* laundry."

Junior stands up and faces Tom. He makes it very clear: he's the one in charge today and there will be no laundry.

"Tom," I say, my voice soft.

Tom stands over Junior and thrusts out his chest. "You go ask him. He'll tell you. He said we could do laundry." His voice is hot, his finger points.

"No laundry," Junior says menacingly.

"Tom! Drop it!" I say.

The two men stare at each other. Tom turns away. Junior glares angrily.

"I'm sorry for what happened last night," Tom says after Junior has locked us up. "The chain was all knotted up. I just can't seem to sleep. I don't know why, but my chain seems to get twisted around all the time."

God, I think. We need to talk about this. I clear my throat. "I *am* a little concerned about what happened last night. We weren't hand-cuffed and I heard noises downstairs—"

"It's all right," Tom blurts, cutting me off. "The chain was just knotted. I didn't hear anything when I opened the door. The coast was clear."

"But Tom, your hearing isn't very good. Especially lately. I'm—"

"I was just trying to unknot the chain. It's all right. Next time I'll be more careful."

"Tom, you're not listening."

Tom turns towards me, daggers shooting from his eyes. "That's enough! Drop it!" he orders. He looks ready to leap out of his chair. I grip the arms of my chair and lean towards him, jaw clenching. "I'm warning you—drop it!" Tom threatens.

Our eyes lock. *Don't do this*, a voice cautions. I take a breath and force my shoulders to relax. "All right," I say, sitting back in my chair. For a long time my body trembles with rage.

—

Harmeet flicks his nails, Norman shifts in his chair, Tom cracks his shoulders. The silence is unbearable. I stare at the brown stains on the bedsheet curtain and concentrate on my breathing. I try to step back, disengage, separate from the conflict, but my mind spirals helplessly, accusation around blame, blame around accusation. It seems impossible. We'll never find a way through this. It makes me despair for the world. If we can't do it, find a way to reconcile, when our survival depends on it and we share a common commitment to non-violence, what hope is there for those whose enmity is written in blood? Tutsi and Hutu, Palestinian and Jew, Croat and Serb.

"Would anyone care for a drink of water?" Norman asks.

Yes, Harmeet says. Sure, Tom says. I can't answer. Not yet. The words won't come. Jim? Norman asks.

"I'd love some, thank you," I manage to say.

Norman pours the water and we pass the cup. He suggests we play the tic-tac-toe game. I turn my mind to the task of laying my cards in rows of five. We play three rounds. When we're done, I take a furtive glance in Tom's direction. He's looking down at his hands. I'm calm now. It's time. I ask him if we can talk. Sure, he says, but not right now. Sometime this afternoon. Our eyes meet. Thanks, that would be great, I say. He nods.

I've prepared my words carefully. Something that's open-ended and doesn't accuse, something that invites. "You reacted really strongly this morning," I say. "I'm curious to know what was going on for you— why you reacted so strongly."

"I felt like I was being verbally assaulted." He pauses. "But I guess really it's the frustration of this chain. Night and day, for sixty days or however long it's been. I try not to let it get to me. At night sometimes the chain gets all knotted up. I'm not sure how it happens—maybe it's the way I sleep, or maybe the chain is too short—and then I can't get my arm in a comfortable position. Anyway, last night I cracked the door open so I could have a bit of light to use the hamam bottle. I was listening to hear if the captors were coming and I didn't hear anything, so I knew everything was fine. When I closed the door and tried to rearrange myself in these crazy blankets, the chain got all knotted up. I thought maybe I could quickly untangle it. I guess I should've asked everyone to lock up first."

"You said it a few times: 'It's all right, it's all right.' What did you mean by that?" I ask.

"I just meant that it's all right, next time I'll make sure the chain doesn't get knotted."

"My concern is that your hearing isn't very good, especially lately. I thought I could hear something downstairs and I wanted you to stop making noise so I could make sure."

"It's all right, I—"

"Would you *please* stop saying that!" I shout. "It's not 'all right'! We were—" I force myself to lower my voice. "We were unhandcuffed. If they had found us like that, it would have been game over. I asked you to stop doing something that I thought was putting us in danger. And you kept on doing it!"

"I'm sorry, it's just that the chain was—"

"I know—all knotted up, and you could hear what was going on, and everything was fine." I stop to take a breath. "You've had it the hardest of all of us, the way they treat you, especially Junior. I have no idea what it would be like to be chained up all the time. You're in the most danger of all of us. But none of us has all the information we need, and our survival depends on being able to make the best decisions that we can. And that means having the best information we can get. Your hearing isn't very good, which means there's stuff you're going to miss. So next time, when someone asks you to stop so that they can hear what's going on—please—for God's sake—STOP!"

"Okay," Tom says. His shoulders fall and his face is contrite. My anger starts to relent.

"Well, for next time," Norman says, "we should just lock up if we are at all worried. Don't wait."

I am staggered. He's right. By hesitating, I put us in more danger than Tom had. "I'm sorry. I never thought of it. I don't know why. That's what I should've done—locked up right away."

"Better to be safe than sorry," Harmeet says.

I turn towards Tom. "Is there anything else? Your reaction was so strong. I'm wondering if there's something else going on, if something's been building up."

No, he says. But there is something else for me. The Valium. I decide to wait. There's been enough turmoil for one day.

# JANUARY 31 DAY 67

Late in the afternoon, Medicine Man enters our room accompanied by Junior and Nephew. He pulls eight hard candies wrapped in gold and silver foil out of his pocket and puts them on the *zowagi* cube. Junior gives us each two.

"I bring you some copy book," Medicine Man says, presenting us each with a child's school notebook, each with a different cover. Mine is an arrangement of plastic purple flowers ringed by a diamond-studded gold necklace. I flip through 120 pages of breathtaking blank-space freedom. I can hardly contain myself. I want to start immediately, playing, leaping, wild cartwheeling-around-in-words.

Junior points to Harmeet. "Father in television," he says, laughing. "This *Hind*." Junior and Nephew mock, ridiculing with their hands his father's turban and handlebar moustache.

"My father was on television?" Harmeet asks.

"Yes, he make some appeal for you," Medicine Man says. Then to me, "Your brothers also on television. And I think maybe your sister-in-law? Is that the proper word?"

"My sister-in-law? Donna? On television?" I ask, incredulous.

Junior points at me excitedly. "*Umma* in television. *Umma hazeen*." My heart breaks. My mother on television? I can't imagine what this must be like for my parents. What comes next I don't fully understand—something about my mother pleading and crying, and a rally for me, "In *Canadi*! In *Canadi*!" with lots and lots of people, all carrying signs, chanting "Jim! Jim!"

Nephew tilts his head and makes a sad face. "Your daughter on television," he says to Tom. Tom nods, face expressionless.

"And you, Doctor," Medicine Man says to Norman. "Your madame on television, and your daughter, and baby."

"That must be my grandson, Benjamin!" Norman cries.

"You very famous. Very famous, all of you," Medicine Man says.

I'm astounded. Communication is happening through the television, an electronic message in a bottle for each of us, released by our families and beamed around the world, received by our captors and delivered to us in person. All through the television.

"We don't want to be famous," Norman says. "We want to go home."

"Three day, four day, and you release," Medicine Man says. "Now I must to go. Is there something else?"

No, we say. Medicine Man says goodbye and the captors leave.

"I wish they hadn't told us," Harmeet says, referring to the appearance of our families on television.

"I concur," Norman says. We fall into a silence bitter with remembering.

# CHAPTER TWELVE

## FEBRUARY 1 DAY 68

It's 8:30 a.m. I'm sitting against the wall with my notebook open on my right thigh. Harmeet is lying next to me with his left arm bent into his chest so I can write. I grip the pen in my fingers. How does it happen? It is astonishing, miraculous even, the invisible current of mind that moves through arm into hand, the dexterity of hand holding pen, the rolling-up-and-down-looping-around flow of pen that lays down letter, the accumulation of letter into word, word into sentence, sentence into paragraph.

*Gross! I write. We've been here over nine weeks. MM came to visit yesterday. Says three or four days more. They're waiting on some money from Canada, and maybe the release of two more women . . . and some other vague "small things." The same song and dance he's fed us since the beginning of our captivity.*

For the first time since our abduction I am excited about the day ahead. I write furiously, breathlessly, greedily. It is pure balm and sheer relief. To move beyond and outside the stifling prison-world of mind. With my pen I can go anywhere, do anything. My notebook is like a magic carpet.

I will have to be careful. I must assume they will see whatever I write. I will write sloppily, in point form, with lots of idiosyncratic abbreviations. Reading it will be difficult, especially for anyone whose first language is not English. Hopefully it will require so much effort they won't bother to try. I must not become attached to keeping it. They will almost certainly take the notebooks away.

Now, with pen and paper, everything about the captivity is suddenly charged with a new significance. The light filtering through the curtains, the sounds of Baghdad outside, the paint-peeling walls, the strange collection of things in our room—I must document everything, every gesture and movement, every interaction and word.

I begin by itemizing the fifteen things that make up our bed. I draw a diagram showing how it is put together and the way we are shackled at night.

Junior enters the room. *"Hamam!"* he barks grouchily. I discreetly close my notebook. "What this? Copy book?" He takes the book and opens it. He bursts into laughter. "What this?" he asks, pointing to my drawing.

It's us, sleeping, lying in bed, I say. He laughs delightedly. Then, seeing the chain I've drawn between Tom's and Norman's feet, his face folds into a frown. "What this?" he asks. My face turns red. It's the chain, I say. Junior shakes his finger. "No," he says. *"Mujahedeen* good." He points to the picture. "This give copy book to *shorta* in Canada. *Mooshkilla."*

"This no *killam.* No *killam* police in Canada," I say.

*"Zane,"* he says, satisfied.


We emerge from our room into the foyer for morning exercise. Junior is sitting on the blue folding chair, absorbed in playing a game on his cellphone. I begin my stretching routine. "What this?" Junior asks, suddenly looking up. I'm standing on one leg, foot braced against the inside of my thigh, arms reaching above my head like an arrow.

"Yoga," I say.

He gets up and stands in front of me, so close I can see traces of red in his beard, flecks of gold in his eyes. He makes a smooching sound and pinches my waist. I lose my balance. "This yoga?" he asks, pointing his arms above his head in imitation of my pose. Our eyes meet. He's standing so close. If I wanted to, I could kiss him on the cheek, or smash him with my head.

"Yes," I say. I look away, pretend he's not there. He drops his arms and steps back.

The sensation of his touch lingers at my waist. It's a strangely intimate encounter. It's as if, for a moment, the boundary between us disappeared, and he was simply a friend spontaneously expressing affection. Who is this man? I wonder. He is my captor and enemy, but he is also a flesh-and-blood human being, a child of God just like me. He's volatile, erratic, immature, in one instant playful, enthusiastic, singing, the next sullen, contemptuous, abusive. Prone to rages at any moment. At times more boy than man. Dread and trepidation follow in his steps. I can hardly stand the sight of him. We sit on eggshells whenever he is on guard duty.

Today is the perfect example. At breakfast I ask if we can write in our notebooks. His face lights up. "Na'am, na'am. Copy book, copy book!" he says. He removes our handcuffs and calls our names in a prim schoolteacher's voice as he distributes our books. He paces back and forth with his hands held pedagogically behind his back, stopping now and then to ask a question or to comment.

"What this?" he asks Harmeet.

"Email. For mother and father."

"This shwaya," he says, referring to the size of Harmeet's handwriting. "What this?" he demands of Norman.

"It's a letter to my wife. For madame."

"Good Doctors, good copy book," he says.

He takes my notebook and shows it to Nephew. They snort and laugh at the diagram I've drawn. The mujahedeen are good, he tells me. I must only write good things about them, that they bring us tea, cook us good food and are always nice to us. Yes, I promise, I will only write good things.

"Talib good," he says, handing my book back approvingly. He turns towards Tom and puts his hands on his hips. "This talib no good," he scolds marmishly, clicking his tongue as he leafs through Tom's notebook. I want to roll my eyes at this stupid game.

In the early afternoon we hear him whistling in the stairway. *What now?* I think. He enters bearing an ornate aluminum tray, our lunch, a large bowl of steaming soup ringed with four spoons and four samoons. Can this really be for us? It is!

He sets the tray on the zowagi cube and points to himself proudly. "Write this in copy book. Mujahedeen make soup." He folds his hands like an altar boy, closes his eyes and makes us repeat, "Bismillah al-Rahman al-Rahim."

Though starving, we sit with our hands on our laps. No one wants to be the first. "How are we going to make sure everyone gets a fair share?" Tom asks.

"It'll be okay," I say. "Just keep an eye out for the slowest person and eat at their pace."

Junior glares at us. "Eat," he barks irritably. We fill our spoons and eat. It's extravagantly delicious: tomato-mutton soup flavoured with basil and numibasra. I could eat a thousand bowls of it. We thank him profusely. He smiles grandly, as if pleasing us is his only purpose. Then, seeing Norman eat his bread with his left hand, he explodes with gestures and lecturing.

In the long of the afternoon he appears twice more, first with a small plastic bottle. He wants to know what it is. The label says *Men's Gel*. "Maybe it's for your hair," I say, spiking my bangs. He looks at me blankly. I turn the bottle over. "'Directions,'" I read. "'Apply before sexual intercourse.'"

"*Shoo?* What this?" Junior says, tugging my arm, unable to repress his curiosity.

"We call it lube," I tell him. Junior doesn't understand. My face reddens. "Lube. It's for sex." His eyes widen.

"With madame," Norman adds.

Junior's face lights up like a Christmas tree. "Sex? With madame?" he cries. He wants to know how it works.

"Well," I say, grasping for words. "You . . . ah . . . put it on before sex." He doesn't understand. I use my hands to demonstrate. Junior runs joyous out of the room, as if he's just won the lottery.

He returns ten minutes later looking puzzled. "Friend, friend," is all we understand. He mimes a big belly and points downstairs. He's talking about Nephew. He rubs his groin, armpits and wrists, showing us where Nephew has applied the men's gel. There's some kind of problem. It's not working. "*Mooshkilla. Leaish?*"

Junior looks at me intently. My face feels hot. I can't believe this is happening. Sex education for insurgents. No, I say, forming a circle with my thumb and index finger. I dangle the index finger of my other hand in imitation of a flaccid penis. The gel has to go on the penis before it goes into the vagina, I explain, sliding a stiffened finger through the circle. He laughs hysterically and runs shouting to Nephew downstairs.

An hour later, we hear him in the stairwell, laughing. Fear surges through my body. We look at each other uneasily. He sounds unhinged, berserk. It happens again. He pokes his head through the door, his face a grinning mask of evil. He stands in front of Tom, legs apart and arms extended, hands wrapped around a gun, eyes murderous. "*Ammmrrriikki,*" he growls, pointing the gun at Tom's head.

"Hello," Tom says, holding his poker face up like a shield. Junior snarls and disappears.

"Are you okay, Tom?" Harmeet asks.

"Yeah. I'm okay," he says, his voice firm and steady, matter-of-fact. "It's the bombing of his house, losing his family. He's traumatized. I'm the symbol of all that. I'm the enemy. When I walk around Baghdad, I watch people watching me. I look military. It's the way I dress, my hair-cut, my manner. Twenty years of military service does that to you."

This explains it, I think. Junior is a traumatized boy, a victim. To be a victim is to endure intolerable shame, humiliation without end, the worst possible thing. A boy who is a victim, in order to become a man, must prove he is not a victim. The clenched fist, the gun, the erect penis, these hard exhibitions of power that climax in the domination of the other, they all say the same thing. See, I am the one who acts, decides, controls, penetrates. See, I am not a victim. I am a man. If you do not believe me, I will show you. Fist, gun or cock, whatever it takes, you will be my victim, or I will die with honour trying. This is how it is for a boy who is a victim: through violence he becomes a man.

I am obsessed. I write feverishly, in point form and scattershot sentences. By the end of the day I have filled fourteen pages with my dense scribbles. I take the book to bed with me, in case Harmeet is awake in the morning and doesn't mind sitting up again so I can write.

The next two days are a blur. I am consumed, swallowed whole in writing. We are a dramatis personae of four hostages and three guards, seven characters in a strange hallucinatory drama where nothing ever happens, actors on a stage no one will ever see.

Seven! We are seven! The biblical number for wholeness and completion. Everything universal and true, everything I need to know to become a whole and complete human being is available to me right here in this room. I don't need to go or be anywhere else. I must write. Every particularity and detail is crucial. I must write it all down before we are released. It can happen at any time.

# FEBRUARY 3 DAY 70

Thank God, Uncle has returned from captor leave. Of all the guards, he has done the most to improve the conditions of our captivity. He was the one who arranged for us to bathe, wash our clothes, trim our beards, the one who rigged up the electric heater, found an old rug to cut the draft under the door, brought Norman a more comfortable chair. "It's because of his days looking after prisoners. He knows what needs to be done," Harmeet says. Uncle told us once he'd been in charge of a group of prisoners during the Iran–Iraq War, when he was a conscript in Saddam's army. Now he receives a regular pension. "*Hubis zane,*" he told us proudly—good money. We asked him what his work was. "Garden, garden," he said, moving his arms as if working a hoe.

We live in a state of continuous apprehension. It spikes every time a captor appears. We never know what their arrival might portend: doom, freedom, nothing at all. Despite this, I usually don't mind when Uncle wanders in to check on us. Sometimes when he enters it is with an agile turn and kick, as though he's dancing a soccer ball on his toes. Sometimes he is silent as a stone, and he'll sit staring at the floor deep in thought, or look at us with a cryptic smile, shake his head with what seems to be a kind of fondness, then leave again without having said a word. Sometimes we'll hear him in the foyer, announcing his arrival with strange blowing and slurping sounds, or if the door is closed he will open it a crack and just his hand will appear, fingers counting down—three, two, one—before he steps into the room. Sometimes it is for just a moment, to open the window or pull the curtain back an inch or two, allowing us a taste

of fresh air and sunlight, and sometimes it is for an extended conversation. He'll mime different animals and ask us their English
names. It's like playing charades. Do foxes live in Canada? he'll ask.
How much does an ostrich egg weigh? Whales are good, they like to
swim—can you swim in Canada? In Iraq we swim all the time. "*Furat,
Furat,*" he says.

He'll spray bug repellent in wild arcs about the room. "*La, la,*" we
protest, coughing. He'll hunt mosquitoes relentlessly and show us their
squashed bodies in his palm. He'll bark, snort, neigh, smack his lips.
"Shhewww, shhewww," he'll say to get our attention. He picks his nose
habitually, even when handling our food. He spits pumpkin seeds, date
pits, excesses of saliva and phlegm onto the floor. He likes smelling the
tips of his fingers, lifting and smoothing the elastic band of his track
pants, patting his substantial belly. Whenever we ask him if there is any
news, his answer is either "*Hubis, hubis*" or his plane-taking-off gesture,
the palm of one hand lifting off from the back of the other hand
accompanied by a whooshing sound. In sharp contrast to Junior, Uncle
is indifferent to Tom, indifferent to all of us in fact. He is a soldier with
a job to do. The particularities of who we are mean nothing to him.
"It's almost like we're his crops," Harmeet says. Only once do we catch
a glimpse of his true feelings. It happens while he is handcuffing us.
His eyes are momentarily apologetic. These are *haji*'s orders, he says.
If it was up to him, he wouldn't lock us up.

Today he asks me what my house in Canada looks like. I draw him
a picture in my notebook of a two-storey brick house with big bay
windows and a peaked roof. He asks for my notebook and pen,
draws a picture of his own home. It's long, rectangular, flat-roofed,
with a second storey jutting up in the middle. There are five windows,
one door, a satellite dish and an antenna on the roof, gases rising
from a metal chimney. The house is surrounded by trees and vines.
In front of it is a wall that extends across the page, with a gate in
the middle. In front of the wall is a road. In the middle of the road,
to the right of the gate, sits a vehicle. It looks like a truck. There's
someone inside the truck.

I ask him if he'll go back to working in his garden after we're released. Yes, he says. First he pulls an imaginary hoe, then he fashions his hand into a gun. He alternates between hoe and gun, urgently, hastily. He is farmer and warrior both. He points to the vehicle in his picture, eyes darkening with rage. He repeats the story over and over. We glean what we can from the handful of Arabic words we know, his gestures and body language. He was stopped by U.S. soldiers on the road outside his house. They made him get out of his car, searched him, forced him to lie on the road face down with his hands folded behind his head. In his good clothes. In the hot sun. For three hours. One of the soldiers put his boot on his head. His face turns purple. He says they forced a woman who was with him, perhaps a member of his family, to breastfeed in public. The soldiers pointed their guns at him, and at the woman. Yes, at a woman! He used to be only a farmer, he tells us, but now he must be a *mujahedeen* too. As long as there are Americans in his country.

Junior brings us "lunch," a stale piece of crumbling flatbread wrapped around some very dry rice, and leaves immediately. I look at it glumly and take a bite. The bread breaks into little pieces and rice free-falls onto the floor. I sweep the rice under my chair with my feet so it'll be out of view. Junior will go ballistic if he sees it. It enrages me. We're in handcuffs and somehow we're supposed to eat these damned scraps without making a mess. There's no way to avoid it.

I look over to see how the others are doing. Harmeet is managing okay. Norman eats whatever falls on the floor. Tom chews mechanically and stares into the distance, oblivious to the rice dropping at his feet. I want to snap my fingers and shout: *Wake up! Can't you see this is only going to make your situation worse?*

Junior returns before I'm able to say anything. He flies into a tantrum. "La Islami, la Islami," he storms, pointing his finger.

"The rice is very dry and the bread is stale," I say as calmly as I can. "We're doing our best, but it's impossible to eat without spilling it."

"*Najis!*" He scowls, sensing I've somehow objected to his insistence on manners. He castigates and we, looking chastened, bend down and clean up the rice. And this is how it works, I think bitterly; here the blindness of the oppressor is revealed, the one who steals life away, debases, if necessary kills. Always it is for the sake of some great project. Sometimes he calls it Civilization, sometimes Democracy or Progress or Truth. If he is religious, he might call it a Crusade or a Jihad. Whatever its name, always by definition it is just.

The oppressor takes the great project seriously. He gives his life to it. It anchors and grounds him, makes him feel good and important, like a real Somebody. Until he is confronted by his antithesis, the one he oppresses, whose degradation and squalor arise as a necessary consequence of the great project. Then, disturbed and dismayed, the oppressor turns spontaneously to contempt. The oppressed is an offence. His existence contradicts and interrogates the great project. This cannot be. The oppressor points his finger in accusation. He does this to protect himself from responsibility, separate himself from the thing he has caused. You are filthy, disgusting, contemptible, he will say. Take a bath, get a job, get a life. Pull yourself together. Use bootstraps if that's all you have. Do this or perish.

The oppressor does not see that his pointing finger is a projection, the exteriorization of something interior. His pointing finger shields him from a truth he dare not admit, that his great project is a lie, that it is the generator of the very thing he despises. The oppressor is like the white-skinned good citizen who sits in horrified judgment of the brown-skinned failed citizen who lies in his streets and on his park benches reeking of alcohol and despair. The good citizen mutters among his own kind, debates solutions in his newspapers and town halls, affirms his good intentions. He passes laws and institutes social welfare programs. When all of this fails to remove the objectionable thing he has brought into being, he grits his teeth and sweeps the failed citizen away. It could be a jail or a ghetto or a reservation, it doesn't matter where, just so long as he is no longer seen. The oppressor does not know that before he arrived with his great project, before the forests were cleared and the park benches and the liquor bottles were unpacked from his bags, the so-called failed citizen had no knowledge or need of alcohol and park benches, because he was at home and lived free in his own land. This is the blindness of the oppressor in every time and every place. He does not see that he himself is the disease, the harbinger of what he reviles.

That night, Tom observes that we have neglected daily prayer and check-in since the notebooks arrived. We all agree that we have to get back on track. Tom starts off the check-in. He says this is the lowest he's been—physically, spiritually and emotionally—since the captivity started. The lack of food, his inability to sleep, Junior's antics; there comes a point when somebody pointing a gun at your head stops being funny. He knows this whole thing is going to end, but when, and what state is he going to be in when it does? He wants to hit the ground running. There's going to be media, decisions to make, everything moving so fast after all this time of nothing happening. He's resolved to work as hard as he can to maintain his connection to God and heal the negative energy he's afflicted with. He concludes by saying he's decided to cut back to one Valium a day. He says he's in a haze all the time; he thinks it's just making him more depressed.

I'm so relieved. There's no longer any need for the confrontation I'd been dreading—and avoiding.

Norman says he's been reconstructing the itinerary of each of his thirteen trips to France in his notebook. Otherwise, he's just trying to disappear in his little corner, trying not to think too much. He says it's sad to think of all the time that's being wasted, how at seventy-five every moment is precious. Baptist spirituality isn't cutting it, he says, at least not here, with its triumphalism and easy answers. He thinks he's becoming an atheist.

As usual, Harmeet doesn't say very much. We're still here, he says, things have been tense with Junior, things will be easier now that Uncle is back. He's been using his notebook to make a list of all the things he needs to do when he gets home. His semester starts in three days. He's missed the deadline; there's no way he can enrol now even if they release us tomorrow.

Our lives are passing us by.

# FEBRUARY 4 DAY 71

"*Shid gul?*" Junior asks us, appearing in the doorway with a stump of cigarette pinched between his fingers.

"*Minundra ani gulak,*" we say, using the reply he taught us.

He takes a last campy drag and flicks the butt into the foyer. "This *zane,*" he says, tracing a path from his nose to his lungs. He flips open the top of a cigarette package and drops two pieces of silver foil on the floor. "This Virginia Smooooth," he purrs, offering each of us a cigarette.

No thank you, we say. He looks vaguely disappointed, pockets the cigarettes and unlocks us for an afternoon *hamam* break. On his way to the bathroom, Norman stoops down to pick up the foil wrappers. He saves everything: the Sensodyne toothpaste box, his empty blood-pressure-medicine packages, the plastic bag our shoes came in. "You never know when you might need something," he once said, after I'd asked him about this habit.

After my turn in the bathroom, I'm astonished to find Junior sitting in my chair yakking away. For a moment I wonder if we have somehow exchanged roles. "Jim!" he exclaims, jumping up when he sees me. "Massage, massage!"

This has become an almost daily occurrence. I want to say no, establish a boundary, tell him I am not his personal masseur. Instead I laugh. "Come on, Jim," he pleads. He sits on the blue folding chair so that he is facing Tom and Norman and Harmeet. He motions for me to stand behind him. I place my hands on his shoulders. How interesting, I think. This is what the captors see when they stand in front of us, over us, above us: four sad, gaunt-looking men wearing black hats, beards and soiled, misshapen clothing. So easy to disdain. We have to be so careful what we say through our faces. They can reveal so much.

I look at my fellow captives and then down at Junior's neck. It would be so easy. To take my hands and crush his windpipe. I chase these thoughts away and, as I always do before I begin, close my eyes, breathe deeply and surround Junior with God's light. *Remember, you are giving him a gift*, I tell myself. *It is when you can no longer do this that you must say no, or accept that you have become a slave.*

"*Shlonik?*" Junior asks Harmeet as I strip the muscles in his shoulders and neck, tight like piano strings.

"*Noos-noos,*" Harmeet says, shrugging his shoulders. Junior asks why. Harmeet imitates Uncle's plane-taking-off gesture. "New Zealand," he says. "No mother, no father, no sister." Junior forms his hands into a machine gun and pretends to fire it at Harmeet. Fear passes through me like a cold wind. Is Junior saying they intend to kill us?

"That's *qatil*. That's murder," Harmeet says.

"This *mujahedeen*," Junior says, insisting that they only kill "*jaysh Amriki.*" He turns to Norman. "Doctors, *shlonik?*"

"Oh, well, I should think I've been better," Norman answers.

"*Leaish?* This no madame?"

"Sadly, yes, no madame."

"I am sorry, Doctors," Junior says. Then, making a sad face, he points to Tom. "What this? This *mozane?*"

Tom nods. Junior asks why. Tom says it's because he can't sleep. Junior points to himself, "This no sleep last night. *La nam,*" he says.

This is important information. If Junior is awake at night, any escape attempt will be exceedingly perilous. As if reading my mind, Harmeet seeks to clarify this with Junior. "*Mbhara?* Yesterday no sleep?"

The word "yesterday" fills me with a grim melancholy. Yesterday, when our lives were our own. Seized by an impulse, I begin to sing the old Beatles song.

"More," Junior says when I'm finished, clapping with delight.

I look at Norman, Harmeet and Tom, hoping they can think of something. They can't. "Amazing Grace" suddenly comes to mind. I begin to sing and they join me.

"Good, good," Junior says when we've finished. "More, more."

# FEBRUARY 6 DAY 73

I take off my shirt in front of the bathroom mirror and run the palm of my hand across my ribs and abdominal muscles. I'm intrigued by the body facing me in the mirror, the bones pushing through a thin veil of skin: clavicle, sternum, ribs, pelvis. I'm turning more and more each day into a skeleton. I wonder how much I weigh, how much more I'm going to lose, if I should be alarmed.

We are hungry, always always hungry. We wake up to it, sit all day in it, sleep in it. The gnawing aching burning empty hollow tingling of it ebbs and flows but never ceases. It is an ugly and detestable sensation that clamours in every molecule of my body. Our minds and bodies are oriented towards the hope of more food the way a compass needle points north.

We've become weak, listless, brittle with fatigue. My heart pounds with the smallest exertion. I must husband my energy carefully during morning exercise. Mass-muscular activity, climbing the first stage of the roof stairway for example, something the captors have recently allowed, is immensely tiring. Three ascents of eleven stairs and my knees are buckling. By the end of the half-hour I'm trembling, light-headed, breathless. It takes most of the morning to recover.

Harmeet asked me if I thought we were being fed a starvation diet. No, I said, horrified at the thought. What they got at Birkenau and Auschwitz, a bowl of watery nettle soup, that's a starvation diet, I said. But then I considered our daily ration: three *samoons* stuffed with an egg-sized portion of potato or rice or the occasional morsel of hot dog. What's that, maybe six hundred calories a day? That's less than a quarter of what an adult male requires. It's enough to keep us going, but not much more.

It perplexes me, why they continually give us so little to eat. A second *samoon* would make such a difference. It can't be that there's not enough food. The captors' waistlines are expanding. It's most noticeable on Junior; once quite lean, he's growing soft and pudgy.

Uncle and Nephew both complain about it. "*Kabir. Mozane,*" Uncle once said, pulling back on his track jacket to show us his growing belly. "*Akeel, nam, akeel, nam. Mozane.*" All they do is eat and sleep.

Nephew too pulled up his shirt to reveal a giant expanse of stomach. "This *kabir. Kabir mooshkilla,*" he said. Harmeet smoothed his sweater against his abdomen to demonstrate how thin he'd got. "*Shwaya,*" he said. "*Shwaya mooshkilla.*" Nephew shook his head and sucked in his stomach. "No," he said, "*shwaya zane.*" I could hardly contain my rage. Don't they know how hungry we are? If they do, they must not care, or else this is what they want; they've figured out that famished hostages are more compliant, easier to control, less likely to fight back or escape. Tom thinks it's because they get a food allowance from Medicine Man and they're spending it on themselves instead of us.

Maybe, if we tell them, they might give us a little more, I say. We debate and scheme endlessly, when and how and who. Each of us resolves to do it, but none of us can. It's impossible to actually say the words: *We are hungry.* It is inexplicably humiliating.

Yesterday, when we were lying in bed, Nephew presented Harmeet with a yellow plastic bag. "*Akeel,*" he said benevolently. I couldn't believe it. They never do this, give us extra food.

"Oh," Harmeet said, his voice strangely flat, "it's some bread."

"Can I see?" I asked, wildly hopeful, visualizing a fresh-baked *samoon* for each of us. I immediately understood Harmeet's disappointment when I saw what was in the bag—a handful of scraps, all different sizes, some splashed with tomato sauce, some with teeth marks, the remains of what they'd eaten for supper, probably to the point of discomfort.

We said thank you and waited for the captors to leave. We didn't want them to see how hungry we were. We watched, eyes riveted to each piece of bread as Harmeet divided the bread into four strictly equal portions. No one ate until Harmeet gave us the sign: "Bon appétit, gentlemen."

I chewed ravenously, eyes staring hard into the distance. I forced myself not to think about how much I needed and wanted this bread, how it had passed through our captors' hands, how they'd torn it from their lips and left it on their plates for garbage. The humiliation of it was unbearable.

—

The day is long. I make lists.

### Some Things You Can Do While Handcuffed
#### (Without the Assistance of the Person You're Handcuffed To)

pray

breathe

rub your fingers together

cross your legs

wiggle your fingers and toes

sigh

slouch

sit up straight

rotate your shoulders

stick out your tongue

make a fist

forgive

use one foot to scratch the
    other foot

cough

dream about being free

### Some Things You Can't Do While Handcuffed
#### (Without the Assistance of the Person You're Handcuffed To)

rub your eyes

scratch your head

stretch your hand above your
   head

pick up something you
   dropped on the floor

drink from a glass of water

zip up your zipper

tie your shoes

eat

stand (if sitting)

sit (if standing)

scratch your back

scratch your neighbour's back

use a pen

cover your mouth when you
   cough

put a hat on your head

### Some Things I Took for Granted About Freedom

washing dishes

answering the phone

opening a window for
   fresh air

riding my bicycle

walking as far as I want to

going to the bathroom
   whenever I want

a hot shower and a clean
   towel

coffee with cream

not being hungry all the time

choosing whom to spend
    time with

being alone when I want to

cooking

answering the door

having friends over for dinner

music

sun shining on my face

sleeping in my own bed

being curled up with Dan

Dan!

playing with Tonnan and Seph
    and Raffi

baking cookies

waiting for the streetcar

hanging clothes on the
    clothesline

taking out the garbage

reading the newspaper

bothering Dan while he reads
    the newspaper

getting caught in the rain

deciding what to wear in the
    morning

shaving

watching Dan shave

green living things

walking in a snowfall

rosy winter cheeks

seeing your breath condense in
    the air

being tired from physical
    activity

sharing a bottle of wine

clean socks and underwear

making a grocery list

setting my alarm clock

coming home after being out
    somewhere

keys in my pocket

And I write.

It is hard to be here. During our afternoon *hamam* interval,
Uncle opened the window to let fresh air circulate through our
cell of gloom. Two feet of open window, street sounds flowing in
direct, unmediated by the window. And light! fresh air light!
glancing, glowing off the building next door, perhaps fifteen feet
away. Oh, my heart/soul just thrills with fresh-air thirst to be free!
This being locked up, four men in a row, each movement of hand
and arm pulling against another hand and arm, elbows always
touching, or just about, it's too much. I'm sick to death of it: the

hunger, the all-day sitting and all-night lying in a sardine row, the utter lack of autonomy, the imposition on Dan, my parents, my brothers and sister, CPT. How strange to see that particular alphabetic formulation. I think hardly at all of CPT anymore, or home, even Dan. I'm just here, in the belly of the insurgency, a seed in waiting, 73 days of it.

—notebook

I close up my notebook. I'm feeling sorry for myself again. It's time to do my inventory. It's the only thing that helps when things get unbearable. Always it starts, *I am alive.* It changes, now and then, depending on the day, how I am feeling, what I can be grateful for. Today it goes like this: *I am not in pain, I am not alone, I am not wet. I have my faith, I am sleeping okay, I am in good health. I am not depressed and I am not afraid. I can see, hear, taste, smell, feel, think. I have a home. I have people who love me and are waiting for me. I am from a country where there is peace.*

I feel better when I am done. It always reminds me: things could be worse.

# FEBRUARY 7 DAY 74

We're lying in bed. Nephew is getting ready to turn off the light and go downstairs. *"Aku akhbar, Haji?"* we ask. It's our perpetual question.

"News good," Nephew says. "Friday go to Canada." He points to Harmeet and me. "Canada okay. Canada *hubis* okay. *La mooshkilla.* Tom *zane, Amriki* good. *Britannia,* Doctor *zane/mozane.*" He waves his hand back and forth to show things are up in the air.

"Harmeet and Jim go Friday?" Harmeet asks.

"No," Nephew says. "All four together." He holds up four fingers. "Canada *hubis* in *Ordoon. Amriki* okay. Norman *zane/mozane.* English *haji la Baghdad.* English *haji Ordoon.*"

"What did he mean?" Norman asks when Nephew is gone. It is unclear and contradictory, impossible to make sense of. It sounds as if they've got the money from Canada, Tom's release has been secured through the prisoner exchange, and now they're just waiting for Britain to come through with a ransom so they can release the four of us together.

"I have a new mantra," Norman says. "It's 'When I get back to Pinner.' It just occurred to me during the Bible study. It was like I snapped awake. This is what I have to do, where I have to keep my focus: when I get back to Pinner! Pinner, it's my new name for God."

"I don't understand," Harmeet says. "What's Pinner?"

"Well, that's the part of London I live in!" Norman exclaims.

"Shall we unlock?" Tom says. "Norman, do you have the Instrument of Grace?"

"I thought you'd never ask," Norman says.

In fact we have several now. We've recently discovered a gold mine supply right at our fingertips: the dozens of curtain hooks in the pleats of the grey curtains we use to cushion our legs at night. We keep them carefully hidden. The original Instrument of Grace, the nail from Harmeet's shoe, is pinned inside the hem of the red blanket. Harmeet keeps a piece of curtain hook in the waistband of his track pants, Norman in a pocket inside his tweed jacket, and we've hidden a forth in the bathroom. Norman is just about to unlock when Uncle flicks on the light. I almost leap out of my skin. Where the hell did he come from! Uncle goes straight to the barricade and grabs a videocassette. He draws a small rectangular box in the air. "*Mooshkilla, mooshkilla,*" he says. Their VCR is broken. He wants one of us to come and fix it. Harmeet, you're the engineer, we say, you better go. Uncle unlocks him and takes him into the mysterious, forbidden world we know simply as Downstairs.

"Wow, that was close," I say. It's past midnight when Harmeet returns.

# FEBRUARY 8 DAY 75

"What happened last night?" I ask Harmeet as soon as he's awake.

"I didn't want to go," Harmeet says.

"What did they make you do?"

"The VCR motor wasn't working for some reason. It's probably jammed. They didn't have a screwdriver to open it, so there wasn't much I could do. Plus they had it plugged in wrong—the 'out' plug was in the 'in' plug—and then they didn't have the right cable. But they have a DVD player, so I watched *Legends of the Fall* with them. Nephew fell asleep and snored really loud through the last half of the film. It wasn't bad. Brad Pitt was in it."

"What was it about?" I ask, suppressing a pang of jealousy.

"Oh, I guess it's mainly a story about guilt. It's set on a ranch in Wyoming. Uncle really liked the cowboys. It was really uncomfortable. I didn't want to be there, with you guys being locked up here. Uncle even gave me some leftovers. I feel a little guilty about it. It was some bread from their supper. When he offered it to me I said I'd share it with you all upstairs, but he said no. He said, 'This is from me to you.' I couldn't say no, so I ate it. I shouldn't have. It wasn't fair."

"I'm glad you took it. No use in all of us starving. What's it like down there?"

"Uncle sleeps on the floor and Nephew sleeps on the bed. The other bed, the one with all the crumbs on it, is used as a table for putting stuff on, food and whatnot. Uncle munched on popcorn for the whole movie. He had a huge bag of it. He offered me some but I said I was full from the bread. It was empty by the end of the movie. They have a *soba* down there going full blast. I was actually hot. If there is a petrol shortage, they certainly aren't suffering from it. They kept the door open a crack."

I curse myself. If only I'd known: the door closed, TV going, Uncle absorbed in a movie, Nephew sound asleep. I could have unlocked, scouted out the kitchen, the rest of the house, maybe even escaped! There's a way out of here, I'm sure of it. We just have to figure it out.

For some inexplicable reason we're given a vast quantity of food for lunch: a *samoon* for each of us, and a bowl of rice and a bowl of lentil stew to share.

At first I am anxious—we're eating from a common dish again, how is this going to work?—but then I relax when Tom divides the food into four equal portions. Nephew, who has brought the food, objects loudly: only Americans divide their food like this. Thank you, we say, ignoring him, the food is very good. He tells us it was made by Uncle. He says he can't eat it because he is Sunni and this is Shia food. He mocks the Shia, beating his chest and whipping his back. "*Kaffir. Majnoon,*" he says of them.

When we're finished, Nephew takes away the dishes and locks us up. There's an unfamiliar sensation in my body. It's almost uncomfortable. It takes me a minute to figure out that my stomach is full.

Before Nephew can leave, Uncle appears at the door. We thank him lavishly. I will cook for you if you ever come to Canada, I tell him, Nephew interpreting for me.

How long does it take to get to Canada? Uncle asks. About twelve hours by plane. How long does it take to fly to Amman? One hour. Is there a plane from Amman to Canada? Yes. How long does it take? About eleven hours. Do I have a mobile? No. Why not? I don't like them. When I'm at the airport, how do I get in touch with you? By a pay phone. I will come pick you up. With a car.

How do I get your phone number? I'll write it down for you when we're released. Good, he says.

All night, a roaring wind, bottles sweeping along pavement, gusts pushing against the window, whistling through invisible crevices, the warbling crash of flying sheet metal.

*I want to be free. Just like the wind.*

# FEBRUARY 9 DAY 76

"Today is Andrew's birthday. He's turning twenty," Tom tells us, stoic, as though announcing some practical fact. Silence fills the room. No one knows what to say. The pain of it is too much. Andrew, without his father on his birthday, not knowing whether he is alive or dead, the grim fear of never seeing him again. Tom told us all about him. Kassie too. I offer a silent prayer for them, for all of our families. I can't imagine what they must be going through. We at least know we are alive. They don't even know that much.

They take Harmeet downstairs to have another look at the VCR player. His report when he returns: "Well, they got a screwdriver and I was able to open it up to have a look. I found a loose connection, and the elastic that turns the spindle is broken. I offered to fix it if they can find another elastic. Nephew and Uncle started bickering about it. Nephew didn't want Uncle to mess with it. I don't think he trusts Uncle to fix it.

"They have a hard life down there. They don't live much better than we do. They have nothing to do. There's no electricity most of the time. They only get two or three channels. It's Junior that brings the movies in. I asked them why they don't get cable. Nephew made a face and said *haji* said no, they weren't going to be here long enough to make it worth getting. So I guess that's a good sign. The only difference is they have a *soba*, and they can eat as much as they want."

"They can certainly leave any time they want," Norman says.

"Maybe not," Tom says. "They might not have a choice anymore, having joined the *mujahedeen*. Who knows, they might be killed if they tried to leave."

Uncle beats his chest and pretends to flog his back. The Shia are crazy, they are friends of the Americans, they collaborate with George Bush. *Ali baba*. Bush is taking our oil. *Bush najis, Britannia najis.* The Sunni are fighting against the Sunni. The Sunni are good. I am Sunni. China is good. We get weapons from China. Bush, Blair, Kuwait, Saudi Arabia, they're all taking oil. *Mozane*. China isn't taking oil. China *zane*. Canada *zane*.

He forms his hands into a machine gun, a rocket launcher, planes dropping bombs. No *salam* in Iraq, he says. He is a *mujahedeen*. Why? Because the Americans have invaded Iraq. He doesn't kill American and British civilians. Why? He points to each of us and then to himself. *Salam*. He's a man of peace, just like us. I'm not going to shoot you, he promises. When the American army leaves, there'll be no more war. America and Britain and Iraq will be friends again. You have to tell Congress, tell Bush and Blair to leave Iraq and there will be peace.

Uncle points to our handcuffs. You came to Iraq and you were kidnapped. *Hubis, hubis,* he says. The money is for guns, mortars, rocket launchers. It's not for me, he insists, shaking his head and waving his finger. Do you understand? he asks. Yes, we say.

When he's gone, Harmeet says, "He's given us his lesson on peace."

There's an explosion. Near enough to shake the windows. Junior instantly raises his hands in the air and shouts *"Allah Ackbar"* three times. God is great. God is great. God is great. A long exchange of gunfire follows.

Uncle and Junior grin at each other. "Mujahedeen," they say proudly. Then, pointing at Tom, "*Amriki jaysh mot.* Good."

"That's just great," Tom says as soon as they leave. "Just what we need—more dead people."

During the night, Norman coughing in his sleep, bursts of air hitting the back of my neck. I can't stand it. I really can't stand it.

# FEBRUARY 10 DAY 77

Junior pulls a switchblade out of his pocket. He flicks it open, examines it for a moment, then lunges suddenly for Uncle's chest, stopping an inch from his heart. Uncle, sitting in a chair, yawns sleepily. Junior draws the knife across Uncle's throat with a villainous grin and then across his scalp. Uncle looks into the distance and picks his nose. Junior locks his arm around Uncle's head and squeezes. Without warning, Uncle explodes out of his chair and they're wrestling. We step out of the way. Uncle slams Junior against the wall. Junior charges. Their arms lock. Junior squirms free and grabs Uncle by the throat. Uncle grips Junior by the wrist, pulls down and twists his arm behind his back. He marches Junior into the foyer and forces him onto the floor. Junior knees Uncle in the gut and breaks free of his hold. They roll across the floor. We look at each other helplessly, no longer sure if they're playing.

I step towards them and wave my arms like a referee. "*Salam, salam*," I cry. They have each other by the throat. Uncle's face is turning purple, drool oozing from his mouth. "Ding ding ding. *Salam, salam*," I cry again.

Junior sits up with a big grin on his face. Uncle sputters, rolls onto his back, wipes his face. Both men are soaked in sweat and gasping.

"Good, good," Junior says between heaving breaths. He clambers to his feet and bounces down the stairs. Uncle lurches into a chair to recover his wind while we go about our morning exercises. We no longer think of Junior as the easiest captor to physically subdue.

Uncle appears with news. What he has to say is electrifying: *Haji* is here, he's going to take a picture of us, then tonight or tomorrow we will be released.

My instinct is to be doubtful: here, yet again, another hot-air promise. Tom, however, is convinced. "Something is definitely happening," he says. Uncle has never been this specific before. The money must've finally come through and the prisoner exchange must be complete. He wants to discuss all the possible logistics of our release tomorrow: what to do if they take us to a safe house, a mosque, a political party office or leave us on the street; how we'll get back to the CPT apartment to get our stuff and debrief; transportation arrangements for getting home.

I'm annoyed. First at Tom's certainty—there's no way he can know for sure tomorrow is the day—and second at the prospect of having to discuss this yet again. We already have a plan, I remind him. From wherever we end up being released, whether it's separately or all together, we'll call Doug in Toronto. He'll get in touch with the team and notify our families. If at all possible Norman will go directly to the airport and get the first flight home; the team can send his luggage on later. Hopefully they'll be able to come and meet us. If not, we can get a taxi to drop us off at St. Raphael's Hospital and walk to the apartment from there; we don't want to attract any attention to it. If that's not possible, we can ask to be taken to the nearest police station. Once we get to the apartment we can call our families, debrief, get our stuff and book a flight home. If any of us are released before the others, we can wait in Amman provided it doesn't take too long.

"You're losing your resolve to stay in the present, Tom," Norman jokes.

"No," Tom says, "this is no different. I'm just suggesting we prepare ourselves as best we can for the different scenarios that might arise."

"I see," Norman says.

"The worst part of this is being treated like a commodity."

Norman explodes. "Oh, please! Would you STOP saying that! You've said it so many times, it's burned into my brain." Norman drills his finger against his temple. "Like a laser. Commodity, commodity, commodity!"

"I'm sorry," Tom says. "It's just that I've never felt this way before. Lots of other people have been made into slaves, but I never have. I never understood before what other oppressed people must go through, not having any control over their lives, not being consulted about decisions that affect them, people in abusive relationships who have to watch everything they do and say. I never knew what that was like, but I have a glimpse of it now."

Norman apologizes. "I'm sorry. Really, I shouldn't object. You—"

"I've come to see this as a 76-day retreat to work on my spiritual life, which wasn't all that much when we started. I just hope it's gotten stronger. And I just hope that when I get out of here I don't fall into my old patterns of self-indulgence and self-gratification."

"When I get out of here," I say, "I'm going to enjoy life as much as I can."

"Baklava," Harmeet says longingly.

"Well, I'm maintaining my pessimism here, just in case," Norman says. "We've heard these things before, haven't we?"

"Not like this. I think we're really close this time," Tom says.

# FEBRUARY 11 DAY 78

Morning exercise. Junior is bouncing, running, doing push-ups, weaving circles around us in the foyer. He stops next to me. "Come on, Jim, massage," he says.

Something tells me this is the time to say it. "This no suicide. *La*, this no go boom," I say, repeating the motions he first used to show a bomb strapped to his body.

Junior shakes his head. "No suicide," he says.

I look him in the eyes. *"Mazboot?"*

*"Mazboot,"* he says. "No suicide." He sits down on the blue folding chair.

*"Inshallah*, this *abu*," I say before I begin the massage. "This *whalid*. This *abu zane*."

"Thank you," he says, grinning.


"I want to tell you something," Tom says as soon as the captors lock us up for the day. "I had this strange experience last night. I was awake, looking up at the ceiling, just lying there, trying to meditate, when . . ." He hesitates, reaches for words. "I don't know how to describe it. It wasn't a dream. It was more like a vision . . ." He stops speaking, self-conscious, unsure if he should continue.

Go on, we say, we're listening.

"You'll probably think this is strange, but I want to tell you because you're my friends. The most amazing thing happened. I couldn't sleep.

I was just lying there, when I heard this voice. I don't know where it came from, but it was clear and unmistakable, almost as if it was a real voice. All it said was, 'I am here, I am here.' And I felt this incredible sense of peace. Total and complete peace. Everything just melted away—all the anxiety and fear—everything. It just kept repeating, over and over, 'I am here, I am here.'"

He looks at us, his face shining. "I think it was God, saying, 'I am here.' I don't know how long it went on, but I've been meditating on those words ever since. I've never felt more at peace."

There is a long, glowing silence. I look over at Tom. He's serene, alert to everything, almost buoyant. I smile, then bow my head. I think I hear it too, the same voice resounding in my own heart. *I am here, I am here.*


The captors come with news. Medicine Man is on his way. We're going to be released, possibly even today!

It's an all-day, nail-biting wait. Wild with the hope of freedom we seize upon every step, voice, door opening and closing. Darkness falls; the diesel generators in the buildings around us come purring to life. "He's not coming," Norman says glumly. As if on cue, we hear the kitchen door slam. We look at each other, hardly daring to breathe.

Medicine Man enters with joking and laughter. Then, facing us, he's suddenly serious, a man of important business. "News good. Everything finished. Our negotiator is back. Everything complete. Today, tomorrow, you will go."

We ply him with questions. He's slippery. Getting specific information out of him is like trying to catch a fish with bare hands. He skates around our questions with generalities, vague promises, soothing pacifications. The negotiator is in Baghdad—he just got the call, two hours before now.

So the negotiations are finished?

Yes.

And the prisoner release?

Medicine Man looks puzzled.

There were two women to be released as part of the negotiation, we remind him.

"Oh yes," he says, as if suddenly remembering. "I think we do something else. Today, tomorrow, I don't know, I carry you, one by one, in the car to the other house."

"In the boot?" I say, alarmed. *Oh God, please, not that again.*

"Yes, in the boot. There is no other way, it is not safe. We have some checkpoint. But this is not a problem. You do this before. We carry you back to the first house, one by one. You will have some shower, we take some picture, we prepare you for you release. Then we take you, all together, in a car, no blindfold. We take you to some mosque. It is not far. I think you know this place."

I groan. *Not the Muslim Scholars Association, the place where we were kidnapped!*

"It is the safest place. We will let you out and you will walk to the mosque. Your negotiators will come and meet you in five minutes."

"What about our things?" Norman asks. "Glasses, passports, cameras . . ."

"Everything is there."

"So today or tomorrow we will go—even tonight," I say, trying not to sound too hopeful.

"I don't know. If it is safe. I will go now and make the trip, see if it is safe to bring you."


"Has Medicine Man ever told us the truth?" Norman's question rings in my ears all night. "We've never been so close," Tom keeps insisting. "I have a bad feeling about this," Harmeet said, pulling me aside during night lock-up, making sure the others couldn't hear.

I don't know what to think. Harmeet and Norman are right to be skeptical. I know it's foolish but I can't stop myself from being hopeful. The desire to be free, like a wild and sovereign beast, will not be tamed. Let it be now, today, this very minute. I am ready.

# FEBRUARY 12 DAY 79

For the first time in captivity, Tom tells a joke. "What's the difference between a Marine and a mushroom?" he asks. We think for a moment and then give up. "Nothing," he says, grinning like a little boy. "They're both kept in the dark and fed bullshit." We laugh, astonished by Tom's levity. We are all of us vibrating with excitement—even Norman. It can't be helped. The hope of release is irresistible. Finally! we tell each other. Finally! We are going home.

"I'm going last," Tom declares. We all agree, without ever having to say it; this is the unbearable thing, to be the one left alone waiting to the end.

Harmeet objects. "I was last the last time. I don't mind. I'll go last this time."

There's no point in arguing. Tom's resolve is incontestable. He changes the subject. "We've moved from being an asset to a liability. Until the deal is done, they're on the hook for us. If something happens to us in the interim, they'll have no credibility for future hostage negotiations."

"I hope to turn into a personal asset very shortly," Norman says.

"Pat's personal asset?" I say.

Norman chuckles. "Yes. She's likely to hit me with a frying pan."

"You'll have to do some extra chores around the house to make it up to her—things you've been putting off that Pat's been after you for," I say.

"I'll beg weakness—or should I say feebleness," Norman says.

"We aren't out of the woods yet," Tom says. "Anything can happen. There are a number of nightmare scenarios, you know, like what happened to Giuliana Sgrena when they were taking her to the airport—"

I roll my eyes. Norman explodes. "We don't need to hear any more nightmare scenarios," he shouts. "We've been through enough nightmare scenarios!"

Tom continues undeterred. "The communication link between the Italian and the American governments broke down. They didn't know what was happening, so when they were rushing Giuliana Sgrena to the airport, the Americans opened fire on her car. One of the Italian security officials threw himself on top of her. He was killed, but she was okay. And that was with only two governments. Our case is much more complex. We've got three governments involved, plus the Iraqi government. That increases the chances that something crazy can happen. It means that when we're released and we're talking with the third-party negotiator, we need to be checking. Do the Americans know about this plan? What about the Canadians and the British? Do the Iraqis know? We need to check that the governments are in communication with each other so that what happened to the Italians doesn't happen to us."

"Fine," Norman says, "but I don't want to hear about any more nightmare scenarios."

"Should we have a meeting to discuss what we're going to do?" Tom asks. "I mean, we have no idea what's going to happen—if we're going to be whisked to the Green Zone right away—we're going to need money in Amman—we should decide who we're going to call first—"

"Tom," I say, trying to keep the exasperation out of my voice, "we've been through all this. We all have Doug's number. It's all so unpredictable. What we've already decided is all we can really plan for."

"We have to expect the unexpected," Tom says.

"Yes, and then expect it to change," I say.

I write a poem in my notebook for my friends Raffi, Tonnan and Sephie, aged 1-and-a-half, 5 and 8.

> Your secret friend stopped by to say
> have a wonderful beautiful
> jump-up-and-down day
> let shine your soul in rainbow ray
> and boy-oh-boy-oh-boy just play
> prance and dance all your live long way

I wonder, how are you? What are you doing today? How I miss you! It has been seventy-eight days. Will I ever see you again? Soon, may it be soon.

Cramps, gut squeezing, a tight, hard fist. I long to lie down flat, ease the stress out of my body. I wave it away but always it comes back, the question buzzing in my head like a horsefly, *Are we going to be taken somewhere to be shot?*

Sometime between Christmas and New Year's, Tom proposed that we issue a joint statement upon our release. He recited the statement from memory, over and over, sentence by sentence. We spent hours cutting, pasting, editing, refining. Tom remembered every word, every change we made. The statement was addressed primarily to citizens of the United States and Britain, calling upon the American and British governments to respect the will of the new Iraqi Parliament by seeking its legislative approval and clearly defined terms for the continuing occupation of their country.

I was never enthusiastic about the statement. It felt like an obligation, a responsibility, something to organize. I imagined having to write a press release, arrange a press conference, call media outlets, follow up with interviews. It was the last thing I wanted to be doing upon our release, if it ever happened. I told Tom I would be part of the statement and I would attend a press conference, but I wouldn't do anything else; he, or the CPT team, would have to do the rest. That was fine with him.

Tom wants to go over the statement one last time. He has it written in his notebook. Harmeet takes a deep breath as if to gather his courage together. Of the four of us, he is the most conflict-avoidant. He has an objection. He doesn't like "Our experiences in captivity have strengthened our commitment to Jesus's teaching of 'loving our enemies' and 'praying for those who persecute us.'" His objection is threefold. One, he's not sure it represents him. Two, it implies that Christianity has the power to say what everybody, including Muslims, should believe, and if you don't, then you're on the wrong side of the truth, and of course we know what happens then. And three, he's not comfortable using religious language in a public document. The first and third objections are secondary, he says, the second is primary.

I understand and accept the first and third objection, I say, but I have difficulty with the second. We're not saying what Muslims should believe, we're saying what *we* believe. We've talked about how, because of liberal guilt, people don't want to make any claims because they're afraid they might exclude or offend somebody, and so they end up trading away their identity altogether. If we take this out, it means we'd be censoring ourselves, that we can't say who we are without offending somebody else.

"But this is being addressed to Muslims," Harmeet says.

"No," I say, "it's being addressed to Britons and Americans."

"Jim's right," Tom says.

"Oh, I must've forgotten that," Harmeet says. "I don't mean to censor anybody. Now that I understand better, it's the first reason. I'm just not comfortable with it. I'm not really a Christian. It's not a claim I can make."

"Then we have to change it," Tom says. Tom asks Norman for his opinion. Norman says whether or not people understand what the quotes mean, they are instantly recognizable, especially for Christians, who are the majority of the population in Britain and the U.S. That gives them a certain amount of power. Using them might make Christians think about their faith in a different way, that it must not be used to justify violence. However, if Harmeet has an objection, he doesn't mind changing it.

We revise the statement to read: "Our experiences in captivity have strengthened our belief that the real enemy of peace is violence undertaken for any reason, regardless of whether it be the violence of an occupying army, or the violence of an insurgent group who uses kidnapping to finance their resistance to that occupation."

"I like it," Harmeet says. "It moves the focus away from our captors. I'm not sure they're my enemy. I feel lighter now. I didn't realize how much it was affecting my mood. I should've brought it up a lot earlier and gotten it over with."

I apologize. When we wrote the statement, I say, we just assumed this sentence included you. Harmeet says he should've said something at the time. We still should have checked with you, I say. It's always hard having to push against an assumption. It puts the onus on you and there's a weight behind it that can be really hard to move.

"You're right," Harmeet says. "It's funny how it took me so long to figure out what I was feeling and why."

I feel lighter too. Now we are ready to face the world, I think.

At five in the afternoon, Junior arrives dressed in a pink shirt, natty suit jacket, pressed trousers, his hair perfectly coiffed. "*Shid ghul?*" he asks, smiling irrepressibly.

My spirits leap madly. Has the time finally come? He gently removes our handcuffs. "Yes Tom, yes Harmeet, yes Jim, yes Norman," he says, cooing our names as he bends over our wrists. He kisses each of us. The quick brush of his cheek against mine is strangely comforting. Then his smile vanishes. He stands tall, shoulders back, points to each of us—a commander issuing an order. "You all go. In car. Tom, then Norman, then Jim, then Harmeet."

We're in terrible danger, I suddenly realize. I sit on my hands to keep from shaking. Everything reduces to fact. Emotion must not exist. It is verboten, unpredictable, a wanton danger. Whatever happens, I am only a video camera recording.

Tom and Norman are told to get ready to leave. Tom changes back into his own clothes and forces his size-twelve feet into his size-nine sneakers. He carefully folds his captor clothes into a neat pile with his notebook, pen and toothbrush: the only things he has left in the world. "You have Doug's phone number memorized?" I ask him. He nods, his poker face dissolving into apprehension.

"Am I going to be able to get my stuff at the CPT apartment?" he asks Junior. Junior looks at him, puzzled.

"My luggage, my clothes, all my things. At the CPT house." Junior does not understand. "The CPT house. Beit CPT. Where all my things are," he says, arms reaching urgently through his voice.

"He doesn't know," I say as gently as I can.

Uncle enters briefly. He points to the clothing on Tom's lap. He asks Tom how he's going to carry his things. *"Chees, chees?"* Does he want a bag to put them in?

Uncle's reference to a bag makes Tom think of his luggage. "My bags," he says. "Am I going to be able to get my bags at the CPT apartment?" Uncle shakes his head and repeats his question. "My bags at the CPT apartment," Tom pleads. "Am I going to be able to get my bags at the CPT apartment?"

"He doesn't know, Tom," I say gently. "He's talking about a bag to put your clothes in."

"Oh, okay," Tom says. His shoulders slump forward and he sits forlornly with his hands folded between his thighs like an obedient child waiting for a cherished permission. He looks so vulnerable, bewildered, lost. My emotion surges. No, force it back, lock it away.

Junior gives Tom the signal that it's time to go. Tom bounces up, his face full of boyish expectation. Junior bends down to look Norman in the eyes. He speaks slowly and deliberately, his face mere inches away. He says he'll be back in half an hour to take him next. Then he turns towards Tom with a pair of handcuffs.

"Well, I guess this is goodbye," Tom says, his face and eyes soft, open, hopeful. His words are like an electric shock. I know what he's thinking: we're going to be released in stages; this will be the last time we see each other until we all get home. Something far more grim flashes across my mind. I chase the thought away.

Tom and Harmeet shake hands. "See you soon," Harmeet says.

I feel very strange. There's an engine inside me roaring full throttle. *No!* a voice screams. *Now!* it commands. *Fight to the death!* Instead I feel, say, do nothing. I stand up like a grey cardboard puppet that's being moved by an invisible hand. "Goodbye, Tom," I say, looking him in the eyes. I wrap my arms around him, for a moment hold him tight. His body is all hardness and bone. There's nothing left of him. It shocks me: this is the first time we've touched each other since the captivity began. It's impossible to do in handcuffs, pat someone on the shoulder or give them a hug. I hold Tom's shoulders for a brief moment. *Be strong, God is with you,* I want to say. I keep reaching for words, but they won't come.

Tom turns to Norman. They shake hands. "Take care, old chap," Norman says. The moment is stiff, awkward, formal.

Junior is waiting with the handcuffs. "Tom, can I give you a hug?" Harmeet asks. They step towards each other and embrace.

Junior tells Tom to put his hands behind his back. *No, please,* I want to cry out, *that's not necessary.* Junior locks Tom's wrists behind his back. He's totally helpless now. Uncle scoops his clothes into a bag. My eyes reach for Tom's, but he doesn't see me. He's scared, lost, already looking ahead. Junior takes Tom by the arm and turns him towards the dark foyer. And then he is gone.


We are squeezed in a giant vise of waiting. With every minute, the vise closes tighter. I can hardly breathe. At nine-thirty, Nephew and Uncle announce that it's time for bed. What's happening with Norman? we ask. They look confused. We point to the little bedroll Norman has made with his woollen tie. He is supposed to go with Tom, we say. They look surprised. No, they say, you're staying here. News good for Harmeet and Jim. Big *Haji* in Baghdad. *Hubis* in Baghdad. Tomorrow or the next day, go to Canada. *Inshallah.* Now sleep, they say.

We set up our bed. No more need to make a place for Tom with the sleeping mat. We can all fit across the futon under the blanket now, and each of us has his own pillow. Harmeet takes Tom's place next to the door. I watch, as if suspended from the ceiling. There's a man locking a metal bracelet around somebody's wrist. The wrist has a mole on it just like mine. The man says good night and closes the door. I fall asleep instantly.

# CHAPTER THIRTEEN

## FEBRUARY 13 DAY 80

And then there were three. There used to be four. Four toothbrushes standing together in a castaway Tupperware container. How I loved the colour of them—there is so little of it in our lives—red and green and blue and purple, so chosen by Medicine Man so we would each have our own to use. They represented our individuality. But now the purple one, Tom's, is gone. A great hole has opened in our lives.

For a moment, grief breaks through. I push it down, bury it deep, pave it over. We just have to keep going.


Tomorrow, tomorrow after tomorrow, a week, Nephew says.

A week? we say. It was supposed to be yesterday. No, yesterday before yesterday.

News good, he says. One million in Iraq, one more million from Canada, we count all the money, phone call from Big Haji, one week and go.

We are staying here, then?

Yes.

And what about Tom?

He shrugs his shoulders. He doesn't know. He was at home, off duty when all of this happened.

He offers each of us a candy wrapped in crinkly gold paper. *No thank you, I want to say, I'm not interested in your pathetic attempt to make everything better.* But I watch, aghast at myself, at the three of us, as we hold out our hands, unwrap and pop them into our mouths, let them dissolve into our bodies. I can't decide whether I am more disgusted with our captors or myself.

"I wouldn't mind to hold on to those," Norman says, pointing to the wrappers in our hands. He folds them up carefully and adds them to the secret miscellany in his pockets.

He produces them later, along with the silver foil cigarette papers he has squirrelled away. "Do either of you gentlemen recall how to make a peace crane?" he asks.

Yes, Harmeet says. It amazes me as I watch them, folding, unfolding, refolding, trying to reconstruct the pattern that a 12-year-old Japanese girl named Sadako Sasaki completed a thousand times before she died. It is a welcome reprieve from the long torment of waiting, the wondering, when are they going to take the rest of us to the other house. She was two years old when her city, Hiroshima, was destroyed by an atomic bomb. When she became sick with leukemia and had to be hospitalized shortly after her twelfth birthday, her best friend told her about the ancient Japanese legend that promises one wish to those who make a thousand origami paper cranes. Sadako got to work immediately. Her wish was for world peace. She used whatever paper she could find. She asked the other patients for the wrappings from their get-well presents and collected the little squares their medicines came in.

Sadako makes me think of Anne Frank, writing away in her red-checker diary at the age of fourteen, telling the story of her life in hiding, two pressure-cooked years in a secret apartment with seven other people, never seeing the sky, living in constant fear of the day they would be betrayed, arrested, deported to Nazi death camps. Her diary was saved by a friend of her family and found its way to her father, the only one of her group to survive, who then transcribed and published it.

Both girls died anonymous and irrelevant, their lives of no apparent consequence beyond the circle of those who knew them. Yet Sadako's hospital bed project has become a world symbol of peace, and Anne's diary is one of the most important testaments of the twentieth century. None of us can know the measure of our lives. None of us can know what our actions might seed.

How does that parable go? A man scatters some seed on the ground. Night and day, whether he is asleep or whether he is awake, the seed of its own accord sprouts and grows, how he does not know.

It gives me enormous comfort. That's us. We are each a seed planted in the ground. While we sit here, while we lie here, day after useless day, suspended in this invisible womb of waiting, something is sprouting, something is growing, how or what we do not know.

As darkness falls, Uncle comes into our room with the lantern. He sets it on the floor, pulls a chair in close and sits down. For a long while he is silent. When he finally speaks, he points towards heaven. "*Allah wahid. Issau, Mohammed, Miriam shwaya.*" He almost touches his thumb against his index finger to show how insignificant they are in comparison to God. "*Allah kabir. Issau shwaya.*"

We strain to understand him, piecing together what we can from his body language and the bits of Arabic we know. No one is like God, he tells us. Allah makes the rain, the wind, the rivers, the animals, the air. Who else does this? He pretends to dig a grave and points to the lantern. Do we want to be buried or cremated? Jesus, Mohammed, Miriam, Moses—they all were buried, put into the fire—where are they now? They're all dead. They are small, *shwaya. Allah kabir, Allah wahid.*

We have feet, legs, hair, eyes, a mouth. So did Jesus and Mohammed. Allah has none of these things. Mohammed and Miriam were married, Allah is not. Issa had a mother, Allah does not. Jesus is not equal to God. *Issa shwaya.* For Muslims, all food must be *halal.* Christians are not *halal.* No drinking alcohol. Muslims must not steal. "*No ali baba.*"

His face is very grave as he speaks. He is telling us the truest and most important things. If only he could speak English he would convince us.

I tear a page out of my notebook and draw a map of Iraq with Baghdad in the middle. I show him how there are different roads coming from different cities, Basra in the south, Kirkuk to the north, Amman in the west and Tehran to the east. The roads begin in different places, but they all lead to the same place, to Baghdad. Baghdad is like God, and the different cities are like the world's religions. Each religion offers a different road leading to God.

"*La,*" Uncle says indignantly. "*Allah wahid. Allah wahid.*" Baghdad is not like God. He goes through the circle of his argument again, point by point, lecturing us with his finger. The harangue lasts an hour. If we were Muslims, he tells us right before he leaves, he would have to release us.

Nephew and Uncle bring us downstairs to watch television. We wonder where Junior is. Could he be minding Tom at the first house? Their room is like a sauna. We take our sweaters off right away and sit facing the television. Uncle has the remote. He switches restlessly through six channels. The choices seem to be news or Arabic soap operas. We don't understand a word, but it doesn't matter. It is a relief simply to be out of handcuffs. I pretend I'm a normal human being who's watching television with some friends.

"*Chai?*" they ask us.

"Yes!" we say. Uncle and Nephew scavenge for some cups. I force myself not to think about how dirty they are. They pour us tea from a blackened aluminum pot that sits on the *soba*. Uncle scoops sugar into our cups from a clear plastic bag, leaving trails of sugar behind each heaping spoonful. The tea slides down my throat like a healing balm, spreading an unfamiliar feeling of vigour.

Tom has been released, Nephew tells us. He's in Amman. We watch the news carefully. I am mesmerized by the image of a jet taking off—the symbol of release, freedom, going home! There are no stories about Tom. We don't know what to think. Perhaps our kidnapping is not of interest to anyone here. Perhaps it will be on the news tomorrow. Perhaps Nephew is lying.

This has been the most discouraging day so far, Harmeet says when we are settled in bed. Tom has been taken away, we don't know what's happened to him, we're back to the three-day/four-day holding pattern. He thought about it all day, how Medicine Man said Tom didn't need shoes. If he doesn't need his shoes, that means they're not planning to let him go. It's clear Tom has been separated from us, we just don't know why or what it means.

For a moment I am awash in grief. *Tom! What's happening to you!* The feeling rises like a cataract and threatens to drown me. But then, something within me, sovereign and inexorable, sweeps it away and buries it deep in my psyche. A time capsule waiting to be opened at another time, on a day when I can walk free under a blue sky.

# FEBRUARY 14 DAY 81

Medicine Man is on his way, Nephew says. He's going to take a picture of Norman. To show "Madame" that he is still alive. They will send it by Internet. "Madame on television. *Hazeen.*"

Medicine Man arrives a short time later with a video camera. "Doctor," he says, "I have to take some picture. This the final video for you." He has three questions for Norman, sent by his wife, that only he knows the answer to: What is his wife's maiden name? Who made Norman's wedding ring? You have an unusual hobby—why?

Medicine Man films and Norman answers. Then he tells Norman to write down the answers on a piece of paper. I ask about Tom. Medicine Man says he is fine, there is no problem, he is at the other house. "We just have some problem with the road. It is not safe to carry you. Maybe today, maybe tomorrow. I must to check the way first."

Norman asks if the negotiations are complete. "The news is good," Medicine Man says. "There is only something, one, maybe two final things. I will come to carry you, maybe today, maybe tomorrow, and you go. I must to take your emails. In three, four years, when all of this is over, I come to visit each of you."

Uncle shows us a zester, something he found somewhere in the house. *Shoo?* he asks, scrubbing his heel with it. Is it for shaving calluses? he wonders. No, we tell him, it's for *portugal*, orange.

Harmeet points to the barricade of chairs in front of the window. Where does all this stuff come from? he asks.

From the people who used to live here, Uncle says.

How long ago was that? Harmeet asks.

Two years ago, Uncle says. The Americans raided the house and killed two people. The owners have four houses in Baghdad. They rented this to *Haji Kabir* for one million dinars a month. They're still in Iraq.

Before us, who else was brought here? Harmeet asks. "*Amriki? Australi?* Italian?"

"*Jaysoos.* Iraqi *najis.* Iraqi *killam.*" After you leave, your chairs will be occupied by others: Australians, British, Germans.

"You are the peaceful people," Nephew says to us. "Harmeet good."

"Harmeet no good," Harmeet jokes.

"Harmeet good," Nephew says. "Jim good, very nice. Norman good. Tom? Tom *hazeen.*" Nephew makes a sad face in imitation of Tom. "*Leaish?*"

His question almost makes me snort. *It might have something to do with being kidnapped*, I almost blurt. "Tom doesn't like to talk very much," Harmeet says.

Nephew is priming us. He wants us to take him into our confidence. We've discovered recently that he has a penchant for gossip. The other day he referred to Junior as Hayder and Uncle as Sayeed. Today he tells us Medicine Man is from a wealthy family, that one of his brothers is an engineer, another a contractor. They have houses in Mosul, Baghdad and Fallujah. He is always moving around. He never sleeps in the same place twice.

"*Shoo?*" Nephew asks, not understanding.

Harmeet leans closer. "Tom *shwaya killam,*" he says.

"Yes," Nephew says, nodding solemnly.

We are brought downstairs. "Movie! Movie!" they say. They settle us in front of the TV and bring us popcorn. It's bizarre. *Movie Night with the Captors.* Tonight's feature is *Transporter 2.* Frank Martin is a one-man martial arts army on a routine mission guarding the six-year-old son of the director of the National Drug Control Policy. Everything goes smoothly until the last day, when little Jack is kidnapped by the evil Gianni, a drug lord with a villainous plan to take over the world's drug trade. Outnumbered at every turn and facing impossible odds, Martin risks life and limb in an inexorable quest to rescue little Jack, thwart the evil Gianni and save the day.

It fascinates and astounds me. Nephew and Uncle are cheering for Frank Martin! The Good Guy going after the Bad Guy who's kidnapped an Innocent Victim. *Somebody's confused*, I think. I look down at my wrists. The red marks from the handcuffs I've been wearing all day are still there. Let's see, that means, yes, I'm one of the Innocent Victims. And Uncle and Nephew, they have the keys and the gun, so that means, yes, they have to be two of the Bad Guys. *Excuse me gentlemen, I hate to interrupt the film, but seeing as you're cheering for Frank Martin and all, I was wondering if perhaps you would maybe consider letting us go, I mean since he is the Good Guy after all, and we are the Innocent Victims . . .*

And then it strikes me. In the movie they're starring in, Uncle and Nephew are with the Good Guys. They're fighting to save their country from the Bad Guys, who have invaded and occupied their country with tanks and Humvees and Apache helicopters. But the American soldiers they are fighting against, they're in a movie too. I've heard them say it, this exact phrase, "We're here to get the Bad Guys," the insurgents, the *mujahedeen*, the men who are resisting their noble quest to bring democracy to a long-suffering people and save the world from Weapons of Mass Destruction.

Good Guy or Bad Guy, soldier or insurgent, they are both working from the same script, there is no difference except in the roles they have assigned each other. They have become the mirror image of the other through the means they have chosen.

## FEBRUARY 15 DAY 82

The captivity changes in Tom's absence. They laugh and tease each other more. Uncle's *hamam* sounds, for example, have become a recent source of great hilarity. Our daily ration of food increases slightly.

Uncle brings us oranges, Nephew carrots and dates. When we see Junior, it is in the evening. An hour or so before they get us up in the morning, a car starts in the driveway, idles for half an hour, then drives away. Our theory is that Junior is spending the day at the other house minding Tom. It is a prospect that fills me with dread.

A new evening routine develops. The captors come to unlock us, we stack our chairs and set up our bed, then we get our toothbrushes and follow them downstairs. If supper is ready, we wash our hands and sit on the floor. Most of our meals now, whether upstairs or downstairs, are served to us from a common plate. We eat with our hands free using pieces of flatbread or *samoon* to take bits of whatever we are sharing: potato, rice, scrambled egg, the fried slices of hot dog the captors call *sausage*. After supper the captors pour us tea—the hot, sweet comfort of it is beyond describing—and they converse with us as if we are friends who just happened to come by for a visit. Then it's two or three mind-numbing hours of Arabic channel surfing. When it's time to go back upstairs, usually around ten o'clock, we brush our teeth in the hallway sink, make a last quick *hamam* visit, and then we're locked up for the night.

It's a coin toss as to where time passes more easily: in the gloom room upstairs, or the captors' living quarters downstairs. The relentless babble of the television is exhausting and the pretence of hospitality infuriating. I find myself longing to return to the stale darkness of our room. There at least, sitting in our handcuffs, everything is very clear, who they are and who we are, the nature of the relationship we are in.

There's one thing that doesn't change: the constant gnawing regime of fear. Sometimes it is a hot rushing dread that courses through your veins like a throbbing toxic ooze, but mostly it's just chronic white noise, something you screen out and stop paying attention to even though it's always there.

We have begun to see, as a result of this increased proximity, that our captors are afraid too. At the slightest sound they're up and moving, bodies on red alert and eyes wide with listening, sneak-peeking through curtains, checking the other rooms or checking outside, sometimes returning with a gun. This reassures me somehow. It means they are just like us: anxious, vulnerable, human.

# FEBRUARY 16 DAY 83

Nephew is unusually jumpy. We suspect he is the only one on duty. As if to assure us otherwise, he tells us Junior is downstairs sleeping. "Hayder *sadika moor-reed*. *Sadika* in hospital. *Sadika* very sick. No sleep for two days." Then he says Uncle is very angry. "Sayeed go to the house."

Which house? The house where Tom is? we ask. No, he says, "house of mother-father." We have no idea what he means.

When Nephew leaves, Norman proposes an "expedition" to the window. We've been watching the shadow of a bird coming and going for several days now; Norman wants to know if there's a nest on the window ledge. We make our way to the window, being very careful not to make any noise with the chain. It's exhilarating, to be crossing this forbidden threshold, a chance to finally see what the world is like beyond these goddamned curtains.

"Well hello, we do indeed have a little nest," Norman says delightedly.

"What else can you see?" I ask, fiercely jealous of Norman's place at the end of the chain, his access to the window and ability to see outside.

"But the nest is empty," he says.

"We'd better get back," Harmeet says.

We are crossing back to our chairs, just about to sit down when we hear, "*Shoo?* What this?" It's Nephew. At the door.

I immediately put my hands above my head as if I've been stretching. "Exercise, exercise," we say. He doesn't believe us. We don't know how long he's been standing at the door. We have to tell him the truth. "Tweet tweet, I like birds," Norman explains, leading him to the window to show him the nest.

"*La!*" Nephew cries, shaking his head gravely. He's going to have to tell Medicine Man. I feel strangely anxious, like a child afraid of his babysitter's report to his parents.

We've watched several action-hero films now. The story is always the same. A lone individual (usually male), of exceptional courage, virtue and strength, is called forth to battle an evil nemesis (also usually male, but sometimes intoxicatingly female). The nemesis has upset the scales of justice, perhaps by killing an innocent victim, or he has an evil plan to take over the world, something which must be stopped at all costs. The action hero faces great peril, is betrayed, captured, wounded, tested to the very limits of human endurance, but in every case defies the impossible and triumphs in the end. Whereas the nemesis is greedy, ruthless, cunning, narcissistic, attended by sycophants, sadistic, vain, ugly, ultimately a coward and doomed to fail, the action hero is selfless, stoic, beyond temptation, proportional in response, humble, pleasing to look at, inexhaustibly determined, courageous beyond measure, inclined always towards mercy but realistic about the necessity of using violence, and destined to win.

I've grown to dislike this mythic staple of the entertainment industry intensely. It is the glorification of the individual. Only the individual counts, triumphs, overcomes, saves the day—never the collectivity. Never a union, a strike, a mass demonstration, people getting organized and working together. In this narrative there is only the hero who acts; only the hero who is chosen, set apart, called forth, elevated from the indistinguishable "common gardener" to make the required difference. We who constitute the rank and file of the inert herd must either equip ourselves for similar action-hero feats or sit on our hands for lack of action-hero capabilities. If we are not an action hero, we are without consequence.

The power of the enemy flows from another kind of rank and file, those who have given their individuality and agency to the nemesis in order to share in his formidable power and wealth. The members of this rank and file, the henchmen, have no name. No one cares about or even notices their destruction by the action hero because they are nothing more than disposable pawns. The action hero is the antithesis of the faceless, sycophantic host who attend the nemesis. He becomes an individual by accepting the call to exert his moral character and physical prowess in the pursuit of the good (i.e., stopping, or if necessary destroying, the nemesis).

It is surely no accident that it is those men who are most disempowered, men sitting around in prisons, men waiting for work, men dying for something to do in drop-ins, men under the orders of another man—in other words, men emasculated by the masculine—who are the most enamoured of, even addicted to, the action hero. He is like an injection of manhood for those whose lives offer no hope of achieving his sublime masculine individuality.

For a man to achieve the *gravitas* of *being a man* he must complete the rite of passage into the fraternity of those who count. In other words, the fraternity of the action hero, the one who risks everything in righteous battle against the nemesis. In the absence of such a true test (for alas, real life is rather mundane), the action film will do. For succeeding in the manner of the action hero, the archetype and arbiter of all things masculine, is surely a conceit for most of us. Let cheering the action hero on from the sidelines be therefore sufficient.

—notebook

It is just before eight o'clock in the evening when Nephew enters the upstairs room with our *samoon* supper. There's been no sign of Uncle or Junior all day. He must be alone. He puts it down on the hostess trolley, unlocks us, tells us to get ready for bed. We set up our bed, go to the bathroom, brush our teeth. We're waiting longingly for our *samoons* when, much to our surprise, Medicine Man comes in.

"How are you?" he asks, standing over us like a monarch. We don't answer. "How are you?" he says again, annoyed. Harmeet asks if there is any news.

Yes, he says. We should carry you to the other house but we cannot. Soldiers in the street, checkpoint, searching the car. Since Sunday I am checking, even today, one hour ago. It is not safe. He looks stressed. He says their chief was captured. Two days ago, at midnight. This is a big problem. We have no one to give the order to carry you. It is a problem like in any army. When you take the chief, the soldier can do nothing. He says there's a committee that will decide who will take his place.

Nephew distributes our supper. They talk together with much laughing as we eat. They talk about us as if we're not there, in the amused way adults will talk about children. When there's a lull in their conversation, I ask about Tom.

He is fine, Medicine Man says. I just see him at the other house. He is resting, watching television, there is no problem.

I ask him how long he thinks it will take. Not more than one week, he says solemnly. He begins to ask us questions: how old are you, are you married, do you have children, what do you do for work. This shocks me. He knows nothing about us. Is it only now, after eighty-three days, that he is beginning to see us as people?

Medicine Man and Nephew converse in Arabic, point to the chain locked around Harmeet's wrist. They're observing how small his wrist is. It's heavy, Medicine Man says, remarking on the weight of the chain.

It's good, Harmeet jokes, flexing and squeezing his biceps as if he's been using the chain to work out. This is just like Guantanamo, Medicine Man says. Our treatment is much better here, Harmeet says.

We got a lecture on Islam from the big man last night, Norman says. Medicine Man says we'll exchange emails and discuss Islam and Christianity when we are released. Norman asks about the political situation in Iraq. It is very difficult, Medicine Man says. Norman asks if the new Iraqi Parliament is working well. No, he says, all of this is very difficult.

Harmeet asks for copies of the *mujahedeen* videos we were shown. He wants to take them home to show people what is going on in Iraq. Yes, Medicine Man says, I will bring for you. We have a new edition now, a sniper edition from Fallujah. I will bring it tomorrow.

I am sleeping here tonight. I am just downstairs. Call me if you need anything, he says.

This confirms our theory that Nephew has been on duty alone. We have to start making a plan, I tell myself. With the Instrument of Grace, the red blanket and the element of surprise, Nephew is vulnerable enough that we can do it, but it will take all three of us. I resolve to bring it up with the others so we can start the process of figuring it out.

# FEBRUARY 17 DAY 84

Much to our surprise, it is Junior who unlocks us in the morning. So much for our theory. Where's Medicine Man? we ask.

Sleeping, he says.

Where's *haji*-with-the-big-belly?

Junior looks at us crossly. We're asking too many questions.

We're out of toothpaste, we tell him. He sends Harmeet downstairs to get some. The door to the common room is open. Harmeet peeks inside. Somebody is asleep. Who is it? Medicine Man? Uncle? Another captor altogether?

We don't see Junior for the rest of the day and it is Nephew who keeps the watch. Who's in the house, we wonder, and who is minding Tom? There are no sounds of coming and going through the kitchen door all day. Is it possible they're using another entrance? It's all very confusing.

I am beginning to wonder if I am growing narcissistic in my captivity. I went to pray yesterday, and initially it all revolved around my captivity: assessing how different people are being affected, and to what extent, and praying for them accordingly. I had to remind myself—my captivity is not the centre of the universe. So then my prayers became more generous, and I felt better.

My interest in our captors is waning, my interest in them as people. I find myself increasingly unenthusiastic about engaging them, trying to reach across this divide with small talk, little jokes, positive interactions. I am, of course, unremittingly polite and obliging, but really all I want is *news*, or release. That's all! It's become draining to relate with them, an imposition—and the suggestion that we will maintain contact after this is all over— well I find the idea ridiculous.

—notebook

Medicine Man talks to us in the light of the lantern, his face all shadow. From the beginning, why do you think the negotiations have taken so long? he asks us. He points to where Tom used to sit. It is because of his government—they will not negotiate. They will do nothing. And the next most difficult government? It is the British. From the beginning you are safe, he says, pointing to Harmeet and me. Your government wants to get you out. But this man here, he says, again pointing to Tom's place, there is the danger for him because of his government.

Norman asks about the video they took of him. There is no problem, Medicine Man says. We take the video to them, they see you are alive, the Canadian and the British are in Baghdad, we carry you to the house, one by one. Then one big push and you go, all together.

Including Tom? I ask. All together, including Tom, he says. The reason this is taking so long is because it must be secret. The CIA must not hear about these negotiations. If they do, they will cut them. The negotiations must be secret.

This seems impossible, like something out of a Tom Clancy novel. We know for sure that a direct link has been established with at least one government, the British, because of the three proof-of-life questions. Is it possible that one arm of the occupation is working against another? The thought chills me.

Norman and I make a plea for Harmeet. Unless he is released by Monday, we tell him, Harmeet will lose his school year. I not know this until you tell to me yesterday, Medicine Man says. Even if you are release tomorrow, you will not make it. The other side will take you to some camp, or the Green Zone, or the UN for your safety, and they will have some requirements before they take you out of Baghdad.

He turns to go. I ask if we might interview him about his views on the political situation, the aims of their group, whatever he'd like to tell us. He shrugs and smiles. To have some talk about the situation here, why it's happened, we need to sit maybe for two, three hours, he says.

We have time, I say. He laughs. This is important, he says. I am here tonight, but . . . maybe tomorrow morning. You have your copy book and write, and we discuss the situation.

Thank you, we say. I am just downstairs if you need anything, he says.

# FEBRUARY 18 DAY 85

We ask each captor once a day if they have any news about Tom. We choose the moment carefully. It has to seem casual and spontaneous, and the captor should have his guard down. Tom called it the captor–captive game—the constant process of reading and tiptoeing around the captors' moods, figuring out how to please and pacify them, what and what not to ask for, when and how to do it, all the possible reactions and risks—what you have to do to survive when you're living under somebody's thumb.

Now, when we ask, they no longer say Tom has been released. Now they say, "Tom in house, Tom *zane, shwaya shwaya* you will go." Junior, back on guard duty for the first time since Tom was taken, points to himself and says, "This go in car to Thomas in *beit*," he says. "Tom *zane.*" His answer dismays me beyond words, to think of Tom being alone with Junior's hatred all day.

Nephew puffs out his chest and pounds on it like Tarzan. If he starts to run and exercise in the mornings, he says, he will be in shape just like me. I ask him how to say "freedom" in Arabic. He doesn't understand. I get one of the locks from our chain and show it to him. I close the gate and say with a sad face, "*La* freedom. *Mozane.*" I open the gate and say with a happy face, "*Na'am* freedom. *Zane!*"

"Yes!" Nephew says, suddenly understanding. He says the word is *hooriya*.

"*Hooriya*," I say, lifting my arms above my head. I love it. It sounds like "hurray." When I am free, I say, we can exercise together.

Yes, he says. Then he points to himself. I am not free. Every day I am here, I can't eat or sleep at home with my family. All the time I am thinking about Tom, Norman, Harmeet, Jim. He points to his wrists as if he is in handcuffs. When you are free, I will be free, he says.

I make a sad face and a chopping motion with my hands—the sign we use to show the passing of many days. "*La, la,*" Nephew says. "One, two, three days and go. Big *Haji*, Sayyed, after one month all go. No house, no *faloos* for us. Finished."

# FEBRUARY 19 DAY 86

Today, for the first time, all three captors eat from our dish: Nephew and Junior take a few small bites at lunch, and Uncle helps himself to a small portion at supper. They do it independently, spontaneously, without comment or pretence, as if they have always done this. It is immensely reassuring. It is a gesture that seems to say, despite these handcuffs and chains, this job we have to do, we are brothers.

Downstairs, killing time in front of the television, Harmeet sitting on the floor near the door, Uncle right behind him in a chair, me and Norman in the middle of the room, also in chairs.

Junior enters in his street clothes, loud, excited, agitated. He takes off his suit jacket and throws it on the coat stand by the door. Everything they wear is draped there: towels, dress shirts, track pants, ties. He has a gun tucked into his belt. He kicks off his shoes, goes to the bed in the opposite corner of the room, puts his gun under the pillow then returns to the doorway. He talks to Uncle as he undresses, face full of anguish and arms moving furiously. He undresses blindly and heaps his clothes onto the rack until he is standing in just his underwear and undershirt. He is oblivious to Harmeet sitting on the floor and stands with his groin just inches from Harmeet's face. His things, covered in a jungle of black hair, bulge like his forearms. I glance quickly at the pillow: the gun, I'm only five feet away from it. Junior pulls his captor uniform out of the coat stand and puts it on. "Jim," he says, shoulders suddenly drooping, "come on, massage."

He flops himself down on the bed with his head facing the television and his feet resting on top of the pillow. I get up from my chair. The gun, it would be so easy to grab, I could have it in my hands before either of them have time to react. If I knew for sure it was loaded, if I knew how to use it, I could order them onto the floor face down with their hands on their heads and we would make our escape, just like in the movies.

Alas, I am a pacifist and I do not know how to use a gun, so I lay my hands on his shoulders and begin to massage. "Good," he says, his face softening, easing into a smile. I keep one eye on the television. The news is on and I want to see if there's anything about Tom. Without lifting his head, Junior rubs his left buttock, the place where his gun must press into his hip all day. "Jim, this, massage," he whines.

I raise an eyebrow in astonishment. "This?" I ask, touching his buttock tentatively.

"Yes, this," he says, in the same matter-of-fact tone one would refer to an elbow or knee. I want to say no, but I can't. The word won't come. I shake my head, aghast at what I am about to do. Surely this is crossing the line, I think. I've fallen headlong into it, Stockholm Syndrome, become an accomplice to my own enslavement.

When I finish, Junior turns onto his side, tucks his knees into his chest, pulls a blanket around his head and curls his hands under his chin. Within seconds he is snoring. Behold the man, *Ecce homo*, armed insurgent, warrior of God, sleeping innocent.

I pick up my notebook and begin to write: "It strikes me that the only thing that separates us is a gun or two, the willingness to use it, and a set of keys. We share the same mortal precarity, are tenants of the same house of captivity, sit chained by the same anchor of waiting." I pause for a moment to think. Yes, we are the same, but we are also separated by two radically different and antithetically opposed desires. I continue writing.

The captor works within two overall dynamics or imperatives. Or we could also say, the captor requires two things from his captive: one primary, the other secondary (though no less necessary). The first: control and submission. The second: absolution.

With regards to the first, the captor needs a secure environment within which to hold the captive. The captor will prefer the captive's willing co-operation, and will offer to entice his co-operation within the limits allowed by the imperative of security, but in the end he will do whatever is necessary to ensure the captive submits and is secure from escape. Once submission is secured, the captor will invariably begin to seek absolutions, or justification for the captivity. This arises as a consequence of the intensely intimate/intense intimacy of the captor–captive relationship. The captor cannot escape the task of having to come to terms with the humanity of the captive. The incarcerated humanity of the captive is an affront to the captor's self-image and conscience. The fear, suffering, hunger, banality, vulnerability of the captive is reflected back to the captor as an interrogation of the captivity project. The reflection of consequences. The captor therefore seeks to confirm the meaning and legitimacy of the captivity by obtaining the absolution of the captive. Absolution offered by the captive in turn confirms submission.

The primary and singular task of the captive is the attainment of safety through release, escape or submission. The captive may adopt a strategy of thoroughgoing submission in order to allay the fears of the captor, and signal his willingness to co-operate in exchange for easements in the regime of captivity. The captive may adopt strategies that involve building bridges and humanizing himself in the eyes of the captor. Humour is a powerful tool in this regard. This strategy is aimed at destabilizing the contempt, or the ideological rationale, that initially motivated and justifies the capture, and obscures the humanity of the captive. It is a strategy based on a simple premise: it is more difficult to harm or kill that which has passed from being an abstraction/object of contempt/demonized other and has become a human being. These strategies are instinctive and pre-conscious.

—notebook

# FEBRUARY 20 DAY 87

I'm not sure, but I think he was trying to be funny. Nephew was explaining why he couldn't bring us tea, even though we hadn't asked for it. He said it was because there was no sugar, which we knew to be a lie, having seen a clear plastic bag full of it when we were downstairs last night. He pulled out a gun, invisible under a bulky sweater and tucked into his waistband at the left hip, and pointed it directly at Harmeet.

"Sugar? No sugar. Give me sugar," he said, pretending to rob Harmeet for sugar.

His gun is worth $2,500, he told us. We looked at him with disbelief. Yes, he said, a peacock fanning his feathers, this twenty-five one hundred. He pointed the gun at the floor and pretended to shoot it seven times. We kill this many *jaysoos*, he said. His cellphone rang. "This *Haji Kabir*," he reported at the end of the call, helplessly self-important. Any news? we asked.

"*Shwaya*," he answered. "One day, two day, five day. Not long." Everything has to be very secret. If the CIA finds out, there won't be any deal. "*Inshallah*, not long, go to the house, one day, sleep, take new clothes and go. Everything okay."

Nephew looked around the room to check that everything was in order. Then, excusing himself with a bow, he left.

Harmeet was furious. "So Nephew has a gun. That's very impressive."

"That was funny, eh? Give me some sugar or I'll kill you," I said.

"I bet it was plastic," Harmeet said.

"It looked pretty real to me," I said.

"They have plastic guns now that look real. He looked so ridiculous with it. All he deserves is a plastic gun. Yeah, you're a tough guy—what are you going to do with a plastic gun?"

"We should have asked him if it was a lighter," Norman joked.

"He did it to assert his authority because he was nervous. Medicine Man probably told him to do it," Harmeet said. "All he needs is a fancy car and he'll be all set for an action film."

In the morning, a window-shaking explosion. Somewhere in Baghdad, a crater smoking with hatred, everything and everyone in its vicinity there is burning, bleeding, metal-twisted, shrapnel-shredded, wailing, running. Another day in the life of a war.

Last night, just as we were leaving to go back upstairs, Harmeet observed that Junior was crying while saying his prayers. "It looks as if somebody he cares about really is sick," he said. When I heard that, I felt this little stab, a spontaneous desire to comfort him, make it better. Of course I am pretty much powerless to offer anything save a prayer, not speaking Junior's language and being his prisoner. It's an interesting mix of emotion: authentic compassion; desire for his good; reverence for his vulnerability; desperation to be away, free from his gun, his orders, his moods, his insecurity, this whole world he is part of that I've been swallowed by.

Last night, sitting on the rug (filthy with crumbs, bits, scraps, the detritus of human habitation), watching *Transporter 2* for the *second* time, I felt like more of a captive than ever, that not only my body but my mind and soul too were chained. And this feeling—that wanted to be screamed in mantra, *I want my life back!*—I took in my hands, folded up and stuffed back down into the deep from which it arose.

I must somehow try to orient myself to the fact that this *is* my life. This is the reality I am in, the reality I must live. (This is the day the Lord has made! It is a blasphemy, but I must nonetheless write it: Yuck!)

Scrape the barrel, then. Take your scrap of bread and wipe up the last vestige of oil from the empty food dish, and cling more desperately to gratitude than to the hope of release. Even if it is nothing more than a crumb that has fallen to the floor, bend down and eat.

But what does it *mean*, to say this is my life, this here and now, these interminable hours of deprival and vain anticipation? I do not know how to answer this question, beyond my morning exercise, brushing my teeth, washing my socks and underwear, trying to order my greasy hair without a comb—the details of trying to maintain some bodily dignity and viability. I do not know, beyond trying to cope and just continue on continuing. I think of #1's question—how can I change my life—and I rephrase it: how can I *live* my life?

I do not know, he said. And neither do I.

—notebook

There's a sudden hubbub downstairs. Medicine Man is here. We can hear his laughter moving through the house and up the stairway. "Ha ha, chuckle chuckle," I say.

"'So then I showed them the gun,'" Harmeet says. "'Ha ha.'"

When Medicine Man enters, he hands me a DVD. On the cover there's a picture of a bearded man with soft eyes. "It is some video about *salam*, the Jesus man," Medicine Man explains. "You will go downstairs to watch it in just five minutes." He turns to leave. Harmeet asks if there is any news. "No," Medicine Man says. "Just suddenly you will go. Phone call and go, all together. The British negotiator—and the Canadian—they are both in Baghdad. Like you, I am just waiting."

What about the video of Norman? Harmeet asks. "We are waiting. They have not answered," he says. Norman asks if there's some reason why they're keeping me and Harmeet if there's no problem with the Canadian government. "As you know, the American man, Thomas, his government will do nothing. They not care about him. The British are cold. You and you"—he points to Harmeet and me—"you are safe from the beginning. So we have a plan from the beginning to take you as a group, to make the negotiating together. If we do not have the negotiations, we kill all of you. So we keep you to release together."

I ask if it would be possible to talk with Tom on the phone.

"Why?" Medicine Man says. "I see him myself, with my own eye. Just today."

Just a quick call, I counter, so we'll know he is okay.

"I know that. I see him today."

"*You* know that," I say, unable to contain my rage, "but I don't know that."

Medicine Man stares at me. "I know that," he says coldly, his voice slicing like a guillotine. Our eyes lock. My jaw clenches. I want to jump up and wrap my hands around his windpipe. *There's no way you're going to win this*, a voice says. I pull myself together, look away, let my shoulders fall.

I hear Norman's voice cutting in. "You've kidnapped me, but it's more like you've kidnapped my wife." He breaks into tears. "I know that I'm alive, but she doesn't. She's the one who's been kidnapped!"

Medicine Man's phone rings. He pulls it out of his pocket, looks down, smiles. It's a text message. "What's this word, 'kidnapped'?" he asks, distracted.

"What you've done to us!" Norman cries. "You take us from the street, handcuff us, keep us locked up . . ."

"This means kidnapped? *Makhtoof*?"

"Yes. Kid-napped," Harmeet says.

Medicine Man puts his index finger against the wall. "How do you spell it?" he asks, writing each letter on the wall as Norman says it. "Yes, I see. *Kidnapped*. I'm sorry, Doctor."

"You see," Norman says, almost pleading, "I know that I'm alive, but my wife has no way of knowing."

Medicine Man's phone rings again. "Who is sending me another text message?" He looks at his phone and chuckles. "It is my girl-friend." He puts the phone away. His face turns serious. "But that is why we take the video. She know, Doctor, she know. She give the three questions only you can answer."

"But has she seen it?" Norman asks.

"The video is gone, Doctor. They have it." He points to the DVD in my hands. "In five minutes you will go downstairs. I must to go. Good night."

The guards unlock us and bring us downstairs. We sit on the floor and help ourselves to a small plate of fried potatoes, eating them one at a time with a stale piece of *samoon*. When it's time for the movie, Nephew and Uncle are excited. "*Issau salam, Issau salam,*" they say. Nephew loads the disc into the player. The room falls silent. I'm tense, fully alert. I have no idea what this narrator is saying or how it might be received by our captors. Uncle points at the screen as Mary is visited by the angel who announces she is going to give birth to a son.

"*Haram. La Islam,*" Uncle says. It is forbidden in Islam to show images of God, Jesus, Mohammed or Mary. What's this? Why are they doing this?

I worry Uncle's indignation will escalate unpredictably. It doesn't. He watches closely, muttering periodically as the movie progresses. Nephew looks torturously bored.

The story unfolds. The first disciples are called. Jesus wanders through countryside and village, teaching, giving sight to the blind, healing the sick, exorcising demons. He walks on water, confronts scribe and Pharisee, calls Lazarus out of the tomb, brings life wherever he goes. I imagine his words. "The last shall be first and the first last." "Love your enemies, do good to those who hate you, bless those who curse you." "Whatsoever you do to the least of these, you do to me." My arms shiver electrically. The acting is wooden, Jesus's eyes are impossibly blue, the special effects are childish—but here it is, the Gospel! The good-news liberation of every human being from every kind of bondage. Somehow it has found us!

Then the inevitable confrontation. Jesus ransacks the outer precinct of the temple. The authorities are enraged. Jesus and the disciples go into hiding, gather around a table for one last supper. This is my body, Jesus says, do this in memory of me. He is betrayed, arrested, condemned, flogged, crowned with thorns, forced to carry the instrument of his execution in a grisly parade of state power. They strip him naked, nail him to a cross, hoist him into the air. *Eloi, Eloi, lama sabachthani?* "My God, my God, why have you forsaken me?"

This is crazy, surreal, too much. To be watching the Crucifixion, in an insurgent safe house, in captivity, under the rule of the gun. "We kill all of you," Medicine Man had said. *Tom! Where are you? How are you enduring all on your own? Or is it much worse? Are you hanging now on a mujahedeen cross, shivering and forsaken, called like the suffering servant to a shock absorber of violence, one who carries the wounds of the world in his body? No, please God, not this. Not for Tom. Not for any of us.*

# FEBRUARY 22 DAY 89

I'm homesick, depressed. I feel like my spirit is dying and I am sick. Yesterday, last night, and to some extent now, I'm in that weird fever world, where my brain feels tender, swollen, brittle; and everything feels granular, angular, bent, warped out of shape. I feel always on the brink of a chill. I couldn't bring myself to exercise this morning— the first time since our little morning regime began. My body, my mind just wouldn't do it.

Last night, Norman said he'd gone back to being in on-hold mode, "which isn't very useful to you two." This, I think, is what I need to do as well. Expect nothing. But how *long* can one go on this way, living off the fumes of vague, repeated promises? We have literally been told three, four days since the first week of our captivity. This, more than anything, is what enrages me, being strung along by the nose, jumping like fools through a never-ending succession of empty hoops, trained pets who'll sit up pretty for a little tidbit of news.

Tomorrow is Medicine Man's "not more than one week" best guess. I, *we*, have got to get out of here. The Simonas went six months. The thought sends me sliding into the abyss. *Another* three months! Our lives have been stolen from us. I am in a rage: at myself, CPT, Bush and Blair, this *mujahedeen* group. The *waste* of sitting here, my right hand chained to the door handle, the left handcuffed to Harmeet. I am a seed buried deep in the bowels of the insurgency, a seed of hoping and waiting. God help me. To endure, persist, love. At the very least, deliver me from despair. Give me wings to carry me through these days. Give me the consolation of your presence. Give me a generous spirit so that I may reach out to the suffering of others, the endless host of those whose lives have been stolen by poverty, war, oppression. Give me to know that I am not the only one, that there is a solidarity of suffering in the Body of Christ, that no matter what happens, the cross is not the final word: There is Sunday morning! There is resurrection! There is Release.

*Shwaya shwaya.* This too shall pass.

—notebook

Uncle thinks we enjoyed the Jesus video so much, we're watching it again tonight. As he loads it into the DVD player, Junior asks me what I would do if the United States invaded Canada. He pretends he's holding a machine gun. Would I not become *mujahedeen*, "Canada *jaysh*?" he says, pointing at me.

No, I say, I cannot kill anyone, not for any reason. "This *Issa salam*," I say. I want to explain to him that there are other ways of resisting—there's the power of non-violence, the power of Gandhi, Dr. King and the Badshah Khan—but where to begin, how to find the words!

"*Majnoon, majnoon,*" he says, laughing and making circles with his finger at his temple.

# FEBRUARY 23 DAY 90

It is Junior who comes to unlock us in the morning. Harmeet tells him it is his sister's birthday today. Junior nods sadly. His sister is very sick, he tells us, the doctors can't help her. To comfort him, Harmeet says he is sorry, we will pray for her today.

*Inshallah*, you will be out for your sister's next birthday, Junior says to Harmeet. He rubs his left buttock and complains of intense pain. Why? he asks me.

I don't know. Could it be from driving?

Yes, back and forth to Fallujah every day. Too much driving, he says.

*Junior has not been watching Tom at the first house then. Tom, what is happening to you? It's been eleven days!*

When they bring us downstairs, I immediately lie on the floor and close my eyes. I don't care about the filth of the rug or what the captors might say. I'm desperate to rest my body. I hear Harmeet explaining to Junior that I am sick. "I am sorry," Junior says to me. "*Bacher duwa, bacher duwa,*" he promises.

Harmeet lends me his sweater for a pillow. Norman gives Harmeet his tweed jacket and Harmeet covers me with it. I surf through the evening on waves of sleep and the babble of television, dimly aware of Junior whispering fervently on his prayer mat.

The captors have left. The door is closed. The darkness is a relief.

*Dear God*, I pray, *help me. I can't stand it here anymore. I want to go home. You order the stars and set the planets on their courses. Please, return us to our lives, our families, our loved ones.*

The image of Junior praying for his sister strikes me like a thunder-bolt. We are both praying to the same God! How can this be, when I am in handcuffs and Junior holds the key, when he is the oppressor and I am the one he oppresses? Is it possible that God can hear both our prayers at the same time? Who is this God we are praying to, lord of innumerable worlds and the incomprehensible reach of the universe? My mind whirls at the inexplicability of it and I fall into the sweet oblivion of sleep.

# FEBRUARY 24 DAY 91

It was a strange night. Felt as if I didn't sleep at all. How to describe it? Low fever incoherencies. My head and my body thoroughly inhospitable, both squeezing, trying to expel my consciousness. Sometime after dawn, I woke up sweat-soaked, and I felt normal— the greatest feeling in the world! I have little mental energy for writing. Another day of no exercises, save some slow walk-shuffling and climbing the stairs a few times.

News from Uncle. Clashes between Shia and Sunni. In Baghdad, Najaf, everywhere. Two days ago, he tells us, a Sunni mosque that was being fixed was bombed. No one was killed. A Jewish, American, Iranian conspiracy. Shia are not Muslims.

Yes, Shia are Muslims, I say.

They are *noos* Muslim, Uncle says. Only half Muslim.

I have Shia friends—they are Muslim.

He's surprised. *Shwakit? Kadim?* Before or now? What do you want for lunch? Potato cooked in oil? *La* oil. Bad for the stomach. Every day oil.

—notebook

# FEBRUARY 25 DAY 92

The sound of martial law in Baghdad. No car horns, no arguments in the street, no donkeys clopping, no ping-ping-ping of propane vendors passing by. According to Junior, 141 Shia were killed in yesterday's clashes. We ask him how many Sunni were killed. None, he says, smirking. It's the newest nightmare scenario: civil war, armed chaos and complete social breakdown making delicate ransom negotiations impossible and exponentially increasing the risk of holding on to three hostage assets.

Baghdad falls silent and I fall into a netherworld of fever. Everything offends and provokes. Harmeet's unfailing politeness, his wiggling toes, the crinkle of his copy book as he flips back and forth through its finger-soiled pages. Norman's incessant gastro-eruptions, all-exactly-the-same-sounding, his fussiness of movement. I'm deathly irritable, sensitive, volatile, capable of spontaneously combusting with rage. I lose track of time. Nothing coheres or matters. The only thing I know is self-pity or rage.

During a break in the curfew, Medicine Man appears with a video camera. He wants us to make an appeal to the leaders of the Gulf Arab States—Sheik Khalifa, Prince of Benzyde Al Inhayon, and Sheik Hamid, Prince of Qatar.

I am furious. What the hell is this! How many more of these stupid, useless, goddamned videos do we have to do! What about "Big *Haji* in Baghdad"? What about "suddenly I get the phone call and you go"?

Medicine Man points his camera at me. I grit my teeth and sit up like a trick poodle. When the required speeches are done, I tell him I am sick, I need medicine, an antibiotic, something for pneumonia. I write the word down for him. He says he will get it as soon as he can.

The next morning I'm too weak to get out of my chair for morning exercise. Junior points to Harmeet and says, "This good. Harmeet *zane*, Harmeet happy. Norman *noos-noos. Zane/mozane.*" Then, pointing to me, "This no good. *Mozane*. Jim *kool yom hazeen.*" He wants me to be happy like Harmeet.

It's too much. I am sick to death of grinning for him, pretending, putting up with his orders, his scorn, his contempt. Anger flashes white and explodes. I stand up and get in his face. "Don't You EVER Tell Me What I Should Feel," I say, enunciating each word with typewritten precision, voice flashing like a sword. "Not when I'M the one who has to wear these FUCKING handcuffs!"

Junior steps back, shocked, eyes wide. I sit down, shaking with rage, ready to kill. He clenches his jaw, threatens me with his fist, deluges me with words I can't understand. *Go ahead,* I dare him with my eyes, *even in handcuffs I will tear you to shreds.* He mutters something and storms out of the room.

Nephew finishes locking us up. Norman and Harmeet ask him if they can lay the futon out in the middle of the room so I can sleep. "Yes," he says, "*mooshkilla, mooshkilla.*" I collapse onto the mattress and fall asleep before Nephew can finish chaining my ankle.

—

The days are a fathomless void and a consuming agony. Prayer is useless. God is dead. There is only suffering without meaning or end. The nights are the worst. I think it's a dream, but I'm not always sure—Medicine Man wearing a surgical mask and an operating gown, holding a scalpel and a bone cutter, butchering me into scores of little pieces that he lines up in perfect anatomical sequence and tortures with electric prods. Again and again and again.

When Medicine Man does come, I'm not sure he's really there at first. He bends down to look at me, his face full of concern. I force myself to sit up. "You have some trouble with my man," he says. "You must to understand. They are the simple man. They do not know these things. This very difficult, very dangerous, they have some stress. I speak to him."

I ask if there's any way I can see a doctor. "This may be something," he says. "We have a doctor who work for us." I tell him that I need an antibiotic and more acetaminophen. "I bring for you," he says. The effort of it is too much. I collapse and fall asleep.

When my rage is spent, there is only despair. I turn to it like a drug. I imagine myself at the edge of an abyss. Everything around me is angry and black, bitter and boiling, except for the abyss, which is warm and sweet. I imagine myself sliding away, falling in, a door opening, the current taking me. Enough of this, no need to hang on anymore, all you have to do is let go. Just say yes and everything will be over. Wonderfully, deliciously, intoxicatingly over.

NO! a voice says. It is like a finger snapping, like a hand flicking a switch. It's a force completely independent of me. It speaks only once. Something stiffens, takes hold within me, and I know immediately: I am going to live.

Bubble wrap packets of acetaminophen and an antibiotic appear, and a wondrous certainty blossoms like a spring orchard. God is not dead after all.

# MARCH 3 DAY 98

Am feeling better. Enough, actually, to declare myself returned to the land of the living. Started a course of antibiotic yesterday that attacks pneumonia—only six pills!

My fever is definitely broken. I awoke this morning without a trace of it and the roundness seems to have come off the swelling in my neck. I had enough energy this morning to do a tiny bit of mild stretching, and some very gentle walking.

My body will recover—fully, I feel I can safely expect—but there's a "but." I think, if I haven't already, I'm at risk of plunging into depression. I *need* to focus on the now, the day, be thankful that I am feeling better, the window is open, birds are singing. There is a cheerful shaft of sunlight illuminating our room. I have two brothers who have been looking after me.

—notebook

# MARCH 4 DAY 99

I suddenly understand the Psalms. I never could before, the repeating couplets that yearn and sigh and rail, the interminable laments, the innocent narrator besieged with enemies and afflictions at every turn. I used to yawn and roll my eyes: please, not again, spare me the high spiritual drama and holy persecution complexes. But now I know. The Psalms were never written for ordinary time, the place most of us live in most of the time, the everyday round of getting up in the morning and falling into bed at night, the hours in between cluttered with the thousands of things we have to do to get through the days and the weeks. No, the Psalms were written for the time of anguish and terror, when life is in peril and mercy is all that matters. They cry out for us when we are in *extremis*, facing the final hour alone and without hope, the time when God dies and there is nothing but suffering.

Alas, I do not have a bible. I decide to try and write my own.

My God, my God,
where have you gone, where can you be?
I speak but you do not hear me,
I call but you do not see.

My heart breaks open with crying,
weeping and gnashing of teeth are its song.
My spirit rolls in ash,
anguish has broken my soul.

The lions come for me,
their jaws dripping with juices.
Hyenas circle in the distance,
eyes watching with greed.

"Come quickly to my aid," I cry.
"My time is at hand!"
But you, riding the heavens by moonbeam,
are too starfield far to hear.

Of me there is nothing left.
I am no more than gnarled bones,
lost and scattered to the far corners of the earth
shining in the moon's forlorn light.

Though you measure the span of the universe
with the span of your finger,
but of my distress know nothing,
there is one last question I must ask, O God,
one thing I must know.

What of the days of my childhood,
when on summer days you held my hand
and wild we ran skipping sidewalk free?

*What of our visits in secret forest glades,*
*the plunge and play in ocean surf,*
*the breathtaking climb of wild mountain heights?*

*What of waiting in the long of the five o'clock grocery line,*
*when in every face and every place you shone,*
*glory all around?*

*Your servant is waiting, O God,*
*waiting for the light of your face.*
*Send forth your chariot now*
*and come quickly to my aid.*

*Deliver me from this grave,*
*release me from this tomb.*
*Death's paw is on my throat*
*and death's door is open wide.*

Always I have felt it, even as a young child, some sense of God's presence in my life. In my breath, my heartbeat, the light and breeze around me, even if only as a whisper of a trace, always, always I have felt, known God was there. Except for these terrible days when I needed him most.

It has to be the most difficult of all human tasks: making sense of suffering. It confounds me, I don't know how, I don't think I can make sense of it. I know only it was pure hell and absolute desolation. But today, the feeling I have always known in the deep of my being has returned. God is alive!

I am filled with strange and wonderful tears. Those days when God had died, they are a gift, a window through which I can see what I never could before: how much I love and need God, and how intolerable life would be without him.

# MARCH 5 DAY 100

One hundred days of handcuffs and chains. One hundred days of being reduced to this penury of waiting. A grisly milestone indeed. But I am secretly exhilarated. We've done it. We're here. We've somehow got this far. As much as the thought sickens me, if I can do this, I can do another one hundred. And if I can do another hundred, I can get through a year.

I decide to commemorate the day with a letter. I think for a long time before I choose my greeting. I finally decide on "My dear Dan." This should not give away too much.

Despite Norman's obstinate assertion that this day is just like any other, one hundred days in captivity does seem like a bit of a milestone, significant at least as a marker of deprivation, and the necessity of enduring deprivation. Why, we ought to celebrate, bake a cake, string up balloons, invite people over . . . but then of course, directions are a bit of a problem, and our existence is a minor anti-state secret, and besides, there's nowhere for people to sit. It would be easier, too, perhaps even possible to celebrate, if there were some end in sight, but alas there is none. Not even an indication of a clue of a possible day of release. The horizon before us is blue and clear with waiting. The only comfort is that when you get to read this, it all will finally be over, the never-ending immediacy of it vanquished by the hand of time. The time between now and then reaches before us into mystery.

I put down my pen. I can't do it. Something's not right. This is not the letter I want to send to Dan. It's too clever, too glib. What I want is to pour my heart out, acknowledge the suffering this must be for him, tell him how much I miss him. I cannot write such a letter. Not here.

I change tack abruptly. I have been considering this for some time now. A letter of appeal directly to the bosses—the invisible higher-ups who are giving the orders, pulling the strings. Something that says, *Please, let us go. Respectfully: Norman Kember, Harmeet Singh Sooden, James Loney, in absentia Tom Fox.*

It sickens me, how hierarchy displaces responsibility, how the people who have to face us each day, deal with our smells, bring us our food, see our underwear and socks hanging about drying, they do not feel responsible for what they are doing. They're just following orders. Someone else, someone above them, someone who doesn't even know what we look like, they're the ones who are responsible, the ones who make the decisions. They sit behind their big desks and swivel in their important chairs, never having to look us in the eye, see our fear, smell our degradation. We are safely abstract, little pawns that can be moved around and disposed of without effect. Every hierarchy is like this. It separates the finger that pushes the button from the bomb, the bomb from the blast, the blast from the carnage. It protects those who are responsible from having to face the consequences of what they decide, and absolves those who implement the decision from feeling responsible for what they do.

I think this is why we have never asked, never said it directly: *Please, could you let us go.* It seems futile, to ask the guards or Medicine Man for the return of our freedom, when it's not their decision. And it is too much to ask. If they are prepared to risk their lives and defy the orders they are obligated to follow, because they are compelled by our humanity and theirs to do the right thing, then so be it. But I cannot ask these men to die for my freedom. They must decide this for themselves.

I begin:

We have been asked to appeal to the governments of the United States, Great Britain and Canada, as well as leaders of various Arab Gulf states, for help in securing our release. As we understand you are the individuals responsible for making decisions about our release, we would like, on this one hundredth day of our captivity, to make a direct appeal to you for our release.

As you know, we came to Iraq on a mission of peace, to build bridges between the people of Iraq and the people of the West, and to try and share with the ordinary people of our countries the stories of ordinary Iraqis in a time of war and occupation. In this way, we wanted to be a small part of turning the tide of public opinion against the continuing occupation of Iraq by the United States and Great Britain. We remain firm in our convictions and our commitment to peace.

In the name of God, the Merciful and Compassionate, Lord of every human being—

I am just about to write it, the crucial words, *let us go!*, when Medicine Man arrives. It's his fourth visit in seven days. He's becoming a regular. Today he says the Canadian negotiations are strong and on track. The minister of foreign affairs is in touch with their negotiator and he wants the matter completed. It's just a matter of transferring the money.

The minister of foreign affairs! My hearts thrills with hope. Is that Pierre Pettigrew? I ask.

No, it is something like Mac-kay, he says.

Mackay? Who's that, I wonder. There must've been a cabinet shuffle.

There's a British lord working on the case, Medicine Man says, the same one who sent the three questions for Norman. "There is some movement, but the British are cold."

I summon my courage to finally ask it: How much money are they negotiating for? "Two million," he answers. "Two million, for each of you."

It's mind-boggling! "Two million, for each of you." We are valuable commodities indeed. This means contact has been established with our governments, they know we're alive and they're trying to get us out. What remains is securing the agreement and negotiating the logistics of transferring the money. My best guess is that it will take another month.

It sickens me when I realize that Medicine Man made no mention of Tom. I'm beginning to suspect that he's been killed.

Harmeet is in the middle of his check-in. "I feel we're quite safe," he says. "As Medicine Man says, we just have to wait."

I take a deep breath. Here is confirmation of what I have long suspected, that Harmeet and Norman are in denial about the reality of our situation. It repulses me, the creeping passivity of captivity, how it infects and corrupts us, like a soothing intoxication, a tranquilizing palliative. There's nothing you can do, it whispers, the decision is out of your hands, relax and let the current take you, you just have to wait, it'll be okay, waiting you can do.

NO! I want to rail and scream. We have to act, get ready, be vigilant for the opportunity whenever it comes. It's impossible to describe, the dismay, the disgust, the rage it evokes, sitting here, day after day, holding out my hands for them to handcuff, the polite smiling and servile obedience. The cry rises from every molecule in my body. *This is not living! I want to live!*

"We are *not* safe," I interrupt, breaking the golden rule of check-ins. "Not for one minute. We could be raided, things could suddenly deteriorate in the political situation, there could be civil war. The captors could have a change of command. They could be forced to kill us to protect their ongoing operations. Until we get out of here, anything can happen."

"I know all that," Harmeet says tightly. "I'm just saying that the negotiations are looking good."

"And I'm just saying we have to be ready to take things into our own hands. We know that Medicine Man is a liar."

The check-in stops. We fall silent for a long time. As my anger subsides, I fall deeper into dismay. It could be that they're right. There are three basic strategies for survival, I think: dig in and fight, run away, or adapt. If I was able to reconcile myself to waiting, adapt the way Harmeet and Norman seem to have, perhaps I'd suffer less. But I can't. I abhor adapting, I'm not built for it. Everything within me wants to act. If I can't fight, I have to flee.

I flop about like a fish that's been landed in a boat. There's no answer to it. Waiting is one survival strategy, escape another. The risks of an escape attempt are momentous, but so are the risks of doing nothing. It's a gamble either way and we have no way of knowing. Regardless of what we choose, we have to face our situation as it really is. Denial can only lead us to doom.

# MARCH 7 DAY 102

Two million dollars. I can't stop thinking about it. It's mountainous, startling, incomprehensible. I am being claimed by my government, despite working for an organization that will not under any circumstances pay a ransom. It sickens me, the thought that the purchase of my freedom will be used to buy more weapons to kill more people. I intend to keep the commitment I made when I joined CPT. I won't ask for it, but neither will I object if a ransom happens. In fact, I am secretly hoping it will. I want too much to be free.

"Do you have any news about Tom?" I ask.

Medicine Man looks stressed. "Yes, he is still at the other house. We have some problems, so we separate him. You know his government will not negotiate for him. The CIA is trying to prevent the negotiation. They do not want the exchange to happen, so it is taking a long time and the negotiation very slow. We announce that we kill him—to separate your case. But we not kill him. He will be released with you. We just make this announcement to some media."

Kassie! Andrew! The weeping, wailing, mortal anguish of such news. It is unconscionable! An outrage! To make them think Tom has been killed for the sake of putting pressure on the Canadian and British governments. And I said nothing. I simply didn't think of it. I was so busy assessing the implications of his statement for my release, so preoccupied with securing my freedom, that I did not see the consequences for Tom's family. Unable to see, therefore unable to act. I am revolted at myself.

Downstairs with the captors. We pay close attention to the news. There's a brief story about us. Twenty seconds or so of the video Medicine Man shot eight days ago, our appeal to the leaders of the Gulf Arab States. It is strange, bizarre, surreal beyond words, to see oneself this way, on television as a hostage, being spoken about in a language you can't understand, from the very place you have been disappeared. Life really is stranger than fiction.

Ominously, there is no image of Tom. Neither do we hear his name spoken. We never ask after Tom's welfare again.

The nightly security protocol changes. The person in the middle—usually me—is no longer handcuffed twice. Harmeet and I can now sleep with one hand free. Norman, chained by his ankle, has both hands free. We no longer use the Instrument of Grace.

# MARCH 8 DAY 103

The captors have moved and taken up residence in what we think used to be the dining room. It is a cavernous space—perhaps fifteen feet wide and forty feet long—divided in half by a custom hardwood cabinet full of shelves and doors for storing dishes. The entrance to the room is just opposite the hallway sink, a few steps from the kitchen. The wall to the far right is banked with red velvet curtains that hang in front of windows that look onto the driveway. There's one sleeping mat against that wall, another in the middle of the room facing the television. The room is illuminated by a fluorescent light that's been hot-wired into a wall-mounted light fixture.

We sit facing the television along the wall opposite the curtains. The floor is covered by an ornate Turkish carpet with red and blue designs. The other half of the room is shrouded in darkness. It appears to be a grand parlour full of stately furniture protected by white sheets.

"I wonder why the sudden change?" I say.

"It was probably easier for them to move to a new room than it was to clean up their old place," Harmeet jokes.

# MARCH 9 DAY 104

It was a completely unremarkable day. I search my notebook for a sign or a clue. There is none. I remember there was a fierce wind-storm in the night. I remember I was still recovering from my illness. The window was open during the day and the light that filtered into the room was warm and healing. Sometimes I sat with Harmeet and Norman, but mostly I slept. The captors were still allowing me that luxury during the day.

I remember that Uncle was taking Harmeet downstairs to do laun-dry. Uncle had discovered a washing machine that actually worked. Harmeet was just stepping into the foyer when I grabbed the two upholstery covers Tom had used as blankets. Here, take these, I said. The nights were getting warmer and I thought it would be a good idea to wash and have them ready as an alternative to the heavy red blanket. I remember smelling the covers, hoping to catch a last trace of Tom's scent. It was faint, but I could still make it out.

They found Tom's body early in the morning. Some reports said it was in a ditch along a piece of wasteland next to a railroad track, others that it was outside a kindergarten. Some said it was in the district of Mansour, others Daoudi. His hands and feet were bound, his body wrapped first in a blanket and then in black plastic bags. The autopsy said there were eight bullet wounds to his head and chest; he had not been dead long—at most a few hours—and there were no signs of physical torture.

Our families and CPT were all given the news at the same time, in the early afternoon of March 10. They were told a body believed to be that of Tom Fox had been found the day before and the process of confirmation with fingerprints and DNA was under way. The team offered to identity the body but U.S. officials said no. The team asked where the body was and they said it was likely already on its way back to the United States. At 8:00 p.m. EST the U.S. State Department con-firmed it was Tom and CPT held press conferences in Chicago and Toronto two hours later.

The officials "misspoke." The body was still in Iraq, at Anaconda Air Force Base near Balad, awaiting transport to Dover Air Force Base in Delaware for an autopsy. When the team found out, Beth Pyles went immediately to see if she could accompany Tom's body home. They said yes, and Beth waited at the base for two days. Then they said no. The Army Reserve Mortuary Unit, whom Beth got to know and greatly respect, allowed her to escort Tom's body into the cargo hold of the plane. His casket was draped in an American flag. The soldiers said good-bye with a salute, and she read from John's Gospel with tears. "The light shines in the darkness, but the darkness has not understood it."

She waited on the tarmac as the soldiers carried a second casket into the plane. To her astonishment, it was the remains of an Iraqi detainee who had died in U.S. custody. He too was being taken to Dover for an autopsy. Even in death, she thought, Tom was accompanying Iraqis. Through more tears Beth recited for both men a verse from the Book of Job: "Naked I came into the world, naked I will depart. The Lord giveth, the Lord taketh away. Blessed be the name of the Lord." And then, in the only Arabic she could think of, *"Bis m'allah . . . Allah ackbar."*

The plane took off at 9:00 a.m. EST on March 12—the same day a memorial service was held for Tom at a Catholic church located near the CPT apartment in Baghdad. Anne Montgomery and Rich Meyer, both CPTers, watched outside the fence as the plane touched down at the base at six o'clock the next afternoon. Tom's children, Kassie and Andrew, and their mother, Jan (accompanied by Rich and CPT co-director Carol Rose), went to see Tom's body on March 16. After the viewing and a time of prayer, Tom was immediately cremated. Some of his ashes were scattered by his children at a favourite spot of theirs called Great Falls, and then at a place in the Shenandoah Mountains that Tom had designated.

On March 19, the team's driver took Maxine and Anita to a place called Hay Eladel, a strip of wasteland located along a railway track located in the Baghdad neighbourhood of Andaluse. This, they had been told, was where Tom's body had been found. It was one of the most dangerous things they did while on team. They covered their heads with *abiyas* and Max wore a *jubba*, the long black coat commonly worn by Iraqi women. They got out of the car briefly to survey the rubble-strewn railway margin. A passerby told them the bodies of Iraqi men were dumped there regularly. They drove to another location a few minutes away to hang the funeral banner. You see them everywhere in Iraq: wide bolts of black cloth with white writing, erected on poles at street corners or hanging from buildings. This one they hung on a wall overlooking an expressway. They wanted as many people to see it as possible. *In memory of Tom Fox in this place*, it read in Arabic. *Christian Peacemaker Teams declares, "We are for God, and we are from God." To those who held him we declare, God has forgiven you.*

In the customary way, the first sentence announced Tom's death; the second sentence offered a traditional condolence from the Quran; the third sentence was a message for his killers reminding them of CPT's unwavering intention. When they went back to get it a week later it was still there, unmolested and intact, exactly as they had left it.

We do not know any of this until much later. Nor do we know that Tom sat down to write on the evening of November 25, the day before our kidnapping, a reflection for CPT called "Why Are We Here?"

It's the ultimate question, really. Why *are* we here? Whether we're cleaning up after dinner or facing a gun, the earth turns, the sun rises and sets, the seasons come and go. We all have to find our way some-how. We have to make sense of the turning, the rising and the setting, the coming and going of our lives, whatever the here is that we've been given to live. It's the task God has breathed into us. True to his serious and thoughtful nature, Tom spent his last night as a free human being deliberating on this question.

I offer it now as his last will and spiritual testament. It was what the arc of his life pointed to, what he fought to live each day we were chained together, what he aspired to, I'm sure, until his very last breath.

The Christian Peacemaker Teams (CPT) Iraq team went through a dis-cernment process, seeking to identify aspects of our work here in Iraq that are compelling enough to continue the project and comparing them with the costs (financial, psychological, physical) that are also aspects of the project. It was a healthy exercise, but it led me to a somewhat larger question: Why are we here?

If I understand the message of God, his response to that question is that we are to take part in the creation of the Peaceable Realm of God. Again, if I understand the message of God, how we take part in the creation of this realm is to love God with all our heart, our mind and our strength and to love our neighbours and enemies as we love God and ourselves. In its essential form, different aspects of love bring about the creation of the realm.

I have read that the word in the Greek Bible that is translated as "love" is the word *agape*. Again, I have read that this word is best expressed as a profound respect for all human beings simply for the fact that they are all God's children. I would state that idea in a somewhat different way, as "never thinking or doing anything that would dehumanize one of my fellow human beings."

As I survey the landscape here in Iraq, dehumanization seems to be the operative means of relating to each other. U.S. forces in their quest to hunt down and kill "terrorists" are, as a result of this dehumanizing word, not only killing "terrorists," but also killing innocent Iraqis: men, women and children in the various towns and villages.

It seems as if the first step down the road to violence is taken when I dehumanize a person. That violence might stay within my thoughts or find its way into the outer world and become expressed verbally, psychologically, structurally or physically. As soon as I rob a fellow human being of his or her humanity by sticking a dehumanizing label on them, I begin the process that can have, as an end result, torture, injury and death.

"Why are we here?" We are here to root out all aspects of dehumanization that exist within us. We are here to stand with those being dehumanized by oppressors and stand firm against that dehumanization. We are here to stop people, including ourselves, from dehumanizing any of God's children, no matter how much they dehumanize their own souls.

I thank God for you, Tom. For your life, your courage, your witness, your friendship. How I wish you had made it too.

## MARCH 10 DAY 105

*Delta Force 3:The Killing Game.* If I had to guess, I'd say the movie was made in the late eighties. The bad guys, this time, are fanatical Islamists intent on waging a global Jihad against Western freedoms. The good guys, a team of Delta Force commandos, have been ordered by the U.S. president to capture an Islamic terrorist mastermind and foil his evil plot to explode a nuclear bomb on live TV in New York City.

At the end of the film, Junior gets his gun from under his pillow and points it at the TV. *Najis,* he howls. *La! La!* he rages. American soldiers are weak, stupid, effete, incapable of the heroic bravery and special forces prowess shown in the film. He stands up, waves his arms, hops up and down, almost to the point of frothing. He puffs out his chest, points to Uncle and himself. They could easily kill ten American soldiers between them, he boasts. Uncle laughs in hearty agreement.

It fascinates me. They have not understood that this movie is about them. They are what the finger of this movie is pointing at, freedom-hating, suicide-bombing terrorists that George W. Bush invaded Iraq to save the world from. They do not see that this movie is the most dangerous weapon being aimed at them, that it is far more powerful than any tank or gun or bomb because it explains and justifies why they must be destroyed. I wish, instead of pointing his gun at it, Junior would leave the theatre altogether.

## MARCH 11 DAY 106

It's official. I'm back in the land of the living, sitting with Harmeet and Norman against the wall in plastic-chair hostage formation. Time here moves more slowly than it does in sick bay, where I could sleep at my leisure.

Medicine Man arrives at about 11:20 a.m. He has a video camera and a newspaper. He's going to film us holding the newspaper. All we have to do is say the name and the date. Who is the video for, we ask. The Society for Peace Between Canada and Iraq, he says. I wonder if this is a government front for transferring the ransom money.

We ask if there's any news. He shakes his head. Britain is still cold. Things are moving slowly with the lord. He is frustrated. "This should only be one month, not two, three, now four. This is the big problem. I talk with my chiefs in a worried way about this—the delay, the risk for us—and they give to me the decision. Now we just take some money—any money—and release. All of you. We have to finish the matter. Now it is just money. There are two people between me and the negotiator, but I am the one who make the decision. It should not be this way, going on for so long."

After taking the video, he holds up the newspaper. "Do you know what this says?" he asks us. He reads the headline—something about how the Sunni political parties have fallen into disarray. "It is very bad," he says, shaking his head. He seems despondent, tired, almost desperate.

Junior is beside himself with boredom. He stands in front of the TV with the remote, clicking through the eight stations. Soap opera, news, soap opera, news, soccer, commercials. He curses the television and throws the remote onto his mat in disgust. He takes his Quran and sits cross-legged on the floor. Nephew lounges on the mat against the wall. The room feels claustrophobic, filled with the bored agitation of its five captives.

Junior puts his Quran to the side and lies cruciform on the floor, covering his face. He gets up, kisses his prayer rug, unrolls it in front of the TV, kneels down and begins his evening prayers with great heaviness. When he is finished, Nephew takes the rug from him and steps out of the room. Junior lies face down on his bed. "Come on, Jim, massage," he says.

"La, la, ani mooreed," I say.

"Massage sit down," he pleads.

I laugh and pretend for a moment that I'm going to sit on him. *What are you doing?* I think, suddenly panicked. *That was not smart at all.* Luckily Junior does not react. I kneel down beside him on the mat. "*Shwaya* massage," I say.

Harmeet asks Junior if he can have the remote control. "*Na'am, na'am,*" he mumbles.

Harmeet takes the remote from his bed. He finds an English documentary about Iranian transsexuals. A young man is being interviewed on the eve of his sex change operation. He's radiant. He tells the interviewer he can't wait for the operation so that he can really begin his life as a woman. There are interviews with his doctor, what appears to be a social worker, his mother. My eyes fill with tears. It's people like him whose lives are the real frontier of human progress, I think.

Nephew returns from saying his prayers just as the documentary is concluding. He's frustrated that there's nothing worth watching on the TV. "*La* cable. *Mooshkilla.*" He takes the remote from Harmeet, changes the channel to al-Hurra news, yawns, scratches his belly, lies down on his mat. And then we see it. The top news story. A poster-board shot with all of our faces and names. The camera focuses on Tom. Then Tom blindfolded and wearing an orange jumpsuit. Then a road, the camera moving in on a spot on the ground and—the channel changes. Nephew is pointing the remote at the television. "*Shid ghul Tom?*" Harmeet says to Nephew.

Nephew sits up. He says something about a prisoner exchange, Tom is okay, he's at the other house, they're just doing a show about him this week, next week it will be one of us. He is lying.

I finish Junior's massage and return to my chair. Junior gets up and puts *Time Cop* into the DVD player for the third time.

# MARCH 12 DAY 107

Nephew asks Harmeet to go downstairs to help him in the kitchen— just before breakfast and again right after. I am jealous. I would give just about anything to be in his place, handcuff free and doing something useful, reconnoitring escape possibilities.

Harmeet gives us a full report when he returns. Nephew said the news was good for me and Harmeet. He made Harmeet promise not to tell Norman: Harmeet and I will be released first, then Norman, then Tom. There's a prisoner in the United States they're trying to get out in exchange for Tom—Omar Abdel-Rahman, the man who was convicted of bombing the World Trade Center in 1993. Harmeet asked about Tom. Nephew repeated his story about how they're doing a profile on each of us. Harmeet told him how Medicine Man had said they were going to announce to the media that they had killed Tom. Nephew repeated the story about the prisoner exchange.

I ask Harmeet what Nephew had him do.

"I washed some dishes first and then helped to clean the floor. He threw some water on the floor. I had this worn-down broom to scrub the floor with and he had a squeegee to push the dirty water into the drain. He didn't seem to want me to do a good job, though. I'd be digging into it, wanting to really clean, and he'd say that's enough. It was quite dirty but he just wanted to do a quick little rinse, it seems."

I have to know. "Do they use hot water for their dishes?" No, he says.

I remember feeling, when we were first promised "copy books" by Medicine Man, a little pang of disappointment. If we had asked, if we had received them earlier, I could have kept a journal chronicling our story, replete with spiritual bons mots and inspiring deep thoughts— something that could be published and, in a vain flight of fantasy, thereby join the pantheon of incarceration journals: Martin Luther King, Anne Frank, Etty Hillesum, Alfred Delp, Eugene Debs, etc.

So now I have paper, a pen, copious measures of time—have had this facility now for thirty-nine days—and I have to face it: I'm pretty darn banal, superficial, weak, limited in my ability to transcend the choking hold, the suffocating confines of our captivity. I won't be writing a great prison journal. This record, if I get to keep it, which I won't know until the day of release, will merely document my self-absorbed efforts to survive, get through the excruciating crawl of time, cope with the various deprivations that define this miserable limbo, illustrate the emptiness and profound limitations of my will, my mind, my emotions, my spirit.

I think of Etty, the amazing generosity and expansiveness of her spirit, how you can see her shining in those last handful of days, a Jewess in a concentration camp awaiting deportation to the Final Solution. I, meanwhile, am preoccupied with my sore throat; whether or not to take more antibiotic; choking down stale *samoons*; bemoaning the lack of food and the thoughtlessness of our captors; wondering if I will finally get a comb today, after asking repeatedly over the course of almost two weeks. How could she? How did she open herself so much and give so much? How was she able to reach beyond the anxieties of physical comfort, survival itself? I at least have the consolation (though possibly illusory) of a hope and an expectation of getting out of here. Etty had to have no such hope, yet she shines with a breathtaking generosity of spirit.

I'm afraid I'm not shining very much. I say this not to berate myself—really, what's the point of that? It is as a statement of fact and a reality for reflection: I'm a compromised compromiser who's willing to barter silence, complicity, co-operation and lassitude in exchange for the hope (promise?) of physical survival, release from captivity.

Case in point: Medicine Man's outrageous statement that they will use a public statement of Tom's death as a strategy for moving the Canadian and British negotiations forward to conclusion. I said nothing. I did not challenge him. I failed to be a voice for Tom's children, for Tom himself.

There are other examples. Every day that I eat, comply, co-operate with the directions of my captors, I am helping to put money in their pocket. This is not what I want. It is profoundly disturbing to think that my life will be bought back for two million dollars, and be used to kill and maim more American soldiers—beautiful young men and women who should be at home figuring out how beautiful and amazing they are—more Iraqi police and soldiers, or Shia, or whoever is determined to be public enemy #1. Blood on my hands.

This is not moral scrupulosity. It is merely a fact. I am a cog that's helping to turn the war machine, and I'm not willing to gum up the works. I want out. I want to go home. I'm willing to accept and live with the facts of this compromise. I don't expect it will keep me up at night. I am weak, afraid of consequences, torture, death. I do not, of my own accord, possess the action-hero testosterone to stand tall in the saddle and go to the wall no matter what. If that time ever comes (as well it may), and if I'm able to stay any course of moral integrity, it will be God's grace and gift that will be acting—nothing of me. What Norman says of himself is absolutely applicable to me: I am feeble. Everything about me is limited: my will, my understanding, my willingness to risk, (especially!) my generosity. Even something as banal as the capacity to entertain myself. There is no power, no capacity I am in possession of that can't be exhausted or crushed. Not even, I'm afraid to say it, my faith, my ability to love.

I think that's what I learned during those days of being sick, feverish, without the relief of painkillers, when my captivity was a constant stench in my nose. I learned that there are and there will be times in our lives when we will merely exist, when we will stumble through a landscape of desolation, when suffering can't be comforted or ameliorated, when we will feel that God has withdrawn, disappeared, when there is no possibility of meaning or hope or anything but somehow, second by second, trying to endure the relentless crush of suffering, and we begin to see/understand that it is entirely possible to be crushed, and maybe that wouldn't be such a bad thing because it offers a way out, an end. Perhaps there is a door of despair for all of us to pass through. It is just a fact, something difficult we can't avoid, a season of a human being's life. Even Jesus cried out, "My God, my God, why have you abandoned me."

Perhaps I am too quick to universalize. Perhaps there are a holy handful who live their lives—and deaths—with the constant comfort and an awareness of God's presence. But I am suspicious of any such claims . . .

—notebook

—

It starts with a question. "Do you see a cat on the wall, there above the window?" I ask.

"Where?" Norman says.

"It's next to the ogre," Harmeet says, pointing to the shape next to it in the water-damaged plaster. Yes, Norman sees it.

"You can see two very distinctive eyes," I say. "The right eye, it makes the cat's face seem quite vicious."

"'Tiger tiger burning bright/in the forests of the night,'" Harmeet says, reciting William Blake.

"'What immortal hand or eye/could frame thy fearful symmetry?'" Norman adds.

"What happened to his rhyme?" I say. "It clunks."

"It's a half-rhyme," Harmeet says.

"That's just what they call it when they can't make their rhymes work," I scoff.

No, Harmeet says, Blake is trying to call attention to those words. The poem is about evil, and the idea that nature holds within it a reflection of its creator, just like a work of literature, or any artistic creation. And so he's asking, what does the existence of violence in the world say about the nature of God? What does it mean to live in a world where a being like the tiger is beautiful—and horrific—at the same time?

"Are there other parts of the poem that clunk?" I ask.

Norman explodes. "Really, I must object to your use of the word 'clunk.' This is William Blake you're talking about. His poetry does *not* clunk!"

I'm taken aback by Norman's anger. "Well, in this instance it does."

"You don't know what you're talking about! When you can write poetry as good as William Blake, then maybe you can criticize."

I turn to him, shaking with anger. "Don't tell ME what I can say or think!" I cry.

"Very well, I withdraw that," he says. "But you need to be more careful about whom you're criticizing."

I hold my tongue. The room fills with an angry silence.

—

Nephew comes in to check on us. We ask him if his house is in Fallujah. Yes, he says.

Where do you stay now, in Fallujah or Baghdad?

"Fallujah," he says. "Madame, children, mother, father—all Fallujah. When it's hot, you come to Fallujah for swimming. Very nice, swimming in the river."

When does Sayeed come back? we ask. He's been away for several days now. *Bacher*, Nephew says. "Sayeed good."

Yes, Harmeet says, he gives us lots of food, lets us wash our clothes, brings us to watch television.

"Yes, yes, *ianni*, Sayeed good," he says. "Hayder angry." Nephew makes an angry face, waves his hand at his head, tenses his shoulders. "Hayder very angry. *Sadika mot.*" He drops his head against his shoulder, closes his eyes and sticks his tongue out.

Did his girlfriend die? Harmeet asks.

"*Shwaya*," he says. She will die soon.

"*Shoo mooreed?*" Harmeet asks.

Nephew traces a path from his breast to his head. She has breast cancer and it's metastasized to her brain. We ask how old she is. Seventeen, he says. We ask if she goes to school. No, he says, she is too sick. That is very sad, we say. Yes, he says, looking down. We tell him we will pray for her. Thank you, he says.


# MARCH 13 DAY 108

Harmeet is taken downstairs by Nephew to help with preparing lunch. This gives me and Norman a chance to talk. "You know, this conflict between you and me," he says, lifting my wrist with his handcuff, "it's really the consequence of these, isn't it? We're two very different people with very different habits and ways of coping with this situation that we're in. That's why."

His voice is gentle, but there's an edge of finality in it, as if this settles everything.

"Yes, I agree," I say. "This is very difficult for all of us. And yes, we are quite different. But I was quite hurt by the way that you talked to me. I felt really dismissed. Attacked, actually. It was so strong and happened so suddenly. It felt like it came right out of the blue, as if there was something more behind it. Is there something more that you need to say?"

"Well, it's just that we're very different people, aren't we?"

"Yes, that's true. Is that your answer to my question?"

"Basically, yes. William Blake is one of my heroes and I guess I didn't like the way he was being attacked."

"I wasn't trying to attack William Blake. I didn't even know it was his poem. I guess, if it had been Gerard Manley Hopkins we were talking about, I'd have jumpped to his defence. I was joking around, taking a potshot at poets who try to justify things that don't quite work."

"But you choose your words very carefully, much more carefully than I do. You really think before you use a word, and when you do, it means something."

"And I chose 'clunk' very deliberately. I don't know much about poetry—nothing at all about Blake—but when I heard it . . . There's this lovely build of phrase—'tiger tiger burning bright/in the forests of the night'—and I felt my ear was being prepared for a beautiful rhyme, and then it doesn't carry through. I was disappointed. And there's the word 'symmetry'—there is no symmetry in the sound. The stanza fails to deliver what he sets up for the ear to hear. So just because it's William Blake—"

"It doesn't mean he can't write a piece of bad verse," Norman says.

"That's right. It was when you said, 'When you can write poetry as good as Blake, then you can criticize,' that's what really hurt. Now as a principle—that you have to be at least as good as the person you want to criticize—that's not a sound principle. How, in the first place, would you make that judgment—what is good, and who is good enough? And really, with that kind of criterion, how could we have any discussion at all about art or literature or film? But I was trying to think, why was I so hurt? And I guess it's probably my writer's ego was attacked—every writer has one. But that's an ongoing struggle."

"Well, we are such different characters, hopefully we can respect each other in our differences," Norman says.

"Yes, we're going to have different opinions about things and we need to allow each other to have those opinions. It isn't always easy to respect each other in that. I hope that you feel respected by me. Maybe there are ways you feel that I don't respect you?"

"No, not really. It's an example of our differences, but not something I—"

"That's what hurt so much yesterday. I felt like you just didn't respect me. I know it's hard—we all fail at that—but please . . ." I hear Nephew and Harmeet coming up the stairs. Rage spews out of me like a gusher of lava. ". . . DON'T you ever tell me what I *can* say or *can't say*. Especially *here!* When we're chained up!" I slam my handcuffed wrist against the arm of my chair, eyes swimming with tears of rage.

"Okay," Norman says.

Harmeet enters first, Nephew follows with our lunch. I open my *samoon*. Reheated white rice. More rage. I have to hold my *samoon* for a long time before I calm down enough to eat it.

What I noted, what's interesting, what I wanted and hoped for most was just an apology. A simple acknowledgement of my feelings. That was not offered. I can manage, continue on normally in my relationship with Norman, get through what we need to in order to eventually, hopefully, get out.

Somehow, sometime in the early evening, my feelings shifted. The hurt let go and I had moved on. I no longer *needed* an apology; I was no longer carrying the injury I had sustained. I can live without receiving an apology, but I can't help noting the fact

I did not receive one. It tells me, I think, that Norman is not someone I can have a friendship with. Funny—I had entertained the idea of visiting Norman when we get out. I have almost no desire to now.

This brings me to reflect on the group nature of this experience. While on one hand, on the whole in fact, having brothers to go through this with has made survival and coping so much easier. It is hard to imagine how hard it would be to go through this alone. (Tom! It's been over four weeks now!) On the other hand, in many ways this has been the most challenging aspect of this experience, and the occasion of some of the most intense emotional pain.

—notebook

# MARCH 15 DAY 110

Today we have a flower! Nephew gave it to me last night, just as Junior was leading us back to our room upstairs. "Here, for you," he said. It was a rose.

I was so surprised, I all but forgot myself. "Why thank you. Nobody ever gives me flowers," I said in my best Southern belle accent, eyelids fluttering. He frowned at me as if I belonged to a deviant species. It was like a slap in the face: Remember where you are, Jim.

I brought the flower close to my nose. Wowmygoodnesswhat-heavenlypleasure! It was like breathing in a choir of angels. "From the garden?" I asked, rubbing the delicate rose skin between my fingers.

"Yes, garden," Nephew said.

"Thank you," I said.

So yes, we have a flower. Floating in a clear plastic cup. A lovely swirl of magenta pink, giving fragrance and beauty for free. Grace indeed, but oh so fleeting: its petal edges are already curling, wilting, turning brown. Everything changes, everything goes, I think. But for right now, today, we have a flower, and that is all that really matters.

# MARCH 16 DAY 111

Curfew today. No car traffic. Scooters and donkey carts only, please. There's a police presence at the intersection, as indicated by occasional loudspeaker instructions. Nothing for sure will happen today.

Our rose has survived another day. We asked Uncle how the garden was. He nodded. *Zane zane, wardeh* (gestures everywhere with hands, sniffs) *zane*. So we are in the season of roses, the season of flowers, spring! Praises be to God.

It also appears to be a season for killing. Was it yesterday, or the day before, that Nephew reported fifteen Sunnis had been killed in Baghdad? People attacked, gun-fired to death in their cars, shot by snipers. Killing—any kind, no matter for what—all killing disgusts me. I'm sick to death of it. Seeing it on the news, hearing about it, watching movies about it. The glorification and idolization of it. The money that's spent on it. The blind orders and justifications for it. There must come a day when killing will finally be seen for what it is: a collective insanity, a moral scourge, a blasphemy against God and against the human.

—notebook

While Norman is in the bathroom taking his bath, Uncle sniffs in his larger-than-life way. *"Shstem, shstem,"* he says, points to the open window in our room, then to the window he's opened in the stairwell leading to the roof, and body-languages the flow of air between them. *"Zane, zane shstem,"* he says, gets up, motions us to follow, leads, pointing towards the open stairwell window, goes up the stairs, we follow, and I get within three feet of the open window, and ah! there's blue sky! a date palm green frond flowing in the breezes! rooftops! the top of a flowering orange tree! *"Shstem,"* he says, and we all breathe deep the sweet spring air.

"Can I look out the window?" I ask. Uncle laughs. No, he says, and gently pulls me back downstairs.

Thus, the first glimpse of our beautiful blue world in 111 days.

—notebook

—

After the bath, Norman is sitting in bare feet, his pants rolled up. His feet and ankles are quite swollen. I ask him if he's noticed this. "Well yes, but my feet generally are a bit swollen. This one especially after I hurt it," he says, lifting his left leg and pointing to a large area of wine-coloured skin on his calf. "I'm not worried about it."

"Okay," I say, "but they do look pretty swollen. Can that be linked to your blood pressure?"

"Heart failure."

"Heart failure?"

He chuckles. "If your blood pressure gets too high, it leads to heart failure, which then causes your feet to swell."

"I'm sorry," I say. "Maybe I shouldn't have said anything."

Norman straightens his legs, turns and examines his feet, comparing them. "They are swollen, aren't they? I had sort of noticed, but I just didn't want to think about it."

Yesterday's movie, *Resident Evil: Regeneration*, filmed on location in Toronto. A surreal treat indeed to be feted with hometown images: City Hall, Nathan Phillips Square, Bloor Street Viaduct, Metro Hall, the Toronto skyline. The world I come from does exist, and it *is* there to return to.

## MARCH 17 DAY 112

Uncle announces that Medicine Man will be coming to do a video. "*Haji* make Hindi movie," Harmeet says, imitating a Bollywood dancer. Uncle laughs.

We prepare our Medicine Man list. At the top of the list, as always: news. Then an update on Tom. Then requests. Reading glasses and combs, a bible and a Quran, a lighter blanket. The contentious issue is whether or not to tell Medicine Man about Norman's swollen feet. Norman doesn't want to—he doesn't think it's a big deal. We think otherwise. It'll put pressure on Medicine Man to come to a resolution. Emphasize your chest pain, tell him that you have a heart condition, you have to see a doctor, we're worried.

Medicine Man arrives at nightfall, followed by Junior and Uncle. "Harmeet," he says, smiling. "I have come to make some Hindi film. Are you ready?" Medicine Man and Uncle exchange laughter. How interesting, I think. Everything we say is being reported to Medicine Man.

"We have to take another video," he tells us. "Just the name and time. This is to show you alive. They have some worry, especially about this one . . . if we kill him." He points to Norman and snaps his finger. He's forgotten Norman's name! "Just this video, we have the money, and you release. All of you. The other video, I not send it."

"The one of just the Canadians?" I ask.

"Yes, I still have it, I not send. This the last one, *inshallah*. News good. I send the video and then not long. Just some little thing . . . taking the money . . . when and where to release you. Now I make the video." He wants me and Harmeet to say our names and the date, Norman to refer to three questions that his wife has sent.

Medicine Man sits on the blue folding chair and replays the video. The three captors talk amongst themselves at great length, their faces solemn. Then Medicine Man stands up. He's about to leave.

"There were a couple of things you said you would get for us— combs, reading glasses, books," Norman says.

Medicine Man takes a breath. "I forget these things. I have been working every day on your case, making some negotiation. Believe me, I not have time for anything. I must to do the important thing. Books, glasses—these are some small thing. Not important. I forget them." He shrugs. "I am bad for that."

"There is one other thing. My ankles." Norman points to his feet. "My ankles are swollen." Medicine Man bends down to look closer. "This is a condition that could be related to high blood pressure," Norman says, pointing to his heart. "This is what I am taking medicine for."

"The heart?" Medicine Man says, peering closely at Norman.

"Yes," he says.

"You need this? Something to check the blood pressure around the arm?"

"Yes," Norman says.

"I bring it."

"Plus a stethoscope," I say. Medicine Man nods, edges towards the door. "Before you go, is there anything more specific you can say about the news?" He leans towards me as I ask the question.

"News good. For all of you. For you," he says, pointing to Harmeet and me, "it has been good from the beginning. Your government is always ready for the negotiation. But now it is good for the Doctor."

"So there is progress with the British?" I ask.

The power cuts out. Medicine Man takes out his cellphone and shines it towards me so he can see my face. "Yes. We will send the video to Canada and Britain. The British have agreed to negotiate. The only thing more is to make the transfer of the money and some details for you release. Everything looks good. I will see you tomorrow."

# MARCH 18 DAY 113

Uncle arrives with "supper"—a common plate of stone-cold fried potatoes and three very stale *samoons*. One of the *samoons* falls on the floor with a thunk. Uncle picks it off the floor, dusts it off and plops the stack of them on the *zowagi* cube so he can unlock us.

The thoughtlessness and disrespect of this sends my anger engines roaring—anger so caustic it threatens to eat me alive. It's the ugliest feeling. I hate how it pulses in my veins, a burning, cauterizing, consuming fury. *Action! Action now!* it screams, lashes, goads. It is the only thing capable of breaking the suffocating hold of our plastic-chair passivity. This, I start to think, is its real purpose. I formulate a test. *When I am angry, it is because of a perception that something is not right. I need something to be different.* I apply it to every situation I can think of, from the whole of my life. In every instance it seems to be true. I am unable to find a single exception.

Maybe this is what anger is, I think, a sacred energy, a vital inner force that irresistibly drives us to act for the change we need. It builds and builds until it is discharged, either in a carefully executed plan, or a blind flailing tantrum. If it cannot be discharged then something worse happens. It dies, and then there is only the open grave of despair. There seems to be no getting around it. You have *to do* something with anger. Sometimes all that's required is the slightest change in perception. This is what happens today. A thought comes to me, free and untethered, like a floating balloon. *You can sit there and rage all you want, it says, but you're the one who will suffer, not the captors. Your moods are of no consequence to them. But they do affect you, and the two men sitting with you.* This is enough. My jets begin to cool and I return again to some semblance of calm.

# MARCH 19 DAY 114

Midday. Medicine Man pops in with his video camera. He films me and Harmeet holding a copy of today's newspaper. "I have some negotiation today with the Canadian embassy," he says. "I must to finish today." He's harried, breathless, sweating. "The British too, but the Canadian one especially, they must to have it done." And then he's gone.

"The British got left behind again," Norman says, his voice sad. I feel a pang of guilt. Neither of us acknowledged the glaring exclusion of Norman from the video.

Uncle returns with a big bowl of rice and a lovely spinach and bean soup. He says a neighbour brought it to the door. Later that afternoon Uncle brings us something else. Three one-inch-square, one-inch-thick rose-coloured confections. "*Helcoom, helcoom*," he says. "This from Mosul." I take it into my fingers. It's dense, spongy, translucent. Uncle watches carefully as we take our first bites. Ecstasy! It is quite simply the most oh-my-God-delicious thing I've ever had. We thank him lavishly. He says he will give us some to take home with us.

Norman pulls up his left pant leg. He shows us, on his calf, a long purplish vein, half an inch wide and six inches long, and a large area of swelling. "Feel here," he says. There's a series of hard lumps under the skin. He's experiencing the same pain he felt during the end-of-December cellulitis episode. His toes are itchy. I give him the antibiotic I didn't use when I was sick.

The captivity is taking its toll. I'm worried about him. He seems to be aging right before my eyes. He's getting more uncertain on his feet and he looks waxy, almost embalmed. Swollen feet, chest pain, what appears to be a second bout of cellulitis. It's as if his body is saying, "I can't take this anymore."

I wonder what happened to the robust young man who set off with his brother for a motorcycle tour of northern Scotland, stopping here and there to scramble up rocky mountainsides; the cross-country runner and track athlete; the bone growth specialist who researched and lectured and administered the St. Bartholomew's Hospital (Barts) Department of Physics; the tireless activist who marched in the street, wrote incisive pamphlets, dressed up as a peace tree at summer festivals and attended dozens of meetings? It's such a mystery, the aging process, how it occurs, the imperceptible accumulation of wrinkle and sag, the greying of hair and coarsening of skin, the stiffening of joint and slowing down of limb.

Cheap grace. It's haunted Norman all his life, Dietrich Bonhoeffer's rebuke of an easy, complacent Christianity that avoids hardships and struggle. He never suffered any consequence for his commitment to pacifism. In fact, it rather worked to his advantage. After completing a degree in physics at the University of Exeter, he registered as a conscientious objector when, at the age of twenty-one, he was called up for the National Service. His application was accepted without question and the tribunal directed him to perform alternative medical work for two years. He started off polishing nurses' shoes and cleaning urine bottles, but then saw a rare posting for a trainee physicist and decided to apply. As chance would have it, one of the doctors who interviewed him was a leading member of the Fellowship of Reconciliation, an international peace organization that formed after the war. His sympathy for Norman's pacifism helped him earn the job and launched his career as a medical physicist. When he finished his service in 1955, he returned to London where he met the world-renowned physicist and Nobel laureate Professor Joseph Rotblat in the peace circles they frequented. Rotblat hired Norman on at Barts and two years later he went on to do his Ph.D. He married Pat Cartwright in 1960 and spent one year as a post-doctoral fellow at Brookhaven National Laboratory (located on Long Island in New York State) before settling into a comfortable middle-class existence as the father of two girls, Sally and Joanna, and a lecturer in nuclear medicine. He succeeded his mentor as head of department when Rotblat retired from Barts in 1976, a role Norman held until his own retirement in 1990.

Caught between the demands of his family life and career on the one hand, and his Christian idealism on the other, Norman fell away from peace activism for many years. The ease and relative affluence of his life seemed incompatible with a life of real discipleship. He went to church, taught at Sunday school and helped out with a children's club—activities that always complemented and never challenged the life he was living. He felt it was hypocritical to involve himself in the peace movement when he wasn't prepared to substantially change his lifestyle. He only returned to it in the 1980s, rejoining the Fellowship of Reconciliation and the Baptist Peace Fellowship after accepting that no one can fully live up to what it means to be a follower of Jesus. Concerned always that he'd been a "cheap peacemaker," he decided in his old age it was time to take a risk for what he believed, just as the young servicemen and -women in Iraq were taking a risk for what they believed.

Well, Norman, here we are. Any thoughts about cheap grace? I could use a little myself right now—how about you?

# MARCH 20 DAY 115 10:00 a.m.

As per yesterday, Uncle comes up in a bleary state, eyes dark-circled, explaining he'd been up till 6:00 a.m.—American soldiers and helicopters. I heard him in the wee hours of the morning, in one of the front bedrooms, metal occasionally banging, the sound of his body shifting. There were helicopters on patrol, hovering near the house, low enough to set off car alarms. I told Uncle I heard him. He said *"Jaysh Amriki,"* body-languaged "keeping watch with a rocket launcher," made a *schoof* rocket-launcher launching sound.

Fuck, that's a little freaky. They're going to fight to their death. This is the biggest threat to our survival. A raid will be a death certificate.

—notebook

We need to get out of here. Pronto, now, today. Tom has most certainly been killed. Medicine Man is becoming desperate. Uncle is on a fight-to-the-death watch. Norman was excluded from the last video. His health is deteriorating. The order for his separation could come at any hour. We're in mortal danger every second that we're here.

Harmeet and Norman think we can just ride this out. They're wrong. My mind has become very clear—we're not going to get out of here unless we take matters into our own hands. My body, however, is not yet ready, and the mere thought of what we have to do sends me into spasms of involuntary shaking.

I am the delegation leader. This is what I have to do. Grapple with the fear, prepare the way, bring the decision to birth within myself first. My mind turns feverishly to making a plan. My body responds with constant invisible trembling.

## MARCH 21 DAY 116

*"Saba il hare,"* we say to Uncle when he comes into the room. *"Saba il noor,"* he answers. He has a rose in his hand. He closes his eyes, inhales deeply, makes loud smacking sounds as if he's about to eat it, smiles, puts it in the plastic cup on the hostess trolley. "Garden, garden," he says. He unlocks us and opens the blue folding chair. He sits and shifts his weight in one motion. The legs of the chair buckle and bend sideways. Uncle recovers his balance, the chair falls, he picks it

up, for a moment tries to fix it, shrugs, tosses it aside. "Finish," he says. He locks us up after morning exercise and then leaves.

We will not see him again.

Vernal equinox: equal day and equal night. The guard has changed. Uncle's gone home and Nephew has taken the captor console.

Staff squabbles. Nephew is in a sour mood because Uncle left the larder bare—no sausage, no meat, no eggs, no tomato, no potato, and apparently no money in the *mujahedeen* kitty to get more. And to boot, as he was opening up the little blue fold-up chair to sit on during morning exercise, I informed him that it was "finished."

"Finished?" he said.

"Yes—Sayeed," and I pointed to the bent leg.

"*Mooshkilla* Sayeed," he said, opened the chair, took it out into the foyer, found it wasn't functional, frowned darkly, sat on the stairs.

—notebook

"My birthday is on Friday," Harmeet tells Nephew. It's part of the ongoing strategy: elicit sympathy, confront with our humanity. Who knows what will be the key that opens the door.

Nephew looks surprised. "Three days Friday?"

"Yes," Harmeet says.

"Good Harmeet," he says. How old will you be? he asks him. Thirty-three. When is your birthday? he asks me. October. Norman? August. "I bring happy-birthday-to-you cake," he says to Harmeet.

Norman does not say anything, but I see him, in the corner of my eye, nodding from time to time. Harmeet and I agree: the worst has probably happened; we're dealing with it in much the same way. It's there, in a mental file folder, a box, a hermetically sealed container. A fact or a possibility, that is all. There's no emotion around or for it. There can't be.

The implication of this fact or possibility is ominous. If Tom has been killed, somebody had to do it. Who then? Medicine Man? Video Man? Number One? One of the initial five who kidnapped us? Somebody else altogether?

The thought makes me shudder. Whoever it was must be waiting in the shadows, ready to kill the rest of us.

We have to get out of here.

As always, we are very quiet when setting up the futon for our afternoon nap. We want to keep our captors from finding out about this sweet afternoon indulgence for fear they will take it away from us. It is this more than anything else that succours my mood. Every step and movement must be coordinated: getting the futon and pillows, opening up the futon, laying down the pillows, unfolding the sheet, lying down on the futon, getting under the sheet. We move like a gangly three-headed creature with six legs and three arms.

Nephew pops his head into the room just as we are lying down. My body tenses, prepares for an angry reaction. "Good good, nice nice," he says, taking the sheet. He flicks it in the air, lets it fall gently upon us, makes sure that it covers our feet and our shoulders. The afternoon light is warm and gold-glowing. I close my eyes. The next hour is utter bliss.

Nephew and Junior are looking for their AK-47. They enter and leave the room, search and re-search their bedclothes, the floor behind the curtains, a cabinet cupboard.

"Should I tell them where it is?" Harmeet whispers to me.

"You know where it is?"

"Yeah, it's in that cupboard over there," he says, pointing to the cabinet. "I saw Uncle put it there when I was down washing the floor earlier. I guess he never told them where he put it before he left."

"Let them find it," I say.

"What kind of operation are they running here? They can't even keep track of their guns."

"I wish CPT training had included instructions on using an AK-47," I say, half-joking, half-serious.

Nephew lies on his mat and covers himself with his blanket. Junior continues to search, casually, wandering here and there as if he is bored. He makes a phone call. The person on the other end of the line directs him to the cabinet. Junior opens the cabinet door. His eyes light up when he sees the gun. "*Najis!*" he says into the phone.

He closes the cabinet door. He doesn't see there's a drinking glass on the floor near Nephew's bed. He knocks it over. The glass shatters on the tile floor. Junior jumps back and curses. It's instinctual, my impulse to get up and help, the courteous thing to do when somebody breaks or spills something. But a foot slams down in my mind. *No, let him clean up his own mess. He's the captor and you're the captive.* I stay in my chair. Harmeet springs up immediately and is on his knees picking up the glass.

My first response is judgment—*Stop, you're crossing the line, Harmeet*— but then I see Junior's reaction. "Thank you," he says, surprised and confused. This is not in the rule book, I think, a hostage offering spontaneous assistance to his kidnapper. Harmeet's action confronts Junior with his humanity and shifts the balance of their relationship. In this moment, he's no longer a helpless and subservient captive but a sovereign individual offering practical assistance to another. It's an example of moral jiu-jitsu.

I experienced this myself when I was sick. Junior asked me for a massage and I said no. Instead of complaining and pleading as I had expected, he said he was sorry and told me to lie down on the floor and sleep. He left the room and returned with a wet cloth to put on my forehead. In that instant my whole orientation towards him changed. I was filled with wonder and gratitude at being cared for when I had expected animosity and provocation. He had turned the tables on me.

A similar thing happened with Uncle. When the captors brought us downstairs one evening, I brought the yellow scrubby from the bathroom with me to clean the hallway sink where we wash our hands before supper and brush our teeth. It always appalled me, the dark veneer of grime that had been accumulating for God knows how long. Without asking for permission, I got the scrubby out and went to work. As soon as Uncle saw me, he wanted to know what I was doing. He stood behind me and watched, unsure at first what to do. He began to point to areas that needed cleaning and then took the scrubby so he could do it himself. "Good," he said when we were done, pleased with the gleaming porcelain result. In that moment we were equals, two men admiring the sink we had just cleaned.

This is what that passage from the Bible is all about, I think: "If your enemy is hungry, feed him; if he is thirsty, give him something to drink. In doing this, you will heap burning coals on his head." If he breaks a glass on the floor, help him pick it up. If he's feverish, get a wet cloth to cool his forehead. If his sink is dirty, clean it. Turn the tables; confront with surprise; provoke wonder, chagrin, even shame. Heap burning coals of love on his head. Do this and you will both be transformed.

Breakfast: a cake that Nephew brought from home, made by his wife, and a *samoon*. Lunch: a big bowl of rice garnished with fried potato bits. Late afternoon snack (first ever!): macaroni with mild chili spice. Supper: rice, macaroni, *samoon*. A stupendous amount of food. I am, for the first time ever, full. And still I could eat, and eat, and eat.

It puzzles me. Why now? Is it a sign they plan to release us? Is this something that Nephew has decided on his own? Do they feel so comfortable with us that they no longer believe we will hurt them or risk trying to escape? Whatever the reason, I don't mind. It feels good not to be so hungry.

## 8:45 p.m.

An hour and fifteen minutes to kill. I used to hate that expression, as if time, God's glorious gift, the lifeblood of life, were a bad weed or a cockroach. But I'm afraid I've come to adopt it here, where time has become the enemy, a dragon that must be slain.

"Come on, Jim, come on, Harmeet," Junior says. What a relief. Time for bed. We follow him upstairs. Junior sits down in one of our plastic chairs while we do our nightly rotation through the bathroom. Taking the cup with the roses into his hand, he wants to know where they came from. From the big man—he took them from the garden, we explain.

Junior nods, smiles, smells it. His face becomes pained. "No, this-I-love-you," he says, gripping his ring finger. He forms an X with his index fingers and places it over his heart. He pretends to pull a ring off his finger. "*Mozane, mozane,*" he says, covering his face with his hands. He makes a big circle with his arms as if to show the circumference of the earth. Life, the world, everything is bad, everything is hopeless, he seems to be saying.

Norman returns and eases himself into his place next to the wall. When I return from the bathroom, Harmeet gets up to take his turn and Junior bends down to chain my foot. "I'm sorry, Jim," he says. He points to himself and shakes his head. "This no mother, no father, no *beit*. No *zowage*, no madame, no *whalid*. Sister *mooreed*. No *sierra*, no business, no *hubis*." He body-languages a rifle, looking through a scope, pulling the trigger. "*Kul yoom Amriki,*" he says. This is what he does every day when he leaves in the car. He's a sniper. He kills American soldiers.

Harmeet returns and takes his place in the middle. Junior handcuffs us together and stands up. "Good night," he says.

"Good night," we say. Junior closes the door and leaves.

"Did I miss anything exciting?" Harmeet asks.

"Just Junior's tales of woe," Norman says.

# MARCH 22 DAY 117

Norman is anxious. It's beginning to seem as if Harmeet and I may be going first, that the negotiations are now on separate tracks. Norman, preparing for this possibility, asks us what we think is likely to happen.

He wants to think through what it will mean for him if he's left behind. Would he be moved? If so, where? What would he need to bring?

In the event that we are released first, there are four things he wants us to tell his wife, Pat:

1. he loves her;
2. he thanks her for forty-some years of life together;
3. he asks for her forgiveness for putting her through this, the consequence of his decision to go to Iraq;
4. while this may be a life that is not of her choosing, he gently urges her to live each day fully, to get on and go on with things as best she can—not to put her life on hold.

The idea gnashes and tears at me. I could, when it's my turn to be in the middle, unlock myself with the Instrument of Grace, sneak downstairs, see if I can get out the door. If I can, I'll run. If I can't, I'll return to my place and lock myself up again. At least then I will know and not waste any more energy wondering of my escape.

The consequences could be catastrophic. The captors will learn about the Instrument of Grace. Norman and Harmeet will be punished, immediately moved (if not killed), perhaps separated. Their conditions will most certainly be more restrictive, maybe even unbearable. All of that will be on my conscience.

But—we're in terrible danger! I want to live! We have to do something!

They don't feel this sense of urgency. They're biding their time, waiting it out, trusting in the course of these negotiations. I could risk it. Maybe one evening. When I'm going to the bathroom. Slip into the kitchen. Go to the door, see if it will open. I'd have five, maybe seven seconds to get to the end of the driveway and climb over whatever gate or wall is there before they figure out what's happening. I'd have to be fast. They will try to shoot me. My heart pounds wildly. It means risking everything. It means leaving Harmeet and Norman behind, exposing them to terrible danger.

The best way is for us to do it together. That way we all share the risk and all share the benefit. But they don't like talking about it. I wish I could convince them. I'm sure, if we just put our heads together, we could figure something out. Something with minimal risk and a high chance of succeeding. Something we could do today, for example, while Nephew is alone with us.

I begin with a summary of our situation: Uncle up all night with his rocket launcher, Medicine Man's lies, the apparent failure of the British negotiations, worries about Norman's health, the precarious political situation in the country. Our time is running out, I say. Unless we take matters into our own hands, we're not going to make it. They're going to kill us. It means risking everything, but I'm starting to think we don't have any option. It's like a puzzle—we can solve it. Once we come up with a plan, we can practise and prepare ourselves.

Then I make my proposal. "I keep thinking about Harmeet's story of when he was a kid, how they would twist each other's shirts so tight that they'd make each other pass out. I'd like to try that, role-play it. We can use the blue blindfolds. Harmeet, if we unlocked you tonight, you could test it out on me, stand behind me with the blindfold, see how long it takes for me to pass out, how long it lasts. I'll pretend to be Junior or Nephew and see if I can reach around behind to stop you. We can try it a few different times in different ways."

"No, I don't think so," Harmeet says, his voice barely a whisper.

"This is not committing us to any plan," I say. "It's just to test something out, to see if it might be an option. Then we can role-play it and perfect it."

No, Harmeet says. I try again to convince him, but Norman interrupts. "He doesn't want to do it," he says, "and neither do I. It's not worth the risk."

"And unlocking every night the way we used to—that was worth the risk?" I say.

There's no budging them. *Bury your heads in the sand*, I want to scream.

———

The impasse hovers about us like a pall. I feel like I am baking in a hot oven of silence. I fight with myself to accept the fact that it is their freedom to say no. I can't.

We need a change of mood. Anyone for a game of Wheel of Fortune or Word Within a Word? I want to ask. I steal sideways glances at Harmeet and Norman. They are closed up, shuttered, somewhere far away. I know it will help us, but I can't bring myself to ask it. What if they say no to punish me? They know I like those games. They were both my idea. I couldn't bear it if they said no. Better to stew in this toxic silence.

Nephew comes up to unlock us. "Hayder coming soon," he says, holding up his mobile. We set up our bed and follow him downstairs. We take our places in front of the television. I open my notebook and begin to write.

"Sometime after 7:00 p.m. Downstairs in haji headquarters, sitting in chairs with good light and no handcuffs, as captive as ever. My mind is largely a blank, perhaps because of thinking about Sheila." (Sheila is the codeword I used for "escape.")

I look up from my notebook. There's a car pulling up the driveway. It has to be Junior, returning from doing God knows what, another long day working in the vineyard of death. I almost laugh. I have this image of Junior entering the kitchen, tired, setting down a bag of groceries, calling out to Nephew, "Hi, honey, I'm home." And Nephew, preoccupied with some task, an apron around his waist, answering absently, "How was your day, dear?"

Junior enters the room with a bag of fresh *samoons*. I say hello and continue with writing. These are the last words of my notebook:

During his check-in, Norman noted that we had a quiet afternoon, perhaps because we were each withdrawn, he as guilty as anyone else. I wanted, at different points, to suggest we play a game, but noting Harmeet and Norman's distance, thought better of it. I looked for, but found no signal of interest, and not wanting to experience the rejection of a no, didn't ask.

There are so many ways I'm a prisoner—so many ways my fears, preconceptions and judgments limit, constrain, handicap, govern me—so many ways I'm enslaved by what-other-people-might-think-say-do. This is the attachment of my identity, my dependence upon favourable opinion, impression, perception of others for the well-being of my ego. This is a prison as surely as this place is. I could've *just asked,* wanna play Wheel of Fortune, let them say yes or no; receive the gift of a yes and accept the honesty of a no. I have so much to learn and so many ways to grow in terms of communication.

Dear God, help me to grow in freedom. The addendum to this prayer I make with some fear and trembling, but I charge ahead nonetheless. Grant me, prepare me, grace me to let go of what I must to receive this freedom. Your freedom, the freedom of being fully the person you created me to be. And the corollary (or the fruit?): allowing others to be *who they are,* embracing them as they are. This is the mutual dialogue, the beautiful give-and-take of freedom.

I think sometimes I get trapped by a dynamic where I *think* another person needs to do or be some particular thing in order for *me* to be who or what I'm supposed to be. This is the difficulty of interdependence, where one's decisions, needs, desires inter-affect the decisions, needs, desires of another, sometimes collide or conflict, and freedom thereby becomes something to negotiate, contend with. This, of course, is the human journey, the dance against limits, until the final embrace of death. It is our nature to strain against and defy that which limits, to break the bond of gravity and fly free transcendent, whether it be through war, art, sport, power, wealth, empire, glory of every shade and shape and texture.

—notebook

—

"Come on, Jim, massage," Junior says to me. He's lying on his bed.

I sigh, close up my notebook, kneel beside him. I work on his back for a long time. This, at least, is one useful thing I can do. I pray for his sister, and for the healing of his spirit. Only then will he be able to lay down his gun.

When I am done, I sit back in my chair and stare vacantly at the television, simmering with escape plans.

We are sitting cross-legged on the futon waiting for Norman, who is taking his turn in the bathroom. Junior sits facing us on a chair, singing his *Shwaya shwaya* song with his eyes closed, head swaying in imitation of Kazem Al Saher, the pop star he idolizes. He opens his eyes and lifts his right forearm towards me. "Come on, Jim, massage, massage," he pleads, pressing his arm to show me how sore it is. I gird myself to say no. Two massages in one day is crossing the line. He gets up from his chair and sits in front of me cross-legged, so close that our knees touch. He holds his forearm out. I laugh. "All right," I say. "*Shwaya.*"

Junior recites the same litany of rue we heard last night—no mother, no father, no house. His voice is pained, aching with despair.

He pulls his arm away, forms his right hand into a gun and points it at his temple. He pulls the trigger, tilts his head, sticks his tongue out, closes his eyes. "This in Canada," he asks, "*Zane? Mozane?*"

He's asking me if it's okay to kill yourself in Canada. "*La, la,*" I say, shocked by his question. "*La suicide. Mozane.* This *haram* in Canada."

He nods. "This good in Canada. This no *Islami.*" He points to himself. "This no suicide. *La Islami.*"

"Good," I say to him. "*Inshallah,* this *abu zane.*"

When Norman returns, I take my turn in the bathroom. When I come back, I'm surprised to find Harmeet and Junior sitting cross-legged together on the mat, Harmeet massaging Junior's forearm just as I had been. "Any good news?" I hear Harmeet ask Junior. He's pressing him for information about our release.

Instead of the usual *inshallah*, or *shwaya shwaya*, his answer is a strange smile. A smile that says yes, it will be soon, very very soon. Harmeet reaches into his pocket and presents him with a peace crane, made from one of the gold candy wrappers. "This is for your sister," Harmeet says.

"Thank you," he says, his face very solemn. He puts the crane into his pocket and locks us up. "Good night," he says, closing the door behind him.

"Good night," we say.

I lie awake for a long time after that, flailing in an agony of indecision. I want to escape and they don't. Our lives are hanging in the balance. I don't know what to do.

# CHAPTER FOURTEEN

## MARCH 23 DAY 118

I'm awake, watching the day's new light gather and grow. Judging by the angle and intensity of the sun, I guess that it's about seven-fifteen.

The kitchen door slams. I'm instantly alert. This is unusual. Junior is never up this early. I wait for the sound of a car door, an engine roaring to life, the kitchen door to slam a second time. Nothing. Only silence.

Then voices, urgent, indistinct. One voice, louder than the others, rippling with alarm, fear, warning. "Hamid! Hamid!" it cries. The ominous whirring of a tank engine.

I shake Harmeet. "Harmeet! There's something weird going on," I say.

Norman and Harmeet both sit up. There's a heavy clang of metal hitting the ground. Boots run up the driveway and pass beneath our window. "It's a raid," I say, standing up.

"Open the door! Open the door!" I hear a British voice shout. The thud of metal pounding against metal. Smashing glass.

My body roars with adrenalin. I don't know what to do. "What should we do?" I cry. I start towards the window. I need to see what's going on. No, I might startle someone with a gun, or something could explode below us, sending glass and shrapnel everywhere. We have to find a safer place. I start towards the door. "Should we go out into the foyer?" I call out. I open the door and look into the foyer. No, the captors could come up the stairs and barricade themselves in the room with us, use us as human shields. There could be gunfire coming from the stairwell. I step back into the room.

A series of rapid-fire explosions. I hit the floor. "What should we do?" I call. "Should we barricade the door?" Another set of explosions.

English voices in the stairwell. They're coming up the stairs. My panic instantly evaporates. We're safe. There are no captors up here. "We speak English," I call out. "We're British and Canadian."

"British Special Forces," we hear. "Is Mr. Kember there?"

"Present," Norman cries.

"We'll be right there, Mr. Kember. Close the door and wait where you are. Don't open it until we get there. We have to clear the rest of the floor."

It takes all of fifteen seconds. We hear a commotion of boots, doors busting open, more percussion grenades, and then they're opening the door, stepping inside, desert-camouflage soldiers in full battle kit. They look at us, their eyes wide with surprise. One of them gives an order. A medic rushes into the room and goes right to Norman. Somebody tells us to sit down. The medic is followed by a soldier with a pair of three-foot-long bolt cutters.

"Is everyone okay?" somebody asks, maybe the medic.

"Yes," we say.

"We'll have you out of here in a minute."

There's a soldier with a camera. He takes pictures of us in our handcuffs and chains. There's a soldier bending close to me. Is it the medic? "Do you know what happened to Tom Fox?" I ask him. "The American who was kidnapped with us. Was he released? Is he at home?"

"No." The voice hesitates. "He's . . . he's dead."

"Are you sure?"

"Yes," the voice says.

"How do they know? Did they find his body?"

"Yes."

I'm about to ask another question. "You can find out more once we get you out of here," he says. The voice changes the subject. "Are you okay?"

"I'm okay," I say.

"Here, let me get you out of those," another voice says. It's the soldier with the bolt cutters. I hold my right wrist out. He places the ratchet into the jaws of the bolt cutter. The handcuff slips out of place. "Here, let's try that again," the voice says. His movements are clumsy. He repositions the handcuff and closes the bolt cutter but the metal is too thick. He's trying to get the whole bracelet off.

"Try doing it here," I say, pointing to the chain that links the two handcuffs.

"Yeah, we can get that off later," he says, referring to the main body of the handcuff. *Yes*, I smile, *with the Instrument of Grace*.

He has trouble getting the bolt cutter into place, his hands are shaking so much. He closes the bolt cutter across the link but the metal is too strong. "Just cut one part of the link, that should do it," I say. He hasn't done this before, I think.

"Sorry . . . " he says. The bite closes a second time and the link snaps.

"Thank you!" I say, immediately standing up. My arms are free! I am free! I clasp the handcuff around my wrist and marvel at the sudden loss of its power. It is now nothing more than a strange metal bracelet.

I look around me. Nothing is clear or distinct. Everything is a haze of commotion and sound. "Get whatever you want to take with you," a voice says.

I have to change, wear my own clothes to freedom. I go to my little pile of clothes in the barricade. Another voice breaks through. "Do you recognize this man?" I look to where the voice is coming from.

There's a man in a white *dishdashda* in the doorway. His arms are bound behind his back. A black blindfold has been lifted onto his forehead. There's a soldier gripping each of his arms. He's not very tall. He looks at me. His face is sad. There are dark circles under his eyes. The lower half of his face is blue with unshaven beard. Who is this man? I know I've seen him before.

"Yes," I hear Norman say beside me. His voice is clear and certain. I look over at him, but he's already turned away, busy with collecting his things. I look back at the man. He nods at me. I reflexively nod back. The soldiers pull the blindfold down over the man's eyes and lead him away. He does not seem to have been tortured or mistreated.

"Was that Medicine Man?" I ask Harmeet, who is changing next to me.

"Shh! We'll talk about it later."

I'm totally confused. "All right," I say. It doesn't matter anyway. We're getting out of here. I strip off my captor clothes and put on my own socks, underwear and pants. I need a belt. With glee I pull the string out of the waistband of my green track pants and pass it through my belt loops. For warmth I wear the Sacred Heart sweater over my collared shirt over my T-shirt over the vest. I joyfully fold up the rest of the captor clothes—green track pants, socks and underwear—and leave them neatly in the barricade. I slip into my shoes, grab my notebooks and pen, and take one last look around me: I want to remember everything. "I'm ready," I declare to the soldiers.

"If you could just wait out in the hall for a moment," a voice tells me.

I go to the *hamam* first. I close the door. I stand over the shit-stained toilet and urinate. I pour water from the *hamam* jug into the bowl to flush the urine down. I go to the sink to wash my hands. I look into the mirror. A gaunt, clammy, bearded, greasy-haired man with blue eyes looks back at me. I laugh. *Hey good lookin'! What's cookin'?* I wipe my hands dry on my pants. I decide to leave the toothbrushes. I turn away from the sink and walk out into the foyer.

There are soldiers everywhere. I look at their faces but I can't find their eyes. These are not fresh-faced recruits. These are battle-hardened vets bristling with years of specialized training and what must be a hundred pounds of equipment—full-body armour, helmets with Plexiglas visors, headset communicators, guns, ammo, fierce-looking knives, pockets everywhere filled with the tools of their trade. One of them brings me a chair. I sit down.

I'm ecstatic. It's over. We're safe, we're free, we're going home. I'm wildly grateful. Astonished. They came, they risked their lives for us. Simply because it's their job. At the same time I am sad, troubled, aching. That it had to come to this, a special forces commando rescue. How strange and paradoxical: we have been delivered by the very thing we were kidnapped for setting our lives against.

"How're you doing? Is everything okay?" a soldier voice asks.

"Oh, yes, just fine," I say, grinning madly. "It's just that I never expected it would end this way."

"It never does," the voice says.

Harmeet sits beside me. He's brought his own chair.

"Shall I bring the toothbrushes?" I hear Norman calling out from the bathroom.

"We'll get you some toothbrushes," a soldier voice says.

"It'll just be another minute," another soldier voice says. "As soon as we secure the perimeter, we'll get you out of here."

There's no rush, I want to tell them. I want to go into every room, look in every nook and cranny, touch and feel and freely see everything. I look around me, look at everything, the once-forbidden foyer doors all broken open, light flooding the terrazzo floor, the high, whitewashed ceilings, the dust-coated walls.

Norman emerges from the bathroom. "I brought the toothbrushes anyway," he tells us. "Just in case."

"Okay, we're ready to go," a soldier voice says.

"Thank you," I say.

"Just doing our job," the voice says matter-of-factly.

We walk towards the stairway, soldiers in front and soldiers behind. I feel like I'm in a dream moving in slow motion. I look around me, wide-eyed, for the first time unafraid. We're walking down the stairs. I turn to look back, one last time, at the foyer we're leaving behind. I look down at the filthy, threadbare carpet that covers each stair tread, the translucent windows at the landing. We turn, go down the second flight of stairs, descend into the grand hallway of this grand house. Ahead of us, twenty-five feet away, is a set of wood and glass doors I never noticed before that open into a formal reception area.

We're down the stairs. Five steps ahead and we turn to the right. To my left, the entrance to the butterscotch blue-curtained room. The door is closed. Three steps ahead to the left. The entrance to the red-curtained dining room is open. The plastic chairs we sat in last night are still in their exact same place. *Goodbye plastic chairs!* Two steps ahead the hallway sink. *Goodbye hallway sink!* Four steps ahead and we're in the kitchen. The door leading outside has been smashed open and shards of tempered glass are strewn everywhere. I look closely at the lock. It's a deadbolt you can only open or close with a key. I take a breath and step across the smashed-glass threshold. Across and out. Into fresh flowing air, good morning sunlight, a breeze on my cheeks, freedom!

I look up. It is stunning, miraculous. I want to open my arms, somersault, jump, dance. Above me blue, an ocean of blue! And green! The green growing fronds of a palm tree!

"We need to keep going," a voice behind me says. I'm standing in the middle of a gauntlet of soldiers lining both sides of the driveway. They're looking at us, smiling. I want to stop, shake their hands, look in their eyes, ask them their names, thank them. But there's no time. We have to keep moving. Through the gauntlet. My feet move me towards an armoured personnel carrier. It's a squat, desert-camouflaged steel bunker on a rolling tread of metal plates, thirty feet away. There's an eight-foot wall to my right. A blindfolded man standing with his face to the wall. He's between two soldiers. His wrists are bound with white plastic ties. He's wearing a white *dishdashda*.

My heart is rent. My feet step towards him. My hand reaches out to touch his shoulder. He jumps. He doesn't know who I am. *I don't mean you any harm,* I want to say. My mouth opens, almost says it, *Medicine Man,* but then I realize he doesn't know that name. The tables have turned. Just like that, in the snap of a finger. My heart is flooded with an immense sorrow. *I don't want this, what's happening to you now. I don't want you to suffer.*

The soldiers beside him are becoming anxious. My mouth opens and closes like a fish gasping for water. The words won't come. My hand pulls away, my feet step back, my body turns towards the armoured personnel carrier and my feet start walking again. With every step the chasm between us widens. I am in the land of freedom now, and he is being taken into captivity.

I join up with Norman and Harmeet. I look around me. We're on the edge of a big traffic circle. There's a monumental piece of architecture on the other side of the circle. I turn towards the house. It's big and respectable, tidy, festooned with flowering roses, surrounded by high walls, indistinguishably ordinary. They tell Norman he's going to ride in the Humvee parked behind the tank. A soldier points Harmeet and me to the armoured personnel carrier. We climb up the ramp into the dark interior.[*]

There's a soldier inside. "Watch your head," he says. We duck. He motions us to sit on a bench seat. He's wearing a helmet and a headset that's plugged into a jack somewhere.

"My name is Jim," I say, extending my hand to him.

"And I'm Harmeet."

"Yeah, I know who you are," the soldier says, shaking our hands.

"What's your name?" Harmeet asks.

"Rob," he says. He looks to be no more than twenty.

---

[*]   In December of 2005, two Muslim men travelled to Baghdad to appeal for our release: Ehab Latoyef of Montreal, and Anas Altikriti of Harrow, England. While in the city, Anas (who was born in Iraq but moved to England when he was 2 years old) went to see his grandmother's sister who lives "approximately four to five houses away from where you were held on the opposite side of the road." According to his aunt, it was early in the morning when the whole street was locked down and the people who lived in the area were ordered not to leave their homes, draw their curtains or look from their windows. After a couple hours passed, she could no longer resist and peeked outside through her upstairs curtain. She saw the house "totally surrounded" and "an Iraqi man in a dishdasha standing with the troops outside the front door, and then a line of people who looked like foreigners being taken to waiting cars, including an old man with totally white hair and another with very long hair."

Anas writes, "When she was telling [me] the story she had no idea that I was involved in this particular hostage negotiation . . . To think I paid my aunt a brief visit and had tea just across the road from where you were, when I was heavily engaged with trying to persuade tribal leaders in Al-Anbar and along Syrian borders to co-operate by informing me of where you might be held, is quite mind-boggling!"

My name! I should've told Medicine Man my name! There isn't much time. "Who's your commanding officer?" I say. "I'd like to ask him a quick question."

"You want me to get 'im?"

"Yes, if you wouldn't mind. I just have a quick question."

The soldier shouts out of the hatch. A face appears in the hatchway. It's a steely-jawed, tough-as-nails warrior face. "What do you want?" he says.

"That man over there," I say, pointing to where Medicine Man had been standing. "Could I talk to that man over there? Just for a second. There's something I need to tell him."

He looks confused. "That man over where?"

"The Iraqi man in the blindfold and handcuffs."

"No," he says. "It's not safe here. Our job is to get you out of here. There'll be time for all that later."

"We can talk to him later?"

"Yes."

The door closes. We're inside the war machine. It takes a moment for my eyes to adjust to the darkness. I look around me. We are sealed inside what must be twelve inches of metal. Everything around us is dark green, machine-tooled functionality. We're surrounded by pieces of equipment held in place with strapping and netting, flat metal boxes, mysterious switches and levers, conduit tubing for wiring, all the hard forms of the tank's inner structural works, CAUTION and DANGER stencilled everywhere, instructions stamped on little metal plaques explaining things, like what to do in the event of a rollover. We have gone from one tomb to another.

"Where are you from?" I ask.

"Indiana," Rob says.

"How long have you been here?"

"Nine months. Going home soon." Silence. "And you?" he asks.

"Four months," I say.

He nods. "Are you hungry?"

Harmeet and I look at each other. Yes, we say.

He points us to a khaki bag. "There's a muffin inside there. It's not much," he says, "but it's all I got. They're not the best. You know, it's army food."

We break the muffin in half. It's chocolate with chocolate chips. I eat it slowly. It is, I'm certain, the most delicious thing I've ever eaten. I look at the packaging. It was made somewhere in Ohio. A muffin, shipped to Iraq from Ohio! The ingredients list is as long as my arm— all long, hyphenated, incomprehensible chemical names. I show it to Harmeet. "They won't have to embalm us now when we die," he says.

Rob points to a rectangle of light behind his shoulder. It's four inches wide and one inch high. "There's a window here if you want to look outside," he says.

I look through what must be a foot of glass. I see a distorted, blurry, convex slice of a small piece of the world outside. Underneath the window is a Velcro flap that functions as a fold-over curtain. I sit back to let Harmeet take a turn. *So this is what the world looks like from inside the war machine,* I think.

We are moving. Rob's mouth is moving. He's shouting something, but the engine roar-clang-pound is deafening. I can feel the power of it shuddering in my bones.

Rob watches out of a window, his attention sharp, focused, purposeful. He says things into his headset from time to time. He opens another Velcro window for us. I watch the world passing by, approximations of buildings, cars, people walking. We stop for a long time at an intersection. Rob's jaw tightens. The tank turns 180 degrees over a traffic median and roars away. His jaw relaxes. We seem to be travelling through a dry, cement-lined water causeway.

I tap Harmeet on the shoulder. "Do you have the Instrument of Grace?" I shout into his ear.

"WHAT?" he shouts back.

"DO YOU HAVE THE INSTRUMENT OF GRACE?"

He reaches into his pocket and pulls out a curtain hook.

"MAY I?" I ask, smiling mischievously.

He nods quickly, eyes alight. He holds out his handcuff for me and

I insert the Instrument of Grace into the keyhole. The ratchet slides free. I hand him the hook and hold out my handcuff. Harmeet springs it open. *Hooriya!*

Our bone-and-teeth-rattling ride seems to take forever. Finally we stop, a half-hour, forty minutes later. The hatch opens. "Thank you, Rob," we say, shaking his hand.

It is a relief to step out into sunlight again. We're in the middle of what looks like a giant parking lot surrounded by blast walls. There's an overpass nearby. In one corner, the rusting and derelict remains of a cement plant. This must be some kind of staging area.

We seem to be encircled by Humvees and tanks. There's a phalanx of soldiers staring at us. I wonder what they're thinking. A soldier steps towards us. His eyes are hard and his face is creased. His body exudes command. He is angry. "I know I'm speaking out of school here," he says, pointing his finger, "but I'm going to say it anyway. You have no idea how many people were involved, how many people risked their lives to get you out. I want you to tell your people that. Just tell them to think about *that* before they decide to send anybody else here. I'm not saying anything else. Just tell them. Tell them to think about all the people that risked their lives to get you out."

My mouth opens and closes. My mind races. How do I begin to respond? *You are the reason I came here, I want to say. So you no longer have to do what you do. It is a paradox. Some men with guns came and took me. Then you came with your guns and took them. You have given me back my freedom. I am unspeakably grateful, but the gun is still in charge and nothing has really changed. We need a world without war. You, me, Junior, Uncle, Number One—all of us do. I wonder, if we sat and talked together for a while, if I could tell you about them, maybe you would see what I have begun to see, that there is no such thing as "Iraqi freedom" or "American freedom," that there is only human freedom. We were created to give life, not to take it. Our freedom begins when we live in accord with this purpose. The gun will never make us free. The gun makes us a slave. A slave of fear going around and around in a spiral of death, becoming more and more like the thing that we hate.*

In this moment it is all too much to know, too much to say. I nod solemnly. "Thank you," I say.

"Let's go!" he shouts to his men, turning away.

A man in civilian clothes steps towards us and shakes our hands enthusiastically. "My name is Dean. I'm from the Canadian embassy. Welcome back! You don't know how great it is to see you guys. We've been working for this day for a long time, and we wanted to make sure there was a friendly face to greet you. Somebody in regular clothes who's not dressed like all these dudes." He smiles and points to the soldiers surrounding us. "It must be a little unnerving for you."

Yes, a little, we say.

"There's just a little more of this. We're going to fly you to the Green Zone in that helicopter over there." He points behind us. "You'll just be with civilians after that. Ever been in a helicopter before?"

No, we say.

"Well, you're going in one today," he says. "We'll have you there in five minutes."

Soldiers escort us to the helicopter. Norman is already there.

"Norman! Long time no see!" I say.

"Greetings. I got to ride right up front in the Humvee," he says, beaming. "I got to see the whole trip—everything. It was quite a tour of Baghdad."

"What did you see?"

"Oh, we went right through the city, through all these shopping districts, turned at different traffic circles. But then we got caught in some kind of traffic jam, so we double-backed and took some sort of back way—it looked like a canal."

Two men in the back hold of the helicopter grab our arms and hoist us up. We're strapped into chairs that pull out of the floor, the engine roars to life and we lift into the air in a whirl of dust. We fly low over the city, no more than five hundred feet. From this height Baghdad is a sprawling ocean of brown rectangular shapes, green sprouting palm trees and ornate mosque towers. A soldier with a leg hanging out the door scans the horizon below us with a heavy-calibre machine gun. Here and there I see people on rooftops hanging out their laundry.

# CHAPTER FIFTEEN

We're in the Green Zone, occupation headquarters. I am marvellously, luminously, deliriously happy. The nightmare is over. We're going home.

I search the horizon around me for familiar landmarks. I recognize, to the northeast, not far, perhaps four hundred metres away, the convention centre where I took delegations and went to meetings at the so-called Iraqi Assistance Center. To the southeast, the empty, bombed-out hulk of the Telecommunications Building. To the south, the Palestine and Sheraton hotels, just a few blocks from the CPT apartment. I wonder if they even know we've been released. Does anyone know?

It used to be called Karradat Mariam. In those days, it was the lush, palmy centre of Saddam Hussein's brutal rule; the home of the Republican Palace, the National Assembly, Baath Party headquarters, government ministries and official palaces, posh villas owned by Baathist elites; a desert Shangri-La of gardens and ponds where ornamental bridges crossed artificial streams and garish military monuments dominated august boulevards. All of which changed on April 9, 2003. The U.S. Army came rumbling into town and Karradat Mariam's powerful inhabitants fled for their lives, leaving behind a luxury ghost town. Homeless squatters were the first to move in—an estimated five thousand of them. Then, over the following weeks and months, the United States and its allies seized whatever had not been reduced to rubble. The American embassy set up shop in the Republican Palace, and so one pharaoh replaced another.

The optimism and goodwill that greeted U.S. forces quickly vanished. Over that first summer the insurgency began its first tentative strikes. The U.S. retreated further and dug in deeper with each attack. They enclosed four square miles of central Baghdad with eight miles of blast wall, surveillance towers and concertina wire.

I had been to the Green Zone twice before, when I was on the CPT team in the winter of 2004. I thought of it as a giant open-air prison. You had to have an appointment, and the person you were going to see had to meet you at the final checkpoint. You waited in line, exposed to the hot, baking sun and whoever might be on a suicide bomb mission that day, and followed a winding gauntlet of razor wire through a labyrinth of earth-berm walls, passing through four checkpoints along the way. If you were lucky, the whole process took half an hour. I only ever got as far as the convention centre, located at the northern end of the Green Zone, a dreary piece of socialist architecture surrounded by perfectly coiffed lawns. This was the only place in Iraq where the Coalition Provisional Authority interfaced with the public it was occupying. It was further separated from the main body of the Green Zone by another set of blast walls.

Harmeet and I are met by a tall, burly man in civilian clothing. "Harmeet! James!" he calls. It's an indescribable pleasure to hear my name being called. "You have no idea how glad I am to see you. Gordon Black. RCMP." He shakes our hands. "Do you know where you are?"

"The Green Zone," I say.

"This is the American Hospital," he says, motioning us towards the front entrance of a modest three-storey building. Ibn Sina it was called, a private hospital that cared for Baathist elites before it was taken over by the Americans. "We've arranged for you all to see a doctor. You guys look pretty good, but we just want to be sure . . ." We follow him through sliding glass doors into a reception area. We're greeted by several concerned-looking medical personnel. Gordon introduces me to a young medic named Jason. I follow him through a cluttered hallway that opens into an emergency operating theatre. I imagine a bomb-blasted soldier on a stretcher, doctors shouting and nurses rushing, blood everywhere.

"It must've been quite an ordeal . . ." Jason says to me. "How are you doing?" He's calm, gentle, a little shy, warm with caring.

"Pretty good, actually," I say. I explain about having been sick, the fever, the mysterious lumps in my neck and under my chin, how the captors brought me some antibiotics and that seemed to clear everything up.

He gives me a hospital gown to change into. "You look like you lost some weight," he says.

"They didn't feed us very much," I say.

He asks about our treatment. "They never tortured us," I say. "Our treatment was . . . consistent, I guess you could say. I guess they wanted to keep their merchandise in good condition."

When I've taken all my clothes off, he puts on a pair of gloves and places each item into a clear plastic bag. "Are you taking my clothes away?" I ask.

"I'm sorry, I should have explained." It's standard procedure, he says. They want them for forensic examination, to see if there might be anything unusual, traces of explosives or gunpowder, DNA from the kidnappers. They want everything, even my underwear. I feel invaded. I don't want to do this. I want to know how this evidence is going to be used. Everything's moving so fast and there doesn't seem to be any choice. I feel as if I have a new set of masters to contend with. I reluctantly agree.

He asks me if I have anything else. "Just these," I say, showing him my pen and solitary handcuff. "I don't care about the other things, but I really want the handcuff back."

He assures me everything will be returned once the investigation is complete. Then he gestures towards my notebooks. "They want everything," he says.

A foot stomps down within me. He's not taking them. "I don't see why this is necessary. I'm the only one who's touched them. I can guarantee there's no gunpowder on them."

"It's okay," he says, relenting. "Just keep them. I'm sure this is more than enough." He gathers together the plastic bags. "Will you be okay if I leave for just a second? I'll be right back. There's somebody waiting for these."

"Oh, sure," I say. It is, in fact, the thing I most want. Simply to be alone. Even if it's for only one minute.

An army chaplain enters the room. He asks me how I am, says it's a miracle that I survived, asks me if I'd like to pray with him. No thank you, I say. He offers me a brown, leather-stitched bible. The feel of the cover is sheer comfort and pleasing luxury. It's beautiful, I say, but I already have one. It seems extravagant, unnecessary to have two; someone might not get one if I take it.

"I have lots of bibles," he laughs. He looks at me closely. His voice softens. "You don't have one now, do you?"

"No," I say. My resistance crumbles. He wants so much to give me something. "Call me, *any time*, if you need *anything* . . ." he says, handing me his card.

"Thank you," I say.

Jason has been waiting discreetly in the hallway. He approaches as soon as the chaplain leaves. "Now, if it's okay, I'd like to check you over, just to make sure everything's okay. Would that be all right?"

Yes, fine, I say. He proceeds to examine me. It feels good to be touched, paid attention to, treated like a human being again. I almost start to cry.

He says I look a little dehydrated. He wants to start an IV. "Actually, now that you mention it, I am really thirsty," I say. He gets me a bottle of water, then carefully slides a needle into my right arm. I brace myself for a stabbing pain, but I don't feel a thing. He hooks up the intravenous and puts a big piece of tape over the needle.

"I've never had an intravenous before," I tell him.

"You've probably never been kidnapped before," he says.

"No," I say, returning his smile.

"I'll be right back. I'm just going to bring these blood samples in for testing."

Gordon approaches as soon as Jason leaves.

"So your family doesn't know yet. Ottawa knows, of course, but we haven't told anybody else." He smiles at me. "When we planned all this out, we wanted you to have the choice. It's up to you. If you like, we can call and let your parents and Dan know, or you can call them yourself. It's totally up to you. You've had your freedom taken away from you for four months. Our role now is to restore that freedom to you."

They don't know yet! I can tell them myself! I look over at the clock on the wall. It's 10:10 a.m. That means it's 2:10 a.m. back home.

I want to make the call, I tell him. His face is shining. He seems overcome with emotion. He hands me a cellphone. He has to clear his throat before he can speak. "You can keep this. You'll probably want to make more than one call. Use it any time, as often as you like. I'll get you the battery charger later."

"I can call them right now?"

"Yes, of course." He steps back. "I'll give you some privacy."

The cellphone is a Nokia. Just like the one I had when I was kidnapped. I dial my parents' phone number. It's ringing. My heart is pounding with excitement. I look over to where Gordon has been standing. He's slipped away.

The phone only rings twice. "Hello?" the voice says. It's my mother. "Hello . . .?"

"Mom . . ."

"Yes? Hello?" she says. Anxious. Urgent.

"It's . . . it's me . . ." I open my mouth, but the word won't come. Not without a flood of sobbing. "It's . . ." Please don't make me say it, *James*, the name you gave me.

"Who?"

I swallow hard and take a deep breath. I can say it now. "It's James," I say.

"James! Is that really you? Oh my God! It's James! Pat, it's James! Where are you? James! Thank God! You're all right?"

"James!" Another voice on the phone. Worried and relieved. It's my father. "Where are you?"

"I'm . . . I'm out. I'm free."

"You're out?" my dad says.

"I'm free! It's over."

"Where are you?"

"I'm in Baghdad. In the Green Zone. It's over."

"Oh, James! It's really you! Thank God! I can't believe it," my mother says.

"And thank Allah," my dad says.

"I'm sorry about all this, what you've had to go through," I say.

"Oh no, James, you have nothing to be sorry for," my father says.

"We're just so happy you're all right. You won't believe everything that's happened. We've learned so much," my mother says.

They begin to tell me about the people who prayed for us, all the cards and letters they received, how people brought them food, sent money, how my brother Matthew cut his trip to Ecuador short, how Ed and Donna came from Vancouver, how they all went on television.

"It'll take a whole day for us to tell you everything," my mom says.

"We even have a cellphone and a computer," my dad says.

"A cellphone and a computer!" I laugh. "The kidnapping has brought you into the modern age." I'm relieved, astounded, amazed. They aren't angry. Not even a little. They're simply grateful.

Then I call Dan. This call is easier. I'm ready, ecstatic. "Hello?" he says, uncertain, nervous. Here it is, finally, the call he's been waiting for—the call I've been waiting for.

"Dan, it's me, it's Jim, it's over!"

"Jim! Where are you? Are you safe?"

"Yes, I'm fine, I'm okay."

"Thank God!" he says. "Thank God!"

I'm standing in a hospital gown, I tell him, with an intravenous in my arm, getting a medical checkup. It's over. It was a military rescue. No shots were fired, no one was hurt. Harmeet and Norman are safe, they're both fine, everybody's fine. He asks me if I know about Tom. The soldiers told us, I say. I ask if they found his body. I have to make sure. Yes, he says. I can hear him knocking on doors, calling to Michael and Jo and Lorraine, my housemates. It's Jim, I'm talking to Jim, he's safe, I hear, then cheers and laughing. I ask Dan to call Doug and let him know. Then

I see Gordon motioning me. I have to go, I say, though I don't want to. I want to keep talking and talking. I feel I have a lifetime of stories to tell.

"I can't believe it. It's really over," he says.

"Yes," I say, "it's really over."


I am in an altered state, delirious with joy, awash in gratitude. A trembling, newborn human being in awe of everything. They tell me, again and again, if there's anything you need or want, any time of the day or night, just let us know. This, truly, is the only thing I want—for everything around me to stop, and to just sit, and bask, in the glory of just-being-alive.

But things are moving fast. Too fast. There are things to do, people to speak to, decisions to make. After four months of nothing-ever-happening, I feel as if I've been strapped onto the wing of a supersonic jet. One of the first decisions I have to make is whether or not to take a call from the prime minister. I am stunned. The prime minister wants to speak to me? Yes, they say. I feel myself panicking, my tongue tying itself in knots. Why? I groan.

There were a lot of Canadians concerned about you, they tell me. The prime minister just wants to welcome you back—on behalf of the Canadian people. I suddenly remember the news clip I saw of the House of Commons early in the captivity. "Who is it? Is it Paul Martin?"

Of course, you don't know, there was an election. You won't believe it, they say. It's Stephen Harper.

"What! Stephen Harper!" I'm in shock. If he'd been in power at the time, Canada would have followed George W. Bush into Iraq. "Tell me he didn't win a majority!"

Just a minority, they say.

I'm immediately suspicious. "Why does he want to speak to me?" I ask. He must have a political motive.

Don't worry, they say, it's strictly a personal call. There'll be no media. He just wants to welcome you back. Think about it. It's totally up to you. But remember, he's really representing the Canadian people.

—

After the hospital, they bring us to the British embassy's guest rooms—a series of metal shipping containers that have been converted into personal quarters. "Pretty ingenious, ah?" Gordon says. "They're inexpensive, safe and surprisingly comfortable." He points to one that was hit with mortar shrapnel.

I close the door. Finally, I am alone. What bliss. The room smells of soap. Everything is scrubbed and dusted and polished and glistening. There's a meticulously made bed, a desk, a reading chair, a private bathroom with a shower—all mine to use! I feel as if I'm in heaven. On the desk are a basket of fruit and a handful of energy and granola bars. I eat one immediately. There's a bag sitting on the chair full of wonders: disposable razors, shaving cream, packages of soap, deodorant, clean socks and underwear, a comb! And, most thrilling of all, the pants and shirt I'd left hanging on the clothesline the day we were kidnapped. Proof that I really did have a life before the kidnapping.

I strip off the clothes I was given at the hospital and jump into the shower. I want to live the rest of my life under that shower. I have to force myself to turn off the tap and swear an oath against taking any more long showers. I am in Baghdad, after all, where it is a sin to waste even a drop of water. I comb my hair for the first time in four months. I stare at my body for a long time, marvelling at the chariot God has given me to move in, the wondrous, incomprehensible fact that I am alive and safe and no longer have to be afraid.

I am just getting dressed when I hear a knock on the door. "Hey Jim, are you in there?" Gordon calls. He sounds impatient. I wonder how much time has passed.

"Be right there," I say. I like it here. I don't want to go anywhere else.

Gordon takes Harmeet and me to a big reception room in the British embassy, where we are joined by Stewart Henderson, Canada's chargé d'affaires to Iraq, and his assistant Sonia Hooykaas. Harmeet looks like a university dude once again in his track pants and sweatshirt. Norman is already there, dressed in the slacks, dress shirt and tie he travelled to Iraq in. He looks stricken, anxious, vulnerable. He's on the phone with his wife, Pat. All he can manage is a stammer. Adrian, Gordon's counterpart at Scotland Yard, has to finish the call for him.*

Adrian pulls me aside. He is worried about Norman. Is there anything he should know, anything he can do to help? I think Norman will be okay, I say. He's just overcome with emotion, needs time, and most of all, he needs to get home to Pat. Adrian nods.

They bring us to a groaning board buffet heaped with salads, cold cuts, rolls, vegetables, dips, sandwiches, soups, casseroles, fruit, pastries and desserts, and, unbelievably, somebody standing by in a white uniform waiting to cut us slabs of prime rib. Do we want to sit inside or out in the sun? they ask us. The sun! we say. We sit down with our plates on plastic chairs arranged around plastic tables next to the dazzling aquamarine of the British embassy swimming pool. This lunch is part of their plan, they tell us, to help restore our freedom, to let us know we have the power to make choices again.

Do we need anything? Sonia asks us. She is a fountain of warmth, laughter, exuberant grace. Shoes, we say at once. "Hmmm," she says, looking at our feet. "I'm not sure what they'll have at the commissary, but I'll have a look. Anything else?" Norman needs a sweater, I need a belt.

She returns an hour later, out of breath, hands full of bags. "I hope this is okay," she says. "It's all they had." She hands us each a pair of Nike Air running shoes. They fit perfectly. She hands me a sand-coloured belt made of webbing. It's all they had, she says apologetically.

"That's great, much better than this," I say, showing her the green string I've been using to hold my pants up. "How do we pay you for these?" I ask, uneasy because we have no money.

They laugh, wave their hands. Don't worry about it, they say.

—

---

* Police officials asked us not to identify them by their last names.

The call comes at two p.m.—six a.m. in Ottawa. I swallow hard as Gordon hands me his cellphone. What does one say to a prime minister whose policies you totally disagree with? "Hello?" I say.

"Hello? James? It's Stephen Harper," the voice says. "Congratulations! Welcome back. This sure is some good news. There were an awful lot of Canadians praying for you. How are you doing? It must've been quite an ordeal. I can't imagine . . ."

"I'm quite fine . . . now . . . that it's over. I'm . . . it's . . . it's great to be alive."

"We're all so relieved that you made it. Though, of course, not all of you. I'm sorry about your friend, Tom Fox."

"Thank you," I say.

"Well, I imagine it's going to take some time to get over something like this," he says.

"Thank you. For everything . . . I mean . . . the government did so much . . ."

"Don't you worry about that. We're just glad you and Harmeet are okay. Be gentle with yourself. Just take things one day at a time. And your parents? Have you talked with your parents? They must be thrilled . . ."

"Yes, they were the first ones I called. That was the best phone call I've ever made."

"I'll bet," he says.

When the call is over, I wonder why I'd been so stressed. He was remarkably easy to talk to—like talking to an ordinary person.


"Do you want to see our operations room?" Gordon asks the three of us. "There are some people there who worked on your release. They'd just like to say hello. We only have to go for a minute."

Sure, we say. We leave one walled and guarded compound, cross a road and enter another, what was once a girls' school. We walk through a courtyard where two mortars landed on the day of Gordon's arrival. "I had just crossed through. If they'd hit a minute sooner, I'd be dead," he tells us, shuddering at the memory.

We follow Gordon into a windowless room. I am nervous, remembering the reprimand the officer gave us before we got on the helicopter; I wonder if these people will be resentful too. We are greeted with cheers, people standing, clapping, wiping tears from their eyes. They shake our hands as if we are returning heroes. I am stunned. The room is divided into about ten workstations. There are phones, computers, piles of paper. There's a map of Baghdad on the wall, specific places marked with coloured pins. This is where the joint-release effort was coordinated. People worked here twenty-four hours a day, manning phones, following up on leads, talking to Ottawa. I can't believe it.

He shows us our pictures, surrounded with printed reports, Post-its, various handwritten notes. "We put these up so we'd have a picture of who we were working for—to help us feel connected to the four of you. It's strange, isn't it," he says. "We've just met you today, but I feel like I've known you forever. It amazes me how you can feel so . . . how much you can feel for a person you've never even met. And now to . . . to have the three of you standing in this very room . . . right beside me . . . I can't express how . . . to have it work out . . . We didn't know what was going to happen, but it worked out, except of course for Tom. In that I failed. I wanted to bring all of you home. But we're not. We're leaving one of you behind.

"You know, I predicted it, a week before it happened, that they were going to kill him. That's part of my job, to try and anticipate what the kidnappers are going to do next. And that forms the basis for what we decide to do next. You can get to know them. If you can get inside their skin, then they can be very predictable. I wish that I'd been wrong, but sadly I was right. It's sort of a grim consolation. It tells me I was on the right track, doing my job properly. In my last report, I came to the conclusion that you had about two weeks. It wasn't imminent, but it was coming. It was becoming clear that we had to act, we couldn't wait any longer. But we weren't going to do anything to jeopardize your safety. That was the goal from the very start, to get all of you out safely. And we wanted to respect your values as much as possible. We didn't want any violence. And there wasn't. We got you out without anyone getting hurt, without a shot being fired. We were successful there. The tragedy is that we weren't fast enough to get Tom." Gordon pats each of us on the shoulder. "But we have you guys."

I look at him and smile, then look down at the floor. I don't know what to say. I could never have imagined that a total stranger—and an RCMP officer at that! —could care so much about my welfare.

Gordon wants to take Harmeet and me to meet some RCMP officers. "They just want to shake your hands," he says. "Do you mind? It'll just be a minute. You don't have to if you don't want to, but they've asked just to see you. It's hard to explain . . . they've worked so hard." I'm not sure, but I think he might be fighting back tears.

Sure, we say. We want to thank anyone and everyone.

They stand in a line, shoulder to shoulder. Five muscle-bulging cop-bodied men in civilian clothes, arms folded across their chests, eyes staring hard into the distance. Gordon formally introduces us and we shake each of their hands. Thank you, we say to each man. They nod in reply. A couple smile tightly. Only one looks me in the eye.

"Are they angry at us?" I ask Gordon.

"No, no," he says. "They're not angry. Not at all. They probably didn't look at you because they would've burst into tears if they did. We don't do emotion very well in the RCMP. Tom over there, he always kids us about that." Gordon points to where, just out of earshot, one of the men we have shaken hands with is leaning on the shoulder of another man, wiping tears from his eyes.

I am astonished to learn that the CPT team never left Baghdad. Harmeet and I are desperate to see them, Norman not so much. They finally come at four-thirty.

"Oh my God! Anita! Maxine!" I say, squeezing each of them. "What are you guys doing here? Have you been here the whole time?" I assumed that if the team had decided to stay they both would've gone home for a break and been relieved by someone else.

"Of course!" Anita says, pretending to be offended.

"We weren't going to leave you here!" Maxine says.

Peggy Gish is there too, whom I'd worked with twice before in Iraq, and a CPTer I'd not met before named Beth Pyles, whom I like instantly. "You're all so brave," I tell them.

"We have to have a picture!" Anita cries, thrusting her camera at Gordon and lining everybody up. "Let me get between my men," she says, squeezing between Harmeet and me.

They present us with our luggage. "Oh, hey, I remember this!" I say, lifting my backpack. I can't wait to look inside.

We move to the plastic chairs beside the pool. Norman stands at the edges and then discreetly disappears. Gordon presents the CPTers with bowls full of ice cream. Maxine laughs delightedly. "Thank you, Gordon!" she says. "But you know, this time we would've come anyway, even without the ice cream!" Maxine explains how they hate making the trip to the Green Zone—it's probably the most dangerous thing they do in Baghdad. Whenever Gordon called to set up a meeting, they would always try to find a reason not to go. Until Gordon started bribing them with ice cream—then they could hardly refuse. They had searched everywhere; ice cream was impossible to find in Baghdad.

We laugh and talk ravenously as the March afternoon fades into twilight. We need hours—there is so much to learn, so much to tell—but at six o'clock Gordon comes with the sad news: it's time for the CPTers to go.

Maxine looks surprised. She says they came prepared to stay the night. Gordon says he is sorry but that isn't possible. Maxine wants to know why—he promised if we ended up in the Green Zone someone from the team could stay with us. He says he is sorry but the Canadian contingent is a guest of the British embassy. If it was up to Gordon, the whole team could stay, but it's not. He looks uncomfortable. Maxine's face darkens. But you promised, she says. Gordon apologizes, says it just isn't possible. Maxine looks betrayed.

I ask if they can come again tomorrow. Yes, sure, not a problem, Gordon says. We'd like to spend the whole day together, I say. That shouldn't be a problem—we'll see what we can do, Gordon says.

"We should take a quick press statement before we go," Anita says, pulling out a notebook and pen. We groan in objection. "Just a couple sentences would be fine. It doesn't have to be anything profound. We've been getting requests all day, from all over the world."

"Really!" I say.

"You guys have no idea, do you? This is a huge story. People really want to hear from you. Just something quick. It'll take the pressure off."

I take a breath. "Okay. How about: We are deeply grateful to all those who worked and prayed for our release. We have no words to describe our feelings of great joy at being free again. Our heads are swirling and when we are ready we will talk to the media."

"That's perfect," Anita says. "Harmeet?"

"I don't know . . . I hate this kind of thing. I like what Jim said."

"This can be from the both of us," I say.

"Okay, now you guys really have to go. The security gates are shutting down for the night. I'm sorry, but we have to end things here," Gordon says.

We hug each other goodbye. Gordon confirms that he'll call the team to work out the arrangements for getting together tomorrow.


We're worried about Norman, Gordon tells us. We don't think it's a good idea for him to be left alone in one of those shipping containers overnight. Arrangements have been made for us to stay with the British ambassador, where, if we want, we can all share one room. Would that be okay?

Of course, we say.

The ambassador, Sir William Patey, is in his early fifties, a bald, vigorous, barrel-chested man bristling with competence and unpretentious charm. He strides towards us, clasps our hands warmly. "Welcome to my humble little abode," he says with a chuckle. "My house is your house. Come on in! Help yourself to whatever you can find in the fridge." He instantly puts me at ease.

His "house" is a cavernous mausoleum of marble pillars, vaulted ceilings, interior balconies, grand sweeping stairways, fountainous chandeliers, heavy brocade draperies—everything in ostentatious excess, utterly lifeless. "It's a bit much, isn't it," he sighs. "It belonged to one of Saddam's aunties. Unfortunately, this was about all we could find. Everything else had already been claimed."

He sits us down around the Gertrude Bell Dining Room Table, "the only thing of real value in the place. The map of Iraq was drawn up on this very table." Stewart, the Canadian chargé d'affaires, is there, as well as Marion, the RCMP officer who will accompany Harmeet home, and Adrian. A butler stands to the side. I can't take my eyes off him—the smile on his face, the perfect ease and serenity of his eyes, a living Buddha radiating effortless grace. The dinner he has prepared for us is incomparable: chicken breast with a white sauce, broccoli, rice pilaf, an exquisite dessert. "The Green Zone is bad for this," the ambassador says, patting his waistline. "Sitting at a desk all day, being driven everywhere."

The ambassador does most of the talking, which is a relief since I'm not in the mood for fielding questions about the captivity. He is the perfect diplomat: funny, urbane, judicious, expansive, discreet. He speaks at great length about the various challenges facing Iraq. His assessments seem frank, well informed, hard-headed. In his hands, the horror and hubris of occupation are transformed into a hopeful and benevolent exercise in nation building where the good intentions of the Western powers (regardless of what their initial purposes might have been for invading Iraq) will eventually carry the day if given half a chance to succeed. If only they could instill an ethic of public service in the nascent Iraqi government, everything else would fall into place. At the end of the meal my head is spinning, and I leave the table wondering, have I somehow got this whole business wrong?

They show us to our rooms on the second floor. Norman is at one end of the building and we at the other. Harmeet and I share an enormous, disorganized room cluttered with miscellaneous wardrobes, chairs, beds and dressing tables that all seem to have come from Ikea.

For the first time today, Harmeet and I have a chance to talk. Harmeet is in crisis. Things aren't going well at home. His brother-in-law has signed a contract with one of New Zealand's national broadcasters giving them exclusive rights to film Harmeet's reunion with his family. In exchange, the broadcaster is flying his father and brother-in-law wherever they want to meet Harmeet. Harmeet told them he didn't want that. They said there was nothing they could do, they'd signed the contract and now they were committed. Harmeet doesn't know what to do.

I ask Harmeet why he said, "We'll talk about it later," when I asked at the time of our rescue if that was Medicine Man standing at the door. Harmeet doesn't think it was a "rescue." At least, he isn't sure. It could just as easily have been a "planned release." Like what happened with Douglas Wood, the Australian who had been kidnapped the year before. At first they said the Iraqi army found him by accident in the course of raiding a house. But then, after researching the story, a reporter uncovered evidence that Wood had been brought to an empty safe house where he could be "found" as part of a pre-arranged release plan. He thinks our "rescue" may have been contrived in the same way. He says maybe the reason I didn't recognize Medicine Man is because it wasn't really him, that maybe they brought somebody in to make us think it was him to convince us of their story. He isn't going to believe anything, one way or the other, until he has proof.

I'm not sure what to make of Harmeet's suspicions. I am confused, reeling. Now, more than ever, I want to know the truth of what happened. I spend the next day trying to find out, probing with different kinds of questions. All I get are vague generalities and well-rehearsed obscurities. It was an intelligence-led operation, Gordon tells me. "You wouldn't believe the fabulous resources available to us through the NATO alliance." By monitoring all the cellphone conversations going in and out of Baghdad, and by tracking different leads, they gradually narrowed in on the group that was holding us, until they were able to catch somebody—Medicine Man—who could lead them to us. It all happened very quickly. They captured him early in the morning, and within a few hours the rescue force was assembled.

Who was he? What was his name? He can't tell me. If a deal was made to let him go in exchange for certain kinds of information, he doesn't want to put him in jeopardy by revealing his name. He says they have to protect their methods so they can be used again in the future.

Who was the group that kidnapped us? He says they called themselves Swords of Righteousness Brigade. No one had heard of them before.

Was there a process of negotiation? No, they only made contact with our captors in the last few days. That was the video they took of Harmeet and me holding up a newspaper on March 19.

What about the video they took of Norman, and the three questions he was asked to answer? They didn't know anything about that, Gordon says. They only established direct contact five days ago.

What about Tom? They have no information about who might have done it.

What else can you tell me? I ask. What else would you like to know? he says.

Everything, I answer. He says he's told me just about everything he can. I feel like I'm trying to scale a wall that keeps getting higher and higher.

Gordon probes with questions of his own. Did they move us? How did they treat us? How many were there? What did we know about what happened to Tom? Did we have any sense of where we were or what was going on in the outside world? Did we see or hear anything that suggested there were other hostages? This is just for his own information, he says. They aren't going to debrief or interrogate us. They don't do that kind of thing.

I am conflicted. Part of me wants to tell him everything, as a way to honour all the work they've done to secure our release. And for the most part I do, hoping I might be able to get more information out of him in turn. But always I am on my guard. I don't know how this information is going to be used. While I have no interest in protecting the captors from the consequences of their actions, there is no way I want them to be executed or sentenced to life in prison. I don't tell him anything that will enable the police or the army to identify the captors. I feel as if we're playing cat and mouse.

—

Decisions decisions. I sit on my bed, staring into space, trying to decide whether or not to change my socks and underwear. It has not even been a day. It seems like an outrageous luxury to change them so soon, after having worn the same things for days and weeks on end. I gather the socks and underwear I was given yesterday with what was in my backpack. It's overwhelming—eight pairs of socks and six pieces of underwear—all in different colours and styles!

Then the decision of whether or not to take a shower. This one is easier. No! It's a crime to use water frivolously. If nothing else, the past four months have shown me how little water it is possible to use.

And then there's breakfast. The butler hands us an embossed menu. There are several kinds of cold cereal; milk or juice; tea—regular or herbal; coffee—regular or decaf; hot cereal; toast with butter or toast without; toast with several kinds of jam; eggs scrambled, sunny side, over easy, poached; eggs in omelette; potatoes mashed or crisp; bacon or sausage or ham; French toast or pancakes. Harmeet and I look at each other and laugh. It is impossible to decide. "Very well, then," the butler says, taking back the menus. "We'll have a little bit of everything."

Gordon stops in after breakfast to see how we're doing. He tells us that Norman is leaving in the afternoon, on a two-thirty flight out of the Baghdad airport. He will have to leave the embassy right after lunch. Gordon asks about our travel arrangements. When do we want to go? Any time after we debrief with the team, I say. Tomorrow would be fine. Harmeet doesn't know. He says he has to work some things out with his family before he can decide. And where would you like to go? he asks us. We'll fly you anywhere you want to go. Toronto, I say. Auckland, Harmeet says.

I ask Gordon if it would be possible for us to see Medicine Man. "No," he says, "he's in American custody. I can't even see him. But we have pictures."

Can we see them? we ask, excited. This is an opportunity to verify if it was indeed Medicine Man standing at the door.

Yes, he can arrange that, he says. He wasn't going to mention it, but since we've asked, he'll show them to us. But it won't be him—it'll be a couple of the guys from the investigative side. I look at him quizzically. He explains that the operation is divided into a negotiating side and an investigative side. He's in charge of negotiation, which involves trying to talk with the kidnappers. He says his goal was much like ours: he wanted to negotiate a non-violent resolution. They'll do anything that doesn't involve a political solution, or what he calls an Unreasonable Demand. So, for example, if the group has a particular message they want communicated, he'll get it out there for them. But if they want the release of all political prisoners, or for a particular country to withdraw its troops from Iraq, anything like that, they can't do it. That's outside their power.

I ask him when we can see the pictures. He says he doesn't know, but it will probably be tonight.

I ask him when our debriefing with the CPT team will be. He says he's still working on it, he'll let us know as soon as he knows. That would be great, I say, feeling slightly alarmed. It's already nine o'clock in the morning and a plan still hasn't been made. Time is passing. I want to spend the whole day together.


In my last act as delegation leader, I suggest to Norman and Harmeet that we might want to debrief, maybe have a little prayer service where we can express our gratitude, ask each other for forgiveness, say good-bye. This might be the last time we'll all be together.

Harmeet seems unenthusiastic but agrees. Norman says he'll think about it. I'm disappointed by their lack of interest. There is no pressure, I tell them. Lunch is at noon. "Any time before then, if you want."

I prepare a little prayer service and debriefing for us just in case. At eleven-twenty I decide to go hunting around. Norman's departure is rapidly approaching. The door to his room is open. "Hello?" I say, peeking my head inside.

I am nervous. I don't know where things stand between us. We've hardly spoken since the release. I wonder if my presence is somehow intrusive to him, a grating reminder of things he'd just as soon forget.

"Hi!" he says. "Would you like to see my room?"

"Sure," I say, stepping onto a plush carpet in a spacious five-star room decorated with ornate plaster mouldings. No clutter here. "I see you got the deluxe accommodations."

He laughs. "Yes, I suppose it comes with being old. And being British doesn't hurt. My guess is that this must have been the master bedroom, but it could just as easily have been the ballroom."

"Hey, you shaved! You look good," I say. He looks fit, steady on his feet, ready to meet the world—much better than yesterday.

"What about you?" he asks, pointing to my patchy beard.

"After I kiss my mother," I say. Then silence, heavy, awkward. "Are you almost packed?" I ask, reaching for something to fill the vacuum.

"Well, yes, but there isn't much to pack, is there," he answers, pointing to the suitcase on his bed. Silence. Norman coughs, looks down at his hands. I look down at the floor. I see Norman's Nike running shoes, smile, look up at his shirt and woollen tie.

"I see you have your new shoes on," I say.

"And I see that you have yours," he says. We both laugh. "They're not quite my style, but they're certainly much better than what we had."

"How I hated those shoes."

"Would you like to sit down?" he asks me.

"Yes, sure, thanks, I would," I say. We fall easily into talking. About the arrangements for our travel home, our families, the British ambassador, yesterday's lunch. He wants to know if I still have my notebooks. Yes, I tell him, but I had to fight to hold on to them.

"I gave them everything. I wish now that I had kept my notebook. I hope I get it back," he says.

The topic turns to the CPT team. "They probably thought I was rude," Norman says. "I certainly didn't stick around very long. I didn't mean to be. It's just that I couldn't . . . I couldn't talk to them right then. Maybe you could thank them for me . . ."

"It's all right, Norman. I know they'll understand. Yes, I'll tell them."

"Perhaps later I'll send them a note."

Silence. I turn to look at Norman. Our eyes meet briefly. I take a deep breath. "I want to apologize to you," I say. "For anything I might have done that made things harder for you. I wasn't always the easiest person to be locked up with, and I . . . I wasn't very generous at times. To you, or to Harmeet."

"Well, none of us was at our best, were we?" His hand briefly touches my shoulder.

"No."

He looks at his watch. "I'm glad they at least let me keep my watch. Well, it's 11:45. Shall we find Harmeet?"

We face each other for a moment. Norman shakes my hand. "We got through it," he says.

"Yes, we got through it," I say, grinning.

"I guess we've had our debriefing, then?"

"Yes, I guess we have."


The British ambassador is travelling back to Britain with Norman. "Thank you. For everything," I say, shaking his hand.

"No problem, any time, come again," he chuckles. "Here's my card. Just call me if you ever need anything. And make sure you sign the guest book."

I turn to Norman. It's a stiff leave-taking. There it is again, that strange absence of emotion. We shake hands and say goodbye. Adrian takes Norman's suitcase and they walk to a waiting SUV, a top-of-the-line occupation model complete with tinted bulletproof windows, armoured body and self-contained air circulation system. A Gurkha opens the gate and the vehicle drives away. Norman never looks back.

I am both relieved and sad. Norman is going home to Pat and my responsibility has come to an end. But I feel his sudden absence intensely. It is too soon; so much has been left unsaid; for better or worse, we are brothers. I turn to go back into the ambassador's house with a big, gaping hole in my heart.

Sonia and Stewart, the Canadian diplomats we met at lunch yesterday, come for us at two-fifteen to take us to the Canadian embassy. They hate driving in the Green Zone. I immediately see why. It's impossible to get anywhere quickly. We crawl behind a military convoy through a slalom course of tire-shredding road plates. They say it is really dangerous to drive in the Green Zone. This surprises me. I ask them why. Stewart points to the fifty-millimetre gun mounted on the Humvee in front of us. They'll shoot you if you get too close, he says.

I don't believe it. This is a constant danger for anyone travelling in Iraq, but here too, in the Green Zone, where everyone is security-cleared? Stewart and Sonia laugh. Why do you think we're driving in this? You're looking at half a million dollars of armoured car. And this is an economy model.

Really? I say. It looks like a normal four-door sedan to me.

"Look again," Stewart says. "Look closely at the windows and doors. You'll see they're quite a bit thicker than the norm. There's an inch of glass there. A month ago we were driving along just like this, and I don't know what happened but the convoy stopped really fast, and we must not have stopped quickly enough or something, because they opened fire on us. We were lucky. We could've easily been killed. The bullets went right through the middle of the car into the back seat. After that, Foreign Affairs said we couldn't go anywhere in the Green Zone unless it was in an armoured vehicle. Another reason why this is one of our more expensive diplomatic missions."

The embassy is located on a small triangle-shaped piece of land surrounded by an eight-foot wall. Behind the wall are two buildings: a garage in a state of serious disrepair and a two-storey house adorned with Romanesque columns. The garden in front of the house is overgrown, and the empty land in the narrowing end of the triangle is full of metal junk that Stewart has no idea what to do with. "The house might look impressive on the outside, but it's really quite modest," Stewart says. It belonged previously to Saddam Hussein's official photographer. They were lucky to get it—it was the last available property in the Green Zone. Nothing is set up yet. No phone line, no generator, no heat, no plumbing. But he comes here to work for an hour every day in the hope that one day it will be a functioning embassy. Eventually, he says, the whole diplomatic mission will live and work here.

Gordon arrives with Beth, Anita, Peggy and Maxine. They bring us into a room they call the library. "We have to sit here because it's the only room that has any furniture," Stewart jokes.

I am eager to start our debriefing—finally! They'll wait for us outside, they say. They don't mind, it's a nice day. We have until four o'clock, and then the team has to go back. It is 2:50 p.m.

"That only gives us an hour and ten minutes," I say, dismayed. They say they're sorry, the checkpoints close early today.

"What happened?" I ask. I was hoping we would have the whole day.

They apologize, this was the best they could do, even to arrange this was very complicated.

"Well then, please wait outside so we can begin," Maxine says. We start our debriefing immediately. There's so much to tell, so much to ask. We pepper them with questions. What about Tom? What do they know about where he was found? How did they find out? When did they learn about the kidnapping? How did they react, what did they do first, how did the authorities get involved? Had the team ever established contact with a third-party negotiator? What do they think about our negotiated-release theory?

Harmeet wants to talk about his dilemma with his family. He tells us he feels as if he's right back in handcuffs; he doesn't know what to do. He's just beginning to explain the situation when Sonia, Gordon and Stewart burst into the room singing "Happy Birthday." Sonia is carrying a square slab of cake decorated with white icing and a pink Canadian flag. We immediately join them in the singing. I have to fight back tears. I've never felt such pride in my country.

Sonia puts the cake down on the coffee table we are sitting around. "Happy Birthday, Harmeet!" they exclaim. She is beaming.

"Thanks, guys!" Harmeet says. He blows out a tea-light candle.

"Here Harmeet, cut the cake," Sonia says, handing him a knife. They sit down. My heart sinks. Our debriefing is over. When and how are we going to figure out Harmeet's problem?

"Thank you for the cake," Maxine says before Harmeet can start cutting. "Now if you don't mind, we still have twenty minutes. We'd like to continue with our debriefing. Privately."

Everything in the room stops. Sonia looks as if she's just been slapped.

"We certainly don't mean to intrude," Stewart says. "We'll give you a chance to finish up and we'll come back in twenty minutes."

I look at Maxine, astonished. After four months of obsequious captor-pleasing, I marvel at how anyone can be so assertive. She's furious. "I can't believe they did that," she says. "Barging in here, taking away even the little time they'd given us. This is the way it's been all along. They could've at least asked."

"I think they wanted it to be a surprise," I say.

"I don't care. They should've asked."

"Let's focus. We don't have much time," Anita says.

"How about if we go until ten-to and then we invite them in to have the cake?" Harmeet says. Everyone agrees.

At ten to four I go outside to get them. Sonia's eyes are red from crying. "I'm really sorry," I say. "We just really needed the time."

"You don't have to apologize," Sonia says. "It's not your fault."

Sonia and Stewart carry on as if nothing has happened. The room fills with laughter as the cake is cut and shared. We gather around Harmeet for a picture. It feels good to celebrate. Like it's my birthday too. In a way it is. I feel new and reborn. Today is the first day of a whole new life.

Two RCMP officers arrive at eight o'clock that evening. I like them immediately. André is soft-spoken, unassuming, cerebral, almost shy.

Tom is a big, warm, open-hearted man—the one I saw crying yester-day. They greet us like old friends. We find ourselves a corner in the ambassador's sepulchral living room. Tom has a file folder on his knee. After a bit of small talk, they ask if we know anything about Jill Carroll, an American journalist who was kidnapped in January.

No, nothing about Jill Carroll, we say.

Did your captors mention anyone else?

Just that they kidnapped a German archaeologist and killed an American contractor in December, and that they had kidnapped two German oil workers in February.

Tom and André nod. Then Tom explains they have some pictures to show us, all of different men, people who are in custody.

*What is this, some kind of photo lineup?* "Gordon told us you had pictures of Medicine Man," I say. I feel set up, betrayed.

It's not a photo lineup, they say. There's one picture of Medicine Man; the rest are of other people who are in custody. This is just for our own purposes. None of this is going to the Americans.

We don't want to identify anybody, we say. We only asked to see a picture of Medicine Man so we can verify for ourselves whether or not the man we saw at the house was him.

Their voices are calm, gentle, so very reasonable. They know how to soothe ruffled feathers. We don't have to identify anybody, they say. In Canada we have certain values. We don't agree with the death penalty, for example. This is just for Canadian purposes. Like for immigration. So that, in the future, we don't unknowingly admit one of your captors to Canada. We want to protect you from bumping into one of them on the street. It's happened before. Lots of people try to come to Canada to escape criminal pasts. And perhaps even more important, some of these men may be innocent. The Americans just pick people up. This is rough-and-tumble, it's the middle of a war. So, by you looking at the pictures, we can eliminate anyone whose picture we have as a suspect in this particular crime. On the other hand, we don't want to release anybody who is likely to do this kind of thing again. I'm sure you wouldn't want this to happen to anyone else, they say.

Harmeet and I look at one another. We need to think. They keep talking, say the same things over and over, their voices repeating in a closed loop. My head is spinning. I have to fight against an almost irresistible desire to please them.

Can we have a minute to talk? I finally say. Harmeet and I step out of earshot. We agree to look at the pictures but we won't say anything until we've seen all of them, and only then to confirm that none of the men are our captors. If we see even one we recognize, we won't say anything.

Tom opens the file folder and passes the pictures to us one by one. He has about twenty of them. I study each face closely. It's a sad exercise. Each man is a locked-up human being, just as we had been, with a story, a family, somebody who misses and needs them. Sometimes I think I can read defiance, sometimes fear, but mostly their eyes are distressingly vacant, not really there. No one looks to have been beaten. "Some of them could be innocent," Tom had said. Most of them undoubtedly are. Colonel Janis Karpinski, the commander of Abu Ghraib at the time of the torture revelations, estimated that 90 percent of their detainees were innocent. I say a prayer for each man as his photo passes through my hands. I don't recognize any of them. Except the very last picture. I am startled by something familiar. Something in the structure of the jaw, cheekbones, forehead. But the eyes . . . the eyes aren't right. It's as if somebody else's eyes have been put into Medicine Man's face. I look at Harmeet. He sees it too. I go back to studying the picture, my heart pounding.

"Do you recognize him?" Tom asks.

There it is again, that irresistible desire to please. I don't know, I say, I can't tell. It sure looks like him, I think, but I can't be sure. I look at Harmeet. He shrugs his shoulders. "I don't know," he says.

I look at André and Tom. "What's his name?" I ask.

"I think they call him Abu Luay," André says, looking over at Tom. Tom nods.

Abu Luay. The father of Luay. It doesn't mean anything. It's just a nickname.

"When was he picked up?" I ask.

Around midnight, they say.

"And he voluntarily gave the information about where we were?"

Not exactly, they say, but they never touched him. They asked him to tell them where you were. When he wouldn't, they said all right, take him outside. That was all they said, take him outside, and then he spilled the beans. This was all the Americans, of course. We've never had any contact with him.

Later, I will read a book written by Mark Urban called *Task Force Black: The Explosive True Story of the SAS and the Secret War in Iraq.* According to Urban, the operation to secure our release was called Operation Lightwater. The British special forces detachment was under "constant pressure from London" to find us. The search involved monitoring cellphone traffic, raiding houses and using seized cellphones to generate network maps to target more suspects. As the kidnapping wore on and Tom was killed, the pace became relentless. In the final two weeks, Squadron B was out every night. Urban says fifty buildings were raided during the course of the operation and forty-seven people were detained. "Tactical questioning"—utilizing the shock of capture by interrogating detainees on the scene—was crucial. He quotes one veteran as saying, "Individuals were exploited to get to him [Kember]—both by putting them under duress and not." They hit the jackpot in the early morning hours of March 23. The target, apparently, was a house in Mishahda, an area about thirty-two kilometres northwest of Baghdad. They found two men they were looking for. "One of them, Abu Laith,* clearly knew something about the kidnapping. Under pressure—people who know about the operation reject the use of such words as 'beating' or 'torture'—Abu Laith began to talk." Presumably using "Abu Laith's" cellphone, the SAS called the captors to tell them they were on the way. "How about you disappear and we won't come after you," they were warned.

I read Urban's book with a grain of salt. Among other inaccuracies, he calls me "Tom Loney" and reports the location of the

---

* Name changed by Mark Urban.

kidnapping as the "university area of Baghdad." We were nowhere near the university.

Tom and André want to know if they can ask us a few questions. It's just for their own information; it's important for them to learn as much as they can from each case so they can do their job better in the future. Hearing from us helps them to complete the picture.

I say okay. It is almost a compulsion—I want, *need* to tell the story—and it seems to be the least I can do, a way to express my gratitude, giving them the other half of the story. We don't know much anyway, I tell myself. Beyond providing them with a complete physical description, whatever we tell them will be of little practical use apart from satisfying their curiosity. They listen carefully, without interrupting. Harmeet listens while I do most of the talking.

At one o'clock in the morning Tom and André say they've kept us far too long, we look tired, they should let us get some sleep. But it is they who need the sleep. I am wired. Neither of us sleep at all that night.


Our departure time is set for 10:30 a.m. The guest book the ambassador told us to sign is on a little table just inside the front door, where his assistant has his office. It feels momentous, to take the pen into my hand, to write my name, to say *I was here, on this day, March 25, 2006,* to officially declare it: my being here matters. My eyes fill with tears. There are no words to say how grateful I am. I write my name under Harmeet's, who has written his under Norman's. Beside my name there is a space to identify myself. "A free human being," I write.

"You'll need to put one of these on," Gordon says, helping me into a flak jacket. "They take some getting used to. How does it feel?" he asks, stepping back.

I take a few steps. It is astonishingly heavy. I feel as if I'm moving through chest-high water on rubber legs. I rap my knuckle against the body of the jacket. "It's like a steel life jacket," I say. I think of the soldiers who rescued us, the full-body armour and all the equipment they wore, how effortlessly they seemed to move, how strong they must've been.

We pile into an armoured SUV. A Gurkha drives us to a staging area. Gordon gets out first. He opens the door for me and holds out his arm. "You want a hand?"

"I'll be okay," I say, declining his help. I slide off the seat and step onto the ground. My knees buckle and I catapult forward. Gordon, standing ready, catches me before I fall flat on my face. "Thanks," I say, sheepish.

"It'll be a while before you get your strength back," he says.

"Don't worry, the same thing happened to me," Stewart says. "The first time I got out of a vehicle wearing one of these things, I just about went head over heels, and it wasn't from love."

A helicopter takes us to the Baghdad airport. As we vault over the city, I remember how at the first house the helicopters would roar overhead in a constant procession and how we always assumed they were travelling between the Green Zone and the airport. Now we are the ones roaring overhead, and somewhere down below us is a house with a picture of the Sacred Heart hanging on the wall where, for a time, we lived in the shadow of death.

We take shelter from the sun under a wood-frame pavilion on the edge of an airfield. It seems to be taking forever. Harmeet nudges me. "See that?" he asks under his breath, pointing his chin towards a concrete separation barrier, the words scrawled in black spray paint. Homos die. Yes, I nod.

Gordon gives us the sign and it's time to go. It's a long walk across the tarmac. I'm glad he insisted on carrying my backpack. My legs are trembling under the weight of my flak jacket and I am growing short of breath.

"That's it over there," Gordon says, pointing to the dark, hulking outline of the plane that will take us to Dubai.

Gordon had never said, and I never asked. I don't know until I see it, the Canadian flag, the Government of Canada logo under the cockpit. My eyes fill with tears. I can't believe it. They sent a Hercules! Here, to Baghdad, to bring us home! We were Canadians in trouble and they came. *They came for us!* I don't know how or when, but I vow to give something back.

"Would you like to go up to the flight deck?" they ask us. Sure, we say, astonished. We follow a crew member up a ladder into the brilliant light of the cockpit. There are four men working in a tight space crammed with instruments, everything metal and glass. I am nervous, ready for a disapproving lecture about our having diverted them from more urgent tasks, wasting government resources. There is none of that. They welcome us warmly and give us headsets so we can communicate with them. Somebody points to the brown world below us and explains that we are following the Shatt al Arab to the Arabian Gulf and that Iran is to our left.

They ask us questions. What's life like in Iraq? How are the people being affected by the war? Why did we go in the first place? I explain about Rick Yuskiw, how he had gone to school with my brother and lived two blocks from where I grew up. He joined the Canadian military and was sent to Afghanistan. His best friend was one of the first Canadians to be killed there. It really challenged me, I say. If Rick was prepared to risk his life serving his country, then I who believed in non-violence should be prepared to take some of the same risks too. Harmeet explains about joining the CPT delegation and wanting to learn first-hand about the realities of Iraqi life under American and British occupation.

What's CPT? they ask. We explain. That takes real bravery, they say.

Someone pulls out a little black book. He opens his flight book to a page where somebody has written, *Thanks for the lift, guys!* Underneath, it is signed, *Stephen.* "Do you know who this is?" he asks me, grinning ear to ear.

"No," I say.

"We brought him into Afghanistan just last week. His first big trip out of the country."

"Stephen Harper?"

"That's right," they say, laughing.

We just talked to him, we say. He called us just after we were rescued.

"Here," he says shyly, handing me his book and a pen, "would you mind?"

"You want me to sign your book?" I say, shocked.

"Yes, if you don't mind. It would be an honour."

There are three more books for us to sign. Then somebody presents each of us with a khaki shoulder patch. 436 *Tactical Airlift*, it reads, *On Target—On Time*. In the middle of the patch is a picture of an elephant with a Canadian flag hanging off each tusk. That's us, he says. We go wherever we have to, do whatever's needed. We're the pachyderm of the Canadian Forces.

Thank you, we say.

Hey, can you do us a favour? they ask. There are two flight crews— A Team and B Team. We're the A Team. We're always joking with each other about who's the best. We are, of course, because we're the A Team. So if you're talking to the media, and you happen to talk about your trip home, if you could just mention sometime that A Team is the best, that'll really burn their asses.

We laugh. We'll do our best, we say.

The original plan was to land in Dubai. That's where Harmeet's father and his brother-in-law have gone to meet Harmeet, where the New Zealand media outlet that paid for their flight is waiting to film their reunion. But Gordon does an end run around the media by changing the itinerary at the last minute. They take us to Abu Dhabi instead, the capital of the United Arab Emirates.

We say goodbye to the flight crew and barely have time to walk the fifty metres from the plane to the airport terminal before the big C-130 is turning back towards the runway. We wave one last time and watch with pride as they mount the sky once again. They weren't on the ground more than five minutes.

We are met by cameras, an official delegation from the United Arab Emirates, and the Canadian ambassador. The latter, a genial, down-to-earth man, drives me, Harmeet and Stewart to Le Royal Méridien Hotel. He tells us all about the UAE as he drives through the gleaming-skyscraper city. Only 20 percent of the population has citizenship, he says. The remaining 80 percent are guest workers from all over the world, most notably India and the Philippines.

We are astonished yet again to learn that we are the official guests of Sheik Khalifa, current president of the United Arab Emirates and emir of Abu Dhabi. We are each given a suite in which to rest before our next flight. Harmeet's flight is at ten p.m., mine at eleven-thirty.

Our final adventure together is a shopping trip with Sonia to a nearby mall. Harmeet needs clothes and I need a belt. It is a bewildering world of consumer opulence and pampering. I walk around, staring at everything like a wide-eyed infant, surrounded by an infinity of choices. After much wandering and hopeless indecision about where to go, Sonia finally takes charge and directs us to a chain store called Giordano. I have to keep reminding myself that I am in Abu Dhabi, not Toronto or Buffalo.

I am glad I only have to decide on a belt. It is a very complex decision. I don't want to waste taxpayers' money, so it can't cost too much, but it has to be of reasonable quality so it will last awhile, and I don't want it to come from a sweatshop, and it has to be something that I am going to wear in the future, so it can't be too thick or too thin, or too small, since I expect to return to my normal weight. And then of course there's the colour, and the style of buckle . . . It takes me half an hour. I feel sorry for Harmeet, who has to choose a shirt and a pair of pants. He agonizes for an hour before Sonia, unable to stand it any longer, orders Harmeet to "Just pick something! Anything!"

Then Harmeet and I walk back to the hotel together. He is distraught. His father is taking a taxi from Dubai to meet him at the hotel. He worries that his father won't understand why he doesn't want to be bought and sold and packaged for some sensationalist media exclusive. He worries that his father will feel slighted, perhaps even dishonoured, and that this will overshadow their reunion. None of this is what he wants.

I leave Harmeet to prepare for his father's visit. He expects his father in an hour. I will come to meet them in the lobby. In the meantime, I decide to go for a walk. I'm desperate to be alone. I exit the lobby and step outside. I am delirious with joy. Finally, for the first time in 120 days, I am really and truly alone. No one to be responsible for, no one to please, no one to fear. I can go left, or right, or stay right where I am, for as long as I care to! I can do anything, go anywhere! I turn towards the ocean. I skip, twirl, dance. I would cartwheel if I felt strong enough. I don't care what *anybody* thinks. I am free!

I walk down a sidewalk through a garden onto the beach. Every step is bliss. Everything is incredible, amazing, astounding, miraculous. I cry with joy for every blade of grass and flower petal and grain of sand and washed-up piece of plastic. I raise my hands to the blue sky above me and send kisses riding on the ocean breeze. I greet all the glass buildings rising around me, the industrial docks reaching into the water, the rusty ships that sit anchored to them. I take my shoes off and run splashing along the water's edge, exulting in the bone-chilling cold. I sit and pour sand through my fingers and say thank you a thousand times.

I sit for a long time. Maybe too long, I start to think. I don't want to miss meeting Harmeet's father. I turn to go back to the hotel. There is an outdoor pool between the beach and the hotel. There are all kinds of people, just lying around, sitting on towels, reading books, smoking cigarettes, chatting! All marvellously, obliviously, gloriously free! And no one afraid! I stop to watch. There are children, splashing, kicking, swimming, jumping in the water, calling out to parents, arguing over a floating toy! A father wraps a towel around his shivering daughter. A mother bends down to her son as he asks a question. A young couple talk animatedly, their legs touching under a table. I am surrounded by ordinary, everyday human love. I can hardly see for my tears. If I wanted to, I think, I could just disappear, right here and now, in a single, joyous burst of light. But I don't want to. I want to go home.

—

We say goodbye in the hotel lobby. Harmeet looks good in his new golf shirt and loose-fitting pants, Sonia's Nike running shoes, the toque he'd worn during the delegation. I keep watching the movements of his hands, marvelling at the fact that there is no longer a handcuff between us. "I'm going to miss you, brother," I say. "There's no one to bring me a glass of water in the mornings anymore."

He laughs. "You kept me sane."

"You too," I say.

He is nervous about going home. His visit with his father has gone well, but there remains real tension in his family. I ache for him. I know that I am going home to the unconditional support of my partner and my community and my family. I so much wish the same for Harmeet. But I'm not sad. Harmeet is going home, and I am going home. The nightmare is over. Our lives have been returned to us.

"Would you like some champagne?" Gordon asks as we take our seats in business class.

I hesitate. "No thanks, I'm okay," I say.

"Come on. We have to celebrate!"

"I don't want to cost the government any more than I already have," I say.

"Oh, don't worry about that. It's already included. There's no extra cost."

I know Gordon is exhausted, but I can't help myself. I pepper him with questions. I ask about his family, his work, what he knows about the psychology of hostage-taking. I tell him more stories from the kidnapping. He asks me what I am going to say to the media. My heart immediately starts pounding. I'd rather not say anything, I say.

He says I should think about it. The media are not going to give up until they get something from me. He recommends that I prepare a brief statement. I don't have to take any questions, just read the statement; that will satisfy them and then they won't bother me after that. I agree that it's a good idea and something I feel I can handle.

I tell him about my conversation with Harmeet, our concerns that it was a negotiated release made to look like a rescue. I tell him about my frustration with not being given any real information about our captors, the events leading up to our release, whether or not a ransom was paid.

He asks me why it matters, since I am free. I say I need to know the truth. He explains again the reasons for not being able to tell me, the importance of protecting their methods, the possible danger posed to informants, the confidentiality he is bound by law and sworn by oath to keep. He swears to me as a Christian that no ransom has been paid. I am convinced. Gordon's personal integrity is something I can believe in.

As for the captors, he says I'll feel differently in the future.

What do you mean? I say.

He tells me that I've been protecting them. He talks about the Stockholm Syndrome, how it is a normal and helpful survival mechanism, how hostages will often attempt to bond with their captors, take on their agenda in the hope it will offer them safety. "Did you ever ask them to let you go?"

"No," I say, stunned.

"Why not?"

"I . . . I don't know," I say. I didn't know how to begin explaining. I wanted to, considered it hundreds of times, but could never bring myself to do it.

"It's okay," he says. "I'm not here to judge. It's going to take time. But you'll feel differently someday."

When we're back on the plane after a stopover in Frankfurt, flying over the Atlantic on the last leg of our journey, Gordon asks if he can read my statement. I wrote it in the business class lounge in Germany. He says it's good but I have to thank the people who rescued us. How can I do that? I say. I haven't thanked anyone in the statement. It's impossible! I don't know where to start. There are so many people, I don't want to value any one person's contribution over another's.

He understands that, he says, but if I don't thank the people who rescued us, they'll think I'm ungrateful, which clearly I'm not. If I don't say thank you, that's what they'll focus on, and they won't hear anything else that I have to say.

I get to work right away and show him the revision. Good, he says.

I see that Gordon is starting to nod off. I suppress my need to talk and let him sleep. I stand up, stretch, sit down, try to read the paper, try to sleep, can't, get up to talk to the stewardesses. I am too excited to sit still. It is really happening. I am going home. Finally.

# CHAPTER SIXTEEN

We're walking through the airport. Uniformed policemen with guns. Someone with a radio. Gordon, Stewart and his wife Giselle, who is also a diplomat and travelled with us from Abu Dhabi. I follow them through airy corridors and sliding open doors. My arms are swinging free. I love that! People are looking at us, looking at me. I walk briskly, pretend not to notice them noticing me, pretend like I'm a regular passenger going to get his luggage.

I see them down a long hall. Dan is to the left, in a blue shirt. My brothers Edward and Matthew are in the middle. Donna is to the right. There are two tall men in suits I have never seen before.

This is it! I can't believe it. I'm beaming. I want to run to them. I want Dan to come running towards me. But he stays where he is. And I just keep walking. It would be too dramatic, I guess. Like something out of the movies.

"It's over, it's over," I say, wrapping my arms around him.

"It's over," he says, holding me tight. We look at each other. He looks good. Just like he always does. Maybe a little greyer. And a little thinner. His eyes are brown. He's smiling. I love that, the way the skin around his eyes crinkles when he smiles.

And then my arms are around Matthew, Edward, Donna, and their arms are around me. I introduce them to Gordon, Stewart and Giselle. I am honoured, grateful beyond words. The people who brought me home meeting the people I've been brought home to. I'm introduced to Larry and Mike, the officers who were the liaison between my family and the RCMP. Yet more surprises.

Gordon leaves right away. He has a plane to catch. He's exhausted, anxious to see his wife, who is recovering from surgery. Stewart and

Giselle slip away too. They promise to come and visit the next time they're in Toronto, and I promise to cook for them. I don't want any of them to go. Not yet. Something's unfinished. They are my last link to Iraq, the rescue, this enormous, bittersweet debt of gratitude. A gratitude I will never be finished with.

We're in a hall with row upon row of fixed chairs. There's no one around us. It's as though we have a whole airport terminal to ourselves. We sit and talk and talk. Our questions run into each other. I want to know everything that's happened. They want to know everything that's happened. This talking together, it's like . . . it's like the kind of breathing a drowning man does once he's safely onshore. I want to just sit here, talking like this forever.

"We should probably get going," one of the RCMP officers says, looking at his watch. "There's a whole bunch of press people waiting."

Oh yeah. A pit opens in my stomach. I really don't want to be doing this.

Dan looks apprehensive. "What are you going to tell them about us?"

"What do you mean?" I say.

"Everyone thinks you're this nice guy from Sault Ste. Marie who's from this nice nuclear family. They don't know anything about me." He tells me about how, in those frenzied first days of our kidnapping, they needed a picture, so they chose the one David and Joseph took of us the night before I left. We were standing together, smiling, shoulder around arm around shoulder. They had to cut Dan out of the picture. No one could know about him. No one could know about our relationship. It just about killed him, seeing that picture on newspaper front pages, knowing he was helpless to speak for me. He too had been disappeared.

I put my hand on Dan's shoulder. "No more prisons."

We walk down a long corridor. When we're halfway, a sliding door opens, revealing a wall of people, cameras, microphones. "Oh my God," I say.

"Are you all right?" I hear my brother Ed say. I feel his hand squeezing my shoulder. It feels good, steadies me.

"Yes," I say. "All I have to do is read. No questions."

We're there. The door slides open again. "There he is," I hear a voice say. Then people calling my name. The click-whirring sound of cameras. A wall of faces. Confusion held behind a yellow-tape cordon. I pull out my statement, clear my throat and begin to read:

During my captivity, I sometimes entertained myself by imagining this day. Sometimes I despaired of ever seeing it. Always I ached for it. And so here we are. For 118 days I disappeared into a black hole, and somehow by God's grace I was spit out again. My head is swirling and there are times when I can hardly believe it's true. We had to wear flak jackets during our helicopter transport from the International Zone to the Baghdad airport, and I had to keep knocking on the body armour I was wearing to reassure myself that this was all really happening.

It was a terrifying, profound, powerful, transformative, and excruciatingly boring experience. Since my release from captivity, I have been in a constant state of wonder, bewilderment and surprise as I slowly discover the magnitude of the effort to secure our lives and our freedom—Tom Fox, Norman Kember, Harmeet Sooden and myself. A great hand of solidarity reached out for us, a hand that included the hands of Palestinian children holding pictures of us, and the hands of the British soldier who cut our chains with a bolt cutter. That great hand was able to deliver three of us from the shadow of death. I am grateful in a way that can never be adequately expressed in words.

There are so many people that need this hand of solidarity, right now, today, and I'm thinking specifically of prisoners held all over the world, people who have disappeared into an abyss of detention without charge, due process, hope of release—some victims of physical and psychological torture—people unknown and forgotten. It is my deepest wish that every forsaken human being should have a hand of solidarity reaching out to them.

My friend and fellow Canadian in captivity, Harmeet Sooden, showed me something yesterday. Our captors gave us notebooks, and

Harmeet opened his notebook to show me two fractions—3/4 and 4/4—that Tom had written. "It was the only thing he wrote in my book," he said. Tom, who had been a professional musician, wrote them as part of a lesson in music theory he gave Harmeet—3/4 time, 4/4 time. Harmeet put his finger over the 3/4 and said, "In the beginning we were 4/4." Then he put his finger over the 4/4 and said, "Now we're this—3/4." We are only 3/4. Tom is not coming home with us. I am so sorry, Kassie and Andrew.

People have been asking, "What's the first thing you're going to do when you get home?" All I really want to do is to love, and be loved by, the people I love. The one specific thing might be to wash a sink full of dirty dishes. After this, I'm going to disappear into a different kind of abyss—an abyss of love. I need some time to get reacquainted with my partner Dan, my family, my community—and freedom itself. I'm eager to tell the story of my captivity and rescue, but I need some time first—that's a subtle hint to anyone who might have a big camera or notebook.

For the British soldiers who risked their lives to rescue us, for the Government of Canada who sent a team to Baghdad to help secure our release, for all those who thought about and prayed for us, for all those who spoke for us when we had no voice, I am forever and truly grateful.

It's great to be alive. *Hamdulillah!*

As soon as I finish, we're moving. Larry and Mike lead us through the reporters like human bulldozers. I follow between them; Dan, Ed, Donna and Matthew follow behind us. The reporters swarm and follow us out of the terminal. There are two black sedans waiting for us. Unmarked police cars. Another surprise. They're driving us right to the door. It feels good to be sitting next to Dan, to be going home, drinking in the familiar sites along the four-lane highways that lead from the airport to our home in Toronto's west end.

We pull up in front of our house. I get out of the car as soon as I can. I reach my hands up to the sky. The day is blue and the sun is late afternoon glorious. I am trembling with relief. Finally I am home. Finally I am out, free, released from the world of the gun.

I look around me. There's only one television camera here. I'm amazed. The media actually respected our request. My friend Sheila Sullivan is standing on the sidewalk. I go over to give her a hug. She bursts into hysterical laughter and runs towards her car. The car door is open, waiting. She's up to no good. I run after her, laughing too. "What're you doing, Sheila?" I say. She's reaching into her car, pushing buttons, trying to play some music. She can't talk, she's laughing so hard. The only thing I can make out is the word "Alleluia." She's trying to play something with "Alleluia" in it.

"You can't do that, Sheila!" I tell her. "It's still Lent." She breaks into more spasms of laughter. The Alleluia begins. I turn to our house. All the blinds are down and the curtains drawn. We walk up the sidewalk to the front steps. Dan opens the door for me. I walk into the house. It takes a moment for my eyes to adjust to the interior light. I look to my right. My friend Sheila Green is standing in the doorway to the living room, all five feet of her. "Hiya stranger," she says, waving to me, smiling impishly, bundled up tight in her winter jacket.

"Sheila!" I say, exploding with joy, opening my arms to hug her. "Did the cats miss me?"

"Yeah, they missed you," she says, nodding, holding back tears.

"Well, I missed you too," I say.

I look behind her into our living room. There are people sitting, standing, crammed everywhere. I can't see the floor. I go to Raffi and Tonnan and Sephie Burghardt Marshall first. They are nineteen months, five years and seven years old. Then to David and Jessica Morales, who are nine and fourteen years old. It is impossible to describe, how beautiful, how wonderful, how amazing it is, to behold a child after the ugliness of captivity. And then the tears come, a hot pouring flood of sweet joy relief. I go around the room, greet each person, blessing and being blessed with tears, my extended Catholic Worker family, my CPT brothers and sisters, the friends who organized and kept vigil and prayed and supported Dan and worked night and day for our release.

When all the hugs and all the greetings are done, I am spent. The adrenalin is gone. I've had two hours of sleep in the past ninety. I'm a trembling wreck. But there's pizza, beer, a party, most of my favourite people in the world gathered together in one place!

I'm standing in the kitchen. There's commotion everywhere. Somebody hands me a plate with some pizza on it. Thank you, I say. Somebody is asking me a question. I'm trying to answer them.

"How're you doing?" Julie says to me, the friend I had dinner with before leaving for Iraq. I'm about to answer when she says, "You look like you need to sit down." She takes me by the hand and leads me to the living room couch. I sit down. Exhaustion washes through my body.

"Do you need anything?" she asks me. There are people all around me.

"Something to drink would be great," I say. A glass of juice appears. I drink it greedily. The sugar is an instant hit of strength. I take a breath, dig deeper.

Dan sits beside me. "How're you doing?" he asks. "Should I send people home?"

"No, it's okay," I say, though I am not really sure what I want. Someone new arrives and asks me a question. I answer it. Then everyone seems to have a question and the stories start pouring out. Each story seems to be interrupted by more questions. This disorients me. *No, wait, I'm not finished yet, I need to tell each one*, I want to say. I feel like a Ping-Pong ball. I see David sitting on the floor in front of me, arms wrapped around his knees, listening closely. I continue on.

I'm flagging. People start to filter out. Madeline, the mother of Seph, Tonnan and Raffi, comes to say goodbye. I stand up. "You know," she says, choking back tears, "today is my birthday."

"It is? Wow—happy birthday!" I say.

"Thanks for coming home. I didn't know . . . wasn't sure this day would ever come." She struggles to get the words through her tears. "I just couldn't bear the thought that . . . that you wouldn't be here . . . for the boys to grow up with you. You mean so much to them—to us."

I don't know what to say. I feel so unworthy of this fierce love. We hold each other again, she wipes away more tears, waves goodbye.

"See you tomorrow, Mad," I say.

"See you tomorrow," she says.

I sit back down. Dan puts his hand on my knee. "Well?" he says.

"Yeah, I think it's time," I say.

"David asked me to give this to you." It's a piece of paper with a pencil drawing of a stick figure holding a two-hundred-pound weight above his head. *Jim is still strong*, it says in careful block-letter writing. I laugh delightedly.

Dan leads me to our part of the house, an old garage converted into a long rectangular living space.

"Hey, we have curtains!" It's the first thing I notice.

"Madeline made those for us yesterday," Dan says. "Part of our media protection program."

I laugh. "It took a kidnapping for us to finally get some curtains. They're beautiful." I turn to look at him. "Everything's beautiful." I am home, in my own room, with Dan. I can hardly believe it.

The first thing I notice is my clothes, Dan's clothes, hanging or sitting folded on the shelves of the open pine wardrobe I built for us when we moved in. "I'd forgotten about these," I say, fingering one of my shirts, a tangible link to the person-I-was-before in a long-long-time-ago life. Everything is the same. Exactly the same. Except for a vigil candle on the dresser. The big, heavy-duty glass kind that you'll find next to the tabernacle in a Catholic church.

"I always had one going," Dan says. "I would bring one into the room with me at night. It was my way of holding you. You can blow it out now, if you want."

"With pleasure," I say, blowing out the candle.

"I'll show you later," he laughs. "I have a whole box of them."

We take off our clothes, climb into bed, arrange ourselves under the sheets. Everything feels strangely anticlimactic, as if there has never been any interruption. As if this is just the end of a regular ordinary day in a long string of regular ordinary days. But it's only six-thirty in the evening, and it's still light out, and my body is tingling with freedom, joy, incredulous gratitude, and I am fighting every second to keep my eyes open as I lie here next to Dan, and the soul balm smoothness of his skin.

"After I brought the candle in, I would always read to you," Dan tells me. "Something Scott gave me that Daniel Berrigan wrote. Shall I read it to you? It's beautiful," he says, bubbling with enthusiasm as he reads the passage that I've used as the epigraph for this book: "Sleep Jonah in the belly of a paradox. Now you need have no purpose, nothing to prove, nowhere to go . . ."

I try really hard to take it in. But I can't. It goes in one ear and out the other, a babble stream of words flowing by. Everything is too much now. Everything.

"What do you think? It's good, eh?" Dan says. He's very excited.

"Yeah, it's . . . nice . . . very . . . nice," I say, unable to keep my eyes open any longer.

"Sleep, Jim," Dan says, caressing my head. "Sleep at last." I nod my head and fall fast asleep.


I'm instantly awake, charged, ready. I have to restrain myself from leaping out of bed. "Are you awake, Dan?"

"Yes."

It's still dark out. I look at the time. It's 5:00 a.m. "Oh good, it's not too late," I say, jumping out of bed. "Come on, Dan. Let's go watch the sun rise."

We grab something to eat and pull our bikes out of the basement. I sit on the seat of my old ten-speed yellow Schwinn, take the handlebars in my hands, put my feet on the pedals. I hesitate for a moment. *Can I still do it?* I push off and it's miraculous, the simultaneous pedal, balance and move, the wheel-turning rush of wind against my face. Yes! Everything works: body, wheels, gravity, the universe. I'm going to be okay.

It's six kilometres to the sunrise spot at the mouth of the Humber River where the Catholic Worker community gathers at dawn every Easter morning to proclaim and celebrate the Resurrection. Dan and I sit on giant limestone blocks along a ragged landfill shore and watch as cobalt turns to mauve, mauve bleeds to pink, pink flows into red and orange and gold-yellow, the fiery arc of sun breaking over the Toronto skyline. Glorious.

We cycle home slowly, telling each other stories. I'm soaking in everything. Blue especially. I'm in love with blue. Blue Lake Ontario waters. Blue open-above sky. Blue, the colour of freedom.

When we get home, I wander around the house in a daze of delight, looking at, touching, feeling everything. Knick-knacks, door handles, countertops. I can't settle anywhere. Everything is a wonder. Everything I do is like for the first time. Parting curtains. Turning on the tap. Making toast. Opening the fridge door. Answering the phone. Dan shows me a big stack of mail and a big stack of newspapers. "When you're ready," he says. I open a letter, flip through the newspapers, check my email. I look at today's newspaper. My picture is on the front page. Everything is overwhelming.

I see that the garbage needs to be taken out. I love this. Tying the bag closed. Stepping outside with it. The clang of the garbage can lid coming off, the thud of the bag falling into the can, the clang of the lid going back into place.

I look up at the sky. Ah, blue, I can't get enough of you. I see, in the middle of the lawn, there's a pop can. I love this too. Walking towards it, bending down, grabbing it with my hand, standing back up. I look down the street. More joy. It's that old man, who passes our house every day, head always down, bent over like a question mark, fighting for every step, his face and hands full of blue veins. I love this old man, and his grizzled old dog pulling him forward, concentrating, breathing hard, just as determined. I watch them make their way up the street.

The old man stops in front of our house. I have never talked to him before. He has not once, that I know of, ever looked up. Nor has his dog. But today they're both looking up. His old dog wants to see me. It's straining against its leash, tail wagging eagerly, ears peeled back, smiling the way dogs do. The old man lets go of the leash. The dog rushes towards me, nuzzles my legs furiously, licks my hand, sits back on its haunches. It wants to be petted. I reach down and rub its head. Its eyes squeeze shut with pleasure.

"I guess he wants to welcome you home," the old man says, smiling, his voice warm· and beautiful and gentle, nonchalant. As if he's always known me.

"Yes," is all I can manage to say.

"It's a beautiful day," he says, taking a deep breath of the blue morning air.

"Yes, it certainly is."

The old dog returns to the old man. "See ya," he says.

"See ya," I say. And on they go, continuing on with continuing on.

When everyone is awake, we go out for breakfast. Dan and I. My brothers and Donna. William, Jo and Michael. A greasy spoon on Queen Street. There's nothing more pleasant: bacon and eggs, home-fried potatoes, toast on the side, coffee, raucous group laughter. Someone nudges my elbow and points to the television. They're playing a clip from my arrival yesterday at the airport. Nobody in the restaurant seems to notice, or care. I am relieved.

I call my parents when we get home. Their voices are a healing balm. I apologize for taking so long to call them. "That's okay, James, we understand. We're just glad you're home," they say. I tell them about the Green Zone, staying with the British ambassador, the Hercules flight out of Baghdad, the stopover in Abu Dhabi, my arrival in Toronto. "When are you coming home?" they ask. I tell them that our plan is to drive up tomorrow. Foreign Affairs offered to fly us, but if we drive we can avoid the media frenzy, and it will also give Dan and me a chance to talk. "Take your time, whenever you get here is fine. We're looking forward to seeing you," they say.

Hobo arrives at noon to celebrate Mass. It is all the same people who were here yesterday. I can't meet or see anyone else. No one new, no one I haven't already been reunited with. No more questions and answers, no more stories, no more small talk, no more hugs. I come into the living room when Hobo is ready to begin and leave immediately when Mass is finished. I can't do it. I am empty, depleted, squeezed dry, suffocating. I need to be outside. I need to be alone. I need to get my hair cut.

I step outside into instant relief. I'm deliriously happy. If I want to I can hop, skip, dance or jump, stare at the sky for an hour, hug a tree, lie on the grass. I go to the corner and turn up Close Avenue. There they are, all the Catholic Worker houses, in their dilapidated, falling-apart glory. I keep on walking. There's a man coming down the street towards me. I smile and nod. He smiles and nods. We pass each other. I hear my name being called. "James? James Loney?" The voice is surprised, delighted.

I turn around. "Yes," I say, perplexed. Is this someone I know, someone I've met before and forgotten?

"I'm so surprised to see you—out, walking around. I didn't think—I'm sorry, I should introduce—I'm a reporter. From Canwest. My name is Robert."

"Well, why not? It's a beautiful day. I'm going to get my hair cut," I say.

His eyes light up. He pulls out his notebook. "Would you mind? Could I talk to you? For just a minute?"

I feel a sudden, dark flash of anger. "No, not today. I have to go now." I turn and walk away.

That feels great. To say no and walk away. Then I think, *That was rather abrupt, maybe I should take his card, so I can call him later, when I'm ready.* I look back. He's gone already. Oh well, no matter, I'm going to get my hair cut.

I'm a supernova of joy. I'm in love with everything. The cracks in the sidewalk. The chestnut trees and the wind-shredded bags flutter-ing helplessly in their branches. The speed bumps. The sun glinting off the cars. The black-pointy Toronto Rehabilitation Institute fence that runs the length of the street. Queen Victoria Public School. The forlorn parkette and the grubby pay phones at the top of the street. The King streetcar rumbling by. The electrical poles full of staples. Holy Family Catholic Church. The litter in the Holy Family Catholic School fence. How I yearned for you!

I've been walking for twenty minutes. I need to sit down. I'm running out of steam. Almost there. Two more blocks. I'm walking in front of the Parkdale Area Recreational Centre. There's a young man out front. He looks to be about twenty-five. He's dressed in a baggy, oversized hoodie, sagging pants, a baseball cap turned to the side. His fingers are stained with nicotine. His shoes are bandaged together with duct tape. He looks at me. I nod and smile. "Brother," he says, "you look great. Let me give you a hug." He opens his arms wide and gives me a gentle squeeze. He steps back. "Have a beautiful day."

"Thanks," I say, stunned. "You too." I keep on walking. I wonder if he knows who I am, or if this is just one of those things that sometimes happens to you in Parkdale. It doesn't matter. It is a blessing I will always cherish.

Finally, at the barbershop, Luigi is puffing on a cigarette, the way he always does between customers. "Hiya," he mumbles, just the way he always does.

"Hi," I say, self-conscious, bracing myself to be recognized.

There are two customers ahead of me. I take off my jacket and sit in a red vinyl chair. The one with the split upholstery and yellow foam peeking through. I love this place. Everything's exactly the same as it was before I left: the faded calendars hanging crooked on the wall, the Christmas cactus in the window, the white and red tile floor, here and there a square missing.

There's a copy of today's *Toronto Sun* lying on the chair nearest the door. My picture is on the front page. I reach for the newspaper, pretend to read it for a while, put it back with the front cover down.

Twenty minutes pass. I need to stand up. I can't sit still. I need fresh air. I step outside.

Across the street, Dan and William are just getting out of Alayna's car. I wave to them. They wave to me. I dash across the street, all smiles. "What's up?" I say.

They look worried. "Is everything okay?" they ask.

"This is the most fun I've had in years," I say. "I'm next in line to get my hair cut. He doesn't recognize me so far. I'm so relieved. Is something the matter?" They look like a couple of mother hens panicking about a lost chick.

"We just came to check to make sure everything's okay. There were a couple of reporters who stopped by the house. Apparently the word's out you're getting your hair cut. They want to know if they can take your picture washing some dishes." I laugh. "Shall we stay with you?" they ask, their faces full of concern.

"I'm fine," I say. "I'll come home as soon as I'm done here." I wave goodbye and walk back into the shop.

Luigi motions to me when it's my turn. I sit in his chair and he covers me with the bib. "How-do-you-a-want-a-the-hair-a-cut-a-today-a?" he says. "Something-a-short-a-or-not-a-short-a?" I only know what he's saying because he always says the same thing.

"Short over the ears," I say, "but not too short on top."

"You-a-have-a-the-long-a-hair-a-this-a-time-a," he says.

"Yes," I say.

He says something about the weather, what a beautiful day it is.

"Yes, it is a beautiful day," I say.

We leave for Sault Ste. Marie the next day. It is one of those glorious March days when sugar maple veins are flowing open. As the Tim Hortons in Parry Sound comes into view, I ask Dan to stop. I have a craving for a sugar-coated sour cream doughnut. When we enter the store, I immediately feel it's a mistake. I feel exposed, on display. Is it my imagination or is every head in the place turning in our direction? I tell Dan I'll wait for him outside.

"Do you mind if I drive?" I say when he returns to the car. "I don't know if I can do it, but I want to try."

"No problem. Here," he says, handing me the keys. I take the wheel. My brain feels spongy, my eyes sluggish. I shift into first and drive us through the parking lot. "Jim! Stop!" Dan shouts. I slam on the brake.

There's a car barrelling out of the drive-thru to my right. I didn't see the stop sign. My whole body is shaking. I put the car in park and immediately get out.

"Sorry, Dan," I say as we pass each other in front of the car. "I can't even get out of the parking lot," I say, laughing contritely.

"The only way you find out is by trying," Dan says.

I talk the whole way, pour the story out from beginning to end, every detail, without interruption. We're passing through Bruce Mines when I finish. We fall silent for a moment. Night has fallen. I watch the highway passing under us through a fleeting tunnel of light. I feel my body relaxing. I have a witness now, someone to hold the story with me, and I am happy. In forty-five minutes we'll be home, the circle will be complete.


Behind my parents' house there's a small three-unit apartment building on a busy street. When we were kids, that property was a vital shortcut in our various comings and goings. When we learned that my father was going to build a fence along the back of our property, we complained loudly. What about our shortcut? Don't worry, he told us, I've got it all figured out. He put a door in the fence.

We park in front of the Anglican church across the street from the apartment building. My sister suggested we come in the back way to avoid the media. Trudging through snow, we enter the backyard through the door in the fence. I stop for a moment. "There they are," I say to Dan. We can see them through the window. Everyone's there— my parents, Claudette and Patrick; my sister Kathleen and her husband Rob; their three children, Adrianna, Olivia and Andrew; Ed and Donna and Matt. My heart races. I open the back door.

My dad sees me first. "James!" he says, throwing his arms around me, engulfing me in his tears. I can't speak. And then it's my mom who is holding me tight. "I love you, James," she says. I feel it in every cell of my body, the love of my parents, the people who gave me life. I give her a kiss. She doesn't say anything about the beard.

"James, do you want some champagne? Ed and Donna got champagne!" Andrew says when all the hugs are done.

"Sure!" I say.

When everyone has a glass in their hand, my dad proposes a toast. "Thank God, and thank Allah, it's over, James is home. To freedom," he says.

"To freedom," we say.

My mom brings me a big bowl of chocolate ice cream. "I think we're going to have to fatten you up a bit," she says.

I laugh. "Thanks, Mom! This is perfect. I haven't had any ice cream yet since I've been home." It is one of the first things I do whenever I visit my parents—help myself to a bowl of ice cream.

The next morning, my father asks me if I'm going to shave. Yes, I tell him, I'm very much looking forward to it.

"What're you going to use?" he asks me.

"I'll just use what's downstairs," I say. My mom keeps disposable razors in the basement bathroom for guests.

"I'll be right back," he says. When he returns, he hands me the razor I remember he used to use when I was a kid—the old-fashioned kind where you have to twist open the head to replace the blade. "You might want to use this. There's a new razor in it."

"I remember this!" I say. Like it was yesterday. Standing next to my father in the bathroom, his face full of lather, his chin lifted and leaning into the mirror, the sound of steel scraping against his beard and the clicking of the razor in the sink as he rinsed it, the pleasing, soap-smelling smoothness of his skin when he was done. The little plastic shaving kit he got me and how grown-up I felt when I would shave next to him in the mornings, my face covered with the lather remaining on his shaving brush. Then the inconsolable tears when the razor fell behind the sink and I thought I'd never be able to shave with my father again. And the sense of being completely restored when he put the razor back in my hands again.

"I thought you might like to have it," he says.

"Thank you, Dad," I say, marvelling at it. "You know, I always kind of hoped that . . . one day I'd be able to use this."

"Well, it's yours now."

I use a pair of scissors first to cut off as much of the beard as I can. Then I use the razor. It feels good. To shave it all away, every last haggard hair, rinse it all down the drain. When I am done, I look in the mirror. Finally, I think. I am beginning to look like myself again.

Later, my brother-in-law asks me what I did with all the hair from my beard. "What do you mean?" I say. "I washed it all down the sink."

"That's too bad," he says. "You should've saved it. We could've auctioned it off on eBay and made a fortune!"

We laugh hysterically. Finally, thank God, hum da'Allah, it's over. It's really really over. And we spend the next days feasting. On laughter, card games, storytelling, afternoon walks in snow-melting sunshine, the full-measure pressed-down shaken-together overflowing goodness of life. The kind of feasting that you can never get enough of. That I so much wish for every human being on our beautiful blue planet.

# CHAPTER SEVENTEEN

I discovered it somewhere in that vast ocean of time: a day without hope, a day so empty and dull and morbid with waiting it is impossible to distinguish. A curtain pulled back, the walls around us dissolved, and I could see with perfect blue-sky clarity the Whole Truth of the Universe. I remember laughing with astonishment. Everything I needed to know about the world and how it worked was right in front of me, literally at my fingertips, hanging on the back of a chair.

On that day, it happened that one of us had occasion to use the *hamam* bottle. This was the 1.5-litre Pepsi bottle the captors brought with the Christmas cake and let us keep after it was empty. We only ever used it as a last resort. As you can imagine, peeing into the narrow opening of a plastic pop bottle when your left and right hands are handcuffed to somebody else is not the easiest thing to do.

On that day, things didn't go so well and the services of our *hamam* rag became needed. This was Tom's undershirt, part of the change of clothes given to us on Christmas Day and made available by Tom when the captors either didn't understand or didn't agree with our need for a rag. We wiped up the spill and draped the rag over the back of a chair until it could be rinsed out later.

Sometime afterwards, Uncle brought us lunch, a *samoon* filled with eggplant fried in oil. I remember it seemed to happen in slow motion. Uncle glanced at his fingers, saw they were greasy, spotted the rag and started to reach for it. *No! Stop! Wait!* I wanted to warn him, but before I could get the words out, Uncle had wiped his fingers on our *hamam* rag. He looked about the room, checked to see that everything was in order, said goodbye and went downstairs.

I was too shocked to say anything. *Uncle just wiped his hands in our piss!* He wanted to clean them, but he ended up doing the opposite thing, soiling himself in our captivity. Our degradation had become his degradation. Uncle couldn't see it, but we could. The oppressed can see what the oppressor cannot. Whatever you do to another, you do also to yourself. Every act of harm, every act of violence, regardless of the reason, soils and corrupts your humanity. And then you pass it on, spreading it like a contagion in everything you touch, in the course of opening a door, shaking someone's hand, making a cup of tea. It happens of its own accord, because it has to, a universal principle of cause and effect. Everything we do, no matter how insignificant, affects everything and everyone else, whether we realize it or not. It cannot be helped or stopped.

It was Lord Acton who famously said that power corrupts. The word "power" comes from the Old French *poer*, "to be able." Every human being needs to be able. To move, think, do, act, decide. Secure the necessaries of life. Establish boundaries, protection, safety. Secure a future for his or her children.

We are born without power. We are born naked, helpless, unable even to lift our heads. From here we embark on a lifelong journey of becoming and growing into autonomous, self-realizing body-selves with wondrous capacities for movement, perception and relation. We move from powerlessness into power in a continuous process of testing, expanding and negotiating the limits of what we are capable of. Anyone who has spent time with a 2-year-old will know this very well. We reach a zenith, and the arc of our lives turns again towards the powerlessness into which we were born, and we become once more dependent, needy, physically indigent. At every point along the way we need power, whether it is for ourselves or someone we are responsible for.

The exercise of power is central to us as human beings. We cannot avoid it. We have to have it. The question is not whether we need power, but what kind. Do we choose the power of *power over*, or the power of *power with*? Do we choose the power of threat, ultimatum and consequence, gun and bomb, or the power of love, solidarity and compassion,

patience and reconciliation? Is it the power of domination and subjuga-
tion, or the power of nurturing and collaboration? Is it the power to
destroy or the power to heal, to take life or give life? The power of
violence or non-violence?

Our captors needed power. They needed the murderous occupation
of their country to stop. They needed accountability, justice, compensation. They needed power, and they reached for the power of violence—the power that corrupts, as Lord Acton so astutely observed.
They used this power to take away our freedom, and then they lost
their own in turn.

I thought about it almost every day, the great biblical story of
Exodus. The Hebrew people had fallen into the slavery of Pharaoh,
building store cities to hold the surplus production of his realm. The
Hebrews cried out to God in their toil and God heard them. He called
forth a leader, a man named Moses, and sent him to Pharaoh with a
simple message: "Let my people go."

How I know this cry. *Let me go let me go let me go!* A cry capable of
blasting down walls and breaking chains. It burned within me like
a fire. Every oppressed and enslaved person knows it. It pulses in
every heartbeat and whispers in every breath, a living mantra of
indignation, anger, hope. It arises militantly, continuously, irresistibly. It will never stop, not for a millisecond, until the day of freedom
finally comes.

Ten times God sent Moses to Pharaoh. "Let my people go," he said.
And ten times Pharaoh said no. Each time he refused, God sent a
plague. First the Nile turned to blood. Then all the livestock died. Then
locusts came and ate everything in sight. Each plague seemed more
terrible than the next, culminating horribly in the death of every first-
born son in Egypt. No one was to be spared. "There will be loud wailing throughout Egypt—worse than there has ever been or ever will be
again," Moses told Pharaoh. When the plague came as promised,
Pharaoh finally relented and allowed the Hebrews to leave. They made
their escape by crossing through the Red Sea. Pharaoh followed after
them until his chariots were swallowed by the sea.

I always used to be troubled by the plague on the first-born. What kind of a God was this? How could an apparently loving and forgiving God reap such a grim harvest of innocents, the wholesale massacre of blameless children in exchange for the freedom of an enslaved people? It seemed like an impossible and abhorrent contradiction. Until Uncle wiped his hands on our *hamam* rag. And then I suddenly understood: the story is about Pharaoh, not God. The plagues are not the vindictive punishment of a malicious deity. They are a consequence, what happens to you when you refuse to let go, a manifestation of the Hamam Effect. You're going to be soiled. You're going to end up with the opposite of what you want. You're going to lose your first-born son, your most precious possession, the thing in which you have invested the totality of your name, your wealth, your existential legacy. You are held by the thing that you hold.

"Is there any news?" we used to ask them. It was our way of saying, "When are you going to let us go?" They each did it, at different times, independently of each other, pointed to their wrists as if they themselves were in handcuffs. "*Inshallah*," they said, Nephew, Junior and Uncle, "when you are free, we will be free." They had the guns and the keys, but they were not free. They lost their freedom—the very thing they were fighting for—as soon as they took away ours. You are held by the thing that you hold.

In the Hebrew scripture, Egypt is the symbol of bondage. It is the place of oppression and debasement that God acts in history to deliver us from. And the symbol of Egypt is the pyramid, a house of domination. Everyone who is in a pyramid is ranked and organized according to a geometry of subservience. The one above rules and the one below obeys. Wealth and ease flow up, while misery and servile labour flow down. This arrangement, called a hierarchy, is rarely questioned, least of all by those who appear to benefit most.

In fact, there is no benefit to living in a pyramid, the house of captivity. It doesn't matter whether you're a pharaoh or a slave, a CEO or an indentured piecework seamstress, an insurgent with a gun or an innocent hostage victim. There is no freedom for anyone in the pyramid because, when you get right down to it, a pyramid is really a tomb, a house for a corpse, a place of despoliation and death for all who inhabit it. If you want to be free, you have to get out of the pyramid altogether.

This is the Whole Truth of the Universe, summarized by Martin Luther King Jr.:

> We are tied together in a single garment of destiny, caught in an inescapable network of mutuality. Whatever affects one directly, affects all indirectly. For some strange reason I can never be what I ought to be until you are what you ought to be. You can never be what you ought to be until I am what I ought to be. This is the way God's universe is made. This is the way it is structured.

This is what captivity taught me. Everything we do affects everything and everyone else. If we want to be free, if we want to live as sisters and brothers in a beautiful blue world, a world without war, we have to let go of the power of domination and reach for the power of loving and healing and forgiving. We have to lay down the gun, the bomb, the institution of war, our faith in the power of violence. Until then we will live in a charnel house of death, a tomb, a pharoah's pyramid, the house of captivity. This is the way God's universe is made, the way human freedom is structured. You are held by the thing that you hold.

# EPILOGUE

Two months after our return, we were informed by the RCMP and Scotland Yard that an undisclosed number of men were being held in U.S. custody on charges related to our kidnapping and Tom's murder.* They wanted us to testify in a trial that would be conducted by the Central Criminal Court of Iraq (CCCI). "The death penalty is on the table," they said, but it was rarely applied. Only six times since the court was instituted by the United States in 2003 had it been imposed, all for high-level al Qaeda operatives.

We had many questions. How many men were there and what were their names? What was the case against them? Was anyone specifically charged with Tom's murder? Had they seen lawyers? What stage was the investigative process at? What was the role of the American government? Would it be a public trial? Would the media be allowed to attend? Could we get a written agreement that our alleged captors would be spared execution in exchange for our testimony?

No, such an agreement was not possible, they said, but we could ask for leniency in the course of testifying. They said our testimony was crucial, witnesses have the loudest voice in the Iraqi system, and the trial might not be able to proceed without us. They hoped we would participate so as to ensure no one else would be kidnapped or killed. They didn't want these men walking free. But they also said a trial could still proceed without us, that a complainant was not necessary when terrorism was involved. Beyond that they told us very little.

---

* In contrast, Mark Urban states in *Task Force Black*, "On 7 November 2006, Iraqi police arrested men alleged to have carried out the kidnapping."

It was a difficult and complex decision, whether or not to participate. We certainly didn't want anyone else to go through what we did, and we thought it important that whoever murdered Tom should be held accountable in some way. On the other hand, we had no desire for punishment. There had been enough suffering and death already, and the prospect of any of our captors being sent to the gallows filled us with anguish. We also had serious questions about the fairness of Iraqi justice and worried that our participation might be legitimating a system that was full of human rights abuses.

We learned everything we could about the CCCI. The UN Assistance Mission to Iraq said it "consistently failed to meet minimum fair trial standards." Amnesty International said at least 100 people had been executed and at least 270 more had been sentenced to death. TIME magazine said, "Hangings are conducted in secret, at a heavily fortified location in Baghdad . . . Only a few officials are notified beforehand, and the vast majority of the names of those executed are never made public."

We decided in the end not to testify. But before making the final decision, Harmeet and I travelled to London to join with Norman in issuing the following statement at a press conference on December 10, 2006, at St. Ethelburga's Centre for Reconciliation and Peace.*

> We three, members of a Christian Peacemaker Teams (CPT) delegation to Iraq, were kidnapped on November 26, 2005, and held for 118 days before being freed by British and American forces on March 23, 2006. Our friend and colleague, Tom Fox, an American citizen and full-time member of the CPT team working in Baghdad at the time, was kidnapped with us and murdered on March 9, 2006. We are immensely sad that he is not sitting with us here today.

---

\* St. Ethelburga's is a medieval church that survived the Great Fire of London (1666) and the Second World War only to be destroyed by a massive IRA bomb in 1993. It was rebuilt in 2002 to inspire and equip people to pursue reconciliation and peacemaking.

On behalf of our families and CPT, we thank you for attending this press conference today.

It was on this day a year ago that our captors threatened to execute us unless their demands were met. This ultimatum, unknown to us at the time, was a source of extreme distress for our families, friends and colleagues.

The deadline was extended by two days to December 10, which is International Human Rights Day. On this day, people all over the world will commemorate the adoption of the Universal Declaration of Human Rights by the UN General Assembly in 1948 by speaking out for all those whose human dignity is being violated by torture, arbitrary imprisonment, poverty, racism, oppression or war.

We understand a number of men alleged to be our captors have been apprehended, charged with kidnapping, and are facing trial in the Central Criminal Court of Iraq. We have been asked by the police in our respective countries to testify in the trial. After much reflection upon our traditions, both Sikh and Christian, we are issuing this statement today.

We unconditionally forgive our captors for abducting and holding us. We have no desire to punish them. Punishment can never restore what was taken from us.

What our captors did was wrong. They caused us, our families and our friends great suffering. Yet we bear no malice towards them and have no wish for retribution. Should those who have been charged with holding us hostage be brought to trial and convicted, we ask that they be granted all possible leniency. We categorically lay aside any rights we may have over them.

In our view, the catastrophic levels of violence and the lack of effective protection of human rights in Iraq is inextricably linked to the U.S.-led invasion and occupation. As for many others, the actions of our kidnappers were part of a cycle of violence they themselves experienced. While this in no way justifies what the men charged with our kidnapping are alleged to have done, we feel this must be considered in any potential judgment.

Forgiveness is an essential part of Sikh, Christian and Muslim teaching. Guru Nanak Dev Ji, the first of the Sikh Gurus, said, "'Forgiveness' is my mother . . ." and, "Where there is forgiveness, there is God." Jesus said, "For if you forgive those who sin against you, your heavenly Father will also forgive you." And of Prophet Mohammed (Peace Be Upon Him) it is told that once, while preaching in the city of Ta'if, he was abused, stoned and driven out of the city. An angel appeared to him and offered to crush the city between the two surrounding mountains if he ordered him to do so, whereupon the Prophet (or Mohammed PBUH) said, "No. Maybe from them or their offspring will come good deeds."

Through the power of forgiveness, it is our hope that good deeds will come from the lives of our captors, and that we will all learn to reject the use of violence. We believe those who use violence against others are themselves harmed by the use of violence.

Kidnapping is a capital offence in Iraq and we understand that some of our captors could be sentenced to death. The death penalty is an irrevocable judgment. It erases all possibility that those who have harmed others, even seriously, can yet turn to good. We categorically oppose the death penalty.

By this commitment to forgiveness, we hope to plant a seed that one day will bear the fruits of healing and reconciliation for us, our captors, the peoples of Canada, New Zealand, the United Kingdom, the United States, and most of all, Iraq. We look forward to the day when the Universal Declaration of Human Rights is respected by all the world's people.

I remember being filled with wonder as the three of us were being interviewed about our joint statement of forgiveness in the London offices of *Al Jazeera*. It was a miracle. To be sitting there, alive, together, all feeling and saying the same things: *We forgive. We have no desire to punish. There's been enough suffering. We will not testify.* And standing behind us was Tom's family—Kassie and Andrew, his former wife, Jan—supporting our decision. We all knew: this is what Tom would have wanted, what he would have done himself.

I was so grateful, so proud. It could easily have been otherwise. Any one of us, for his own good reasons, might have chosen a different course. It was a profound confirmation for me. We got through okay. They took Tom away from us, but they did not take away our ability to forgive. We did not lose ourselves. We were not infected with the poison of hate. They may have changed our lives, but they did not change us.

I wasn't sure at first. That I could say the words, "I forgive." I wanted to, the desire was there, but to take that unconditional and final step into a strange and unfamiliar land, without a map, without knowing what the consequences would be, whether for good or for ill—it took time for me to be ready, to be sure.

It is an audacious thing, a momentous leap of faith, to say to the one who has harmed you, I forgive. To say, I no longer hold you. You may go, your destiny is your own, there is an open horizon before you. You are free. Go without expectation, obligation or libation. Be accompanied only by this wish and blessing: May you be healed of your violence. May you be reborn in the knowledge of your forgiveness. May you start anew in a joyous life of giving life. Where you go, the road that you take now is up to you.

I was encouraged by Dan, for whom this was never a question. By my mother and father, who said, "We're just glad it's over. We aren't angry. We worry about what will happen to them." By my brothers and sisters, who said much the same. By Jan, who said, "This is so important, so essential to who Tom is, we have to do this." By Kassie, who said, "There's an awful lot of blame to go around. I don't think we can just pick out one or two people and hold them responsible."

And so, by the grace of God, the words came. I forgive. Not only to me, but to Harmeet and Norman as well. And something extraordinary happened: the captivity suddenly made sense. It had a purpose. It had become a seed of healing, a seed of forgiveness. I pray that God will take this seed and multiply it. A hundred times what was sown. And each of these in turn a hundred times.

Bishop Desmond Tutu once said, "There is no future without forgiveness." Let the future begin, today, with each of us laying down our hatreds, our pointing fingers, our desires to punish. Only then can we break from the mad spiral of retribution, eye for an eye and tooth for a tooth, bullet for a stone, bomb for a bullet. Only then can the future begin, a real future, a world without war where all can live in the glorious freedom of the children of God, never again to be afraid.

# ACKNOWLEDGEMENTS

It staggers me how so many people did so much on our behalf—working, praying, keeping vigil for us in countless ways during that long dark winter of 2006. In Colombia, Kenora, At-Tuwani and Hebron, Chicago and Toronto, Auckland and London, Whitehorse and Whitethorn, Durham, Red Lake, Amman, places too numerous to mention. Even if I had all the time and space in the world, still it would be an impossible task, to acknowledge and thank everyone. To those I have forgotten or overlooked, I humbly ask your forgiveness. Though my memory and ability to see are limited, my gratitude is not.

To the One in whom we live and move and have our being, the Current, the Light, the Love that holds us always. For the gift of life.

To Harmeet and Norman, my dear brothers. For supporting and helping and tolerating me under the most difficult circumstances. For surviving and forgiving with me. For answering countless questions and subjecting yourself to the task of reading this manuscript. For your generosity in allowing me full rein to tell my story.

To Tom, dear brother. For your ever-reaching spirit. For your readiness to take the hardest place. For your witness.

To all those who prayed.

To all those who gathered at street corners and public squares, in churches, living rooms and schools to keep vigil.

To Maxine Nash and Anita David, who remained on team throughout. To Greg Rollins, the first to receive the news. To Peggy and Art Gish, Michele Naar-Obed, Allan Slater and Beth Pyles, who went to Baghdad and worked on the team at a time of incalculable risk. For your astounding bravery. To all of my CPT sisters and brothers.

To CPT's partners, neighbours, translators, drivers and friends in Iraq. To Abu Hani, the team's landlord and anchor, and to his family. To Bahar Al Kindy, wherever you may be. To the "Independent Activates," who held public vigils for us in Firdos Square, and the one member who offered to exchange his life for ours. To the sheiks, NGO staffers and the many, many people throughout Iraq who cannot be named for security reasons. For advising, consoling, inquiring, providing information, making appeals and standing by the team in myriad ways. For following every thread.

To Doug Pritchard, who slept on the floor of his office for the first thirty-one days. To Carol Rose, Rebecca Johnson, Claire Evans, Robin Buyers, Kryss Chupp, Brian Young, Jane MacKay Wright and Ruth Buhler, who along with Doug served on the CPT Crisis Team for all or some part of the kidnapping. To my other colleagues at the Toronto and Chicago offices, Scott Albrecht, Mark Frey, Bob Holmes, Rich Meyer, Jessica Phillips and Sara Reschly. To Kathleen Kern in Rochester. For your tireless accompaniment and friendship, the joy of sharing this good work with you.

To Claudette and Patrick. For giving me the gift of life and loving me into the person I have become.

To Aunt Shirley. For your unceasing prayers.

To Kathleen and Robb. To Adrianna, Olivia and Andrew. To Ed and Donna (and now little Parker!). And to Matthew. For putting up with a pesky older brother, and for carrying the burdens of the captivity with such grace. To Jerry Stein. To all those whose love and support helped them to endure.

To the people of Sault Ste. Marie, the new friends and old, the neighbours and colleagues and complete strangers who brought food, sent cards and flowers, offered a kind word. To Father Burns.

To Jo Roberts, Len Desroches, Sarah Shepherd. To all those who dropped everything.

To my Catholic Worker community, who rallied around Dan and the CPT Canada office staff. To Michael Armstrong and Lorraine Land, my housemates who kept the homefires burning. To Chris Andersen, Cathy, Bradley and Martin Ashkeway, Amritha Baghwan, John Bird, Don Bowyer, Amy Brown, Janis Dahl, Madeline and Richard Burghardt Marshall, their children Seph, Tonnan and Raffi, Julia Churchill, Helyn Fisher, Genevieve Gallant, Liz Garrison, Stephanie Gris, Hobo, Rebecca, Toomas Karmo, Rob Kleysen, Scott Marratto, Diego Mendez, Heryka Meranda, Miriam Morales, her children, Jessica and David, Alayna Munce, Jo, Rob Shearer, Sarah, Joanna and Luke Stocking, their children, Jacob and Amy.

To the friends who wrapped Dan with so much love and carried us in your heart. To Joseph Stelpflug and David Martin. To Lyn Adamson, Colleen Barrett, Nik Beeson, Mark Chilton, Rory Crath, Julie Egan, Pamela Girardi, Miguel Gordillo, Sheila Green, Anna Jarvis, Claire Huang Kingsley, Joey MacDonald, Dee Marchand, Alexandra Morrison, Denise Nadeau, Matt Schaaf, Elizabeth Stocking, Dwyer and Sheila Sullivan, Ryan Weston, Daryold Winkler.

To all those who supported the work of the Toronto office around the clock, brought food, offered technical assistance.

To Sascha. For playing your fiddle. To Shawn O'Connor. For holding my picture on a rainy night.

To Dan's family, Rosemary, Carl, Jason and Trisha.

To all those who rearranged their lives and did everything they could.

To Carolyn Egan, John Humphrye and all of the sisters and brothers at the Steelworkers Hall. For your unstinting generosity and every manner of assistance.

To the many, many people who supported the Chicago office. To Gene Stoltzfus. For coming out of retirement to help lead Shine the Light. To Julie Hurlbut. For much-needed massages. To Kathy Kelly, Joel Gulledge and the folks at Voices for Creative Nonviolence. For advice, friendship and support.

To Dale Fast. For monumental media monitoring.

To b.h. Yael and John Greyson. To all those who assisted with the filming, editing and transmission of family appeals.

To Alyssa Burgin and Wilson Tan. To Robert Fisk, Roy Hallums, Giandomenico Pico, Karen Ridd and Terry Waite. To all those who offered crucial advice.

To Ehab Latoyef of Montreal, and Anas Altikriti of Harrow, who travelled to Iraq to make an appeal for our release.

To the signers of the Yemen Statement arising from the Al-Quds International Foundation conference, December 2005. To Sheikh Yusuf Al-Qaradawi, chairman of the Al-Quds International Foundation; Sheikh Faysal Mawlawi, secretary general of the Islamic Group in Lebanon; Sheikh Harith Al-Dari, head of the Association of Muslim Scholars in Iraq; Khalid Mishaal of Palestine, head of the Hamas Political Bureau; Musa Abu Marzuq of Palestine, deputy head of the Hamas Political Bureau; Maan Bashur, secretary general of the Arab Nationalist Congress; Hasan Hudruj of Lebanon, Hezbollah; Mahmud Al-Qumati of Lebanon, Hezbollah; Father Antwan Dhao of Lebanon; Sheikh Abdulhadi Awang of Malaysia, the Islamic Party; Professor Aleef-ud-Din Turabi of Kashmir; Dr. Mohamed M. O. Jamjoom of Saudi Arabia, businessman; Dr. Khalid Abdurrahman Al-Ajami of Saudi Arabia, university professor; Dr. Muhsin Al-Awaji of Saudi Arabia, Islamic writer and thinker; Dr. Abd Al-Quddus Al-Midwahi of Yemen; Muhammad bin Ali Ijlan of Yemen; Dr. Abdullatif Al Mahmud of Bahrain, Islamic Society; Abdulmunem Jalal Al-Mir of Bahrain, Palestine Solidarity Association; Dr. Muhammad Al-Sheikh Mahmud Siyam of Palestine, former Imam of Al-Aqsa Mosque; Khalid Mahmud Khan of Pakistan; Dr. Zafrul-Islam Khan of India; Dr. Azzam Tamimi, the Muslim Association of Britain; Haitham Yassin Abu Al-Raghib of Jordan; Saud Abu Mahfuz of Jordan; Boulafaat Abdulhamid of Algeria, engineer.

To Hassan Almrei, Mahmoud Jaballah, Mohammed Mahjoub, security certificate detainees in Canada. To Moazzam Begg, survivor of Guantanamo. To Abu Qatada, Muslim cleric suspected of ties to al Qaeda detained in the United Kindgom.

To the Grand Mufti of Jerusalem, Ekrima Sa'id Sabri. To Cindy Sheehan. To UN Secretary General Kofi Annan. To Mohammad Mahdi Akef of the Muslim Brotherhood. To the 9/11 families. To the World Council of Churches, the Canadian Council of Churches and the National Council of Churches (USA). To the forty-three British Muslim and Christian leaders who issued a joint statement calling for justice for Iraqi detainees, and our release. To the Jewish groups and individuals who expressed private support. To the more than 170 individuals and groups, religious and secular, who made public appeals.

To Noam Chomsky, Craig and Cindy Corrie, Naomi Klein, Arundhati Roy, Howard Zinn. To the more than forty thousand people who signed the online petition.

To Janet Somerville, who organized an ecumenical prayer service at St. Michael's Cathedral in Toronto. To Father Damian MacPherson and the religious leaders from sixteen denominations that attended.

To Judy Da Silva. To Robert Williamson and Annette Pahpasay, their son Darcy. To Roberta Keesick and Barbara Fobister. For asking for my name. To Napoleon Ross. For receiving the name. To Maria, Mary Ann and Lillian Swain, cougars at large. To all of my friends in Grassy Narrows and Kenora.

To the great Sullivan, Murphy, MacPherson and Barrett clans.

To members of Toronto City Council who passed the hat for CPT. To Mayor David Miller, who matched the total as his own personal contribution.

To Tom Artiss and Lyn, organizers of the Peace and Release coffee house fundraisers. To Belladonna and the Awakening, Big Rude Jake, Andrew Cash, Jason Collett, Julia, Dala, Mamma Dee, Michael Franti, Greg Keelor, Sara Marlowe, Sarah Masr, Scott, Michelle Rumball, Vincent Ryskin, Smokey Dymny, Jen Woodil, Hawksley Workman, Din Yalonen, Joe Zupo and Kevin McGrath. For sharing the gift of your music. To the El Mocambo.

To Bob Kellerman.

To Teresa Dremetsikas, Rosemary Meier, Marty Farahat and Kathleen O'Malley. For trauma care at critical times. To Quaker House. For a place to rest.

To Sheila Abdullah, Jenny Elliott, Kim Lamberty and Justin Alexander. For coordinating CPT's media work in Amman, Jordan. To Jameel and the staff of the Al Monzer. For your exuberant hospitality and eager helpfulness.

To Paul Martin, prime minister of Canada. For "doing everything we possibly can."

To Dan McTeague, parliamentary secretary to the minister of foreign affairs tasked with protecting Canadians Abroad, and his intrepid assistant, Glenn Bradbury. For leaving no stone unturned.

To Stephen Harper, prime minister of Canada. To Peter McKay, minister of foreign affairs. For bringing us home.

To Robert Desjardins, Serge Paquette and Helen Harris. To Robert Kerr. To all those at Consular Affairs. For being a lifeline to my family.

To Mike Flaherty and Larry Busch, RCMP officers, at all hours available for my family.

To Scotland Yard.

To Task Force Black, the men who busted down the door, cut us out of our chains and whisked us to safety. To all the soldiers involved. To all those who had a role in securing our release and must remain unknown because of the nature of your work. To Ronald Van Straalen of the Ontario Provincial Police. To Gordon, Tom, Andre, Marion, all the RCMP officers who volunteered to serve in Baghdad. To Paul.

To everyone who was involved from the Canadian Foreign Service. To Stewart Henderson and Sonia Hooykaas. For thinking of everything.

To William Patey.

To the Hercules A Team.

To Michaëlle Jean and Jack Layton. For your words of welcome.

To the producers, editors and media workers in Canada whose understanding of the story, and whose discretion in withholding the fact of my sexual orientation, likely saved my life. To Radio Canada, which my parents respected and appreciated above all others. For remembering us every day. To Karen Pauls. To Tony Burman, CBC editor-in-chief. For offering a word in our defence. To all those who were part of telling the story.

To Jan Stansel. For your warm, loving embrace.

To all those who assisted us in preparing our joint statement of forgiveness. To Simon Barrow, Jan Benvie, Anita, Mohamed Elmasry, Ehab, Maxine, Doug, Sheila, Beth, Itrath Syed, Greg, Saara Siddiqi, Jan.

To Jonathon Bartley and Simon, directors of Ekklesia in Britain. For keeping watch, impeccable advice, arranging everything.

To Edwina Hughes of Peace Movement Aotearoa. For coordinating media work in New Zealand.

To Dr. Aris. For your advice about the Iraqi legal system.

To Peter Rosenthal. For your indefatigable generosity and invaluable counsel. To Ramsey Clark. For helping us make a very difficult decision. To Paul Slattery. To Peggy Nash and her assistant Ricardo Filippone. To all those who answered inquiries and helped us in our search for news about our captors.

To Charlie Angus, Wayne Marston, his assistant Katy Kydd-Wright, Tony Martin. For restoring my faith in politics.

To all those who hosted me in my travels.

To Ched Meyers and Elaine Enns. For remembering every year.

To Tara Detwiler, Jon Ennis, Ignatius Feaver and Kathleen. For your healing attention.

To Tricia Gates Arciga. For *118 Days: Christian Peacemaker Teams Held Hostage in Iraq*. To all those who contributed their stories.

To Matthew. To John Carten and the Scarboro Missions community. For giving me a place to get started.

To my Redwoods sisters and brothers, members of the Order of Cistercians of the Strict Observance. For holding me in a womb of prayer, during the captivity and after. For welcoming me when I was a spiritual refugee and everything was failure. For allowing me to roam free in the redwoods. To Veronique. For flowers, 5:00 a.m. coffee, gingersnap cookies, anticipating my every need and being my first reader.

To Michael Harank, who gave me a place to stay, when coming and going. For your friendship.

To Anne McDermid. For the gift of your advice when I was so unclear.

To Anne Collins and Diane Martin, who said, after reading the first fifty thousand words I had written, "We would like to continue to be of use to you."

To Nicole Langlois, my agent. For "getting me."

To Ron Hay. For your generous counsel along the way.

To Michael Schellenberg, editor with the patience of a saint. For gentle, unerring guidance, structure, and wondrous knack for helping me figure it out for myself.

To John Sweet, comma artisan without peer. For a copy edit that felt like being wrapped in a warm blanket.

To Andrew Roberts. For a captivating cover design.

To Amanda Lewis. For pulling it all together.

To David Parsons. For the gift of your photography.

To all of the hardworking and fabulously talented staff at Knopf Canada. For rendering an embarrassingly long and mangy draft into an actual book: magic indeed!

To all those who read the manuscript at different points and offered comments. Carrie Whitney Brown, Jo, Dan, Stephen Donahue, John, Doug, Sarah, Andrea Siemens, Denise Nadeau.

To Thaer and Sheila Abdullah. For assistance with the glossary.

To Alayna. For sharing your hard-earned wisdom about writing.

To Daniel Berrigan. For your astounding words and the permission to use them. For your witness.

To Paul Martin, Marina Nemat, Jean Vanier and Lois Wilson. For your words of blessing.

To sweet William. For your fierce, beautiful heart. For doing everything that you possibly could.

To Dan. For sharing your life with me. For your unconditional love. For Walt Whitman and "The Great Day." For holding me. For being my first witness and walking with me every step of the way. ("anywhere/ I go you go, my dear; and whatever is done/by only me is your doing, my darling.")

Thank you.

I scarce can take it in.

# PERMISSIONS ON QUOTED TEXTS

JAMES LONEY is a Canadian peace activist, writer and member of Christian Peacemaker Teams (CPT). Based in Toronto, he has served on violence-reduction teams in Iraq, Palestine and First Nations communities in Canada.